The Russian's World
LIFE AND LANGUAGE

The Russian's World

LIFE AND LANGUAGE

Genevra Gerhart

Harcourt Brace Jovanovich, Inc.

NEW YORK   CHICAGO   SAN FRANCISCO   ATLANTA

To Jim

Drawing on Cover and Title Page Courtesy of Intourist, USSR
Company for Foreign Travel, New York

Illustration credits and acknowledgments appear on page 243.

ISBN: 0-15-577983-4

Library of Congress Catalog Card Number: 73–13208

Printed in the United States of America

Preface

My son has an archery target with a yellow bull's-eye. Around the bull's-eye are other red, blue, and black concentric circles. My desk dictionary defines *bull's-eye* as "the center of a target," and *target* is defined only as something at which one shoots. But with the other concentric circles gone, that remaining yellow spot is no longer a bull's-eye. The dictionary assumes that the reader knows the language background—that targets are made up of concentric circles whose arrangement makes a bull's-eye out of a mere yellow spot.

The first goal of this book is to explain in what physical ways the Russian world differs from ours, both the given world of nature and the world of objects the Russian and his forebears have created to cope with it. Those who know a "Russian stove" are not shocked to find grandma sleeping on it. Many of the animals common in the USSR do not exist in the Western Hemisphere. Likewise, a Russian's home is filled with different objects than our own.

So the Russian visible world is different. Next we discover that not only are the Russian objects different but the uses of the objects and the attitudes toward them differ also. Starlings become nice little birds. Fish eggs taste good. Put a thermometer in a Soviet Russian's mouth and he will spit it out and/or request an explanation. The Russian log cabin is not picturesque in the common Russian view, but rather a remnant of an impoverished past that is too close for comfort. The contemporary urban Russian wants to be associated with Russian stoves, log cabins, and felt boots about as much as young Americans want to be associated with Viennese waltzes.

Finally, a language has many relationships within it that are not part of most language textbooks. Not only is the naming system different but the choice of acceptable standard names differs also. For example, the Russian Фома́ is of the same origin as Thomas, but the real American equivalent is more like "Clem" or "Rube." Calling upon the Almighty is both standard and acceptable; calling upon the Devil is not. Russians use Arabic numerals much as we do, but a problem in long division as written by a Russian seems, at first glance, incomprehensible to us.

Why the book was written

What I thought was extensive preparation for teaching Russian proved inadequate within the first few days of my initial class. (Native Russians on the staff pointed out that I was assigning names that in today's English would be as uncommon as "Ebenezer" or "Bedelia"!) I began to realize how much background information I needed, and worse, that it was the kind of information I could not get without hours of questioning and research. (This estimate turned out to be incorrect by several orders of magnitude: it took years.)

For whom the book was written

Though the book deals with what is "common knowledge" to most Russians, we can use the information in various ways. The traveler, even one who knows no Russian, might want to investigate sections that describe practices and attitudes relating to transportation, housing, clothing, leisure, education, or holidays. Even readers of *War and Peace* in English might be more comfortable if they were able to find their way through the forest of Russian names. Students of Russian can indulge their individual interests on topics ranging from "how to read math problems in Russian" to a description of Russian folk costume. I hope Russian instructors will find in this book many of the answers to questions their students have been asking. Students who major in Russian should understand much of this general background. However, anyone studying Russian should have easier access to many of the aspects of a foreign culture that make language study satisfying.

The reader should investigate what amuses him and disregard those parts that are boring (or beyond him). With few exceptions, the material from chapter to chapter is not cumulative and need not be read in any special order. Almost all passages in Russian have been translated so that those who know little Russian can profitably use the book. A bullet indicates that the accompanying passage is translated in the appendix, and the only major assumption is that the reader is acquainted with the Russian alphabet. Passages in Russian were chosen as examples of statements made in English. When they contain any new information or insight on the subject under discussion, they are always translated. We urge the reader at any stage to try to read the Russian, for he will often discover that context suggests some meaning that a limited vocabulary does not.

How the book was written

The material in the book is an attempt to present "what every Russian knows" about some aspects of life that he assumes other Russians know, with emphasis on what I felt were the needs and interests of Americans. The material was presented so as to take advantage of what is known in English. The basic text is in English, while illustrations and examples are in Russian.

Obviously, not all the topics that concern everyday life and language are discussed in this book. To cover them all adequately in one volume would have required a tome too expensive to buy and too heavy to carry.

A Russian will complain that I have too much material on subjects that to him are old-fashioned. But he knows what old-fashioned is; we must have it shown to us. A Russian will also complain of mistakes. I will not err by denying my humanity, but I have done everything possible to eliminate misleading or mistaken information. Essentially all research was done using pre- and postrevolutionary Russian sources directly. This includes both study of printed matter and interviews with Russians themselves.

The whole manuscript was reviewed in detail by Russians in the USSR and in the USA. Much of what is written, however, is Russian opinion, on which absolute and total agreement will come only with the millennium. I have tried to record the consensus and would be grateful to those who find and report to me any errors of fact, language, or judgment.

No conscious effort has been made to espouse the virtues or vices of either the new or old regimes, of either the New World or the Old World. Sometimes one is startled by changes (in regime) or differences (in worlds) but at other times even more startled by the lack of change or difference.

Sources

For ethnographic information I have drawn heavily on S. A. Tokarev's *Ethnography of Peoples of the USSR* published at Moscow State University, Moscow, 1958. С. А. Тóкарев, *Этногрáфия нарóдов СССР,* издáтельство Москóвского университéта, Москвá, 1958. I will refer to it as: Тóкарев, *Этногрáфия нарóдов СССР.* Another useful source of ethnographic information gives many more details but requires considerable sifting. It is from the series *Peoples of the World: Peoples of the European Parts of the USSR,* volume I, edited by V. A. Aleksandrov and others, and is a product of the N. N. Miklukho-Maklay Institute of Ethnography of the Academy of Sciences, Moscow. *Нарóды мúра: Нарóды европéйской чáсти СССР,* том I, Институ́т этногрáфии úмени Миклу́хо-Маклáя, Академия Нау́к СССР. Издáтельство

"Наýка," Москвá, 1964. I will refer to it as: Алексáндров, *Нарóды европéйской чáсти СССР.* For general use as a guide, both a picture book and a reference, to man-made objects or items for man's use in the USSR, I highly recommend the *Commercial Dictionary* in nine volumes, edited by I. A. Pugachev and published by the State Publishing House of Literature on Commerce, from 1956 to 1961. *Товарный словарь,* глáвный редáктор И. А Пугачёв, Госудáрственное издáтельство торгóвой литератýры, Москвá, 1956–1961. For examples of much of the contents of this book I recommend early school textbooks used in the USSR and more advanced literature anthologies. Otherwise, material for this book has been gathered from a very wide range of sources—everything from household manuals to *War and Peace.*

Acknowledgments

The finding, sorting, and organizing have been neither simple nor easy in spite of the subject matter, seemingly a mere compilation of the Russian banal. Common references are often out of date or do not agree, or they assume that the reader has the language background that was the object of research. Russians themselves sometimes disagree or fail to see the problem presented to the non-Russian. At other times the topics under discussion push national pride or shame to excesses. I needed help.

I am especially grateful to Dr. Paul McRill, Foreign Language Specialist for the Seattle Public Schools and formerly Director of the Washington Foreign Language Program (of the University of Washington), which operated under a grant from the Ford Foundation. Paul's assurance that I was on the right track was great spiritual help, and a grant from the WFLP was material help at a time when both were essential. Work on the book would have been impossible without Wladislaw Krasnow, now of the University of Texas, and Xenia Bednekoff, both of whom willingly answered numberless questions. For their reviews of the manuscript and for their corrections, comments, and suggestions, I am deeply indebted to Nina Andreeva, Mrs. Tatiana Bevan, Lensey Namioka, Vadim Pahn, Dr. Harold Swayze, Natalie Tracy and Marina Waugh of Seattle and/or the University of Washington, and to Dr. Konstantin D. Hramov and Emilia Hramov of Yale University. I have also benefited from comments on organization, presentation, and facts made by the following Russian teachers: Nancy Levin, Helen McIntyre, Olga Penrose, and Rosanne Royer. For information or suggestions I also wish to thank Dr. Donald Bevan, Pamela Butler, Dr. Paul Gribanovskiy, Dr. Roger Hagglund, Dr. Jack Haney, Dr. Willis Konick, Dr. Lew Micklesen of the University of Washington, and Dr. Josef Sauter of Friedrichshafen, West Germany. And finally, I am very grateful indeed to the American Friends Service Committee and in particular to Myrtle McCallin for allowing me to participate in the 1970 USA-USSR Teacher Exchange. It was the experience of a lifetime. To my family goes the deepest appreciation for the gift of time; I now return to them the use of the dining-room table.

The accuracy of fact and judgment is due to all those I have mentioned and to the others I could not mention; the onus of inaccuracy must fall to me.

G. G.

Note:
1. A passage marked with a bullet • has been translated in the appendix.
2. Usages and stresses given here are meant to reflect colloquial Russian; by colloquial I mean standard spoken Russian as used in the USSR.
3. Some of the sources were printed outside the USSR, and others were printed in the USSR. In quotations I have followed the capitalization system *used in the source*. Outside the USSR we have "God, Lent, Easter, Christmas." Soviet sources use "god, lent, easter," and so on.

Contents

Что ни го́род, то но́ров, что ни дере́вня, то обы́чай.

Every city has its character; every village, its customs.

1

The man himself

Он сам

This chapter deals mostly with nomenclature—the names for parts of the body, what people carry with them, and some terminology for their relations to others. The essence of a man is not to be found in the names he gives to his parts. For those who would like a well-written, interesting, and knowledgeable book on that subject, Wright Miller, *Russians As People* (New York: Dutton, 1961) is recommended. Language students can find some small amusement in discovering that the Russian does not commonly identify knuckles or cuticles or that he does distinguish two shades of blue eyes. Perhaps, however, the significance of terminology is greater when it relates to members of the family: four different words distinguish mothers and fathers-in-law for instance. The ways in which both medals and identification cards are used can also say something about a people. The subjects included here are:

Anatomy
Hair, eye, and skin color
Personal cleanliness
Cosmetics
Jewelry
Medals
With them, they carry . . .
Identification cards
Age
The man and his family

Anatomy
Анато́мия

It is sometimes difficult to make an exact translation from English to Russian in dealing with parts of the anatomy. English, for example, separates parts that Russian does not, as in arm/hand рука́ (*pl.* ру́ки), leg/foot нога́ (*pl.* но́ги), finger/toe па́лец (*pl.* па́льцы), and chest/breast грудь. There *are* words to specify a hand кисть and foot ступня́ when it is vital to make the distinction: "У меня́ боли́т ступня́" is "My foot hurts." But context is most often relied upon to supply that distinction: "У неё дли́нные но́ги" is "She has long legs," while "У неё больши́е но́ги" is "She has big feet." Many of the words for parts of the body involve accent shifts in the plural or oblique cases. In all the drawings of parts of the body that follow, the key below gives the English translation and then the nominative plural form if there is any change in the stress or the stem, or if the plural is not formed by merely adding ы or и to the stem.

Sometimes it is easier to recognize or remember terminology when we can see where it came from. Thus, freckles весну́шки derive from spring весна́, which is the time they are expected to appear; подборо́док is the place under one's beard борода́, namely, chin.

The words cited here are the standard ones. In everyday speech Russians tend to use more slang words, and even the relatively casual student of Russian can expect to hear them. Often such words are the ones that properly apply to animals. Very common is мо́рда for mug, but literally, an animal's face (намо́рдник muzzle); физиомо́рдия is a comical rendition of физионо́мия + мо́рда. Snout ры́ло is an abusive term for face. Animal paws or feet are ла́пы: "Get your paws off me!"—"Убери́ свои́ ла́пы!" Брю́хо is, properly, an animal's stomach or underside, but it also can be "belly," especially a large one, in referring to humans.

Babies' parts are often in their diminutive form: нос—но́сик, те́ло—те́льце, лицо́—ли́чико, рука́—ру́чка, нога́—но́жка, голова́—голо́вка.

The body
Те́ло

A Soviet third-grade reader that describes and identifies many of the parts of the body included here introduces the subject this way:

● Ка́ждый челове́к до́лжен обяза́тельно знать строе́ние своего́ те́ла. В те́ле различа́ют го́лову, ше́ю, ту́ловище и две па́ры коне́чностей: ве́рхние коне́чности, и́ли ру́ки, и ни́жние коне́чности, и́ли но́ги.[1]

The head, face, and neck
Голова́, лицо́ и ше́я

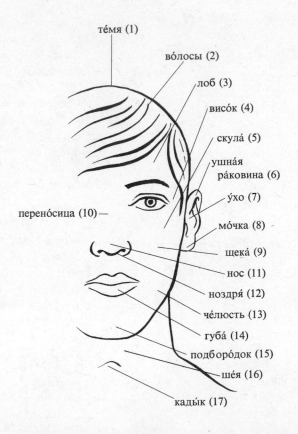

те́мя (1)
во́лосы (2)
лоб (3)
висо́к (4)
скула́ (5)
ушна́я ра́ковина (6)
у́хо (7)
перено́сица (10)—
мо́чка (8)
щека́ (9)
нос (11)
ноздря́ (12)
че́люсть (13)
губа́ (14)
подборо́док (15)
ше́я (16)
кады́к (17)

[1] Е. Е. Соловьёва и др., *Родна́я речь III* (Москва́: Учпедги́з. 1964), стр. 249. *Родна́я речь* is a graded series of Soviet readers used in all schools where Russian is the native language.

(1)　crown (*no pl.; gen.* **те́мени**)
(2)　hair (**оди́н во́лос** one hair)
(3)　forehead (*pl.* **лбы**)
(4)　temple (*pl.* **виски́**)
(5)　cheekbone (*pl.* **ску́лы**)
(6)　(outer) ear
(7)　ear (*pl.* **у́ши**)
(8)　earlobe
(9)　cheek (*pl.* **щёки**)
(10)　bridge of nose
(11)　nose (*pl.* **носы́**)
(12)　nostril (*pl.* **но́здри**)
(13)　jaw
(14)　lip (*pl.* **гу́бы**)
(15)　chin (*pl.* **подборо́дки**)
(16)　neck
(17)　Adam's apple (*pl.* **кадыки́**; *formal* **Ада́-мово я́блоко**)

Also:

заты́лок　back of the head (*pl.* **заты́лки**)
бараба́нная перепо́нка　eardrum
морщи́на　wrinkle
я́мочка　dimple
двойно́й подборо́док　double chin
весну́шка　freckle
пе́рхоть　dandruff

The eye
Глаз

The eyes **глаза́** have many features that are commonly distinguished (the most common form, cited first):

бро́ви　eyebrows (*sg.* **бровь**)
ве́ки　eyelids (*sg.* **ве́ко**)
ресни́цы　eyelashes (*sg.* **ресни́ца**)
белки́　whites of the eyes (*sg.* **бело́к**; *formal* **белко́вая оболо́чка**)
ра́дужная оболо́чка　iris (*informal* **ра́дужка**)
зрачки́　pupils (*sg.* **зрачо́к**)
глазно́е я́блоко　eyeball
рогови́ца　cornea (*formal* **рогова́я оболо́чка**)
хруста́лик　lens
сетча́тка　retina (*formal* **се́тчатая оболо́чка**)
зри́тельный нерв　optic nerve

The mouth
Рот (*pl.* **рты**)

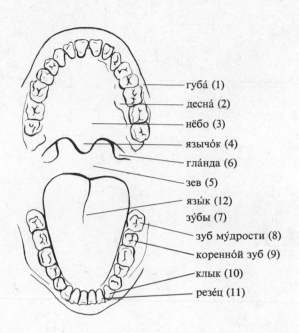

губа́ (1)
десна́ (2)
нёбо (3)
язычо́к (4)
гла́нда (6)
зев (5)
язы́к (12)
зу́бы (7)
зуб му́дрости (8)
коренно́й зуб (9)
клык (10)
резе́ц (11)

(1)　lip (*pl.* **гу́бы**)
(2)　gum (*pl.* **дёсны**)
(3)　palate (*pl.* **нёба**)
(4)　uvula (*pl.* **язычки́**)
(5)　throat opening (**зева́ть** to yawn)
(6)　tonsil (*formal* **минда́лина**)
(7)　teeth
(8)　wisdom tooth
(9)　molar
(10)　canine tooth (*pl.* **клыки́**)
(11)　incisor (*pl.* **резцы́**)
(12)　tongue (*pl.* **языки́**)

Also:

слю́нные же́лезы　salivary glands
моло́чные зу́бы　baby teeth (*formal*)
зубо́к, зу́бик　baby tooth (*pl.* **зу́бки**)
вставны́е зу́бы　false teeth
мост　bridge
коро́нка　crown

The trunk
Ту́ловище

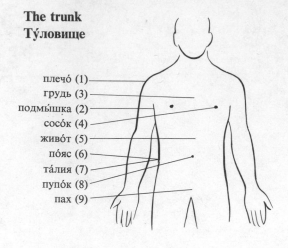

плечо́ (1)
грудь (3)
подмы́шка (2)
сосо́к (4)
живо́т (5)
по́яс (6)
та́лия (7)
пупо́к (8)
пах (9)

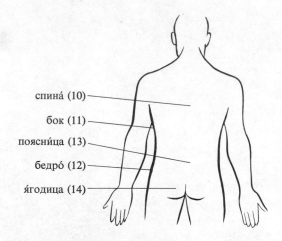

спина́ (10)
бок (11)
поясни́ца (13)
бедро́ (12)
я́годица (14)

(1) shoulder (*pl.* плечи)
(2) armpit, general underarm area
(3) breast/chest
(4) nipple (*pl.* соски́)
(5) stomach (*pl.* животы́)
(6) waist/belt (*pl.* пояса́)
(7) waist
(8) navel (*pl.* пупки́; пупови́на umbilical cord)
(9) groin (*pl.* пахи́)
(10) back (*pl.* спи́ны)
(11) side (*pl.* бока́)
(12) hip (*pl.* бёдра)
(13) small of the back
(14) buttock

The arm/hand
Рука́ (*pl.* ру́ки)

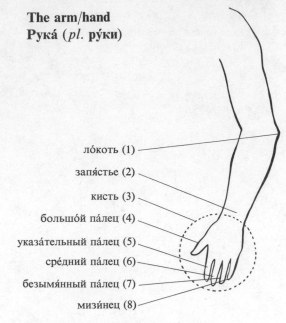

ло́коть (1)
запя́стье (2)
кисть (3)
большо́й па́лец (4)
указа́тельный па́лец (5)
сре́дний па́лец (6)
безымя́нный па́лец (7)
мизи́нец (8)

(1) elbow (*pl.* ло́кти)
(2) wrist (*pl.* запя́стья)
(3) hand (*specific*)
(4) thumb (*pl.* больши́е па́льцы)
(5) index finger
(6) middle finger
(7) ring finger
(8) little finger (*pl.* мизи́нцы)

Also:

кула́к   fist (*pl.* кулаки́)
ладо́нь   palm

The finger/toe
Па́лец

The fingers or toes па́льцы seem to have fewer features distinguished than the English counterparts: fingernail но́готь (*pl.* но́гти) and moon лу́нка are distinguished. The cuticle does not have its own word in Russian but ко́жица (usually, thin skin, peel, or husk) can be used. The ball of the finger can be translated as поду́шечка па́льца, and a hangnail can be заусе́ница. For fingerprints, отпеча́тки па́льцев is used.

The leg/foot
Ногá (*pl.* нóги)

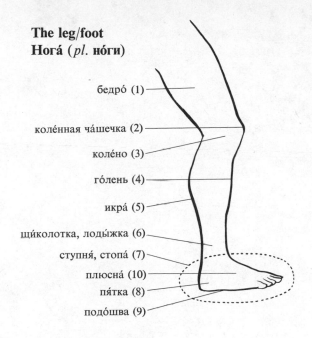

бедрó (1)
колéнная чáшечка (2)
колéно (3)
гóлень (4)
икрá (5)
щи́колотка, лоды́жка (6)
ступня́, стопá (7)
плюснá (10)
пя́тка (8)
подóшва (9)

(1)   thigh (*pl.* **бёдра**)
(2)   kneecap
(3)   knee (*pl.* **колéни**)
(4)   shin
(5)   calf (*pl.* **и́кры**)
(6)   ankle
(7)   foot (*specific*) (*pl.* **ступни́**)
(8)   heel
(9)   sole
(10) metatarsus (*pl.* **плю́сны**)

Also:

подъём   instep
большóй пáлец (ноги́)   big toe
мáленький пáлец (ноги́)   little toe

The skin
Кóжа

● Когдá человéку жáрко, то кóжа покрывáется мáленькими кáпельками пóта. Выделéние пóта имéет для нас óчень большóе значéние. С пóтом удаля́ются из тéла врéдные для нас вещества́. Пот выделя́ется из кóжи чéрез мáленькие отвéрстия—пóры. В жару́ пот испаря́ется и при э́том охлаждáет кóжу.[2]

[2] Соловьёва и др., *Роднáя речь III*, стр. 261.

The skeleton
Скелéт

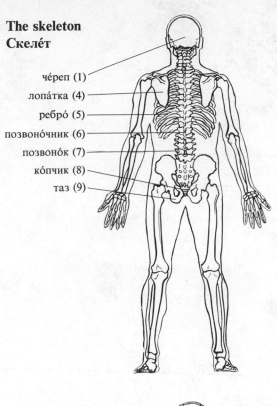

чéреп (1)
лопáтка (4)
ребрó (5)
позвонóчник (6)
позвонóк (7)
кóпчик (8)
таз (9)

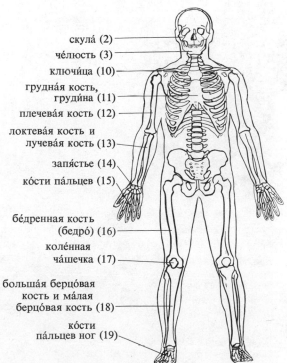

скулá (2)
чéлюсть (3)
ключи́ца (10)
груднáя кость, груди́на (11)
плечевáя кость (12)
локтевáя кость и лучевáя кость (13)
запя́стье (14)
кóсти пáльцев (15)
бéдренная кость (бедрó) (16)
колéнная чáшечка (17)
большáя берцóвая кость и мáлая берцóвая кость (18)
кóсти пáльцев ног (19)

(1) skull (*pl.* **черепа́**)
(2) cheekbone (*pl.* **ску́лы**)
(3) jawbone
(4) shoulder blade
(5) rib (*pl.* **рёбра; грудна́я кле́тка** rib cage)
(6) spine
(7) vertebra (*pl.* **позвонки́**)
(8) tail bone or coccyx
(9) pelvis
(10) clavicle
(11) breastbone or sternum
(12) upper arm bone
(13) lower arm bones (ulna and radius)
(14) wrist bone (*pl.* **запя́стья**)
(15) finger bones
(16) thighbone or femur (*pl.* **бёдра**)
(17) kneecap
(18) tibia (shinbone) and fibula
(19) toe bones

Also:

суста́в joint
хрящ cartilage and gristle
фала́нга finger bone

The digestive system
Пищевари́тельная систе́ма

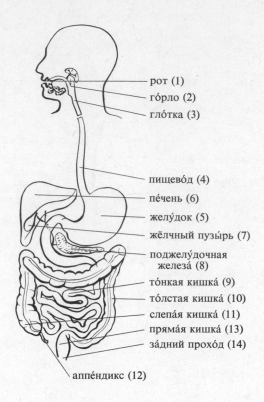

рот (1)
го́рло (2)
гло́тка (3)
пищево́д (4)
пе́чень (6)
желу́док (5)
жёлчный пузы́рь (7)
поджелу́дочная
железа́ (8)
то́нкая кишка́ (9)
то́лстая кишка́ (10)
слепа́я кишка́ (11)
пряма́я кишка́ (13)
за́дний прохо́д (14)
аппе́ндикс (12)

The respiratory organs
О́рганы дыха́ния

Following the air **во́здух** from the nose on down, there is:

носогло́тка nasal passage
гло́тка pharynx (**глота́ть** to swallow)
го́рло throat
горта́нь larynx
голосовы́е свя́зки vocal chords
дыха́тельное го́рло windpipe (*formal* **трахе́я**)
бро́нхи bronchial tubes
лёгкие lungs (*sg.* **лёгкое**)

● Мы ды́шим во́здухом. Дыши́те и наблюда́йте за собо́й. То мы вдыха́ем во́здух (вдох), то выдыха́ем его́ (вы́дох).[3]

(1) mouth (*pl.* **рты**)
(2) throat
(3) pharynx
(4) esophagus
(5) stomach (*pl.* **желу́дки**)
(6) liver
(7) gall bladder (*pl.* **жёлчные пузыри́**)
(8) pancreas (*pl.* **поджелу́дочные же́лезы**)
(9) small intestine
(10) large intestine
(11) caecum (*a distinction not commonly made in English*)
(12) appendix (*formal* **червеобра́зный отро́сток**)
(13) rectum
(14) anus

[3] Соловьёва и др., *Родна́я речь III*, стр. 260.

Also:

кише́чник digestive tract
кишка́ intestine
испражне́ния feces (*polite*)
кал feces (*medical*)

The brain and spinal cord
Мозг

The Russian word in its literal sense refers to all the gray matter in the brain and spinal cord; the plural **мозги́** usually indicates brains as food. Gray matter is divided into cerebrum **головно́й мозг**, cerebellum **мозжечо́к**, medulla oblongata **продолгова́тый мозг**, and spinal cord **спинно́й мозг**. Other neurological terms include the nerve **нерв**, nervous system **не́рвная систе́ма**, and solar plexus **со́лнечное сплете́ние** (from **со́лнце** for sun and **сплести́** to braid or plait).

The urinary and reproductive organs
Мочевы́е и половы́е о́рганы

Some of these organs are shared by males and females such as the kidney **по́чка**, ureter **мочето́чник**, bladder **мочево́й пузы́рь**, and urethra **мочеиспуска́тельный кана́л**.

Others are not. Male organs include the prostate gland **предста́тельная железа́**, penis **(мужско́й половой) член**, and testicle **яи́чко** (*pl.* **яи́чки**); female reproductive organs are the ovary **яи́чник**, Fallopian tube **труба́ яи́чника**, womb **ма́тка**, and vagina **влага́лище**. Urine **моча́** and semen **се́мя** are the products.

The blood
Кровь

The Russian circulatory system **кровено́сная систе́ма** involves many words that are easily recognizable: **ао́рта, ве́на, арте́рия, капилля́ры**. Heart **се́рдце** and spleen **селезёнка** are harder to recognize as cognates, which they are. However, the jugular vein as a traditional object of savage attack has an interesting counterpart in **со́нная арте́рия**, the "sleep" artery (English, carotid).

Pressure on this artery (which is right next to the jugular, by the way) is supposed to put one to sleep according to Russian popular science. This reaction is also the basis for the name of the artery in English: kar(os) = stupor. (Do not try this interesting stunt: it is possible not only to induce sleep but also to cause cardiac arrest.)

The muscles
Му́скулы, и́ли мы́шцы

Both words derive from the same root, "mouse," as the English word "muscle."

● Вы зна́ете, что снару́жи всё те́ло покры́то ко́жей. Прощу́пайте у себя́ ру́ки и но́ги. Под ко́жей вы нащу́паете что́-то мя́гкое. Это му́скулы. На конца́х му́скулов сухожи́лия.[4]

Hair, eye, and skin color
Цвет воло́с, глаз и ко́жи

The Russian terms one uses to describe the coloring of people can be confusing for English speakers. For hair color, black hair can be either "У него́ чёрные во́лосы" or "Он брюне́т" (while our word "brunet" refers to brown or dark brown hair). Brown hair is commonly either **кашта́новые во́лосы** (chestnut **кашта́н**) or **шате́н(ка)**. ("Она́ шате́нка" is a somewhat high-flown French and foreign term.) In fact, all these words of French origin—**брюне́т, шате́н, блонди́н**—are somewhat citified, so that for brown hair, **тёмные во́лосы** is perhaps even more common. Redheadedness—"Она́ ры́жая. У неё ры́жие во́лосы"—is less common than it is in America, but its rarity does not make it a treasure. Red hair is a liability for children, who are teased with, "Ры́жий, кра́сный, челове́к опа́сный" (**опа́сный** dangerous). The term for light brown hair **ру́сые во́лосы** covers a rather wide range from dark blond to light brown, including what we call "dishwater" blond; this color is both common and nondescript (from our

4 Соловьёва и др., *Родна́я речь III*, стр. 253.

point of view), but it is by no means undesirable to the Russians. Blond hair can be described in several ways: "**Он блонди́н. У него́ светло-ру́сые во́лосы**" is standard nomenclature for blond hair as is **све́тлые во́лосы. Белоку́рые во́лосы** is a light blond, and the term is complimentary, while **белобры́сый** is a very light blond and uncomplimentary, often applied to small boys and similar pests. **Льняны́е во́лосы** (**лён** *cf.* linen) is, of course, flaxen hair, but the term is not quite as poetic and unusual in a land of flax. Gray and white hair are both **седы́е во́лосы**. When hair is turning from its usual color to gray or white, one can add **с седино́й** or **с про́седью** (**чёрные с седино́й, ру́сые с про́седью**).

Eyes, too, have a set of colors different from ours. Hazel eyes have no description, but Russians distinguish kinds of brown eyes and blue eyes in ways we do not. The song "**О́чи чёрные**" means "black eyes," eyes so dark that one cannot distinguish the iris from the pupil. (**О́ко, о́чи** is a very old and now poetic word for eye. One now says, "**У него́ чёрные глаза́.**") The more usual brown eyes are **ка́рие глаза́**. Blue eyes come in two shades: the common light blue eyes are **голубы́е глаза́**; much less common and held in very high regard are **си́ние глаза́**, eyes that are darker blue. Eyes can also be gray **се́рые глаза́** or green **зелёные глаза́**.

Facial complexion **цвет лица́** is thought to be at its best when it is light-colored—"**У нее хоро́ший цвет лица́**"—and pink-cheeked **с румя́нцем**. A dark complexion is **сму́глый цвет лица́**. Light skin color can also be **белоко́жий** or **светлоко́жий**, and dark skin is **тёмная ко́жа**. "**Он бле́дный**"—"He is pale."

The formal major racial distinctions are **европео́ид, монголо́ид, негро́ид**. Normal speech naturally uses other words. To distinguish a white man from others, one uses **он бе́лый**. A Negro can be **он негр** (**она́ негритя́нка**) or **он чёрный**, though the latter indicates less respect. Very commonly blacks (from Africa) are called **африка́нцы**. Since the racial minority in the USSR is Oriental, it is they that have the largest number of somewhat derogatory words applied to them: **косогла́зый** slant-eye; **азиа́т**; **жёлтый** yellow; **нацме́н** is a Sovietism (**национа́льное меньшинство́** national minority) now somewhat obsolete and derogatory; and others. If you see an Oriental in the USSR and you wish to mention his race without being offensive, **челове́к восто́чного ви́да** can be used. American Indians are **он инде́ец, она́ индиа́нка**, and **они́ инде́йцы**. Our term "redskin" (which is slang if not derogatory) goes directly into Russian as **красноко́жий** and with the same connotation. For people from India, **он инди́ец, она́ индиа́нка**, and **они́ инди́йцы** are used. The words for a Hindu are **инду́с, инду́ска**, and **инду́сы**. (Be careful not to confuse either Western or Eastern Hemisphere Indians with **инде́йка** or **индю́шка** a turkey!)

Personal cleanliness
Ли́чная гигие́на

Personally speaking, Russians are clean (using the more familiar European nations as a standard). To them, personal dirt is a Bad Thing. In the past Russians did not sew themselves into their underwear as some early Americans are reputed to have done. Traditionally, bathing was both regular and frequent, that is, at least once a week, typically on Saturday. But bodily cleanliness was one thing and keeping clothes and bedding clean was quite another. It is this laundry problem that accounted for the former prevalence of bedbugs, lice, and the like. The traditional major avenue to cleanliness was the Russian sauna **ба́ня**.

The traditional bathhouse
Традицио́нная ба́ня

The oldest and most common form of **ба́ня** was a small, one-room log hut built some distance from the living quarters **изба́**, for fire protection, and close to a water supply. The major piece of equipment was a stove made principally of stones **печь-ка́менка** in which the fire was built. A pile of stones was placed on top of this "stove," and once the stones were hot, some of them were used to heat water (for washing) in a trough. Then water was poured over the rest of the stones to produce the necessary steam. The traditional stove was without a chimney; the stove opening was near the door and the smoke went out the door. Naturally, one did not use the bathhouse until the fire had done its heating. The major furniture was a built-in bench **ла́вка** to sit on while washing and a shelf **поло́к** to sit or lie on while steaming: "**Он сиде́л на полке́.**"

The modern bathhouse in the country now has a chimney and the added convenience of a dressing room **предба́нник.**

Bathing actually involved several processes and getting clean was only one of the objects of the procedure. First one washed oneself for reasons of cleanliness, then one steamed oneself for reasons of health. Steaming was and still is considered a major therapeutic device. (Steaming was so essential that the Russian stove was used as a steamer in those regions where fuel was at a premium or where it was too expensive to build a bathhouse separately.) In the course of steaming, the bathers thrashed themselves or each other with a bundle of (usually birch) twigs **ве́ник** to bring the blood to the surface.

The use of a bathhouse seems to go back as far as Kievan Russia. Peasants too poor to build their own bathhouse either joined with others and built one or used the public bathhouse. One indicator of reasonable hospitality was an offer to heat the bathhouse for the traveler. No small amount of superstition was connected with the bathhouse. For one thing, it was supposed to be inhabited by an evil spirit **ба́нный, ба́нник,** who would bewitch (or befoul) clothes if worn into the bathhouse. At one time, the reason for dousing oneself was to be cleansed of the evil that the **ба́нный** had somehow loosed. In some places, one could not go to church on the same day that the bathing occurred for the same reason.

The contemporary bathhouse
Совреме́нная ба́ня

Happily, the Russian bath **ба́ня** is still in operation, somewhat modified in normal use but still preserving the elements basic to its original form.

Private bathhouses are now rather infrequent; the common bath is a public bath **обще́ственная ба́ня.** (Do not confuse this bath **ба́ня** with the bathtub **ва́нна** found in a regular bathroom **ва́нная.**) Before setting out for the bath, take your soap **мы́ло,** a towel **полоте́нце,** and the equivalent (in use) of a washrag **моча́лка.** (Originally that consisted of strands of linden fiber **моча́ло** that softened when wet; now **моча́лка** is often a kind of sponge **гу́бка.**) It is usually possible to rent or buy this equipment at the **ба́ня** itself, though most people bring their own. Upon entering, you first check your coat, then proceed to the cashier's window **ка́сса** and pay for the services or facilities you will be using; you might want a pedicure, a hairdo, a massage, or a private bathroom **но́мер** in addition to or instead of the use of the public bath. The **ба́ня** itself has two separate divisions, **о́бщее мужско́е отделе́ние** and **о́бщее же́нское отделе́ние,** both of which consist of three basic sections: (1) the dressing room **раздева́лка** where the woman in charge is a **ба́нщица** (and with whom you may leave your valuables); (2) the main washing room **мы́льня, мы́льная** filled with rows of benches **скаме́йки,** on which there will be washtubs **тазы́,** and equipped with faucets **кра́ны** along one wall and a shower **душ** along another; and (3) a steam room **пари́льня** (written on the door) or **пари́лка** (in normal speech). Historically, one washed first and then steamed afterward, but now some people steam first and then wash. The steam room **пари́лка** has a large stove-cum-furnace for producing heat and steam, the latter obtained when bathers who so desire it throw water on the heated stones in the stove. The steam room also has wooden benches or steps **поло́к** (*sg.*) that one can mount. The higher you go, the hotter it is. In the steam room

Russians often use a bundle of birch twigs **ве́ник** to thrash one another. When you think you have cooked enough, proceed to the washroom. Fill a tub **таз** with water and start washing, head first, and with many changes of water. Do not hurry or your "Americanness" will show; this is a peaceful, relaxing time. Use the shower **душ** to rinse off and return to the dressing room **раздева́льня** (formal) or **раздева́лка** (colloquial). On your way out you can relieve the enervated feeling by a drink at the buffet that usually accompanies a bathhouse. On your return home, your Russian friends will say, "**С лёгким па́ром!**"—a wish of good health bestowed upon those who have just bathed or steamed in a **ба́ня**.

The public bath described here is currently used by two large groups of people: those who simply like the steam bath and those whose housing does not include a bathroom. There are enough people in each group to keep a large number of bathhouses operating even in major cities. But you should take note of the fact that many contemporary Russians look upon the **ба́ня** as old-fashioned and even, therefore, somewhat backward.

Cosmetics
Косме́тика

The use of cosmetics appears to be more limited in the USSR than it is with us. But this seems to be most directly related to availability in the first place and considerable inexperience in the second. In the major cities, at least, it is both chic and acceptable to use makeup **грим** and, most noticeably, to dye or bleach hair: "**Она́ кра́сит во́лосы**"—"She dyes her hair." Auburn hair (within the range of **кашта́новые во́лосы**) is currently very popular.

Various creams **кре́мы** are often required in makeup **гримиро́вка** and skin care **ухо́д за ко́жей**:

крем под пу́дру foundation cream
защи́тный крем protective skin cream
пита́тельный крем moisturizer

крем от зага́ра suntan lotion
крем от весну́шек freckle remover
крем для рук hand lotion

Other basic equipment includes:

каранда́ш для брове́й eyebrow pencil
тушь mascara
щётка для ресни́ц, щёточка eyelash brush
тень eye shadow
пу́дра powder
пу́дреница compact
пухо́вка powder puff
губна́я пома́да lipstick
румя́на rouge
лосьо́н makeup remover
духи́ perfume
лак fingernail polish
ацето́н fingernail polish remover
пи́лка fingernail file
щипцы́, щи́пчики tweezers

Men require less:

крем для бритья́ shaving cream
бри́тва razor
ле́звие razor blade
одеколо́н, лосьо́н shaving lotion

Cosmetics are not all that is involved in appearance, however. Americans tend to shave and pluck with considerable fervor, taking second place only to the French who seem willing to do anything for beauty's sake. Russian women do not consider all that plucking necessary. (Leg shaving is almost totally American.) And overweight is not a national ideal; the young, for instance, especially try to avoid the problem. Nevertheless, throughout the population there is a very strong feeling that someone who is thin is also therefore sickly. "**Она́ попра́вилась у нас!**" can mean "She put on weight (literally, got better) while she was here!"

Jewelry
Ювели́рные изде́лия

Extremes in personal decoration of any kind are neither common nor acceptable. Little jewelry is worn, often only one of the following: a brooch **брошь, брóшка**; a bracelet **браслéт**; a necklace **ожерéлье**; a chain **цепóчка**; or beads **бýсы** (*sg.* **бусúнка**). (**Кольé** is a fancy necklace, especially one made of precious stones.) Generally, the Russian precious stones **драгоцéнные кáмни** are our precious stones: diamond **бриллиáнт**, pearls **жéмчуг** (*sg.* **жемчýжина**), ruby **рубúн**, emerald **изумрýд**. However, a traditional and popular Russian ornament is cut and polished amber **янтáрь**, actually not a stone but a fossil resin, most of which comes from along the Baltic Sea coast. Green malachite **малахúт** is also a traditionally popular stone.

A note on rings: if the ring contains no major stone and is essentially a metal band, then the word is **кольцó**. Technically speaking, if it has a stone, especially a prominent one, then it is a **пéрстень**. (Therefore, our engagement rings are **пéрстни**.) Russian wedding rings **обручáльные кóльца** are used by both men and women. They usually consist of a single gold band and are worn on the fourth finger of the right hand, not the left. (During the 1930's, the wearing of rings was frowned upon as bourgeois, religious, superstitious, or a combination thereof.)

Earrings are among the most commonly seen jewelry. They come in two types: **сéрьги** (**однá серьгá**) are those earrings made for pierced ears; now, however, the other kind for unpierced ears **клúпсы** (*sg.* **клипс**) are quite popular.

As already noted, Russians use little jewelry. However almost everybody, especially children, has a small collection of **значкú** (*sg.* **значóк**). These are small pins, sometimes merely decorative little enamels of animals, humans, or other designs. Most often they are commemorative of some person or event—the flight into the "cosmos," for instance, or the insignia of an art festival. Small schoolchildren **октябрáта** wear one such pin with a picture of Lenin as a little boy with curls. A red star figures prominently in the **комсомóльский значóк** worn by Komsomol members. **Значкú** are also a form of award; thus, a "Master of Sport," for instance, gets a **значóк Мáстера спóрта**. These pins are pro-

duced in such profusion and are sufficiently popular and inexpensive that they make a favorite item for souvenir collecting and exchanging both among Russians and tourists.

Medals
Орденá, медáли

Another common phenomenon in Russian personal decor is the wearing of medals. The original medal **óрден** (less often, **медáль**) is usually not worn except for parades or similar occasions. Instead, one will often see the little colored bands **лéнты** or **лéнточки** in a jacket lapel or the like. These medals, as you have doubtless heard, are awarded not only for some outstanding military service but also for significant contributions in civilian life—all the way from Hero of Motherhood **Мáть-герóиня** (for delivering and rearing ten children when one or two children are the limit for most families), to the Order of the Red Banner of Labor **Óрден Трудовóго Крáсного Знáмени**. There are many such medals (see "For Valor, Heroism and Fortitude," *Soviet Life*, November, 1969). The best-known among them are:

Óрден Лéнина   the highest government award

Óрден Боевóго Крáсного Знáмени   the highest military award

Óрден Трудовóго Крáсного Знáмени   civilian parallel to the above

Óрден Крáсной Звезды́   a high military decoration

Óрден «Знак Почёта»   the civilian parallel to the above

You will notice, also, that not only people but entire factories and even cities and republics are awarded medals. **Москвá—гóрод герóй**.

Medals for civilians are by no means a Soviet innovation, except in the choice of recipients. Read, for instance, "**Áнна на шéе**," one of Chekhov's short stories.

With them they carry . . .
При себе́ но́сят . . .

A man's wallet **бума́жник** is the larger vest-pocket size and contains what you would expect. Coins **моне́ты** often go in pockets without benefit of a container. Other common necessities are, of course, a handkerchief **носово́й плато́к**, a comb **расчёска** (a somewhat more common term) or **гребёнка** (which also refers to what holds hair in place), glasses **очки́**, a watch **часы́**, and a pen **авторучка**. Keys **ключи́** are usually fewer in number and larger in size than are ours.

Women's purses **су́мки** (*sg.* **су́мка**) carry those objects that men must plant on their person. Money will be kept in a coin purse **коше-лёк**. In addition to a comb, women usually carry a mirror **зе́ркало**, their lipstick **губна́я пома́да**, and powder **пу́дра** in a compact **пу́дре-ница**. In cities almost all women and some men also carry a light net shopping bag **се́тка** or **аво́ська** (from **аво́сь** meaning: **мо́жет быть**) just in case they come across something on their way around town that is worth buying. And, even though more consumer goods are on the market all the time, finding and buying them is still treated as a matter of chance and luck.

Identification cards
Докуме́нты

As in English, when someone asks "Who's that?" the answer will be either a name (**Ива́н Ивано́в**) or a job title (**дире́ктор шко́лы**) or any outstanding relationship requiring description (**жена́ нача́льника** the boss's wife). But there are many occasions where official documentation of identity is required; this occurs much more frequently in the USSR. In fact, we should make it quite clear that identification papers are no less than vital to a Soviet citizen. Their loss is regarded as calamitous, for without them a person gets no job, no place to live, and so forth. During World War II those people who lost their papers risked the title and the treatment of "spy." The hero of Simonov's novel *The Living and the Dead* **Живы́е и мёртвые** spends a major part of the book trying to reestablish his identity and regain his party documents. The most universal identifier is the passport.

The passport **па́спорт** here referred to is also called the interior passport, that is, the one used within the USSR. For foreign trips, the Russian has to exchange his **па́спорт** for an exterior passport **заграни́чный па́спорт** as he leaves the country. The exchange again takes place when he reenters.

The internal passport is issued to everyone sixteen or over living in cities. Young people in the country have theirs kept for them by the local rural council **сельсове́т** until they finish school. This document is a requirement for traveling anywhere within the country. Rural stay-at-homes do not require them until they do travel. In everyday use, the passport will establish identity for receiving money orders and parcels at the post office, withdrawing money from the bank under certain circumstances, registering at hotels or dormitories, getting a job, renting equipment, and so forth.

The residence permit for foreigners **вид на жи́тельство для иностра́нца** that is shown here is much like a Soviet passport. The latter contains about the same information but also includes the "nationality" of both one's parents in addition to one's own. In the USSR "nationality" does not refer to citizenship. Instead, it answers the question, "Of what descent are you?" Possible answers are, for example: **ру́с-ский, украи́нец, эсто́нец, таджи́к, евре́й**. (Jews are therefore thought of as a nationality rather than a religion.) The nationality of either parent can be chosen for use in the passport.

Perhaps the next most commonly held identifier is the trade-union card **профсою́зный биле́т, профбиле́т** that shows you to be a member of the trade union attached to your place of work. Such membership is not compulsory, but advantages accrue to those who belong. Another important document, a record of employment **трудо-ва́я кни́жка**, is kept at the personnel office **отде́л ка́дров** at one's place of work.

Actually a foreigner's residence permit, this document is similar to an internal passport па́спорт.

Somewhere in the family archives is kept a birth certificate, colloquially called **ме́трика** and formally entitled **свиде́тельство о рожде́нии**.

People in certain positions require special identification. Thus a student needs his dormitory pass **про́пуск в общежи́тие**, university pass **про́пуск в университе́т**, library pass **чита́тельский биле́т**, and so forth. The Komsomol member needs his **комсомо́льский биле́т**, and males subject to the draft must have their draft card **во́инский биле́т**. Many people carry a prepaid public transport pass **проездно́й биле́т** that allows them to use a bus, trolley, or subway without further payment. Travel is made cheaper this way and more convenient, since one need not carry a store of small change.

Membership in the Communist party **парти́йность**, though granted to only about 5 percent of the population, is very important to the member. His proof of membership is **партбиле́т**. It is always carried on his person.

Job applications can be very revealing: they indicate what the employer wants or needs to know about the applicant. The following is the first paragraph from В. Аксёнов, *Колле́ги* (Москва́: Сове́тский писа́тель, 1961). The people here are three young men just out of medical school. They are filling out applications for their first job.

Кто они́ таки́е?

● В анке́тах они́ писа́ли: год рожде́ния—1932-й; происхожде́ние—из слу́жащих (Ка́рпов—из ра-

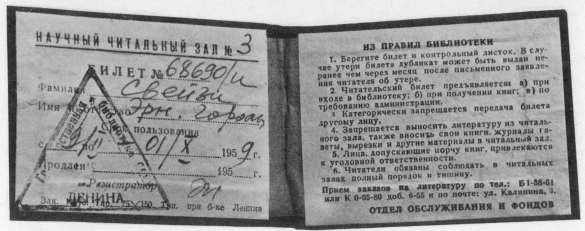

A library pass читáтельский билéт

бóчих); партúйность—член ВЛКСМ с 1947 гóда; учáстие в вóйнах—не учáствовал; судúмость—нет; имéет ли рóдственников за гранúцей—нет; и еще нéсколько «нет» до грáфы «семéйное по-ложéние» в котóрой всё онú писáли—хóлост. Автобиогрáфии их умещáлись на половúне странúчки, а расскáзывали онú о себé так. . . .

Age
Вóзраст

The standard words for people at advancing ages are:

ребёнок	ребёнок
дéвочка	мáльчик
дéвочка-подрóсток	подрóсток
дéвушка	ю́ноша
дéвушка	молодóй человéк
жéнщина	мужчúна
старýха	старúк

They are mentioned here only because of dis-tinctions commonly made in Russian that are not made in English. Technically speaking, our word "baby" should be груднóй ребёнок since ребёнок can be applied up to adolescence. A girl is дéвочка before puberty and дéвушка after puberty. As you can see, an obvious mistake in this distinction could be funny or even insulting. If you wish to specify a girl at puberty, дéвочка-подрóсток is used. Older married women some-times jokingly speak of each other as girls дéвочки, but even the aged saleswoman must be called дéвушка to get her attention since there is no better word. The word for a boy at pu-berty ю́ноша is much more commonly used than is the term дéвочка-подрóсток for girls. These are by no means all the words that refer to people at different ages, but the others are diminutives, pejoratives, or words with much more special-ized uses.

Младéнец, малю́тка, малы́ш are all affec-tionate and frequent substitutes for ребёнок; дитя́ (*pl.* дéти) is now used poetically in such locutions as дитя́ прирóды a child of nature; девчóнка is a bad little girl,[5] while девчýрка and девчýшка are good little girls; дéва and девúца are both poetic and old-fashioned words for дéвушка except that стáрая дéва is equivalent to "old maid"; дéвка can be either a mild pejorative for дéвушка or a prostitute.

As you know, the grammatical plural of ребёнок is ребя́та; but ребя́та is more fre-quently used meaning "the guys," "the gang," or "the kids." Дéти is the plural of ребёнок in practice. Notice that there is no word for child, someone beyond the baby stage, except in the plural—дéти; детворá is a collective and collo-quial singular for the small children.

[5] Current songs are also using it as an endearing term for a gay, happy-go-lucky type.

The man and his family
Челове́к и его́ семья́

Two charts, "One man's family" and "One woman's family," give the many titles Russians can use to identify those related by marriage. In the days of the expanded family (in *War and Peace*, for example) the Russian used these many different words for a woman's relatives and for a man's relatives. Today's nuclear family tends not to make so many distinctions. Words in parentheses are no longer commonly used except among peasants, where the usage is not incorrect, merely old fashioned.

It is interesting to note that from **сноха́**, **схоха́ч** is derived, a nasty word for a man who takes advantage of his daughter-in-law in a way that is normally reserved for her husband.

Though the origin of **неве́стка** is disputed, one explanation is: **неве́стка = не + ве́дать** (not + to know).

One man's family

(These are titles of those related to one man shown as ▼. X indicates marriage. Horizontal lines separate generations. Arrows indicate children from a marriage. Parentheses indicate outmoded usage.)

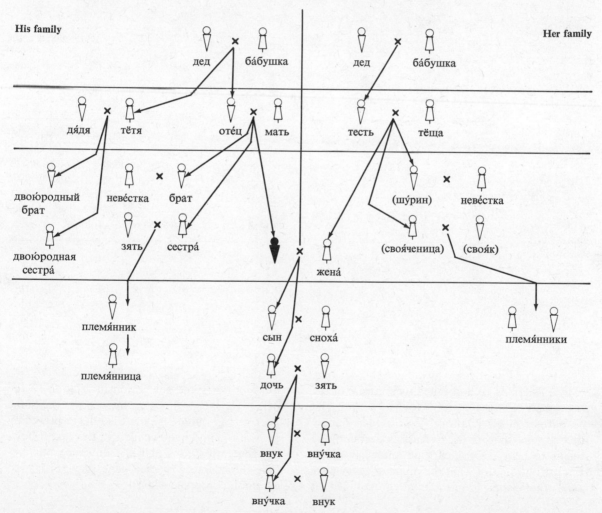

His family   Her family

One woman's family

(These are titles of those related to one woman shown as 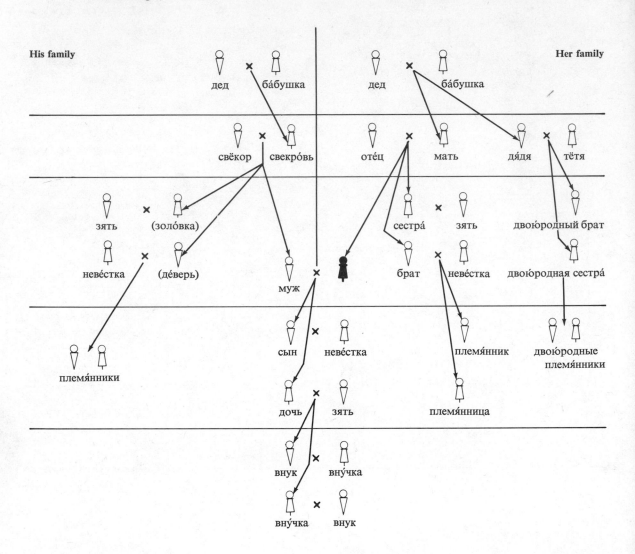 . X indicates marriage. Horizontal lines separate generations. Arrows indicate children from a marriage. Parentheses indicate outmoded usage.)

His family   Her family

дед   бáбушка   дед   бáбушка

свёкор   свекрóвь   отéц   мать   дя́дя   тётя

зять   (золóвка)   сестрá   зять   двою́родный брат

невéстка   (дéверь)   муж   брат   невéстка   двою́родная сестрá

племя́нники   сын   невéстка   племя́нник   двою́родные племя́нники

дочь   зять   племя́нница

внук   внучка

вну́чка   внук

The Russians are not much more aware of the titles their relatives might have than we are. The "Chart of blood relations" was made to show the system that is used. Russian terminology seems to have a significant advantage over the English: no matter what the modifier (**двою́родный**, **трою́родный** . . .), the noun modified at least indicates the generation in relation to the person spoken of. Thus, **брат** is in the same generation, **дя́дя** is in the next preceding generation, and **племя́нник** is in the next following generation. In English, many such relatives fade into degrees of cousinage that are lost to common comprehension.

Chart of blood relations in Russian and English
(The arrows separate generations; dotted lines connect them.)

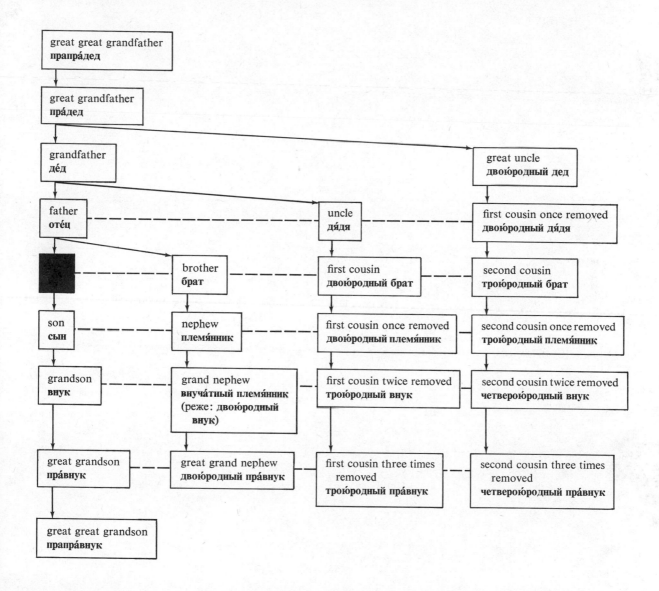

great great grandfather **прапра́дед**		
great grandfather **пра́дед**		
grandfather **де́д**		great uncle **двою́родный дед**
father **оте́ц**	uncle **дя́дя**	first cousin once removed **двою́родный дя́дя**
■	brother **брат**	first cousin **двою́родный брат**	second cousin **трою́родный брат**
son **сын**	nephew **племя́нник**	first cousin once removed **двою́родный племя́нник**	second cousin once removed **трою́родный племя́нник**
grandson **внук**	grand nephew **внуча́тный племя́нник** (реже: **двою́родный внук**)	first cousin twice removed **трою́родный внук**	second cousin twice removed **четверою́родный внук**
great grandson **пра́внук**	great grand nephew **двою́родный пра́внук**	first cousin three times removed **трою́родный пра́внук**	second cousin three times removed **четверою́родный пра́внук**
great great grandson **прапра́внук**		

2

Names
Имена́

Every Russian has one given name. That is not very startling information, except to those who read Russian novels in English. These people are bewildered by what seems to be an endless array of names for one person. Name usages and forms in the Soviet Union are quite different from ours, so this chapter is intended to both guide and explain. Russian, of course, has a different selection of popular names; **Васи́лий** in Russian and Basil in English do not enjoy the same status, in spite of their similar origin. Russian is also blessed with a variety of name forms that change according to status, formality, and attitude, so that one can be insulting, respectful, or endearing merely in the choice of name form. Part of learning Russian, then, is learning to use the right form or, at least, understanding when a Russian does.

For teachers who use Russian names in their classes, the first two columns from the "Table of names" in this chapter can be made available to students. Let them choose their own Russian class names. Until they have been chosen, address the students by their last names, as is frequently the practice in the Soviet Union. The student should always address the teacher by his first name and patronymic **и́мя и о́тчество**. Teachers might also point out that if their students ever go to the Soviet Union, the Russians will tend to call them by their real (American) names: **Пит, Дик, Джейн**. A foreign name, after all, has its charms.

For the non-Russian, Morton Benson, *Dictionary of Russian Personal Names*, with a guide to stress and morphology (Philadelphia: University of Pennsylvania Press, 1964), is a useful reference work. This book solves the problem of where to stress Russian surnames; 23,000 are listed with stress indications. Details are also given on declining surnames. The book includes as well a very handy alphabetized list of personal name diminutive forms indicating to which full name or names these refer. It is the next best thing to having a Russian on hand.

Here, the various aspects of naming are discussed in the following order:

What's your name?
Как вас зову́т?

This is the more familiar way of asking the question in Russian. Several answers to it are possible (which will be discussed):

Са́ша
Алекса́ндр
Алекса́ндр Миха́йлович (Петро́в)

It is more formal to ask:

(Прости́те), как ва́ше и́мя (и) о́тчество?
(Прости́те), как вас по и́мени и о́тчеству?

Somewhat old-fashioned and therefore ironic versions of asking for patronymics include:

Как вас велича́ют?
Как вас по ба́тюшке?
Как вас по отцу́?

If you are inquiring after a last name you say:

Как ва́ша фами́лия?

Forms that names can take[1]
Ра́зные фо́рмы имён

You have probably already noticed that Russians seem to have a wide variety of names to choose from when they are talking to each other. Middle-aged **А́нна Ива́новна** might have been

[1] These comments relate to the "Table of names."

called **Ню́ра** or **А́ня** by her classmates at sixteen, but at eight her friends often called her **А́нька** or **Ню́рка**, while her mother might have used any of those names plus many others: **А́нечка, Ню́сенька,** and so forth. What are all these names and how are they used?

The formal given name
По́лное ли́чное и́мя

The first column in the "Table of names" lists the formal given name, **по́лное ли́чное и́мя** (literally, the full personal name). This is the official name, the one listed on birth certificates, marriage licenses, or any official paper; for example: **А́нна, Ве́ра, Евге́ния, Алекса́ндр, Михаи́л.** The formal name is actually often used in conversation, especially if it is one of a small group of names—**Ве́ра, Ни́на, Глеб,** for instance—that has no commonly accepted shorter forms. This formal name is the only one used in combination with a patronymic **о́тчество.** Your signature in Russian usually includes the first letter of this full-name form and the surname: **В. Ива́но́в.**

The patronymic
О́тчество

This name type, also listed in the first column, is formed from a father's given name to which are added the endings **-ович, -евич, -ич** (Ива́-

нович, Никола́евич, Илья́ч) for a man, or -овна, -евна, -инична, -ична (Ива́новна, Никола́евна, Илья́нична, Са́ввична) for a woman. (The -ович, -овна are added to names ending in a consonant, the -евич, -евна to names ending in -й or a soft consonant, and -ич, -инична, -чна[2] are added to some names ending in -а or -я.) If your given name is А́нна and your father's name is Ива́н, then you will be А́нна Ива́новна. If your name is Михаи́л and your father's name is Никола́й, then you will be called Михаи́л Никола́евич, and so forth.

The patronymic is constantly used in spoken Russian. It is always polite and respectful to call someone by his и́мя и о́тчество. Americans must take special care to remember these two names when being introduced. It is this combination of names that you must use to speak and refer to that person thenceforth. Use this combination and the Вы form of address unless you are specifically told to use the more familiar ты. (In Chapter 9, see "When to use ты.") The patronymic is usually not included in one's signature.

The patronymic alone used to be a term of address among the peasants and petty bourgeois. It usually referred to older people and was always both respectful and familiar. Thus, in *Doctor Zhivago*, we read:

● —Вам Его́ровна зна́ки де́лает,—шепну́л Ю́ра.... На поро́ге стоя́ла Аграфе́на Его́ровна, ста́рая седа́я го́рничная.[3]

This use of the patronymic alone often appears in the Soviet press to invoke these feelings of folksiness, familiarity, and respect: Lenin is referred to as (наш) Илья́ч.

Diminutives
Уменьши́тельные фо́рмы

The second column in the "Table of names" gives the most common diminutive forms of the names in the first column. The less common

[2] -чна is pronounced as -шна.
[3] Бори́с Пастерна́к, *До́ктор Жива́го*, 2nd ed. (Ann Arbor: University of Michigan Press, 1958), p. 56.

diminutives are in parentheses. It is upon these diminutive forms that the endearing name forms ласка́тельные фо́рмы and the pejorative name forms пренебрежи́тельные фо́рмы are based. Thus if the formal name is Григо́рий, the most common diminutive is Гри́ша; from the latter are formed the endearing Гри́шенька, Гришу́ня, and the pejorative Гри́шка.

Notice that some formal names, especially the shorter ones, do not commonly have a diminutive. Instead, the endearing and pejorative forms are taken from the original name.

Generally speaking, the diminutives are used with members of one's family or good friends. Americans should not use the diminutives when speaking to a Russian unless told to do otherwise, or when obvious circumstances require them (when addressing a child, for instance).

ENDEARING NAME FORMS   ЛАСКА́ТЕЛЬНЫЕ ФО́РМЫ

The third column lists only the most common endearing names. As an example of why not all such possible forms can be included the list below gives some of the endearing varieties of the word па́па. Of course, not all these possibilities are equally popular, but the list does give an idea of the possible range.

Па́па

Папа́ша	Папу́ленька	Па́пушка
Па́пенька	Папу́лечка	Папу́шенька
Папа́шечка	Папу́льчик	Папа́ня
Папа́шенька	Папу́лька	Папа́нька
Папа́шка	Папу́лик	Папа́нечка
Папу́ся	Папу́ня	Папа́ненька
Папу́сечка	Папу́ненька	Папа́нюшка
Папу́сенька	Папу́нь	Папа́нчик
Папу́сик	Папу́нька	Пап
Папу́сь	Па́пка	Па́пище
Папу́ля	Па́почка	Па

Russians themselves seem to enjoy making up name forms, but you should confine yourself to those listed.

The fourth column includes only the most commonly heard pejorative names, those ending in -ка. "Growing up with a name in the USSR" describes how these are most often used.

There are still other pejorative name types. For instance, **Алёха**, **Федю́ха**, and **Кирю́ха** carry the notion that those mentioned are big, and even stupid, clods. But as with almost all pejorative endings, the intended meaning depends almost entirely on the situation. There are also dialectical variations. These names can be an endearment to a very close friend. What they do not connote is respect for someone you do not know well.

The table does not contain a name form especially common among children. When calling to each other children will often abbreviate the diminutive in the second column. For example, there is **Маш!** or **Марь!** for **Мари́я** or **Ма́рья**; **Владь!** for **Вла́дя**; **Тань!** for **Та́ня**; or **пап!** for **па́па**.

A table of names
Табли́ца имён

Names most educated Soviet Russians are likely to choose for their children are listed in the table. The choice is highly subjective, and since names do go in and out of fashion, one is quite likely to come across others; however, most other names are relatively rare or carry the heavy burden of strong social or religious connotations. This is only a general guide, not a complete exposition of all possibilities. Many of the names cited here may be spelled in other ways. Usually the formal church spelling of the name (see "Choosing a name before the Revolution") is somewhat longer: **Дими́трий** and **Дми́трий**, **Илия́** and **Илья́**, **Иродио́н** and **Родио́н**. The table provides the spelling that is now most often used.

The most popular names are underlined. Names or their diminutives that are often associated with peasants are followed by an asterisk. Name forms in parentheses are less commonly used but are encountered often enough to be worthy of mention.

Table of names—men's names   **Табли́ца имён—мужски́е имена́**

Full name, patronymic По́лное ли́чное и́мя, о́тчество	Diminutives Уменьши́тельные фо́рмы	Endearing forms Ласка́тельные фо́рмы	Pejorative forms Пренебрежи́тельные фо́рмы
Алекса́ндр Алекса́ндрович Алекса́ндровна	Са́ша, Шу́ра, Са́ня (А́лик)	Са́шенька, Са́шечка, Шу́рочка, Са́нечка, Сашу́ня	Са́шка, Шу́рка, Са́нька
Алексе́й Алексе́евич Алексе́евна	Алёша, Лёша	Алёшенька, Лёшенька	Алёшка, Лёшка, Алёха, Лёха
Анато́лий Анато́льевич (-иевич)[1] Анато́льевна (-иевна)[1]	То́ля	То́лик, То́ленька, То́лечка, То́люшка	То́лька
Андре́й Андре́евич Андре́евна	Андрю́ша	Андрю́шенька, Андре́йка	Андрю́шка
Анто́н[2]	Анто́ша (То́ша)	Анто́шенька	Анто́шка
Арка́дий Арка́дьевич (-иевич) Арка́дьевна (-иевна)	Арка́ша	Арка́шенька	Арка́шка

[1] -иевич is used but -ьевич is preferred.
[2] Hereafter, except as noted, the patronymics of names ending in a hard consonant are formed by adding -ович or -овна.

Full name, patronymic По́лное ли́чное и́мя, о́тчество	Diminutives Уменьши́тельные фо́рмы	Endearing forms Ласка́тельные фо́рмы	Pejorative forms Пренебрежи́тельные фо́рмы
Бори́с	Бо́ря (Бо́ба, Боб)	Бо́ренька, Бо́речка	Бо́рька
Вади́м	Ва́дик (Ва́дя)	Ва́денька	Ва́дька
Валенти́н	Ва́ля	Валёк, Ва́лечка, Ва́ленька	Ва́лька
Вале́рий	Вале́ра (Ва́ля, Ле́ра)	Вале́рочка	Вале́рка
Вале́риевич (-ьевич) Вале́риевна (-ьевна)			
Валерья́н	Вале́ра (Ва́ля, Ле́ра)	Вале́рочка	Вале́рка
Васи́лий	Ва́ся	Ва́сенька	Ва́ська
Васи́льевич Васи́льевна			
Вениами́н	Ве́ня	Ве́нечка, Ве́нюшка	Ве́нька
Ви́ктор	Ви́тя	Ви́тенька, Витю́ша	Ви́тька
Вита́лий	Ви́тя	Вита́лик	Вита́лька
Вита́льевич (-иевич) Вита́льевна (-иевна)			
Влади́мир	Воло́дя, Во́ва	Воло́денька, Во́вочка, Воло́дик	Воло́дька, Во́вка
Владисла́в	Вла́дик, Вла́дя, Сла́ва	Вла́денька, Владю́ша	Вла́дька
Все́волод	Се́ва	Се́вочка	Се́вка
Вячесла́в	Сла́ва, Сла́вик	Сла́вочка	Сла́вка
Генна́дий	Ге́ня, Ге́на, Ге́ша	Ге́нечка	Ге́нька, Ге́нка
Генна́диевич (-ьевич) Генна́диевна (-ьевна)			
Гео́ргий, Его́р*	Жо́ра, Жорж, Го́ша, Го́га (Го́ра)	Жо́рочка, Его́рушка, Го́шенька	Жо́рка, Его́рка, Го́шка
Гео́ргиевич Гео́ргиевна			
Ге́рман	Ге́ра (Ге́ша)	Ге́рочка	Ге́рка
Глеб	Глеб	Гле́бушка	Гле́бка
Григо́рий	Гри́ша	Гри́шенька, Гришу́ня, Гришу́та, Гришу́нька	Гри́шка, Гришу́ха
Григо́рьевич Григо́рьевна			
Дми́трий	Ди́ма, Ми́тя	Ди́мочка, Ми́тенька, Митю́ша	Ди́мка, Ми́тька
Дми́триевич Дми́триевна			
Евге́ний	Же́ня (Ге́ня)	Же́нечка, Ге́нечка	Же́нька
Евге́ньевич (-иевич) Евге́ньевна (-иевна)			
Ива́н	Ва́ня	Ваню́ша, Ва́нечка, Ваню́шечка, Ваню́шка, Ива́нушка	Ва́нька
И́горь	И́горь, Го́га, Го́ша (Го́ра)	Игорёк, Го́шенька, Го́гочка, Игорю́шка	Го́шка
И́горевич И́горевна			
Илья́	Илю́ша, Илью́ша	Илью́шенька, Илю́шечка	Илю́шка
Ильи́ч Ильи́нична			

Full name, patronymic Полное личное имя, отчество	Diminutives Уменьшительные формы	Endearing forms Ласкательные формы	Pejorative forms Пренебрежительные формы
Климент	Клим	Климочка	Климка
Константин	Костя	Костенька, Костюша, Костюшка, Котик	Костька, Котька
Лев Львович Львовна	Лёва	Лёвушка	Лёвка
Леонид	Лёня	Лёнечка	Лёнька
Леонтий Леонтьевич (-иевич) Леонтьевна (-иевна)	Лёня	Лёнечка	Лёнька
Максим	Макс	Максимочка	Максимка
Михаил Михайлович Михайловна	Миша	Мишенька, Мишутка	Мишка
Мстислав	Слава	Славочка, Славик	Славка
Никита Никитич Никитична	Ника	Никитушка	Никитка
Николай Николаевич Николаевна	Коля	Коленька, Николаша	Колька
Олег	Олег	Олежек, Олёженька, Олёжечка	Олёжка
Павел Павлович Павловна	Паша	Пашенька, Павлик, Павлуша, Павлушенька	Пашка
Пётр Петрович Петровна	Петя	Петенька	Петька
Родион	Родя	Роденька	Родька
Роман	Рома	Ромочка, Ромаша	Ромка
Ростислав	Слава, Ростя	Славочка, Ростик, Славик	Славка
Сергей Сергеевич Сергеевна	Серёжа	Серёженька	Серёжка
Станислав	Стасик (Слава, Стась)	Стасинька	Стаська
Степан	Стёпа	Стёпочка	Стёпка
Фёдор	Федя	Феденька, Федюшка	Федька, Федюха
Эдуард	Эдик	Эдинька	Эдька
Юрий Юрьевич Юрьевна	Юра	Юрочка	Юрка
Яков Яковлевич Яковлевна	Яша	Яшенька	Яшка

Full name По́лное ли́чное и́мя	Diminutives Уменьши́тельные фо́рмы	Endearing forms Ласка́тельные фо́рмы	Pejorative forms Пренебрежи́тельные формы
А́да, Аделаи́да	А́да	А́дочка	А́дка
Алекса́ндра	Са́ша, Шу́ра, Са́ня	Са́шенька, Сашу́ра, Шу́рочка	Са́шка, Шу́рка
Али́на	А́ля (Ли́на)	А́ленька	А́лька
А́лла	А́ля	А́лочка	А́лка
Анаста́сия, Наста́сья	На́стя, Та́ся, (А́ся)	Настю́ша, На́стенька, Та́сенька, Настю́шка, Тасю́ша, Та́сечка	На́стька, Та́ська
А́нна	А́ня, Ню́ра (Ню́ня, Ню́та, Ню́ша, Ню́ся)	А́нечка, Аню́та, Аню́точка, А́ннушка, Ню́рочка	А́нька, Ню́рка
Бе́лла (Бе́ла, Бэ́ла)	Бе́ла (Бэ́ла)	Бе́лочка, Бэ́лочка	Бе́лка, Бэ́лка
Валенти́на	Ва́ля (Тина)	Валю́ша, Ва́лечка, Валю́шенька	Ва́лька
Вале́рия	Ва́ля, Ле́ра	Ле́рочка, Вале́рочка	Ле́рка, Вале́рка
Варва́ра	Ва́ря (Ва́ва)	Варю́ша, Ва́ренька, Варю́шенька	Ва́рька
Ве́ра	Ве́ра	Ве́рочка, Веру́ша, Веру́шенька	Ве́рка
Верони́ка	Ни́ка, Ве́ра, Ви́ка	Ни́кочка	
Гали́на	Га́ля	Га́лечка, Га́лочка, Га́ленька	Га́лька, Га́лка
Да́рья	Да́ша	Да́шенька	Да́шка
Жа́нна	Жа́нна	Жа́ночка, Жану́ся	Жа́нка
Евге́ния	Же́ня	Же́нечка, Женю́ра	Же́нька
Евдоки́я (Авдо́тья*)	Ду́ся, Ду́ня*	Ду́сенька, Ду́нечка, Дуня́ша, Дуня́шенька	Ду́ська, Ду́нька
Екатери́на, Катери́на	Ка́тя	Катю́ша, Ка́тенька, Катю́шенька	Ка́тька
Еле́на (Алёна)	Ле́на (Лёля)	Ле́ночка	Ле́нка
Елизаве́та (Лизаве́та)	Ли́за	Ли́зочка	Ли́зка
Зинаи́да	Зи́на	Зи́ночка	Зи́нка
Зо́я	Зо́я	Зо́енька, Зо́ечка	Зо́йка
Изабе́лла, Изабэ́лла	Бе́лла (Бе́ла, Бэ́ла, И́за)	Бе́лочка	Бе́лка
И́нна	И́нна	И́нночка, Ину́ся, Ину́ля	И́нка
Ине́сса	И́на	И́ночка, Ину́ля, Ину́ся	И́нка, Ине́ска
Ираи́да	И́ра, Йда	И́рочка	И́рка
Ири́на (Ари́на*)	И́ра	И́рочка, Ири́ша	И́рка
Капитоли́на	Ка́па (Ли́на, То́ля)	Ка́почка	Ка́пка
Ки́ра	Ки́ра	Ки́рочка	Ки́рка
Кла́вдия	Кла́ва (Кла́ня, Кла́ша)	Кла́вочка, Клавдю́ша, Кла́вденька	Кла́вка
Кла́ра	Кла́ра	Кла́рочка	Кла́рка
Ксе́ния (Акси́нья*)	Ксе́ня (А́ся)	Ксю́шенька, А́сенька	Ксю́шка, А́ська
Лари́са	Ла́ра (Ло́ра)	Ла́рочка, Ла́ринька	Ла́рка
Ли́дия	Ли́да (Ли́ля)	Ли́дочка	Ли́дка

Full name По́лное ли́чное и́мя	Diminutives Уменьши́тельные фо́рмы	Endearing forms Ласка́тельные фо́рмы	Pejorative forms Пренебрежи́тельные формы
Ли́лия	Ли́ля	Ли́лечка	Ли́лька
Любо́вь	Лю́ба	Лю́бочка, Люба́ша	Лю́бка
Людми́ла	Лю́ся, Ми́ла, Лю́да	Лю́сенька, Ми́лочка, Лю́дочка	Лю́ська, Ми́лка, Лю́дка
Ма́йя	Ма́я	Ма́ечка	Ма́йка
Маргари́та	Ри́та	Ри́точка, Риту́ля	Ри́тка
Мари́на	Мари́на (Ма́ра, Ри́на)	Мари́ночка, Мари́ша	Мари́нка
Мари́я, Ма́рья	Ма́ша, Мару́ся, Ма́ня (Ма́ра, Му́ся, Му́ра)	Ма́шенька, Мару́сенька, Ма́нечка	Ма́шка, Ма́нька
Наде́жда	На́дя	На́денька, Надю́ша	На́дька
Ната́лья (Ната́лия)	Ната́ша (На́та, Та́ша)	Ната́шенька	Ната́шка
Нэ́лли, Нэ́лли	Нэ́ля, Нэ́ля	Нэ́лочка, Нэ́лочка, Нэ́лечка	Нэ́лька
Ни́на	Ни́на	Ни́ночка	Ни́нка
Но́нна	Но́нна, Но́на	Но́нночка, Нону́ся	Но́нка
О́льга	О́ля (Лёля, Ля́ля)	О́ленька	О́лька
Поли́на	По́ля	По́ленька, По́лечка	По́лька
Раи́са	Ра́я	Ра́ечка	Ра́йка
Ри́мма	Ри́мма	Ри́мочка, Риму́ля	Ри́мка
Светла́на	Све́та (Ла́на)	Све́тик, Све́точка	Све́тка
Со́фья	Со́ня	Со́нечка	Со́нька
Тама́ра	Тама́ра (То́ма, Ма́ра)	Тама́рочка	Тама́рка, То́мка
Татья́на	Та́ня (Та́та)	Та́нечка, Таню́ша	Та́нька
Э́лла	Э́лла	Э́ллочка	Э́лка
Э́мма	Э́мма	Э́мочка	Э́мка
Ю́лия	Ю́ля	Ю́лечка, Ю́ленька	Ю́лька

Growing up with a name in the USSR
И́мя и во́зраст

It is probably the smallest babies that are exposed to the largest and widest variety of names. The child might hear his full first name (first column, "Table of names") at birth and not again until he goes to school at seven. Russian mothers delight in using the most endearing name forms they know and then feel free to make up others if established ones are not enough. Pasternak illustrates this phenomenon:

● Она́ обожа́ла Ни́ку и из его́ и́мени Инноке́нтий де́лала ку́чу немы́слимо-не́жных и дура́цких про́звищ, вро́де Й́ночек и́ли Но́ченька.[4]

The small child hears his name in the endearing form (third column, "Table of names") so often that he might think it his official name. Chukovskiy, in *From Two to Five*, cites one such child:

● Слу́шай, ма́ма, когда́ я роди́лся, отку́да ты узна́ла, что я Ю́рочка?[5]

[4] Пастерна́к, *До́ктор Жива́го*, стр. 18.
[5] Корне́й Чуко́вский, *От двух до пяти́*, 17-ое изд. (Москва́: Детги́з, 1963), стр. 320.

He will hear **Юрочка** throughout his life, first from his mother and later, though infrequently, from his wife (who will usually call him **Юра**).

When he is old enough to socialize his mother will introduce him to new friends as **Юра** (second column). He will address those other children in like manner until he considers them good friends, at which point he and they will often switch to the usually derogatory name (fourth column). To his friends and siblings he will be **Юрка**. (The derogatory **-ка** endings are actually used in several ways: they can be used among children to say "You're my pal"; among adult friends who might be saying something like "You're crazy, but I like you anyway"; and by adults toward particularly offensive children. The neighborhood brat would probably be so referred to by almost everyone. Use of this form, however, does not meet with society's approval; it is considered crude. Therefore a teacher would avoid using it even though a pupil might well deserve it.)

In class Yuri's teacher will often refer to him by his last name alone, or sometimes as **Юрий** or **Юра**. The younger he is, the more familiar the teacher will be. Out of class the teacher might call him **Юрий**, **Юра**, or **Юрочка** depending on the situation—**Юрий** or **Юра** if emotion is not involved, and **Юрочка** if he has been hurt, for instance. He will always address his teacher and adults not in his family by their full name and patronymic.

At puberty many things change, not the least his name. Now his friends call him **Юра** or **Юрий** most of the time; **Юрочка** and **Юрка** remain for special rather than normal use.

He comes into his own when he starts work; then he will normally be addressed by his full name and patronymic: **Юрий Иванович**. Only his relatives and good friends have the privilege of using the diminutive forms of his name.

Women's names are used in the same way as men's. Most women take their husband's surname when they marry, but it is fairly common in the Soviet Union to marry and keep one's maiden name (as professional women do in the United States). You should not think it unusual that a wife has a different surname from her husband. The least common alternative for a woman when she marries is to connect her surname to her husband's with a hyphen. This is done when there is thought to be some advantage in retaining both names.

Choosing a name before the Revolution
Вы́бор и́мени до револю́ции

Before the Revolution, the choice of names that could be given a child was limited to a list of saints' names **свя́тцы** that had been approved by the Eastern Orthodox Church **Правосла́вная це́рковь**. Each saint had his day on the calendar,[6] and those who had been named after that saint celebrated this day more commonly than they did a birthday **день рожде́ния**. It was called a name day **имени́ны**. When the person celebrating his name day was male, then he was an **имени́нник**; if female, she was an **имени́нница**.

The Russians, then, or more specifically the Russians that adhered to the Russian Orthodox Church, could use only saints' names to begin with. But there were other limitations mostly having to do with social status but also sometimes related to occupation.

There was a relatively small number of names that were both popular and acceptable at all levels of society. For men such names were:

Алекса́ндр	Григо́рий	Ники́та
Алексе́й	Дми́трий	Па́вел
Анто́н	Ива́н	Пётр
Андре́й	Кири́лл	Са́вва
Васи́лий	Константи́н	Серге́й
Влади́мир	Макси́м	Степа́н
Гео́ргий	Михаи́л	Фёдор
(Ю́рий)	Никола́й	Я́ков

For women such names were:

Алекса́ндра	Еле́на	Мари́я
Анастаси́я	Елизаве́та	О́льга

[6] The Julian calendar. See "Time" in Chapter 11.

Анна	Зинаи́да	Раи́са
Варва́ра	Кла́вдия	Со́фья
Ве́ра	Любо́вь	Татья́на
Екатери́на		

Ла́зарь	Ро́за
Мануи́л	Руфь
Моисе́й	Са́рра
Соломо́н	Эсфи́рь
Эммануи́л	

There also was a set of names that would only be found in major cities and in higher society. Men's names of this sort were:

Анато́лий	Вениами́н	Ипполи́т
Аполло́н	Вита́лий	Кла́вдий
Арка́дий	Все́волод	Лев
Вади́м	Вячесла́в	Леони́д
Валенти́н	Евге́ний	Рома́н
Валериа́н	И́горь	

Women used:

Аделаи́да	Евге́ния	Ли́дия
Антони́на	Ираи́да	Людми́ла
Ариа́дна	Кале́рия	Магдали́на
Валенти́на	Ксе́ния	Олимпиа́да
Ва́сса	Лари́са	Ю́лия
Е́ва		

Some names were most often associated with the clergy. Monks had names like:

Ага́пий	Гермоге́н	Никоди́м
Агафо́н	Зоси́ма	Ни́кон
Агафа́нгел	Иерони́м	Ти́хон
Амвро́сий	Илиодо́р	Феодо́сий
Анаста́сий	Не́стор	Филаре́т
Варлаа́м		

Nuns were called:

Ага́пия	Глике́рия	Нимфодо́ра
Афана́сия	Диони́сия	Фео́ния
Вириме́я	Лео́нтия	Ювена́лия

Orthodox Russians (in essence, all Russians) also tended to avoid certain names, considering them Jewish in spite of the fact that many such names were in the list of saints **свя́тцы**. Such names were:

Абра́м	Ди́на
Ада́м	Ли́я
Дави́д	Мариа́мна
Исаа́к	Рахи́ль

There were some names, as listed by Černyšev,[7] that were ordinarily only found in use among the peasants. (The spelling here follows that in the **свя́тцы**. In everyday use many of these names are slightly shorter and there are occasional vowel and consonant changes, too.) These included for the men's names:

Авра́м	Иусти́н	Пармён
Агафо́н	Карп	Пота́пий
Амвро́сий	Кири́лл	Пи́мен
Архи́п	Козьма́	Проко́пий
Афана́сий	Ла́зарь	Про́хор
Вла́сий	Лука́	Симео́н
Гаврии́л	Лукиа́н	Созо́нт
Гера́сим	Мака́рий	Спиридо́н
Глеб	Макси́м	Стефа́н
Дании́л	Марк	Тара́сий
Диоми́д	Матфе́й	Тере́нтий
Диони́сий	Миро́н	Тимофе́й
Евдоки́м	Митрофа́н	Тит
Евфи́мий	Наза́рий	Ти́хон
Заха́рий	Нау́м	Три́фон
Игна́тий	Ники́та	Трофи́м
Иларио́н	Ники́фор	Фо́ка
Илия́	Нил	Фаде́й
Иа́ков	Они́сим	Фома́
Ио́сиф	Парамо́н	

Among the women's names were:

Ага́фия	Евдоки́я	Параске́ва
Агриппи́на	Евфроси́ния	Пелаги́я
Акили́на	Иули́тта	Стефани́да
Ани́сия	Ма́рфа	Фёкла
Васили́са	Матро́на	Феодо́ра
Глике́рия	Мела́ния	Феодо́сия
Да́рия		

Some names popular among the peasants also began to connote qualities commonly attributed

7 V. Černyšev, "Les Prénoms Russes, Formation et Vitalité," *Revue des Études Slaves*, v. 4, fasc. 3 et 4 (Paris, 1934), p. 212.

by the upper classes to the peasantry, such as dirtiness, stupidity, and ineptitude. A few of these names were:

Агафо́н	Ага́фья
Софро́н	Акули́на
Созо́нт	Афроси́нья
Харито́н	Мала́ния
Фалале́й	Нени́ла
Феду́л	Ули́та
	Фёкла

One of the sayings Даль recorded was: **"И по ры́лу знать, что Созо́нтом звать"**—"You can tell by his ugly mug that his name must be Созо́нт."

The peasants and petty bourgeois used a wider selection of names because they followed the custom of choosing a name for a child according to his day of birth. The church calendar would usually supply several names to choose from[8] and superstition held that not to choose one of these names would deprive the child of good health, protection, and the like.

The following page was taken from a calendar used by emigré Russians; it gives the date according to the Julian calendar (Old Style), the Gregorian calendar (New Style), and also lists religious festivals for the day. The calendars are a convenient device for showing when your friends will be celebrating their name day.

A common church calendar lists not just one, but sixty-two Saint Ivan's days and not just one, but nineteen Saint Mary's days. It is no wonder that non-Russians tend to think of any Russian as Ivan.

Gogol humorously described how a half-hearted attempt to follow the tradition of using the church calendar produced the unfortunate name of **Ака́кий Ака́киевич**, the "hero" of his story "The Overcoat." The names **Мо́ккий, Со́ссий, Хоздаза́т, Трифи́лий, Ду́ла, Вараха́сий, Павсика́хий,** and **Вахти́сий** sound absolutely ridiculous to a Russian.

• Свято́го проро́ка Иереми́и, му́ченика Ва́ты мона́ха, свяще́нному́ченика Мака́рия, Митрополи́та Ки́евского (1497 г.), преподо́бного Пафну́тия Боро́вского (1477 г.), свято́й цари́цы Тама́ры Грузи́нской. Ико́ны Бо́жией Ма́тери Царевококша́йской или Мироно́сицкой; Византи́йской и Андро́никовской.

Чте́ния: Дея́ния XII, 1–11; Иоа́нна VIII, 31–42.

Четвёртая седми́ца по Па́схе (Преполове́ния)

Choosing a name after the Revolution
Вы́бор и́мени по́сле револю́ции

The Revolution affected names almost as much as it did life. No longer were Russians confined to the use of church names. Some new ones were in order.

One change was, happily, only temporary. In

the 1920's it was not uncommon to name one's child after revolutionary events, leaders, and ideals. Thus **Владле́н** is **Влади́мир** + **Ле́нин**, **Нине́ль** is **Ле́нин** spelled backwards, and **Ким** is formed from the initials of **Коммунисти́ческий интернациона́л молодёжи**. Women's names like **Лени́на** and **Стали́на** appeared; **Дотна́ра** is **дочь трудово́го наро́да**. Most of such names disappeared as quickly as they came. One no longer hears **Э́ра**, **Иде́я**, **Поэ́ма**, **Робеспье́р**, or **Тру́да**. Nor would one dream nowadays of naming his child **Карм** (**Кра́сная А́рмия**), **Ревди́т** (**революцио́нное дитя́**), and the like.

Other more important changes have occurred, however. Since more people live in cities than before, and since there is greater social mobility, the higher-class names are more popular than ever and the names that seem to insist on one's peasanthood (**Харито́н**, **Заха́рий**, **Ма́вра**, **Акули́на**, and many others) are becoming less common.

Not long ago Western names were temporarily popular—**Кла́ра**, **Не́лли**, **Э́мма**, **Эми́лия**, **Альбе́рт**, **Арту́р**, **Леона́рд**—though these names are not common. Very popular names now are those that go far back into history—**Влади́мир**, **Все́волод**, **И́горь**, and the like. Generally, names still carry the connotations that they did before the Revolution. **Акули́на** is still a peasant, and **Соломо́н** is still a Jew. As for birthdays and name days, those who remember their name days often celebrate them. More often, one has a birthday **день рожде́ния** but not infrequently refers to it as his **имени́ны**.

The passage that follows offers instruction to lady authors of romantic novels for naming characters in their stories. It gives many clues to contemporary feelings about names and their various diminutives.

На после́днем сло́ге
(Сове́ты а́вторам да́мских рома́нов)

● Положе́ние писа́тельницы я бы сравни́ла с положе́нием многоде́тной ма́тери. Ведь пре́жде чем ее де́тища начну́т де́йствовать, их ну́жно оде́ть, обу́ть, накорми́ть, дать им жилпло́щадь, и хоть каку́ю-нибудь обстано́вку. А кто это

до́лжен сде́лать? Ну, коне́чно, мы, авторе́ссы.

Геро́й роди́лся—на́до его́ назва́ть.... При́нципы подбо́ра имён, пра́вда, не но́вы. Положи́тельного геро́я мо́жно назва́ть Андре́ем, Алексе́ем, Па́влом, в кра́йнем слу́чае, Серге́ем (хотя́ в э́том после́днем слу́чае он обяза́тельно до́лжен поги́бнуть. Почему́-то Серге́и всегда́ ги́бнут.) Называ́ть положи́тельного геро́я Ива́ном, Петро́м, а тем бо́лее Кузьмо́й или Про́хором не рекоменду́ется—чита́тельница мо́жет бро́сить чита́ть. Э́ти имена́ испо́льзуются на подсо́бных рабо́тах. У Андре́я (Алексе́я, Па́вла) мо́жет быть друг, сла́вный паренёк из рабо́чих (железнодоро́жников, поэ́тов, колхо́зников, аспира́нтов сельскохозя́йственного ву́за—нену́жное вы́черкнуть). Рабо́та его́ заключа́ется в том, что он выслу́шивает изложе́ние нау́чных взгля́дов, техни́ческих заду́мок и заве́тных ча́яний положи́тельного геро́я. Э́ти страни́цы чита́тельницы, как пра́вило, пропуска́ют.

Полуположи́тельных геро́ев, очелове́ченных отде́льными недоста́тками, рекоменду́ется называ́ть имена́ми вро́де И́горь, Леони́д, Анато́лий. Уменьши́тельные их имена́ зави́сят от того́, како́го элеме́нта в геро́е бо́льше—положи́тельного или отрица́тельного. В пе́рвом слу́чае Леони́да бу́дут называ́ть в семье́ и в дру́жеском кругу́ Лёнькой или Лёхой. Но е́сли в нём бо́льше плохи́х черт, то уменьши́тельное и́мя ему́ даётся странова́тое, вро́де Леони́дика или Лю́сика. Е́сли в рома́не есть отрица́тельная тёща, то тако́го зя́тя она́ бу́дет называ́ть Лео́, с францу́зским ударе́нием на после́днем сло́ге.

Имена́ отрица́тельных геро́ев уже́ хорошо́ обка́таны—э́то Эдуа́рд (Э́дик), Арно́льд да ещё, пожа́луй, Вади́м. Таки́е имена́ даю́тся развра́тникам, тру́сам и кандида́там нау́к, кото́рые, как всем изве́стно, положи́тельными геро́ями быть не мо́гут. Развра́тники и абстракциони́сты должны́ име́ть фами́лии позаковы́ристее—Ке́дро-Ливано́вич или Венесуэ́льский. Зажи́мщикам самокри́тики и управдо́мам мо́жно дава́ть фами́лии вро́де Глы́га или Щуп.

В же́нских имена́х то́же есть свои́ то́нкости, свои́ нюа́нсы. Вы что ду́маете—назва́ли свою́ геро́йню Елизаве́той, и на э́том де́ло ко́нчилось? Е́сли она́ положи́тельная, то бу́дут звать э́ту Елизаве́ту Ли́зой; е́сли с мяту́щейся, го́рдой душо́й, то быть ей Ли́кой; а е́сли открове́нно отрица́тельная—то Ли́лькой и́ли, прости́ го́споди, Ли́ззи. Рокову́ю же́нщину по па́спорту чи́слящуюся Елизаве́той, мо́жно ещё называ́ть Ве́той.

Я про́сто удивля́юсь, что не́которые начина́ющие авторе́ссы не понима́ют бе́здну, раз-

деля́ющую Анаста́сию, кото́рую до́ма зову́т
На́стей (больши́е се́рые глаза́, железобето́нное
целому́дрие, непримири́мость к тому́-сему́), с её
тёзкой, друго́й Анаста́сией, кото́рую до́ма зову́т
А́стой (зелёные, ко́со поста́вленные глаза́, чёрный сви́тер в обтя́жку, разгово́р о Ка́фке и не-
коммуника́бельности).

Васи́лий	Васи́льевна	Васи́льна
Григо́рий	Григо́рьевна	Григо́рьна
Арсе́ний	Арсе́ньевна	Арсе́нна
Евге́ний	Евге́ньевна	Евге́нна
Влади́мир	Влади́мировна	Влади́мирна
Фёдор	Фёдоровна	Фёдорна
Бори́с	Бори́совна	Бори́сна

Pronouncing first names and patronymics
Произноше́ние имён и о́тчеств

The first name and patronymic together (**Ива́н
Ива́нович**) are the normal title used in talking
to or about an adult who is not a close friend or
a member of the family. The combination is
rather long and is also used very frequently.
As a result these names, especially the patronymic, are shortened somewhat (**Ива́н Ива́ныч**).
The following table gives examples of types of
this phenomenon taken from a classic reference
on Russian pronunciation, Р. И. Аване́сов,
Ру́сское литерату́рное произноше́ние (Москва́: Учпедги́з, 1954). This pronunciation is used
in standard spoken Russian; emphasis, clarity,
or a formal occasion can require the more distinct enunciation of each syllable.

Pronunciation of men's patronymics when used with first names

From the name	One writes	One says
Ива́н	Ива́нович	Ива́ныч
Степа́н	Степа́нович	Степа́ныч
Анто́н	Анто́нович	Анто́ныч
Макси́м	Макси́мович	Макси́мыч
Михаи́л	Миха́йлович	Миха́лыч
Па́вел	Па́влович	Па́лыч
Алекса́ндр	Алекса́ндрович	Алекса́ныч
Андре́й	Андре́евич	Андре́ич
Серге́й	Серге́евич	Серге́ич
Алексе́й	Алексе́евич	Алексе́ич
Никола́й	Никола́евич	Никола́ич
Васи́лий	Васи́льевич	Васи́лич
Ю́рий	Ю́рьевич	Ю́рич
Дми́трий	Дми́триевич	Дми́трич

Some men's first names, those that end in a
consonant or **-й** with stress on the stem, are not
declined in the oblique cases in normal speech.
Thus, **к Ива́ну Ива́новичу** is **к Ива́ныва́нычу**;
от Степа́на Григо́рьевича is **от Степа́н Гри-
го́рича**. But if the stress is on the ending of the
first (given) name, then it too must be declined
in speech; thus: **ко Льву́ Ива́нычу**, **за Льво́м
Петро́вичем**, **от Петра́ Никола́ича**.

A few men's first names are pronounced differently when used with patronymics; for
example: **Михаи́л**, but one says **Миха́л-Нико-
ла́ич**; **Па́вел**, but **Па́л-Петро́вич**; **Алекса́ндр**,
but **Алекса́н-Петро́вич**.

Surnames and their nationality
Фами́лии и национа́льность

The majority of Russian surnames end in **-ов/
-ев**, **-ин** (**Ивано́в**, **Фоми́н**). Russian surnames

Pronunciation of women's patronymics when used with first names

From the name	One writes	One says
Андре́й	Андре́евна	Андре́вна
Матве́й	Матве́евна	Матве́вна
Алексе́й	Алексе́евна	Алексе́вна
Серге́й	Серге́евна	Серге́вна
Никола́й	Никола́евна	Никола́вна
Вячесла́в	Вячесла́вовна	Вячесла́вна
Владисла́в	Владисла́вовна	Владисла́вна
Святосла́в	Святосла́вовна	Святосла́вна
Семён	Семёновна	Семённа
Ива́н	Ива́новна	Ива́нна
Рома́н	Рома́новна	Рома́нна
Макси́м	Макси́мовна	Макси́мна
Алекса́ндр	Алекса́ндровна	Алекса́нна
Михаи́л	Миха́йловна	Миха́лна
Па́вел	Па́вловна	Па́лна

also often end in **-ский**, but Russians themselves consider such names to be Polish (**Разумóвский**), Belorussian (**Могилéвский**), or Jewish (**Тарнóвский**); **-ский** endings are also associated with noble origin (**Милослáвский**) or the church (**Благовéщенский**).

Typical Ukrainian surnames end in **-ко, -енко, -ак/-як, -чук** (**Гуркó, Шевчéнко, Вишня́к, Корнейчýк**).

Armenian names often end in **-ян** (**Хачатуря́н**) and Georgian names in **-вили, -вали, -дзе, -яни, -ани**. (Stalin's real name was **Иóсиф Виссариóнович Джугашви́ли**.)

Moslems, or former Moslems, tend to add Russian endings to their original names (**Ахмадýлина**).

Typical Polish and Belorussian names end in **-ский** and **-ич** (**Якубóвский, Иванов́ич**). The **-ич** ending is also strongly associated with Serbo-Croats (**Дрáганич**).

Names ending in **-ьш, -ис, -ус, -ас** with an unfamiliar stem often turn out to be Latvian or Lithuanian (**Бéрзиньш, Пожáйслис**). Many German names are associated with the Baltic republics. Estonian and Finnish names are also typified by unrecognizable stems, but they sometimes can be identified by the use of many double consonants and vowels.

There are, of course, many different national groups within the Soviet Union proper. If you want to ask for someone's nationality, you say: **"Какóй вы национáльности?"** Possible answers are innumerable, but include: **"Я латы́шка," "Он эстóнец," "Они украи́нцы,"** and **"Онá грузи́нка."** But if you are familiar with the names of the Soviet republics, most of your problems are solved.

Russian surnames
Ру́сские фами́лии

The beginning Russian student is often delighted at the uses to which his newfound knowledge can be put. Consider the joy that accompanies the discovery that **тóлстый** and **Толстóй**

come from the same root. Count Leo Fat? And as vocabulary increases, so does the number of parallels that can be drawn; thus: **Хрущёв** 〉 **хрущ** = the May beetle (so destructive to agriculture), **Грибоéдов** 〉 **гриб** + **есть** = mushroom-eater, and so forth. This joy is modified, however, by the problems of declining Russian surnames; those that have the most common ending (**-ов/-ев** or **-ин**) also have declensions that are part noun declensions and part adjectival declensions. Consider the Wolf family, for instance. The adjectival endings are underlined.

	Masculine	Feminine	Plural
N	Вóлков	Вóлкова	Вóлковы
G	Вóлкова	Вóлковой	Вóлковых
D	Вóлкову	Вóлковой	Вóлковым
A	Вóлкова	Вóлкову	Вóлковых
I	Вóлковым	Вóлковой	Вóлковыми
P	Вóлкове	Вóлковой	Вóлковых

There is a relationship between the unending variety in the root meanings of surnames and their half-adjective and half-noun declension.

The relationship can be traced to the fifteenth century. The naming system at that time was not yet standardized. Usually every child did have a given (Christian) name **и́мя** chosen from the list of saints and bestowed upon him at birth. In addition, the use of a nickname **прóзвище** was also widespread if not universal. This nickname might be one assigned early by parents and used to the exclusion of the Christian name for fear the Devil might find out who the child was and thereupon snatch his soul; thus, names used might be **Малю́та** the little one, **Третья́к** the third child, and so forth. Or the nickname was acquired in time according to any circumstance that usually determines nicknames—physical description, character traits, occupation, and others; thus: **Косóй** crosseyed or walleyed, **Беззýб** toothless, **Овчи́нник** dealer in or maker of sheepskins, and others. (The penchant for assigning nicknames did not disappear. Just before the Revolution, one could ask for a peasant's name and get the answer, "His street name or passport name?"—"**Уличное или паспортное?**")

Another kind of name was also used, especially when one tried to be more specific, often for official reasons when names like "Mary, Squirrel" were not sufficient. The third name was a short-form possessive adjective ending in **-ов/-ев** or **-ин** that identified the father. This adjectival patronymic appeared in the same case as the bearer's given name: **Семён Савельев сын** Simon, Saveliy's son; **Марица Онисимова дочь** Maritsa, Onisim's daughter. The words "son" or "daughter" were frequently omitted and the nickname occasionally followed: **Семён Савельев, Кривой**. Still another possible name form was a similar short-form adjectival patronymic (**-ов/-ев, -ин**) based on the father's nickname rather than on his Christian name (**Сухов, Шишкин**). And the final possibility was the addition of one's father's nickname patronymic (that is, one's grandfather's nickname). This last name form always appeared in the genitive case. For example if the family names were:

Иван Перепеча (grandfather),
Борис Иванов сын Перепечин (father),
Фёдор Борисов сын Перепечина (son),

then:

Иван, **Борис**, **Фёдор** are given or Christian names;
Перепеча is a nickname;
Иванов, **Борисов** are patronymics;
Перепечин is a nickname patronymic;
Перепечина is the father's nickname patronymic.

This conglomeration of names might be interesting to us, but they were troublesome for their bearers. The most important drawback was that there was no established name form that invariably identified the family. The use of numerous patronymics was optional and even variable; some were used on one occasion and others used on another. Only the father and son relationship, or at best the identity of grandfather, was firmly established by the name. Each new generation brought a new set of names. This might be enough for a small village, but it was not enough in a growing state.

What happened is probably obvious: the grandfather's nickname patronymic often became the surname, losing in time its genitive ending and eventually becoming felt as a noun denoting the family even though its declension retained some adjectival endings: **Волков, Грибоедов, Смирнов, и т.д.** Many Christian name patronymics followed the same process: **Николаев, Иванов, Петров, и т.д.** Now one is expected to remember that Russian surnames ending in **-ов/-ев** or **-ин** have a part noun, part adjective declension.

These remarks have been an unforgivable reduction of В. К. Чичагов, *Из истории русских имён, отчеств и фамилий* (Москва: Учпедгиз, 1959), a fascinating book on Russian onomastics.

To answer a question you should be asking, the **-ович** or **-овна** endings that now form the current patronymics were originally confined to the very high nobility alone—great princes, princes, and boyars. The saying remains: "**наши вичи едят одни калачи**" (**калач** a rich bun). The use or denial of these endings was used to flatter or insult. As time went on, the form spread downward to all classes.

Names for pets
Клички

In English we associate certain names with certain animals. "Bossie" has to be a cow, "Dobbin" a horse, and "Rover" a dog. These are traditional names. Russians, too, have a set of names particularly associated with certain animals. (In the following table of animal names an asterisk is placed after such traditional names.) Of course they also have a much larger set of names for pets or animals, and there is no real limit to the possibilities.

Notice that many of these names have to do with the color of the animal; that is especially true of horses and cows. The color of horses is **масть**: **"Ло́шадь како́й ма́сти?"**—" What color is the horse?" There are many such colors: **ворона́я (масть)** is black, **бу́рая** is black and brown, **гнеда́я** is bay (reddish brown), **си́вая** is gray, **савра́сая** is light bay with black mane and tail, **пе́гая** is spotted, and **кау́рая** is light brown. In the expression **"Си́вка бу́рка, ве́щая кау́рка"** from *Конёк-горбуно́к* by Ершо́в, the words **си́вка**, **бу́рка**, and **кау́рка** are horse names that are derived from horse colors, and **ве́щий** is "one able to prophesy."

Animal	Живо́тное	Кли́чка
horse	ло́шадь	Гне́дко, Вороно́к, Рыжу́ха, Ры́жик
cow	коро́ва	Бурёнка,* Рыжу́ха, Беля́нка, Краса́вка, Бу́ська, Зо́рька, Ми́лка
pig	свинья́	Хавро́нья*
rooster	пету́х	Пе́тя* (Петушо́к)
chicken	ку́рица	Хохла́тка, Пестру́шка
bear	медве́дь	Ми́ша,* Михаи́л Пота́пыч (Papa bear), Мишу́тка (Baby bear)
tomcat	кот	Ва́ська,* Пушо́к (Fluffy), Ба́рсик
cat	ко́шка	Ма́шка,* Му́рка,* Му́шка, Ми́лка

If you want to give your dog a Russian name, here are some general notions of the meaning of common names for dogs with a note on genders to which they may apply.

Кли́чка	Пол	Значе́ние
Ша́рик*	м	шар (ball, balloon)
Кашта́нка	м и ж	кашта́н (chestnut)
Жу́чка*	м и ж	жук (beetle)
Ара́бка	м и ж	"Blackie"
Каб(ы)сдо́х	м	"Drop dead"
Ми́лка	ж	ми́лый (darling)
Полка́н	м	пол + коня́ (centaur)
Бу́лька	ж	*Boule de neige* (snowball)
Буя́нка	ж	буя́н (ruffian)
Дружо́к*	м	друг (friend)
Зо́рька	ж	заря́ (dawn)
Ту́зик	м	туз (ace)
Бу́ська	ж	бу́сы (beads)

There is also a fashion to call dogs by Western names:

Джон   Те́ри
Ральф   Си́льва
Джек   Джу́ди
Ка́йзер

3

Clothing

Одéжда

Before the Revolution there were essentially two main types of clothing a Russian might wear. The peasants, that is, the majority of Russians, wore what is described in the section on traditional peasant clothing. It was all homemade and for the most part handspun; stories of Russian folklore often show the spinning in process. And every village had people who made woven bast shoes and felt boots. Village stores supplied some materials and fixtures, but the great mass of Russian peasant clothing was a do-it-yourself affair that had little to do with the vagaries and refinements of upper-class clothing.

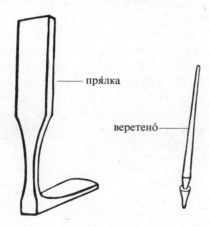

пря́лка

веретенó

The Russian distaff пря́лка *and spindle* веретенó

A grandmother, who lives in the far north, shows a contemporary young man how the spinning is done.

At the other end of the spectrum were the clothes worn by the upper classes, which, after Peter and then Catherine, were essentially the Western European clothing of the day. The relatively small middle classes of the nineteenth century wore some Western clothes but often combined them with clothes of peasant design.

Then came the Revolution, the attachment to the West was essentially broken, state money was spent on heavy industry (rather than on clothing), decimation came with World War II, and isolation followed that. When Stalin died, the door finally opened a crack and the flood of wonder and curiosity began, accompanied by the demand for a few of the refinements of living the Western world seemed to have. Today you may walk down the street of a major city in the USSR and not necessarily be aware (from the clothing) that you are not in a Western European city.

One of the problems for language students brought about by the innovation and imitation is that some of the terminology for clothes has not really settled down yet. One man's **фуфа́йка** is (or rather, used to be) another man's **ко́фта**. (The following discussion tries to show when such variations exist.) Another problem is that though terminology and even design are often borrowed from the West, their application and use do not necessarily correspond to those of the Western source. Pajamas **пижа́ма** provide an example. After the Revolution, the Russians took up the idea of pajamas and used them not just for sleeping but also quite logically for long-distance train travel (not to wrinkle good clothes) and for beachwear (for the same reason). As a result, **пижа́ма** can resemble sportswear. But a recent book whose task is to describe good behavior insists that pajamas are for the bedroom alone. Presumably the only reason for this stricture is that this is the way pajamas are used in the West.

In this chapter, contemporary clothing is discussed first, including terminology for kinds of clothing and then sizes, materials, styles and patterns; the basic Russian folk costume for both men and women is then considered briefly.

Contemporary clothes
Совреме́нная оде́жда

Standard "outer" wear for men[1]
Ве́рхняя оде́жда для мужчи́н

мужско́й костю́м   a man's suit

---

[1] A discussion of kinds of pants, shirts, and so forth follows under separate headings.

двойка: пиджа́к и брю́ки   a jacket and a pair of pants
тройка: пиджа́к, жиле́т и брю́ки   a jacket, a vest, and a pair of pants
ве́рхня руба́шка, соро́чка   a shirt
га́лстук   a tie
носки́   socks
ту́фли   shoes

Одноборотный костюм
A single-breasted suit

Костюм тройка
A three-piece suit

Повседневный костюм
An everyday suit

**Standard underwear for men
Нижняя одежда для мужчин**

майка a sleeveless undershirt
трусы pants or shorts
нижняя рубашка, сорочка an undershirt with sleeves
кальсоны long underwear, long johns
эластичные трусики (*literally* elastic pants) fulfill the function of athletic supporter as do **плавки** trunks

**Standard "outer" wear for women
Верхняя одежда для женщин**

женский костюм a woman's suit
 жакет a jacket
 юбка a skirt
блузка, джемпер или свитер a blouse or sweater
чулки hose
туфли shoes

Note:
жакет a woman's suit jacket
пиджак a man's suit jacket

The Russian **платье** is generally equivalent to dress, except that another word **халат** can be used for almost any dress (knee length or full) that opens down the front. **Халат** can also be used for everything from a bathrobe to a surgical gown for both men and women. An item in traditional women's clothing, the **сарафан** now refers to anything that in America would be called a "jumper," namely, a sleeveless dress with straps over the shoulder that, in the daytime at least, requires a blouse or sweater under it.

**Standard underwear for women
Женское бельё**

бюстгальтер, лифчик a brassiere (**Лифчик** can also be used for "outer" wear, such as a woman's bathing suit top or a child's sunsuit top. **Бюстгальтер** is for underwear only.)
трусы, трусики underpants
пояс a belt, girdle
 пояс с подвязками, пояс с резинками a garter belt
 гигиенический пояс a sanitary belt

гра́ция a corset (Both girdles and corsets are less commonly resorted to in the Soviet Union than in the United States.)

комбина́ция, комбина́шка a slip

Special purpose clothes
Ра́зные ви́ды оде́жды

For sleeping, women wear a nightgown **ночна́я соро́чка** (less often called **руба́шка**). Men might wear a nightshirt with the same name or a pair of pajamas **пижа́ма**; they are also likely to wear their underwear for that purpose (or nothing at all, of course).

For swimming wear, a bathing suit is **купа́льный костю́м** or **купа́льник**, but if you wish to specify a man's swimming suit, then **пла́вки** is used. (The latter is usually considerably briefer than ours.) A woman's two-piece suit consists of **тру́сики с ли́фчиком**.

The general term for work clothes is **спецоде́жда** or **спецо́вка**. (Work shoes are **спецо́бувь**.) Work clothes, of course, vary according to the job. Laborers commonly wear overalls **комбинезо́н** (sometimes including a jacket). Laboratory workers and doctors wear a **хала́т**. An apron is either **пере́дник** or **фа́ртук**, the latter perhaps slightly more common. Leotards **трико́** are worn by ballet dancers and gymnasts.

BABY CLOTHES   БЕЛЬЁ ДЛЯ НОВОРОЖДЁННЫХ

Sometimes Russian babies are swaddled **свива́ть**, that is, tightly wrapped so that only the head is left free to move. Swaddling is not universal, however, and is even rejected by a home medical reference (*Популя́рная медици́нская энциклопе́дия*). Wrapping **пелена́ние**, with the arms left free, is recommended. Diapers and receiving blankets have the same title in Russian, **пелёнки**. A diaper is a small **пелёнка**, and when folded around the baby it has the title of **подгу́зник** (from **гу́зно** a bird's rear end).

Aside from crawlers **ползунки́** the only other clothing unique to babywear is a short-sleeved undershirt **распашо́нка** that opens down the back. Otherwise, diminutives of common words are used: **руба́шечка, штани́шки, ко́фточка**.

SCHOOL UNIFORMS   ШКО́ЛЬНАЯ ФО́РМА

In major cities, schoolchildren wear uniforms. The winter uniform for girls consists of a brown dress **пла́тье** with a black apron **фа́ртук** for everyday and a white apron for special occasions. Boys wear a white shirt **руба́шка** and a blue gray jacket **пиджа́к** and pants **брю́ки**. If summery weather persists, then white blouses or shirts and dark blue skirts or pants/shorts are worn. The latter ensemble is also the Pioneer uniform. The red Pioneer tie **пионе́рский га́лстук** is knotted at the neck, resembling our Campfire Girl ties.

MILITARY UNIFORMS   ВОЕ́ННАЯ ФО́РМА

The illustrations indicate common terminology for military uniforms. Other clothing associated with the military includes:

мунди́р either specifically the jacket for a full dress parade uniform or the entire outfit as a whole

ки́тель a uniform jacket, single breasted, with no belt and usually a standing collar

шине́ль a uniform overcoat, usually somewhat longer than civilian overcoats

фура́жка
пило́тка
гимнастёрка
мунди́р

брю́ки
брю́ки, брю́ки галифе́ или шарова́ры
сапоги́
боти́нки

Солда́т   Офице́р

тельня́шка, тéльник a sailor's striped knit undershirt

руба́ха a sailor's middy

бескозы́рка a sailor hat (козырёк brim)

Kinds of coats
Вéрхняя одéжда

The usual word for the everyday overcoat is пальто́: зи́мнее пальто́, лéтнее пальто́, деми-сезо́нное пальто́. Полупальто́ is also a coat but somewhat shorter. Fur coats are discussed in the section on furs in Chapter 10. Other coats are:

плащ a raincoat (непромока́емый плащ a waterproof raincoat)

дождеви́к (less commonly) a raincoat, often not as substantial as the плащ

пы́льник a light summer coat, so light that it has no lining

наки́дка a cape

плащ-пальто́ a raincoat

плащ-наки́дка a rain cape

бу́рка a black felt cape with broad boxlike shoulders, originating in the Caucasus, that provides especially good protection from wind and rain for horseback riders

бушла́т a heavy, very short, dark coat worn as an overcoat originally by sailors and later by small boys also

Kinds of jackets
Жакéты, кýртки . . .

As shown in the pictures, a man's suit jacket is пиджа́к and a woman's suit jacket is жакéт. There is a third kind of jacket кýртка very frequently referred to and used by both men and women. It differs from the first two by its design: one should be able to button or zip it up all the way to the neck. Its major purpose is for sportswear (especially by women), though some uniform jackets that go up to the neck are also called кýртка. Another word for jacket is тужýрка, which can either resemble a double-breasted suit jacket (when worn by the military) or any lightweight кýртка.

Телогрéйка, ва́тник, and фуфа́йка are short, warm work jackets often with a cotton-padded lining sewn to the outer layer of cloth. (Фуфа́йка can also be a very heavy coarse-knit work sweater.)

The блýза is a light, loose, often indoor jacket, worn by both men and women. (Блýза can also refer to a sweater.)

Kinds of sweaters
Кóфты, сви́теры . . .

In American English a sweater is a sweater, and nobody would confuse it with a blouse, a shirt, or a jacket. But the Russian usage is not quite so clear. Perhaps the most widely accepted term for the all-inclusive sweater is кóфта (кóф-точка more often, since the кóфта belongs to a woman), but кóфта also applies to a blouse. Others insist that the equivalent for sweater is фуфа́йка, although this is an obsolete usage. Some relief from the dilemma can be obtained by using the specific words for special kinds of sweaters:

сви́тер any turtleneck sweater, currently a very popular design

пуло́вер any sweater, often a man's, that is collarless and does not open all the way down the front

джéмпер for men, a V-neck sweater; also, a woman's pullover sweater, usually with short sleeves (especially one that is worn in place of a blouse and is therefore relatively decorative)

трикота́жный, вя́заный жакéт a cardigan sweater, more often a woman's, which may or may not have a collar

трикота́жный, вя́заный жилéт a cardigan sweater, often a man's, without sleeves and collar

безрука́вка a sleeveless sweater, often a man's (when this word applies to a sweater)

Kinds of shirts and blouses
Руба́шки, блýзки . . .

руба́шка almost any kind of shirt—daywear, nightwear, and underwear (бéлая руба́шка, ночна́я руба́шка, ни́жняя руба́шка)—that is either knit or woven; primarily but not exclusively applied to men's shirts

соро́чка   used by some people interchangeably with **руба́шка**: **ве́рхняя (ни́жняя) соро́чка**; usually, however, an undershirt

соро́чка   a girl's or woman's undershirt, though sometimes extended to refer to a slip

ма́йка   a sleeveless, knit undershirt

блу́зка   a woman's or girl's blouse

блу́за   either a light, loose-fitting overshirt for men or women or, less commonly, a sweater, often one that opens down the front.

мани́шка   a dickey or a shirt front used by both men and women

футбо́лка   a long- or short-sleeved knit shirt, originally for playing soccer

те́нниска   a man's short-sleeved knit sport shirt, sometimes worn for tennis, a newly popular game

ковбо́йка   a cowboy shirt for men and boys, made of plaid, often with a button-down collar and buttoned pockets

се́тка   an undershirt made of especially large netting

Kinds of pants
Брю́ки, штаны́ . . .

Almost any outer pants are **брю́ки**, and almost any underpants are **трусы́** (for women, **тру́сики**). Another general word for pants is **штаны́**, but this term is much less formal. New business pants might be **брю́ки**, while old baggy pants are **штаны́** (though **штаны́** can also be underpants). **Панталóны** is a somewhat formal and foreign term usually for women's and children's underpants. **Рейту́зы** (German: *die Reithosen*, riding breeches) are usually long knit pants for women, children, and ice skaters, though they can also be knit pants as underwear. The terminology for pants in the shape of riding breeches has not yet congealed so that they are referred to in a number of ways: **брю́ки-галифе́**, **бри́джи**, **шаро-**

вáры, **брю́ки в сапоги́**. Shorts as outer wear are called **шóрты**. American blue jeans **джи́нсы** are very popular among the young and modish males.

Headwear
Головны́е убо́ры

Headgear comes in many varieties and, due to climate perhaps, Russian emphasis and variety are different from ours. In winter, at least, head covering is a vital necessity, and it is in winter (fur) hats that the variety is most remarkable.

The usual Western (business) hat is **шля́па**. (Women tend to call their hats **шля́пка**.) What we call a fur hat, however, is **ша́пка**. The most common kind of **ша́пка** is **уша́нка** or **ша́пка-уша́нка**; this is the hat most often associated with Russian men and boys. The fur (or furlike) brims are normally turned up and tied on the top and turned down for protection only when it is very cold. Another well-known **ша́пка** is the **папа́ха**, a high, conical karakul hat that has become associated with high officers on parade. There are many others; you can assume that any fur hat (especially a man's fur hat) has a special name—**куба́нка**, **украи́нка**, **го́голь**, **боя́рка**—but even most Russians aren't sure which are which. The Russian **ша́пка** need not be made of fur; it may also be knitted.

Other hats distinguished by any Russian are:

ке́пка, ке́пи   a very common hat in the USSR, shaped like a golf cap

фура́жка   the hat military officers and policemen in the United States wear

пило́тка   an overseas cap

капюшо́н   any hood

тюбете́йка   a skullcap, common among Central Asians, that is more highly decorated than the Jewish yarmulke **ермо́лка**

чалма́, тюрба́н   a turban

шлем, ка́ска   a helmet (the former, the more general word, while the latter is mostly restricted to an army helmet in World Wars I and II and a fireman's hat)

Scarves of various sorts are the most common (and in the winter, vital) kind of headwear for women. To some extent shape tends to determine terminology. The square piece of material has the general title of **головнóй платóк**. It may be light, just to keep hair covered in the summer. A smaller decorative (and folded or made to be triangular) variety is the **косы́нка**. This is the one most like our bandana. A very large square of material is the **шаль**, worn on either or both head and shoulders, mostly for warmth in winter and decoration in summer. Rectangular in shape is the **шарф**, worn mainly by women about the neck and head. What we think of as a winter scarf fits this category as does our stole. The smaller, more utilitarian scarf for men is the **кашнé**.

Socks and stockings
Носки́ и чулки́

Носки́ is equivalent to socks, while **чулки́** can be either stockings or hose. Nylons are **нейлóновые чулки́**, while **капрóновые чулки́** are similar but heavier; panty hose is **колгóтки**. ("I have a run in my stocking" can be "**На чулке́ поéхала петля́**," "**На чулке́ спусти́лась петля́**," or "**У меня́ чулóк поéхал**.")

Гóльфы or **получулки́** are our knee-highs, worn mostly by children.

Портя́нки replace stockings for wear with the knee-high boots that don't lace **сапоги́**, and with felt boots **вáленки**. **Портя́нка** is a rectangular piece of cloth about forty by ninety centimeters that is wrapped about the foot in place of stockings. This wrapping is used in the army (and elsewhere) and requires considerable know-how to put on. It has three advantages: (1) wear and tear is more evenly distributed than with stockings, (2) different sizes are not required, and (3) the wearer can rearrange the wrapping if absorbed perspiration begins to freeze.

Footwear
Óбувь

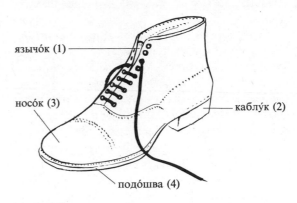

язычóк (1)

носóк (3)

каблу́к (2)

подóшва (4)

Боти́нок

(1) tongue
(2) heel
(3) toe
(4) sole

Also:

стéлька innersole
шнурки́ shoelaces

Shoes seem to present the same problem that hats do; there are more kinds that have different words to distinguish them rather than fewer words requiring modifiers for distinction.

The most common word for everyday shoes, both men's and women's, is **ту́фли**, especially if the shoes do not require laces. Oxford shoes are also called **полуботи́нки**. House slippers, especially those with a heel, are also **ту́фли**, **домáшние ту́фли**. Slippers **шлёпанцы** consist of nothing but soles and toes.

Боти́нки are (usually men's) leather shoes that go up to the ankle. When women wear them, they are specifically for trudging in slush and snow. This word is also applied to the category of ski boots, skating shoes, and many kinds of footwear that go up to the ankle, no matter what their purpose. **Бу́тсы** or **бу́тцы** for playing soccer are in this category. Boots that are not worn over another pair of shoes and that do not lace down the front are **сапоги́**: **рези́новые сапоги́**, **меховы́е сапоги**, **зи́мние сапоги́**, **сапо́жки**.

Felt boots **ва́ленки** are the Russian contribution to the art of keeping warm on a low budget in very cold weather. The American acquaintance with felt is poor preparation for the Russian object. How do you make boots out of hat material? By making the felt much thicker in the first place and stiffer in the second. Felt boots are traditional winter wear among the peasants. This unfortunate background accounts for their rejection among people in the cities except among those whose work allows or requires their use. Children and grandmothers are not as accountable for style; to them warmth is more important. Children can often be seen wearing **ва́ленки** with rubber galoshes fitted over them.

Rubbers and galoshes that are worn over other shoes come in two major varieties. The smallest and lowest cut are **гало́ши**, **кало́ши**. These are the most nearly equivalent to our rubbers, except that the Russian variety is both lined and stiff so that they will not stretch. If the galoshes have height to them, at least up to the ankle, then they are **бо́ты** for men and **бо́тики** for women.

For lighter footwear **санда́лии** are sandals, **сандале́ты** are women's sandals with heels so that they resemble regular shoes with holes in them, and **босоно́жки** are nothing but soles with straps to hold them on. Tennis shoes with high uppers are **ке́ды** (Keds!) and are usually reserved for serious sport use. **Та́почки** are very common everyday wear around the house. They have flat soles, cloth uppers, and are sufficiently simple that they are sometimes homemade. The word **та́почки** is also used for the very large slippers that go over tourists' shoes worn on some tours of historic buildings.

To tie your shoes Russian style, start out making the first knot just as we do; then make a large loop of each lace and tie them together just as you tied the first knot.

Holders and fasteners
Застёжки

по́яс belt
хля́стик belt loop
подтя́жки suspenders (*less frequently* **по́мочи**)
подвя́зки garters
пу́говица, пу́говка a button
 Брю́ки всё ещё застёгиваются на пу́говки (**Застёгивать** to fasten).
 Застегни́ руба́шку!
 Пу́говицы застёгиваются в пе́тли (**петля́** loop, buttonhole).
пря́жка a buckle
 Пря́жки ча́ще всего́ употребля́ются на пояса́х, но иногда́ и на бо́тах, боти́нках, и т. п.
мо́лния, застёжка мо́лния a zipper
 Застёжка мо́лния сейча́с о́чень популя́рна.
 Он стал застёгивать «мо́лнию» на ку́ртке.
кно́пка snap, snapper
 Блу́зки ча́сто застёгиваются на кно́пки.
крючо́к и пе́телька a hook and eye
шнурки́ shoelaces
 Он ещё не уме́ет зашнуро́вывать ту́фли. (He doesn't know how to lace his shoes yet.)
 Завяжи́ ту́фли! (Tie your shoelaces!)
 Развяжи́ ту́фли! (Untie your shoelaces!)

Sizes
Разме́ры

Sizes of clothes are quite different from ours, but there is a certain amount of regularity in them. First remember that when things are measured, they are measured in centimeters: **"Где мой сантиме́тр?"**—"Where is my tape measure?" For most clothes (shirts, dresses, coats), the size is the number obtained by taking the bust or chest measurement and dividing by two. Thus, men's coats, women's dresses, and shirts all range in size from 44 to 56 (even numbers only). Other measurements are used for length or collar size, for instance, but they are secondary and their range depends on what is being sold. Hose and stocking sizes are obtained by measuring the length of one's foot in centimeters (odd numbers only). Shoe sizes are, unfortunately, another matter: measure the length of your foot, divide the result by two and then multiply by three. Shoes sizes range from 38 to 47 for men and from 33 to 42 for women. You may order your gloves straight from ГУМ; for some reason, glove sizes are the same all over the world. Hat sizes are obtained by measuring in centimeters the circumference of the head at the mid-forehead level. For adults the range is from 53 to 62. Children's sizes are smaller, of course, but they are obtained the same way.

Does a woman who wears size 40 shoes have big feet?

Materials
Ткани

Sometimes fashion magazines are especially interesting reading for foreigners. Here are some materials mentioned in the course of one such magazine: **креп, джéрси, фланéль, твиды, буклé, шифóн, вельвéт, габардин, синтéтик, велюр,** not to mention **брюки из эластика.** Those are mostly various weaves, of course, and the original material from which they are woven carry suitably unrecognizable names:

хлопчатобумáжная ткань (woven) cotton
   (**хлопчатобумáжная, бумáжная рубáшка**)
  хлóпок raw cotton
  вáта drugstore cotton
  бязь, вóльта, сатин, ситец cotton materials
шерсть wool (**шерстянóй костюм**)
шёлк silk (**шёлковая рубáшка**)
лён linen (**льнянóе полотéнце**)
искýсственный, вискóзный шёлк rayon
капрóн, нейлóн both nylon, but the former is coarser and cheaper (**капрóновые чулки, нейлóновая блýзка**)

Knitted materials are separated into those that are machine knit **трикотáжный** and hand knit **вязаный.**

Items of fur, especially the more elegant kinds, are not readily available to the Russian consumer; rather, they are a good source of foreign currency for the government.

Styles
Стили в одéжде

По одёжке встречáют, по умý провожáют. (You can't judge a man by . . .)

Styles in the USSR are a difficult subject to discuss. For one thing, they are changing, as do all styles, but perhaps even more rapidly in the Soviet Union than in the United States. That is because the Russians have farther to go on the path to popular variety. Twenty years ago it was easy enough to typify Russian style as drab or uniform. Today that is not true. More materials are now available and the demand for and acceptance of variety and "stylishness" have tremendously increased. The trend is toward more variety, more color, and more experimentation.

There are some constants, however, that relate to clothing and style. One is the winter weather. It is hard to imagine that boots and very warm coats might disappear from the Soviet wardrobe. Some kind of warm legwear is also necessary. And hair styles will always be affected to some extent by the physical necessity of wearing something to keep one's head warm.

Another two factors in style persist but are more subject to change than is the weather: shape and containment. The Russian female figure tends to be full, and Russian women tend to dislike the manmade restraints (girdles) on that fullness. Countering this tendency is the trend, especially among the young and in the cities, toward the slimmer figure. Current fashion magazines in the USSR feature fashion models that approach the gaunt apparitions in *Vogue*.

Style is also affected by availability and cost. Popular styles are frequently hard to get (especially in the country), and the cost of clothes in relation to income is high. Ready-made clothes are naturally of government manufacture, a limiting factor on extremes in design. The popular trend now, however, is to have clothes made to order from a local seamstress **портни́ха**.

What deductions might a Russian make about another Russian from the clothes he wears? Old-fashioned clothing (**плато́к, ва́ленки**) worn in the city identifies someone recently from the country and therefore thought of as backward, even uncultured; someone too old or too young to care; or someone for whom comfort and convenience are most important. Ten years ago, those who wore conspicuously Western clothing were likely to be suspected of equally Western sympathies. That is no longer true. Western clothing styles are currently the height of fashion. American jeans are now the best gift you could possibly make to a young teen-age Russian male. The following conversation might easily

be imagined: American student of Russian, "Can you tell me where I can get a pair of **ва́ленки**?" (They are, after all, very Russian and he has never seen them.) The Russian answers, "What on earth do you want that old stuff for?"

Sewing and patterns
Шитьё и вы́кройки

ли́ния та́лии waistline
ли́ния бёдер hipline
перёд front
спина́, спи́нка back
вы́тачка dart
скла́дка pleat
подги́б, подши́вка hem
подо́л hemline
сги́б тка́ни fold (of material)
вста́вка insert
сбо́рочки gathers
карма́н pocket

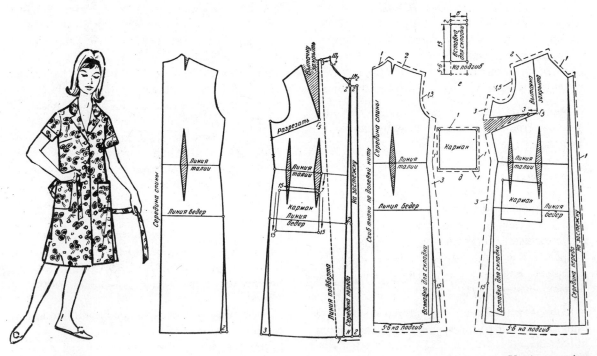

Хала́т для до́ма

Хала́т для до́ма

There are two kinds of patterns in the USSR. The traditional one **вы́кройка** usually refers to a small-scale design that the seamstress must enlarge to fit the required proportions. The sewing section of a current book on basic home economics (from which the above pattern was taken) is divided in sections that show how to make kinds of sleeves, collars, skirts, and so forth. Girls' home economics classes include instruction on how to use this kind of pattern **вы́кройка**. The other kind of pattern **патро́нка** is a pattern as we know it, issued in various sizes and as large as the piece of material that it is to shape. Sometimes **вы́кройка** is used for **патро́нка**.

Not everybody sews well enough or likes to sew. It is quite common to buy material, find a pleasing design, and then take the two to a dressmaker **портни́ха**.

The Russian folk costume
Ру́сский наро́дный костю́м

Clothes worn by peasants in the second half of the nineteenth century will be described here primarily because styles and customs are represented that are often encountered by the student of Russian (in literature and in folk dance ensembles, for example) and yet are farthest from his own experience. The period chosen is significant too because peasant clothing really has not varied much from that of either several hundred years earlier or seventy-five years later.

The American would be hard put to find a contemporary Russian wearing the entire ensemble of clothes discussed here. Many features of the costumes do persist, however. It would be difficult to imagine that the Russian shirt **руба́ха**, **руба́шка** had completely disappeared from everyday use. And even though woven bast shoes **ла́пти** are doubtless looked down upon as a vestige of an impoverished past by the Russians themselves, they were so comfortable and cheap that their current rarity can only be attributed to the general decline of small business operations.

Only major national differences—Russian, Ukrainian, and Belorussian—and only the most basic components of clothing will be discussed. These descriptions will enable you to distinguish Russians from Ukrainians and Belorussians, married from unmarried women, and northern Russian women from southern Russian women.

Underwear **ни́жнее бельё** will not enter the discussion because there was none. Defense against the cold came by adding another layer of outer clothing.

For those interested in greater detail and a discussion of smaller regional and class variations, see Тóкарев, *Этногрáфия нарóдов СССР* and Алексáндров, *Нарóды европéйской чáсти СССР*.

Russian men's clothes
Ру́сский мужско́й костю́м

The Russian men's shirt **руба́ха** opened partway down on the side left of center. If it had a small collar, it was called **косоворо́тка** (literally,

Russian men's wear: руба́ха, штаны́, ону́чи, ла́пти

sideways collar) and was somewhat more elegant than the shirt with no collar **голошéйка** (literally, bare neck). For holidays the shirt might have embroidered collars, sleeve ends, and front panel. The Russian wore his shirt outside his pants with a belt over both of them.

Russian pants **штаны́** were fairly narrow and were either tucked into the tops of boots or held in place below the knee by strings that also held **ону́чи** in place. **Ону́чи** were relatively long and narrow pieces of cloth wound around the foot and lower leg in place of stockings.

The most common footwear in the summer were **ла́пти** (*sg.* **ла́поть**), a cross between shoes and slippers woven from **лы́ко**, the fibers of the linden (lime or basswood) tree **ли́па**. Each village had its **ла́пти**-maker, and, as already mentioned, the **ла́пти** were comfortable, cheap, and readily available. For winter Russians wore **ва́ленки**, which were also locally produced. Leather boots were used when it was less cold by those who could afford them; leather has the nasty habit of freezing and cracking in very cold weather.

Hats were of wool felt in summer, relatively high and conical; in winter they were of fur,

sometimes with earflaps. Underneath his hat, a man's haircut resembled that obtained by putting a bowl over his head and cutting off the remainder. The Russian peasant usually let his beard grow, especially if he was older.

For lighter wear the Russian had a cloth coat **кафта́н** fitted at the waist and flaring at the bottom. In winter he wore the **шу́ба**, a fur coat with the fur side inside. In very cold winter weather, especially for travel, he wore a very long coat **тулу́п**, usually consisting of nothing but a sheepskin, fur side in, over his usual coat. The **тулу́п** was also used as a blanket.

Cossacks' clothes resembled the Ukrainian rather than the Russian clothes.

UKRAINIAN MEN'S CLOTHES   УКРАЙНСКИЙ МУЖСКÓЙ КОСТЮ́М

The Ukrainian shirt **соро́чка, руба́ха** differed from the Russian in that (1) it was gathered at the neck; (2) the neck opening was in the center, rather than off to the left side; (3) it tended to be more highly embroidered; and (4) it was always tucked into the pants. A sleeveless jacket **безрука́вка** was often worn over the shirt. Ukrainian pants **шарова́ры** were very wide their whole length, especially by comparison with the Russian pants; they were also tucked into their boot tops. Footwear consisted of boots during the winter and on summer holidays, while **по́столы**, a sort of leather moccasin, was for everyday use in the summer. The Ukrainian equivalent for the Russian **кафта́н** was the **сви́та**, an often highly decorated cloth coat. For winter, a sheepskin coat **ко́жух** was a heavier version of the **сви́та, сви́тка**.

BELORUSSIAN MEN'S CLOTHES   БЕЛОРУ́ССКИЙ МУЖСКÓЙ КОСТЮ́М

The Belorussian could be distinguished from his Russian and Ukrainian cousins in several ways. His shirt, for example, was worn outside his pants (unlike the Ukrainian), and its opening was traditionally in the center (unlike the Russian). His pants were narrow (like the Russian).

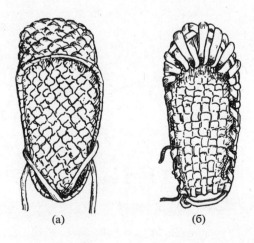

(a)   (б)

Ру́сские ла́пти: (a) моско́вского ти́па, (б) за́падного ти́па

Russian women's clothes
Ру́сская же́нская оде́жда

NORTHERN RUSSIAN WOMEN'S WEAR　**СЕ́ВЕРНАЯ ЖЕ́НСКАЯ ОДЕ́ЖДА**

The women's clothing that we think of as typically Russian is actually that of northern Russia. The basic components were the shirt **руба́шка** and the **сарафа́н**. (The terms **руба́ха** and **руба́шка** *were* interchangeable.) The long-sleeved shirt was actually much longer than the English word "shirt" would suggest. Over the shirt came a **сарафа́н** whose design resembled a jumper except that the skirt was much longer.

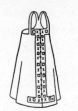

сарафа́н косокли́нный

сарафа́н кру́глый

and hair—a kind of hat plus drapery called **ко-ко́шник**, which was often ornamented with shells, beads, and the like. Unmarried women wore their hair in a single long braid down the back with ribbons intertwined. They might also wear a crown-shaped headdress, which left the top of the head uncovered. In any case women's hair had to be restrained in some fashion, usually in braids, because long and loose tresses were considered unseemly. (They are still rare; women's hair today is usually either relatively short or else braided or tied up in some way.)

A northern Russian girl wearing руба́ха, сарафа́н

Among the several types popular in the middle of the last century, the **косокли́нный сарафа́н** was cut on the diagonal to achieve fullness at the bottom. A little later came the **кру́глый сара-фа́н**, cut straight up and down and gathered at the top with rather narrow shoulder straps.

For holidays, married women in the north had elaborate and large devices to cover their head

кокошники　　　　　ки́чка

Же́нские головны́е убо́ры конца́ XIX—нача́ла XX в.
Women's headwear at the end of the nineteenth century and beginning of the twentieth century

Southern Russian women's clothes
Ю́жная же́нская оде́жда

Women in southern Russia did not wear a **сарафа́н**. Instead, over the shirt they wore a skirtlike affair **понёва** made of panels of material gathered at the waist but not necessarily stitched up the front. That opening was covered

A southern Russian woman wearing рубáха, понёва, пере́дник

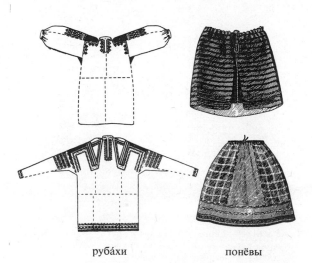

рубáхи   понёвы

by a **пере́дник**, an apron that ran almost the length of the costume. The **рубáха** covered what the **понёва** didn't. This assemblage however was worn by married women; for unmarried women, the **рубáха** and **пере́дник** sufficed.

Southern headgear for the married was the **ки́чка**, a headdress characterized by a cap often in the shape of horns. The cap also held up additional highly decorated material whose purpose was to hide hair. Southern Russian ornamentation was especially gay, with wide use of feathers, beads, and the like.

UKRAINIAN WOMEN'S CLOTHES   УКРАЙНСКАЯ ЖЕ́НСКАЯ ОДЕ́ЖДА

Ukrainian women wore clothes that resembled those of southern Russia. The paneled skirt was called a **плáхта**, but the design (in panels) and purpose (for married women) were the same. The apron **фáртук** usually began at the waist; the costume often included a sleeveless jacket. They wore the same coats, shoes, and so forth as the men.

On holidays unmarried Ukrainian women wore a distinctive headdress that has become associated with them: a small wreath of flowers to which were tied gaily colored ribbons that hung down the back. This is part of the basic costume for any Ukrainian folk dance group.

BELORUSSIAN WOMEN'S CLOTHES   БЕЛОРУ́ССКАЯ ЖЕ́НСКАЯ ОДЕ́ЖДА

The Belorussian **рубáха** was often highly embroidered. Over it was worn a skirt **андарáк**, which often had bright stripes, and over that was an apron, either short (beginning at the waist) **фáртук** or long **нагру́дник**.

Hair and the married woman
Головно́й убо́р заму́жней же́нщины

Women's headgear was dominated by one single factor that was true for all the eastern Slavs. A married woman could not appear before her husband's relatives or before strangers without having all her hair covered. (Uncovered hair was "sinful.") It is thought that this custom derived from a more ancient one in which hair was given some sort of magical power. Since early custom required that a wife be acquired from among the girls in a village outside one's own, it would follow that all married women were strangers and therefore not to be trusted with their power running loose. You can assume that if a woman is pictured with any significant portion of her hair uncovered, then she is not yet married. (Women's hair as such was not the problem, just strange women's hair.) This custom probably accounts for the rather large number of bandanas still to be seen among the peasant women today when weather or working conditions would not seem to require them.

4

Housing
Жилище

When a Soviet Russian says he is going home, what does he expect to find when he gets there? Russian housing is significantly different from ours in several major aspects, among them, size. Housing has been a terrible problem for the Soviet government. Major industrial construction for many years took precedence over housing, and World War II made further inroads on the already minimal supply of housing. Of course, housing has improved since then, but the single major theme has been to put as many people in as little space as possible. For the Russian, often this means that mothers-in-law live in the same room as their married children. Marriage, divorce, and having children are often directly related to the amount of housing space available. An ad that says **сдаётся угол** means that a part (literally, a corner) of a room is available for rent, and **"Молодо-жёны снимают угол"** means, actually, "The newlyweds are renting a part of a room." Most Russians, especially those that live in the city, think of a family of four as an upper limit in size. The civil courts are filled with adjudications over who has how many or which square centimeters of housing space for his use.[1] The amount of housing space is steadily growing however, so that young couples are beginning to expect a separate room for mother-in-law. But regardless of who lives with whom, the average Soviet apartment still seems very small and crowded.

Although the Russian does not have much room, neither does he pay very much. Rent is rarely more than 4 to 5 percent of income. (Care must be taken, therefore, in comparing Soviet incomes to American incomes. Housing for the Russian is not spacious, but it is very cheap.)

A third major difference is that many of the conveniences—indoor plumbing, hot water, or even running water—that we think of as basic parts of housing are not that basic in the USSR. City buildings and new major constructions have these services, but outside the

[1] For greater and more fascinating detail, see George Feifer, *Justice in Moscow* (New York: Delta, 1965).

cities, especially in smaller and older houses, they are frequently absent. Indeed, housing is one of the major fields in which the great disparity between city and country life is evident; but it is also true that conditions are changing rapidly.

In this chapter, the various kinds of housing available to the Russian are described. A typical new self-contained apartment is discussed first since that is the most common type of new housing. Types of rooms, their contents and equipment are shown. The older communal apartment, which also forms a significant fraction of available housing, is then dealt with, followed by hints on how to find any city apartment. Lastly, the classic features of the peasant "hut" are shown with changes in contemporary rural housing.

A new self-contained apartment
Отде́льная кварти́ра

Most Russians are looking forward to moving into this kind of housing. Many already have, of course. The apartment consists of at least one room, or more often two rooms (sometimes more), plus a kitchen, bathroom facilities, and hallway. (The last three are not counted in describing the number of rooms or the number of square meters of housing space.) It is different from the communal apartment **коммуна́льная кварти́ра** to be described later in that the hallway, bathroom facilities, and kitchen are not shared: it is self-contained.

The illustration shows a possible arrangement of furniture in a new two-room apartment. Notice that this apartment is supposed to be large enough for four people—in this case, a mother, father, grandmother, and small son.

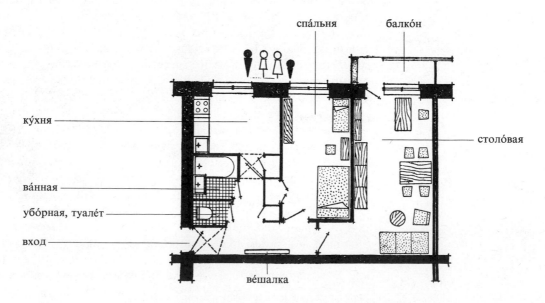

спа́льня   балко́н

ку́хня

столо́вая

ва́нная

убо́рная, туале́т

вход

ве́шалка

Кварти́ра для семьи́ из четырёх челове́к

In the entrance hall
В прихо́жей

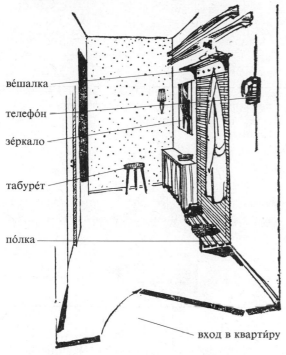

вешалка

телефо́н

зе́ркало

табуре́т

по́лка

вход в кварти́ру

Прихо́жая в совреме́нной кварти́ре   *The entrance hall in a contemporary apartment*

The entrance hall **прихо́жая** is small, with no coat closet; instead, a coat rack **ве́шалка** is used. The coat rack often has some arrangement of boards to protect the walls from wet raincoats (and vice versa). Hats are placed on a shelf **по́лка** above, and overshoes and street shoes often have a rack or shelf below. Other typical furniture for an entrance hall includes a stool **табуре́т** and a mirror **зе́ркало**, which often also has a shelf under it. If there is a telephone in the apartment, it is likely to be attached to the wall near the entrance.

● Воше́дший в кварти́ру вытира́ет но́ги о полови́к, снима́ет гало́ши, пальто́ и то́лько тогда́ прохо́дит в ко́мнату. Éсли гало́ш нет, то вытира́ют боти́нки о ко́врик на ле́стнице.[2]

[2] И. Н. Фёдорова и др., *Домово́дство* (Москва: Просвещение, 1967), стр. 371. (**Полови́к** is a rather long, narrow rag rug, especially one for wiping shoes; **ковёр, ко́врик** refers to any rug.)

The main room
Столо́вая

In the dear dead days beyond recall, some people had houses with a number of rooms to which they assigned various purposes. Guests **го́сти** were received in the "guest" room **гости́ная** and meals were eaten from a table **стол** in the "table" room **столо́вая**. There is now one basic room filling both purposes and both names therefore can be applied to it, though the latter is more common. (The term **о́бщая ко́мната** is also used but has the ring of "official-ese.")

This room carries the major burden of living: it is a living room, dining room, bedroom, and study combined. Anything that resembles a sofa in the daytime doubles as a bed at night. Storage is an immense problem. If the family has one, or more rarely, two children, their beds are often placed in a corner **де́тский уголо́к**, sometimes separated by drapes or a large piece of furniture from the rest of the room.

Столо́вая (и́ли) о́бщая ко́мната. *Note the child's bed behind the curtain. This design makes the room appear larger than usual.*

The traditional heart of the room is the dining table (**обе́денный**) **стол**, usually found in the middle of the room with the other furniture arranged around the wall.

DECOR ИНТЕРЬÉР

It is difficult to typify the "Russianness" of Russian decor. There seems to be no one style that predominates; too much depends on whose decor one is describing. Older city apartments have a heaviness to them—reminiscent of Late Victorian in England, often with darker colors and hanging fringes here and there. The style of newer city apartments is closer to nondescript. Here the effort to pack a modicum of furniture into very small rooms is the most impressive feature. Newer furniture design is similar to both Scandinavian models and Sears Roebuck.

A common decorating device is the display of Persian-type rugs **ковры́** on the wall. A recent satirical article in the press described someone as "sophisticated" who put the rugs on the floor rather than on the wall! The floors themselves always seem to be parquet, and small area rugs are used, if any at all.

A constant item in Russian decor is the house plant. Every Russian dwelling from the country house to the city apartment almost invariably has some kind of house plant, from the lowly geranium **гера́нь** to a palm tree **па́льма**.

WINDOWS ÓКНА

Winters are cold and Russians like it warm indoors, so the traditional windows are double windows, often with the inside set of window frames removable for the summer. Both sets have a section in them, the **фо́рточка**, that can

Фо́рточка

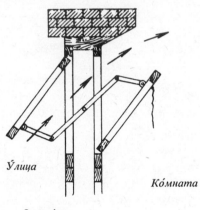

У́лица

Ко́мната

Фраму́га

be separately opened. A new device **фраму́га** to accomplish the same purpose is also being installed in some new buildings.

LIGHTING FIXTURES ПРИБÓРЫ ДЛЯ ОСВЕЩÉНИЯ

A lamp is simply **ла́мпа**, a table lamp **насто́льная ла́мпа**; but a light bulb is **ла́мпочка**. Judging from the terminology for many light fixtures, illumination would seem to come from France:

торшéр a floor lamp
бра a wall lamp

люстра a chandelier
плафо́н a ceiling light
свети́льник a large lighting fixture, especially one attached to or suspended from the ceiling
выключа́тель a switch
шнур a cord
розе́тка a (wall) socket
ви́лка a plug

Включи́(те)/зажги́(те) свет! (Turn on the lights!)

Он включи́л/зажёг ла́мпу. (He turned on the lamp.)

Она́ вы́ключила/погаси́ла свет. (She turned off the lights.)

Вы́ключи(те)/погаси(те) свет! (Turn off the lights!)

FURNITURE   МЕ́БЕЛЬ

The following is a list of furniture[3] that can be bought as a set and is the recommended amount for a two-room apartment. (Remember that halls, bathrooms, and kitchens are not considered rooms when the size of an apartment is under consideration.)

серва́нт a sideboard buffet
обе́денный стол a dining room table
сту́лья chairs
дива́н-крова́ть иди друго́е изде́лие мя́гкой ме́бели a sofa bed or some other overstuffed furniture
кни́жный шкаф a bookcase
пи́сьменный стол a desk
стол и́ли ту́мба для радиоприёмника или телеви́зора a table or stand for a radio or television set
односпа́льные крова́ти (и́ли одна́ двуспа́льная и односпа́льная) single beds (one double bed and one single bed)
комо́д-туале́т a dressing table or dresser
прикрова́тные ту́мбочки nightstands, bedstands, small cabinets
платяно́й шкаф, гардеро́б a wardrobe closet/cabinet

[3] И. И. Середю́к, *Культу́ра ва́шей кварти́ры* (Киев: Будиве́льник, 1967), стр. 24.

Notice that space-wasting armchairs кре́сла are not on the recommended list nor is the two-storied buffet буфе́т.

CLOSETS   ГАРДЕРО́БЫ, ПЛАТЯ́НЫЕ ШКАФЫ́

New apartment buildings are using more built-in cabinets in the kitchens and closets in the bedrooms, but they are still very new and comparatively rare. Usually clothes are kept in a large movable wardrobe cabinet гардеро́б, платяно́й шкаф as they are in other parts of Europe. Clothing is hung on a coathanger пле́чики, ве́шалка.

The bedroom
Спа́льня

In two-room apartments, the second room is often a children's bedroom. (Usually a second room is not available unless there are at least three to four people in the family.) If the second room is used by adults, then it will often also contain a desk пи́сьменный стол, a dressing table комо́д-туале́т, or chest of drawers комо́д.

BEDS   КРОВА́ТИ, ПОСТЕ́ЛИ

There are two words for bed, often used interchangeably: крова́ть refers essentially to the frame and legs of the bed, while посте́ль refers to what you might put on it—blankets, sheets, mattresses, and so forth. Other kinds of beds are:

односпа́льная, одина́рная крова́ть a single bed
двуспа́льная, двойна́я крова́ть a double bed
тахта́ a daybed
дива́н-крова́ть a sofa bed
раскладу́шка a folding bed
кре́сло-крова́ть a combination armchair and bed
откидна́я крова́ть a wall bed

HOW TO MAKE A BED   КАК УБИРА́ТЬ ПОСТЕ́ЛЬ

The Russian system[4] for making a bed is much easier than ours. A lower sheet простыня́

[4] It is also used by many other nationalities.

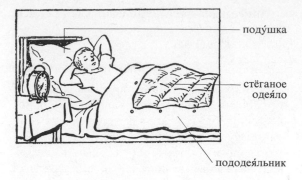

подушка

стёганое одеяло

пододеяльник

is affixed to the mattress **матра́с, матра́ц** as is ours. The Russian upper sheet **пододея́льник** is actually a sort of envelope for the blanket, which buttons onto the blanket **одея́ло** or comforter **стёганое одея́ло**. (A bedspread **покрыва́ло** may cover these.) This top arrangement is not tucked under the mattress. So, to make the bed, just spread this enveloped blanket out evenly. (Our flat two-sheet system, however, is also sometimes used in the USSR.) The (square) pillow **поду́шка** is buttoned into its pillowcase **на́волочка** and seems to average at least twice the size of our bed pillows.

Bathroom facilities
Убо́рная, туале́т; ва́нная

Usually, bathroom facilities are divided between two rooms: the toilet **унита́з** is in one small room **убо́рная, туале́т**, and the bathtub **ва́нна** and sink **умыва́льник**[5] are in another **ва́нная**. (Especially polite usage avoids the words **убо́рная, туале́т**; "conveniences" **удо́бства** can be used.) Toilet paper **туале́тная бума́га** is now commonly available at stationery stores (and elsewhere), but home toilet paper still often consists of the daily newspaper, carefully torn into rectangles and put in a large envelope that hangs on the toilet room door. The bathtub-and-sink room often is also the storage room for any washing equipment, perhaps a washing machine **стира́льная маши́на** or a

Russian washing tub **коры́то**, which has the shape of an abbreviated trough. (According to a book of Soviet statistics,[6] in 1970 slightly over one-half of Soviet families had washing machines. Some Soviet citizens have insisted that washing machines are used even in households without running water, and still others report that most washing is done in the bathtub. Commercial laundries **пра́чечные** have a reputation for being inexpensive but hard on clothes. Commonly, people send bed and table linens, towels, and men's shirts to the laundry. Diapers are done at home.)

The kitchen
Ку́хня

The kitchen is a relatively uncomplicated affair. It often seems to have the appearance of a room that had originally been designed for some other purpose, perhaps because most kitchens are usually not supplied with built-in cabinets, and the tenant usually supplies his own. Pipes are often on, not in, walls. Most kitchens that are not shared are very small rooms but there is a move afoot to make them large enough so that they may also serve as the dining room.

Remember that the kitchen furniture, equipment, and techniques described here suit Russian usage, conditions, and food. Counter space is very small and almost always covered with oilcloth **клеёнка**. And notice in the paragraph below that the preferred method for washing dishes requires scrubbing with a brush under a stream of hot water. Standing water per se is thought of as unsanitary (to the chagrin of American travelers who can find no sink stoppers).

HOW TO WASH DISHES　　　КАК МЫТЬ ПОСУ́ДУ

● Лу́чше всего́ мыть посу́ду и прибо́ры мы́лом и щёткой под струёй горя́чей воды́. Но, к сожале́нию, не во всех ещё дома́х име́ется водопро-

---

[5] A kitchen sink is a **ра́ковина**.

[6] Я. А. Иоффе, *Мы и плане́та*, 3е изд. (Москва́: Изда́тельство полити́ческой литерату́ры, 1972), стр. 227.

вод с горя́чей водо́й, и́ли водогре́й. Поэ́тому иногда́ мо́ют посу́ду в та́зиках. В любо́м слу́чае у ребя́т на́до выраба́тывать пра́вильные приёмы, кото́рые облегча́т и уско́рят весь проце́сс мытья́: спра́ва поста́вить гря́зную посу́ду, пе́ред рабо́тающим—таз с тёплой водо́й (с раство́ром горчи́цы и́ли со́ды), ря́дом, леве́е—второ́й таз с горя́чей водо́й для ополаскивания; сле́ва же ста́вить вы́мытую посу́ду.[7]

The passage notes that soda or (dry) mustard **горчи́ца** is used as we use soap or detergent. The use of mustard as a cleaning agent[8] is also commonly extended to floors and clothes. But soda or mustard is not used to the exclusion of soap **мы́ло** or detergent **детерге́нт**. The common word for cleaning substances in powdered form is **порошки́**. Laundry soap (or detergent) is **стира́льный порошо́к**. In practice, brand names are often referred to, for example, **Я стира́ю в Ло́тосе** or **Я стира́ю в Та́йде** (**стира́ть** to launder).

[7] И. Н. Фёдорова и др., *Домово́дство* (Москва́: Просвеще́ние, 1967), стр. 304 (a guide for teachers of home economics in grades V–VIII).
[8] It is the physical rather than the chemical properties of mustard that make it usable as a cleaner.

KITCHEN FURNITURE AND UTENSILS	КУ́ХОННАЯ МЕ́БЕЛЬ И ПОСУ́ДА

Stoves **пли́ты** in the cities are commonly heated by gas; those in newer apartments have an oven. When a stove is a stove in our sense of the word (two to four burners **конфо́рки, горе́лки** and an oven **духо́вка**), then it is a **плита́**: **га́зовая плита́, электри́ческая плита́, дровяна́я плита́** (**дрова́** firewood). Whether for reasons of economy, space, or availability, however, other devices are sometimes used—for example, a hot plate **электропли́тка**. (Other devices are also used where there is no gas or electricity supply. See "Contemporary rural housing" in this chapter.) Where space is at a premium a smaller table-model oven **электродухо́вка** might be used in conjunction with a hot plate; a **чу́допе́чка** is a specially constructed pan for baking on top of the stove using the heat from a regular burner.

The remaining furniture is not as complicated:

шка́ф   a kitchen cabinet or cupboard
буфе́т   a tall piece of furniture, sometimes found in the kitchen, that holds table linens, silverware, and sometimes food
ра́ковина   a kitchen sink
холоди́льник   a refrigerator

Pots, pans, and containers include:

кастрю́ля   the usual cooking pot or pan
сковоро́дка, сковорода́   the former, a frying pan, not necessarily including a handle **сковоро́дник**; the latter, a very large frying pan
котёл   a large, heavy metal stewpot, a Dutch oven, or a kettle
гуся́тница   a roaster
кофе́йник   a coffeepot
ча́йник   a teapot or teakettle, **заварно́й ча́йник** a teapot
лист (желе́зный)   a cookie sheet
про́тивень (желе́зный)   a large flat pan with low sides for making **пироги́**
фо́рма   a mold for **желе́, пу́динг**
коро́бка   a box or canister for storage
ба́нка   a glass jar
подно́с   a tray
подста́вка   a holder or pad for resting hot pans
кры́шка   a lid
ми́ска   a bowl

For dealing with food in preparation, one uses:

мясору́бка   a meat grinder
кофе́йная ме́льница   a coffee grinder
соковыжима́лка   a juicer
си́то и решето́   both sieves, often referred to together, with low round sides and a flat bottom—**решето́** (*pl.* **решёта**) used for coarse sieving, **си́то** for fine sieving
цеди́лка   a strainer, especially for bouillon
дуршла́г   a colander
сту́пка с пе́стиком   a mortar and pestle
деревя́нный молото́к   a wooden hammer for pounding meat
се́чка и коры́тце   a special knife with a handle

in the middle and a curved blade **се́чка**, made for use with a wooden bowl (or trough) **коры́тце**; for chopping vegetables, mainly cabbage

тёрка a grater

шумо́вка a shallow ladle with holes, for removing scum or retrieving **пельме́ни** (a sort of Russian ravioli) from boiling water

ска́лка a rolling pin, with or without handles

ве́ничек a wire whisk

сбива́лка a beater

разливна́я ло́жка, разлива́тельная ло́жка, поваре́шка a ladle

лопа́тка a spatula for cooking or serving

ку́хонные ножи́ и ло́жки kitchen knives and spoons, the former not usually differentiated except by size: **большо́й нож, нож, ма́ленький нож, но́жик**

For opening things, there are:

што́пор a corkscrew

консе́рвный нож a can opener

ключ for prying off a lid

To clean up with, one may use:

моча́лка a washrag, sponge, or any scrubbing device; formerly strips of bark, now often dried vegetable sponge

ёршик a brush with bristles going in all directions

щётка a brush with a hard back, bristles on one side

суши́лка usually a drying rack for dishes, but sometimes a plate-warmer; also, a clothes dryer

таз a dishpan in shape and mostly in use

ведро́ a (garbage) pail

SET THE TABLE! НАКРО́Й НА СТОЛ!

The "Fanny Farmer" of the Soviet Union, *Кни́га о вку́сной и здоро́вой пи́ще*, recommends the following table equipment (in addition to a tablecloth **ска́терть**) for serving six people. The meal that requires all this equipment is hardly an everyday affair, however.

таре́лки глубо́кие, 6 dinner soup bowls (that is, large, shallow, and rimmed)

таре́лки ме́лкие, 6 dinner plates

таре́лки заку́сочные, 6 hors d'oeuvres plates (resembling our salad plates)

таре́лки пирожко́вые, 6 meat pie plates (resembling our butter plates)

таре́лки десе́ртные, 6 dessert plates (resembling our salad plates)

лото́чек для се́льди, 1 a long, narrow, oval dish (to suit the size of salt herring)

сала́тники, 2 salad bowls

ми́ска супова́я, 1 a soup tureen

со́усник, 1 a gravy or sauce boat

блю́до кру́глое, 1 a round platter

блю́до ова́льное, 1 an oval platter

блю́до для хле́ба, 1 a bread dish

бульо́нные ча́шки с блю́дцами, 6 bouillon cups and saucers

судо́к для пе́рца, горчи́цы и у́ксуса a condiment holder (usually for vinegar, mustard, salt and pepper)

графи́н для воды́ a water pitcher (**графи́н** is in the shape of a decanter, but size differs according to use)

графи́н для фрукто́вого со́ка a pitcher for fruit juce

графи́н для во́дки a decanter for vodka

рю́мки для во́дки vodka glasses, stemmed liqueur glasses in shape

рю́мки для вина́ small wine glasses

фуже́ры large wine glasses

бока́лы для шампа́нского champagne glasses

ножи́, ви́лки столо́вые и десе́ртные по 6 dinner and dessert knives and forks, six each

Though the Soviet Fanny Farmer didn't include spoons, they are:

ча́йная ло́жка a teaspoon

столо́вая ло́жка a soup spoon

супова́я ло́жка a soup ladle

десе́ртная ло́жка a dessert spoon, not quite so large as a soup spoon

The communal apartment
Коммуна́льная кварти́ра

Most older apartments are communal. In one apartment there may be several individuals or even families, all sharing the use of the kitchen, hallway, and bathroom facilities, and the telephone if there is one. This is where the problem of close quarters is really severe. The use of common facilities must be scheduled, and there must be a clear definition of what belongs to whom, how it should be maintained, and so forth.

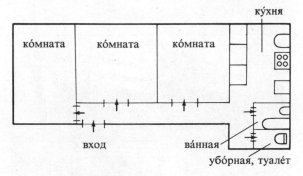

Коммуна́льная кварти́ра

The problem is not just the squabbles that arise over communal facilities but also the lack of privacy when a family (two to four people) are living in one room. Russians are an adaptable people, however. (The American perhaps attaches a different significance to the space problem than does the Russian. Historically, the great mass of Russians have lived at very close quarters with each other. They seem to have developed a way of satisfying what we see as the "need" for privacy. The American requires physical space for privacy; he feels obliged to pay attention to others in the room. The Russian seems to internalize this requirement; he does not feel the same obligation to entertain while in the company of others. He is also more likely to be unhappy without other people around.)

The description of this type of apartment is the same as for new apartments except that:

(1) The individual rooms tend to be larger and have higher ceilings; both these features are highly desirable since contemporary rooms are very small and their low ceilings are oppressive. Kitchens are also larger, but the problems that arise when they must be shared far outweigh this advantage.

(2) Since the buildings are older, the utilities supplied them are often not adequate and therefore kerosene stoves and other equipment described under "Contemporary rural housing" are occasionally used. The apartment need not necessarily have a bathtub.

(3) Since much of modern housing has the reputation of being jerry-built, the older buildings are often thought of as being more solidly constructed and therefore less likely to require repair.

(4) Decor will tend to be older, larger, and heavier.

Addresses and finding the apartment
Адреса́

Some addresses, usually those for centrally located older buildings, are arranged as are ours, namely, the street number also indicates the entrance to the buildings. However, many buildings, both new and old, have other types of addresses.

For mailing purposes, the name of the city (or region, village, and so forth) is followed by a postal zone number: **Москва́ Г-125**. Most addresses then give the street name (**ул. Чайко́вского**) followed by the building **дом** number (**д. 28**) followed by the apartment **кварти́ра** number (**кв. 136**). Sometimes the building number will look like this: **Ле́нинский пр. 64/2** (**Ле́нинский проспе́кт, дом шестьдеся́т четы́ре дробь два**). Such numbers indicate a corner: the building number on Leninsky prospekt is 64 and the 2 is the number of the same building on the cross street side. Most buildings have a number of entrances to them, many of which may be found in the courtyard or around the back of the building. And since 64 refers to an entire building, the address number 49 on the same street can be a long walk away.

The peasant house
Крестья́нский дом

The Russian peasant hut **изба́** had certain fairly regular features to it that our words "hut" or "log cabin" naturally don't convey. The peasant household described here is the forerunner of the contemporary farmhouse; it is also the peasant building of Russian fable, folklore, and literature. After all, this is where most Russians lived in the middle of the last century. (Because of the lack of attention given to housing by the Soviet government, many people still do live in them. That fact, however, is not a matter of pride to the government or to many Russians you are likely to meet. Your interest in peasant huts and their Russian stoves is, unfortunately, likely to be considered "slumming.")

Russian peasant housing offers a wealth of fascinating material for the ethnographer, some of which is worth exploration by language students. Only the major or most common themes will be discussed here. For more detail, refer to publications of the ethnographic institute, Институ́т этногра́фии и́мени Миклу́хо-Макла́я, Акаде́мия Нау́к СССР.

Exterior
Вне́шний вид

Russians did not live in isolated farmhouses but in villages. There were two kinds of villages in Old Russia: a **село́** was a village with a church and a few stores; it was therefore larger than a **дере́вня**, a village too small for a church. Villages were often located near a river or stream with the peasant houses lining one or both sides of a street that ran parallel to it.

Either **дом** or **изба́** can be applied to a peasant house. **Дом** refers to the whole building and is especially used when the building is large (as in the north) or when the speaker wants to avoid peasant connotations; **изба́** can refer either to the peasant house as a whole or to the main living room therein.

At first glance, the American is likely to call the Russian **изба́** a log cabin, for indeed the central and northern Russian houses were made of logs chinked with moss **мох** or with hemp **конопля́** and without a foundation in our sense of the word. For instance, tree stumps were often used as well as stones.

Use of tree stumps at foundation corners must have inspired the folk stories of the hut on chicken legs избу́шка на ку́рьих но́жках *where the witch* Ба́ба-яга́ *lived.*

This illustration to a Pushkin fairy tale clearly shows a зава́линка—*earth shored up by boards around the base of a peasant house. It is still to be seen in the USSR but one must know enough to look for it.*

Roofs were traditionally made of straw **солóменная кры́ша** or of planks **тесóвая кры́ша** and were capped by a ridge beam. The front end of this beam, the end that extends toward the street, was often carved in the shape of a horse or rooster head, a remnant of the pre-Christian belief that such figures could bring good fortune or ward off misfortune.

A distinctive feature of Russian peasant houses was a **завáлинка**, a mound of earth held in by boards that was built around the outside of the house up to the level of the floor inside. Its purpose was to prevent cold winter air from circulating underneath the hut. In the summer it served as a bench for sitting.

In southern Russia and the Ukraine wood was scarce and peasant houses were made of combinations of brick and adobe made from clay and manure.

DECOR   УБРÁНСТВО ДÓМА

The southern houses **избы́** (**избá** is **хáта** in the Ukraine) were whitewashed and then decorated with brightly painted designs **рóспись**. Further north any paint was confined to shutters. Instead, decoration consisted of fancy woodcarving **резьбá** especially of beam ends, rims, and

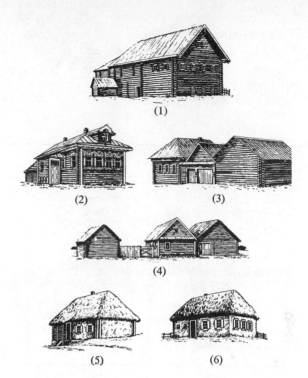

(1)

(2)   (3)

(4)

(5)   (6)

These are types of peasant houses that were common in various parts of Russia at the end of the nineteenth and beginning of the twentieth centuries: (1) northern regions, (2) central black-earth regions, (3) Perm oblast, (4) western regions, (5) southern black-earth regions, (6) the Kuban region. The two-sided roofs are standard in most places except the south.

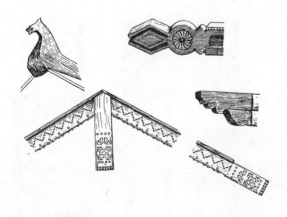

Украшéния сéверного жили́ща *Decorations on a northern house*

almost any shutters. The art of woodcarving was very highly developed in the northern regions of Russia.

SIZE   РАЗМÉРЫ

Variations in size also occurred from north to south. Southern buildings were usually smaller while those in the far north were huge two-storied affairs. (The farm animals could be kept from freezing by bringing them closer to the only supply of heat, in the same building as their owners.) For central Russia, the most common **избá** was one-storied, with its wood floor constructed a few feet above ground level. (The space below **подвáл, пóдпол** was used for storing vegetables, especially potatoes and other root vegetables.)

The variations in size that seem large in the preceding figure are not due to real differences in housing, at least for people. The peasant household **крестья́нский двор** could include just a house and garden, perhaps a small fence and some outbuildings; this was common in the south. In central Russia there might be a house, a high gate, and farm outbuildings connected to each other by a fence, often in such a way as to enclose an area **двор**. The very large northern houses included the farm outbuildings **двор** and the peasant house **изба́**, all under one roof.

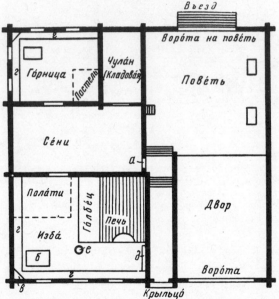

The top (main) floor in a northern Russian peasant house
а. входна́я дверь, *б*. стол, *в*. божни́ца, *г*. ла́вки, *д*. посу́дник, *е*. рукомо́йник

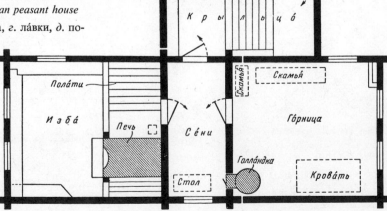

A central Russian peasant house

The most common farm building had three basic parts: (1) the heated hut **изба́**, one large room where all cooking, eating, and sleeping took place; (2) an unheated entrance room **се́ни** (*pl. only*) that might be used for sleeping in the summer or also some storage; and (3) either a barn area **двор** or a storage and summer sleeping room **клеть**. (In later use, toward the end of the nineteenth century, the **клеть** often became a **го́рница**, usually a heated room for receiving company and sleeping.) This three-part design (**изба́** + **се́ни** + **клеть/двор**) was the most common one. The very poor had to manage on just a one-room hut or a hut and an entrance room.

божни́ца   an icon shelf
воро́та   a gate or a large barn door (*pl. only*)
входна́я дверь   entrance
въезд   a ramp
го́лбец   a structure alongside the stove, for lying on, containing an entrance to the lower floor
голла́ндка   a stove for heating
го́рница   a second room, for sleeping or company
двор   the part of building used as a barn
крова́ть   a bed

крыльцо́ a porch

ла́вка a built-in bench

печь a Russian stove

пове́ть a loft

пола́ти a very large overhead shelf (*pl. only*)

посте́ль a bed

посу́дник a cupboard

рукомо́йник a dispenser suspended over a large bucket, used for washing

се́ни an entrance room (*pl. only*)

скамья́ a (movable) bench

чула́н a storage room in a peasant hut (**кладо-ва́я** is the usual word)

In the peasant hut
В крестья́нской избе́

Let us imagine what you would see if you went into one of these peasant houses. (The arrangement discussed here is the most common one for north and central Russia.) From the road you walk up a short path along the side of the house to a small covered porch **крыльцо́**. The first room you enter is the entrance room **се́ни**. It is from the **се́ни** that the living quarters **изба́** are entered. (The threshold **поро́г** is at the entrance to the **изба́**, not at the entrance to the **се́ни**.) Take one step inside and you will be facing the street. Either to the immediate right or left of you is a huge Russian stove **ру́сская печь** the size of a furnace; it takes up one-fifth to one-fourth the area of the room. (The whole room is not large, usually square and ranging from sixteen to twenty-one feet a side.) Benches **ла́вки**, often built-in, line the remaining walls of the room. In the corner diagonal to the stove there is a table with perhaps an additional free-standing bench **скамья́** and/or some stools **табуре́тки**. In the same corner (called the **пере́дний**, **кра́сный**, **Свято́й**, or **Бо́жий у́гол**) is an icon with a small oil lamp **лампа́дка** suspended in front of it and often also draped with a heavily embroidered "towel" **полоте́нце**. The wall opposite you (the front wall) usually has three small windows and the side wall opposite the stove has another one or two. Above the

Пере́дний у́гол, Архáнгельская губе́рния

В избе́ се́верного ти́па. *A Russian stove is to the left, the sleeping shelf* пола́ти *above.*

windows along the walls are small shelves **по́лки**. Directly over your head is a very large shelf **пола́ти** (*pl. only*) usually extending from the stove to the opposite side wall.

Which way did the Gingerbread Man (**колобо́к**) go?

● Надое́ло колобку́ лежа́ть, он и покати́лся с окна́ на ла́вку, с ла́вки на́ пол, по́ полу да к дверя́м. Перепры́гнул че́рез поро́г в се́ни, из сене́й—на крыльцо́, с крыльца́—на двор, со двора́—за воро́та—да́льше, да да́льше.[9]

[9] О. Ка́пица, *Ру́сские ска́зки про звере́й* (Ленингра́д: Детги́з, 1951), стр. 19.

● Надое́ло колобку́ лежа́ть; он и покати́лся с окна́ на зава́линку, с зава́линки на тра́вку, с тра́вки на доро́жку и покати́лся по доро́жке.[10]

THE RUSSIAN STOVE РУ́ССКАЯ ПЕЧЬ

The Russian stove, a great mass of clay **гли́на** or brick **кирпи́ч**, is common to all the eastern Slavs as their answer to very cold winters. Its location,[11] orientation,[12] and decoration[13] differed according to locale, but every **изба́** had one. It was used any time any form of heat was required—for baking bread, cooking for both humans and farm animals, in some areas taking a steam bath. In addition, it kept the **изба́** warm, grandma slept on it, it dried both foods and clothes, and often it protected small farm animals from the winter cold.

Ру́сская печь в ста́рой крестья́нской избе́, Кали́нинская область

The earliest and/or poorest Russian **изба́** used a stove that operated without the benefit of a chimney pipe. This type was called **курна́я изба́**,

горшо́к

ухва́т

The long-handled **ухва́ты** are used for taking hot pots **горшки́** from deep inside the Russian stove

чёрная изба́. Smoke went out either through the door or through a hole in the roof, which was closed once the smoking had stopped. By the end of the nineteenth century, the use of a stovepipe was more common. **Бе́лая изба́** was a house that had a chimney.

The great size of the Russian stove made it a heat holder and distributor. Food was cooked and bread was baked deep inside the stove after the fire had died out and the embers and ashes were pushed over to one side. Therefore very long-handled devices were used to get the food in and out or to clean the oven. Some of the equipment used with a Russian stove included:

ухва́т   a long rod, with one end in the shape of a large U that fits around the base of pots, for taking pots out of the stove

сковоро́дник   a long rod with a hook and lever at one end for removing skillets from the oven

лопа́та   a broad wooden shovel for loading and unloading loaves of bread

кочерга́   a poker (*gen. pl.* **кочерёг**)

метёлка   a broom

TRADITIONAL COOKING КУ́ХОННАЯ У́ТВАРЬ EQUIPMENT

Traditional cooking utensils were usually relatively large in size and few in number. People did not eat off individual plates. Rather, each person had his own spoon and dipped into the common bowl **ми́ска**. Members of the family took turns at dipping, with the eldest first; child-

---

[10] А. Чу́хин, *Малю́тка* (Симферо́поль: Крымизда́т, 1964), стр. 190.

[11] In the Ukraine, the stove was most often in a corner opposite, rather than next to, the entrance.

[12] South-central Russian stoves often faced the side wall rather than the front wall.

[13] Ukrainians whitewashed their stoves and often painted colorful designs **ро́спись** on them. Richer peasants often tiled the outside of their stoves.

ren who took food out of turn faced rebuke. A character in *Ра́ковый ко́рпус* by Solzhenitsyn explains that he does not know his interlocutor very well: **"А почему́ я до́лжен вам ве́рить? Мы с ва́ми из одно́й ми́ски щей не хлеба́ли."** ("Why should I trust you? We haven't eaten cabbage soup from the same bowl.")

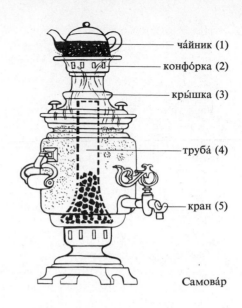

чайник (1)
конфо́рка (2)
кры́шка (3)
труба́ (4)
кран (5)

Самова́р

квашёнка

ми́ска

руко́мойник

ко́вшик

кри́нка

ча́шечка
с пе́стиком

THE SAMOVAR   САМОВА́Р

(1)   teapot
(2)   teapot holder
(3)   lid
(4)   central tube
(5)   spigot

Also: **заглу́шка**   lid for the central tube

A ceramic stewpot **горшо́к** was the basic container for cooking in a Russian stove. After the fire had been made early in the morning and the stove had warmed up, the embers were pushed over to one side and the **горшо́к**, most often with a cereal **ка́ша** inside it, was put into the oven, using the long-handled **ухва́т**. The following are only the most common or most obvious cooking utensils:

пло́шка   a flat bowl
чугу́н   a cast-iron (stew) pot
сковорода́   a large metal frying pan
ко́вшик   a short-handled ladle
кры́нка, кри́нка   a pitcher, usually without handles, especially for milk
кувши́н a pitcher with handles for serving other liquids

(4)

(3)   (5)   (2)

The Russian samovar **самова́р** (self-cooker) was a relative newcomer (late eighteenth century) to the Russian household. But when it came, it stayed, for the samovar was an economical way to get hot water quickly.

The samovar made hot water for tea, but the tea was never inside the samovar. A charcoal fire built in the central tube heated water that surrounded the tube in the body of the samovar. Naturally, smoke poured from the samovar chimney while the fire was being made, so that in the summer the samovar was started outside the house and in the winter its draft chimney (an extension of the central tube) was connected to a pipe in the Russian stove.

A very strong tea mixture was made in a small teapot that was then kept warm resting on top of the samovar. A small amount of this strong tea was poured into a cup and then diluted with hot water from the samovar.

THE "KITCHEN" КУ́ХНЯ

The area between the stove and the wall it faced was for cooking. It had extra shelves for cooking utensils and maybe a small cupboard **посу́дник** for dishes. This area occasionally was separated from the rest of the room by a screen of some sort, but not usually.

THE FRONT "ROOM" ПЕРЕ́ДНИЙ У́ГОЛ

In the corner at a diagonal from the stove was the dining area. This was considered a place of honor: it was rude for a stranger to advance toward it without specific invitation. Here all the eating, the ceremonies, and the parties took place. An icon **ико́на, о́браз** was placed on a shelf **божни́ца** in this corner. Seating at the table was on benches or stools. (Chairs were a city invention and not a part of peasant furniture.)

Benches **ла́вки** were often attached to all the wall space not already occupied by the stove, each one had a name that varied from place to place, though the use of the benches was less variable. The long bench **до́лгая ла́вка** on the side wall opposite the stove was often where the women did their spinning, mending, and weav-ing. The bench **ко́ник**, **ку́тник** from the doorway to the side wall was reserved for the man of the house. It was here that he repaired and cleaned his tools and equipment; therefore this was the part of the house reserved for dirty jobs.

WHERE DO THEY SLEEP? ГДЕ СПЯТ?

Nothing has been said about beds. At the beginning of World War II when the German soldiers first began to investigate peasant houses (in the western USSR) for their own use, they could not find the beds. The stove and table were obvious enough, but where did these people sleep? The answer was almost dramatically simple: on any flat surface. Grandmother or grandfather slept on the stove, the warmest and most desirable sleeping place. The children slept on the large shelf **пола́ти** just over the door. The baby slept in a cradle **лю́лька** hung from the ceiling, and the rest of the family used the benches and, if necessary, the floor.

LIGHTING ОСВЕЩЕ́НИЕ

Lighting during the long winter months was a major problem. Oil for lamps was too expensive to burn except in front of the icon, and kerosene

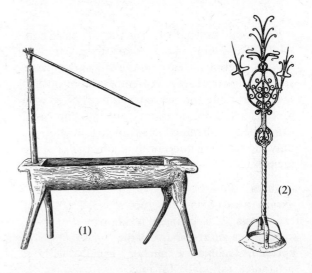

Приспособле́ния для держа́ния лучи́ны *Devices for holding sticks:* (1) свети́льно с коры́том, (2) стари́нный свете́ц

lamps were a relatively modern invention. Instead, long dry sticks **лучи́на** were used. These sticks were both cheap and readily available, but they were also dangerous and very short-lived: a new one had to be lit every fifteen minutes or so. In describing life in an average village in Leningradskaya Oblast in 1927 a correspondent asserted:

● То́лько в не́которых дома́х жгут кероси́н. Про́чие освеща́ются лучи́ной или за́светло ложа́тся спать.[14]

PLUMBING   ВОДОСНАБЖЕ́НИЕ

Water was obtained from a well **коло́дец** usually somewhere outside the house. Two types of well rigging are common in Russia. One is the wind-up kind with which we are familiar. Another very common device **жура́вль** uses a counterweight to help pull up the bucket of water. The figure below shows a very old model of this type, but the type itself is common today. The long poles suspended at an angle often seen in pictures of Russian villages indicate the sites of wells.

From the well, women carried the water in buckets **вёдра** (*sg.* **ведро́**) that hung from both ends of a kind of yoke **коромы́сло** to a barrel **чан** located either in the entrance room or near the **изба́** door. Inside, often near the Russian stove, was a **рукомо́йник** (literally, a hand-washer), some kind of dispenser hanging over a large bucket.

Sanitary facilities (toilets) varied with time and place. Some areas had none whatsoever. The following was written in 1926 regarding this problem about an area now known as Kalininskaya Oblast, just north of Moscow:

● Специа́льные убо́рные ста́ли то́лько о́чень неда́вно появля́ться в нове́йших постро́йках. Для э́того отгора́живается сте́нками оди́н из концо́в ма́ленького мо́стика на дворе́. В ста́рых постро́йках никаки́х осо́бых отхо́жих мест не́ было; и в э́тих це́лях испо́льзовался весь двор.[15]

In other areas, especially in the north, a special place (a hole in the floor) was provided somewhere in the **двор**, almost always near an outside wall to make cleaning easier. The accumulated soil was removed in the winter with pickaxes and baskets when, mercifully enough, everything was still frozen. Especially in the summertime, outhouses **нару́жные убо́рные** were also used.

The house "spirit"
Домово́й

Every house had to have a **домово́й** (and sometimes also a **домова́я**). Most people thought of this creature as having some real form or substance (unlike our amorphous ghost), but his actual description varied considerably according to locality. Generally he was thought of as relatively small, animallike, and endowed with special powers. He would carry on conversations with mice or crickets who also were house dwellers. In any case, every house had to have one, and he had to be treated with care lest he leave. The following passage gives

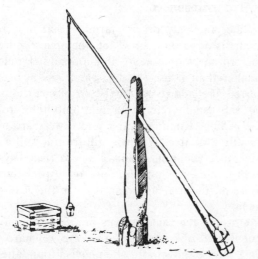

Стари́нный коло́дец

[14] As cited by И. Бугрова, "Дереве́нские встре́чи," *Ленингра́дская пра́вда*, 1 января́ 1968, стр. 2.

[15] Ве́рхне-Во́лжская этнологи́ческая экспеди́ция, *Крестья́нские постро́йки Яросла́вско-Тверско́го кра́я* (Ленингра́д: Госуда́рственная акаде́мия исто́рии материа́льной культу́ры, 1926), стр. 46.

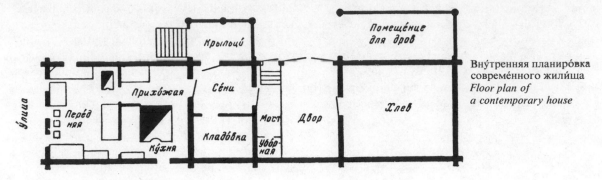

Вну́тренняя планиро́вка
совреме́нного жили́ща
*Floor plan of
a contemporary house*

Labels in floor plan: Улица, Крыльцо́, Помеще́ние для дров, Прихо́жая, Се́ни, Пере́д няя, Кухня, Кладо́вка, Мост, Убо́р ная, Двор, Хлев

one local description of the **домово́й** and his invitation to a newly built house. In this region a yard or barn spirit **дворово́й** was also part of the scene.

● Любопы́тно при переселе́нии на но́вое ме́сто приглаше́ние дворово́го и домово́го. Хозя́ин стано́вится пе́ред воро́тами двора́, кла́няется три ра́за в ра́зные сто́роны, повора́чиваясь че́рез ле́вое плечо́ и зовёт: «Ба́тюшка домово́й и ма́тушка домова́я, ба́тюшка дворово́й, ма́тушка дворова́я, со всем семе́йством, пойдёмте к нам на но́вое жили́ще, с на́м(и) жить.»
. . . Представле́ние о домово́м и дворово́м ещё живёт в широ́ких ма́ссах, и представля́ются они́ как бы двойника́ми хозя́ина. Они́ пока́зываются иногда́, но не к хоро́шему, и при э́том лицо́м похо́жи на хозя́ина. И по хара́ктеру и по скло́нностям, они́ таки́е же, как и хозя́ин—е́сли тот небре́жно отно́сится к скоти́не, то и дворово́й начина́ет пошаливать; но относи́ться к ним, во вся́ком слу́чае, ну́жно уважи́тельно, ина́че они́ мо́гут и уйти́.[16]

Contemporary rural housing
Совреме́нное се́льское жили́ще

A house in the country these days may range from the traditional peasant house just described (in the 1920's there was such widespread poverty and lack of materials that even then a few chimneyless **курны́е и́збы** were being built) to something greatly resembling the city apartment discussed in the first section. Most contemporary rural housing is a cross between the two.

[16] *Крестья́нские постро́йки Яросла́вско-Тверско́го кра́я*, стр. 47, 48.

What remains
Что остаётся

If it is a single family dwelling, then the stove is still there, though it might be a less romantic concrete block affair. It is now often situated in the center of the house, since one of its present purposes is to help divide the house into separate rooms. In fact, the major difference between the old and the new is the effort to create more privacy by dividing up the housing area into separate rooms.

What has changed
Что измени́лось

Since the only private farming that now remains is done on a small lot, the area required for storage, equipment, and animals is much smaller than it used to be. There has also occurred the added advantage of electrification, but this usually refers to a light bulb hung from the ceiling. Running water and sewers are not usually available. Water is still from a well and the toilet **убо́рная**, **отхо́жее ме́сто** (*vulg.* **ну́жник**) is either in an outhouse or, especially in more northern areas, somewhere in the covered **двор**.

Outside, the **зава́линка** is not very common, but if you look for them, they are not hard to find. Houses now more often have a foundation.

Furniture has taken on a citified air, with chairs, beds, and sofas the rule rather than the exception. There is now a greater variety of cooking equipment. Houses not supplied with electricity, or with not enough of it, now commonly use the following devices to cook with (in addition to the Russian stove):

кероси́нка the most common substitute for a hot plate, usually a one-burner kerosene stove with a cloth wick

при́мус like the **кероси́нка**, except that the wick mechanism is more advanced

керога́з also a kerosene burner, but more economical to run

The kitchen, instead of the **рукомо́йник**, might now have a **мо́йка**, another word for kitchen sink (also called **ра́ковина**), used especially when there is no running water; thus it often includes a reservoir in a cabinet above to supply water, and a bucket in the cabinet below to catch the waste. The same device in a bathroom or bedroom is the **умыва́льник**. **Рукомо́йник** now is a water dispenser with a valve and lever at the bottom. It is often attached to a wall or pole outside the house and is used for summer washing.

5

Education

Образовáние

It would perhaps be an understatement to say that the USSR places strong emphasis on education. The pressure for education comes not only from the government, which wants and needs qualified workers, but also from the people themselves. Back-to-school day, the first of September, is practically a national holiday. Support for education is rooted in traditional respect accorded scholars and learning by the upper classes (as in Western Europe). Contemporary Russians are also aware that education is a way to a better job. Though any useful work is promoted in theory as a Good Thing, in the public mind some things are better than others. Thus engineers have more esteem than skilled mechanics, even though the pay for their work may be less.

The regard for education, at least in the upper classes, predates the Revolution. The institution now known as the Academy of Sciences, USSR, for instance, was founded by Peter the Great in 1724. Before the Revolution, Russia had the full range of schools, from primary schools to technical institutes and universities. It was, after all, possible for a Lomonósov (1711–65), born of a peasant family in a fishing village in the far north, to become one of the great scholars of history. He was, however, a genius, and it seems that even though Russia has had room for genius, it was not a fruitful breeding ground for the more commonplace competence. The framework of educational institutions existed but was not filled out with the muscle of the masses, partially because money and sometimes nobility were required for advanced education, and partially because education was not part of the lower-class mystique. The following quotations demonstrate several things at once: (1) the 1897 census revealed considerable illiteracy, (2) the Soviets tend to choose figures that put the Old Regime in the darkest possible light (but that is to be expected), and (3) one must pay great attention to modifiers in Soviet statistics to avoid misinterpreting them.

● По дáнным пéреписи 1897 г., в Росси́и бы́ло грáмотных мужчи́н 29,3%, жéнщин—13,1%; в э́то же врéмя грáмотных мужчи́н-рабóчих бы́ло 59,9%, жéнщин-рабóтниц 34,9%.[1]

[1] Алексáндров, *Нарóды европейской чáсти СССР*, стр. 475.

● По да́нным пе́реписи 1897 г. да́же в Европе́йской ча́сти страны́ на 1000 челове́к приходи́лось гра́мотных: мужчи́н—227, же́нщин—117.[2]

Just before the Revolution, things had improved somewhat, and it was not terribly difficult for the poor man to get at least a few years of schooling. In 1920, in the 8 administrative regions of the European part of the RSFSR, approximately 54 percent of the people aged 9 to 49 were literate (70 percent of the men, 40 percent of the women).[3]

Before the Revolution, many groups had set up two- to four-year courses in the rudiments of learning, including the local government school **зе́мская шко́ла** and the church parish school **церко́вноприхо́дская шко́ла**. The real problem came with secondary education. That began at about the age of ten in a gymnasium (**класси́ческая**) **гимна́зия**, where classes concentrated on a classical (both Latin and Greek) education, or in a **реа́льное учи́лище**, where a more technical education was given. Nobility was not required for most of these schools but money usually was. And since most peasants needed the labor their children could provide, they were rarely sent to school even when it was otherwise possible to do so.

Lenin saw that he could not build a strong industrial country without a technically well-trained populace from which to draw. Efforts to bring literacy to the masses led to the establishment of **шко́лы ликбе́за** (**ликбе́з—ликвида́ция безгра́мотности**) in 1920, which flourished by the end of the decade. These were schools whose principal aim was to teach reading and writing, mostly to adults, especially to those who were beyond normal school age but who were illiterate. At the same time special schools **рабфа́ки** were formed to prepare peasants and workers for university level work.

● Осо́бое ме́сто в о́бщем образова́нии взро́слых за́няли рабо́чие факульте́ты (рабфа́ки), кото́рые впервы́е бы́ли организо́ваны в 1919 г. при не́скольких ву́зах. Декре́т Совнарко́ма «О рабо́чих факульте́тах», при́нятый в сентябре́ 1920 г., закрепи́л их существова́ние в госуда́рственном масшта́бе. Пе́ред рабфа́ками была́ поста́влена зада́ча подгото́вить к учёбе в вы́сших уче́бных заведе́ниях рабо́чих и крестья́н, что име́ло огро́мное значе́ние для созда́ния но́вой сове́тской интеллиге́нции.

Сре́днее образова́ние взро́слых до середи́ны 20-х годо́в росло́ дово́льно ме́дленно, гла́вным о́бразом за счёт рабфа́ков. . . . В 1928/29 уче́бном году́ в РСФСР бы́ло 107 рабфа́ков (39,9 тыс. уча́щихся), в 1932/33 уче́бном году́—609 (204,9 тыс. уча́щихся).[4]

---

[2] *Наро́дное образова́ние в РСФСР* (*1917–1967 гг.*) (Москва́: Просвеще́ние, 1967), стр. 2.

[3] *Наро́дное образова́ние в РСФСР*, ред. М. П. Ка́шин и Е. М. Чеха́рин (Москва́: Просвеще́ние, 1970), стр. 162.

[4] *Наро́дное образова́ние в РСФСР* (*1917–1967 гг.*), стр. 14.

By 1930 the government was able to declare that a primary education was obligatory for all (**всео́буч—всео́бщее обяза́тельное нача́льное обуче́ние**), and by 1949 all children in the Russian Federation (РСФСР) were to have seven years of education.

● Постановле́нием ЦК ВКП(б) от 25 ию́ля 1930 г. с 1930/31 уче́бного го́да вводи́лось всео́бщее нача́льное обуче́ние, в города́х же и рабо́чих посёлках бы́ло введено́ всео́бщее семиле́тное обуче́ние (повсеме́стно обяза́тельное семиле́тнее обуче́ние введено́ в РСФСР в 1949 г.).[5]

These were merely the first steps in the establishment of the educational system that has evolved (with not a few changes) into the present one, which will be described here in greater detail.

There are two aspects of Soviet education that will not be dwelt upon in the course of the discussion but that permeate the entire educational structure. One is that the Soviet educational system, philosophically, at least, does not believe in intelligence quotients. Therefore, pupils are not separated according to ability levels, nor do teachers (relying on IQ tests) tend to expect more of certain children than they do of others. From our point of view this concept might put too heavy a burden on those children we think of as slow, but it has the advantage of not condemning to mediocrity those who have not scored well on predictive examinations.

The other major difference in Soviet education is what seems to us an extreme uniformity of courses and curriculum and a resultant lack of choice on the student's part. All secondary school pupils must take chemistry, physics, mathematics, and other prescribed subjects. (There are special schools that emphasize certain subjects, but this emphasis is mostly in addition to the regular curriculum.) All students take what in the United States is a college preparatory course. The small number of electives in secondary schools is just a chance to take more of the same courses already in the curriculum. Therefore, Soviet schools require no school counselors or college advisors. There are no choices to advise upon. Choice does come, in a sense, at the end of secondary schooling when the student must select a career. But having chosen a field, his courses are again all laid out for him. Electives in college can be taken, but they are above and beyond normal course work.

Soviet education is obviously a huge subject; only some general idea of Soviet schooling and its terminology will be given here. For more details interestingly and clearly explained, consult Nigel Grant, *Soviet Education* (Baltimore: Penguin Books, 1964). For an interesting comparison of Soviet and American primary and second-

[5] *Наро́дное образова́ние в РСФСР (1917–1967 гг.)*, стр. 6.

ary schools, see Urie Bronfenbrenner, *Two Worlds of Childhood* (New York: Russell Sage Foundation, 1970).

Here, different aspects of Soviet education are discussed in the following order:

Levels in education
Curriculum
Grades
Administration
In and out of school
Different types of schools

Levels in education
Ступéни образовáния

The table of grade levels shows where Russian children are both in relation to each other and in relation to their counterparts in the United States. The table lays out the full range of possibilities, but only primary and secondary schooling is required of everyone.

Nursery
Дéтские ясли

If a mother has no one at home to look after her small child while she works, she will enroll him in a nursery **дéтские ясли** for children from six months to three years old. The service is not free, but is very inexpensive. It fulfills the physical need for a babysitter, and the training emphasizes good habits and groupmanship. Parents often try to avoid enrolling their children in nurseries because they feel that such young children need home care and attention.

Kindergarten
Дéтский сад

Some real effort at education begins here—letters and numbers, even simple "combinations," often in fact as much as we accomplish in our first grade. The fee varies from 2.50 to 10 rubles a month, depending on income. The children usually stay all day until a parent can pick them up after work. A teacher at this level is a **воспитáтельница** and a pupil is a **воспитанник. Дошкóльник** is any preschool-age child.

In 1970 about half of urban children and about 10 percent of rural children under seven were enrolled in nurseries and kindergartens (mostly in the latter where the demand is greatest). Kindergarten and nursery facilities are often combined.

Grade and high school
Восьмилéтка, десятилéтка

Real school begins at age seven. From this point on, schooling is free. Parents are expected to buy books, supplies, and uniforms, however. Attendance is obligatory for eight years (or until the end of the school year in which the child reaches sixteen), normally eight grades, and may be continued for two more years.

There are several "schools" shown in the table—**начáльная школа, (непóлная) срéдняя школа, пóлная срéдняя школа.** They are an administrative convenience to indicate the level of schooling. Students usually attend the same school building for the mandatory eight years—**начáльная и непóлная срéдняя школа**; those that continue for two more years **пóлная срéдняя школа** also remain in the same school building. (Some schools in the country go only to the eighth-year level and continuing students

Grade level: USA		Age	Grade level and type of school		Those attending are called	When done they get
		28			докторант	до́кторская сте́пень, степень до́ктора
		27				
		26				
		25				
		24	аспиранту́ра[4]	вуз[2]	аспира́нт	кандида́тская сте́пень, сте́пень кандида́та
Graduate		23				
School		22				
College	Senior	21	выпускни́к[8]		студе́нт[5]	дипло́м
	Junior	20	четвероку́рсник	вуз[2]		
	Sophomore	19	третьеку́рсник			
	Freshman	18	второку́рсник	те́хникум	уча́щийся[7]	
Senior High	Senior 12	17	первоку́рсник	учи́лище		
	Junior 11	16	10 по́лная сре́дняя	проф-тех.		аттеста́т зре́лости
	Sophomore 10	15	9 шко́ла	учи́лище[9]	учени́к[5]	
	Freshman 9	14	8 непо́лная		шко́льник[5]	свиде́тельство
Junior High	8	13	7 сре́дняя	восьмиле́тка[3]		
	7	12	6 шко́ла			
Grade School	6	11	5	десятиле́тка[1]		
	5	10	4			
	4	9	3 нача́льная			
	3	8	2 шко́ла			
	2	7	1			
	1	6			дошко́льник[6] воспи́танник	
	kindergarten	5	де́тский сад			
Nursery		4				
School		3	де́тские я́сли			
or		2				
Day Care		1				
Center		6 months				

[1] Десятиле́тняя шко́ла (formally, Сре́дняя общеобразова́тельная трудова́я политехни́ческая шко́ла). It is the basic ten-year school, soon to be the level of education required for everyone. Now it is the most likely and direct way to college (that is, вуз).

[2] An acronym for вы́сшее уче́бное заведе́ние, an "institution of higher learning." University-level training is provided either at a university университе́т or at an institute институ́т. When speaking English, Soviets often confuse our high school with their вуз.

[3] The "eight-year school" and currently the level of education required of everyone. Formerly, required education was only seven years and the school therefore was called семиле́тка.

[4] Graduate student training. Though often delayed two years after graduation from college as shown, it can also begin right after finishing undergraduate work.

[5] Студе́нт is a university-level student; шко́льник, учени́к are high-school level and below: "Он в пе́рвом кла́ссе"—"He is in the first grade"; "Он на пе́рвом ку́рсе"—"He is a freshman (in college)."

[6] A preschool-age child, whether or not he attends nursery school or kindergarten.

[7] Most often used to refer to vocational or trade-school students.

[8] Either a graduate of or a last-year student in a вуз (вы́пустить to release, let go, let out).

[9] Профессиона́льно-техни́ческое учи́лище. See text.

must transfer elsewhere.) The major difference between the primary school **нача́льная шко́ла** and the upper grades is that the primary grades have the same teacher all day (except for physical education, music, and foreign languages when possible or necessary), while the upper grades have subject specialists. The upper grades also have longer hours (see the curriculum table in the next section).

At the end of eight grades the pupil **учени́к, шко́льник** has several choices. He can quit altogether and find work while continuing his secondary education in a night or correspondence school if he wishes. He can go straight into a vocational school, sometimes obtaining his high-school diploma **аттеста́т зре́лости** there. Or, especially if he has done well, he can continue for two more years his essentially academic education in the **по́лная сре́дняя шко́ла**. The latter is the most likely and the most direct route to a higher education in a **вуз**. The vocational schools are worth some comment before discussing this direct route to higher education.

Vocational schools
Сре́дние специа́льные уче́бные заведе́ния

The operative words are **сре́дние** and **специа́льные**, the former indicating that one of the schools' purposes is to continue academic instruction through to the equivalent of the ninth and tenth grades (that is, until the high-school diploma has been earned), the latter stressing additional training in a particular kind of work. These schools fall into two categories: **те́хникум**, which trains for highly skilled technical or clerical jobs such as electronic technology, some engineering, food processing, finance, and the like; and **учи́лище**, which provides training in nursing, medical technology, library work, and lower-level elementary school teaching.

Courses in these schools vary from two to four years, usually depending on whether or not the student has already obtained his ten-year education.

A third kind of vocational school is perhaps better called a trade school **профессиона́льно-**

техни́ческое учи́лище, where emphasis is almost entirely on learning a trade such as carpentry, plumbing, and so forth. Most of student time is spent as an apprentice and wages are paid accordingly. The length of the course varies widely from a few months to several years, depending on the subject. Technically, one can go from any of the те́хникум, учи́лище, профессиона́льно-техни́ческое учи́лище schools into a вуз, but in practice the large majority of students (most often called уча́щиеся) in these schools go straight into a job.

Evening and correspondence schools are very widely used, especially by those who for some reason never finished the ten-year school. The те́хникум and учи́лище often have evening divisions вече́рние и сме́нные отделе́ния, and there are also special correspondence schools or divisions of schools зао́чные сре́дние специа́льные уче́бные заведе́ния. The latter tend to have much greater contact with their pupils in the course of study than do ours. The use of these part-time schools is widely encouraged by the government since the participants are making their contributions to society while improving their capacity for future contributions. Very wide use of evening вече́рнее отделе́ние and correspondence зао́чное отделе́ние courses is also made at the university level, where about half the students get their degree дипло́м this way. Naturally, the studies take longer to complete, but one day off a week and an extra month of vacation are granted to correspondence and night-school students. The students themselves, however, consider this a much less desirable way to get their college education.

Higher education
Вы́сшее образова́ние

The direct route to a higher education is the completion of all ten grades of school, including the по́лная сре́дняя шко́ла. The student is then about seventeen years old and has his аттеста́т зре́лости. At this point, he is technically eligible to enter a higher educational institution вы́сшее уче́бное заведе́ние or, more commonly, вуз. That can be either a university университе́т, which offers a broad spectrum of subjects in the sciences and the humanities, or an institute институ́т, which specializes in two or three aspects of a single subject. Medicine, engineering, agriculture, and the like are more often studied at institutes than at universities, where emphasis is more on the humanities and on the pure rather than applied sciences. (Our general word "college," meaning any place of higher education other than a trade school, in Russian is институ́т: "Are you planning to go to college?" is "Ты собира́ешься поступа́ть в институ́т?")

A high-school diploma does not guarantee access to higher education. During the Khrushchev era, the student was encouraged and sometimes forced to get work experience for two years before entering academic life. But the practice, though educationally interesting, turned out to be scholastically unsound. The students did best who came directly from high school. Although this practice has been largely discontinued, another obstacle remains. The real hurdle for the student now is to pass the competitive entrance examinations, for there are many more would-be students than there are openings in the universities and institutes. (Private tutors are frequently hired to help pass this hurdle.) Though universities are generally held in greater esteem than the institutes, some of the

This is a typical announcement from an institute. Notice that most subjects can be studied while the student continues working. Necessary documents are listed, as is the fact that the institute does not have its own dormitory.

Моско́вский институ́т электро́нного машинострое́ния
ОБЪЯВЛЯЕТ ПРИЕМ на 1-й курс
с отры́вом от произво́дства по специа́льностям:
«ПОЛУПРОВОДНИКО́ВОЕ И ЭЛЕКТРОВАКУУМНОЕ МАШИНОСТРОЕ́НИЕ»,
«ПРИБО́РЫ ТО́ЧНОЙ МЕХА́НИКИ»,
«АВТОМА́ТИКА И ТЕЛЕМЕХА́НИКА»,
«СЧЕТНО-РЕША́ЮЩИЕ ПРИБО́РЫ И УСТРО́ЙСТВА»,
«КОНСТРУИ́РОВАНИЕ И ТЕХНОЛО́ГИЯ ПРОИЗВО́ДСТВА РАДИОАППАРАТУ́РЫ»,
«ЭЛЕКТРО́ННЫЕ ПРИБО́РЫ»,
«АВТОМАТИЗИ́РОВАННЫЕ СИСТЕ́МЫ УПРАВЛЕ́НИЯ»,
«ПРИКЛАДНА́Я МАТЕМА́ТИКА»;
без отры́ва от произво́дства по всем перечи́сленным специа́льностям, кро́ме специа́льности «Автоматизи́рованные систе́мы управле́ния».
На специа́льность «Прикладна́я матема́тика» без отры́ва от произво́дства принима́ются ли́ца, име́ющие вы́сшее техни́ческое образова́ние.
Общежи́тия институ́т не име́ет.
Заявле́ния принима́ются:
на обуче́ние с отры́вом от произво́дства — по 31 ию́ля.
на обуче́ние без отры́ва от произво́дства — по 31 а́вгуста.
Необходи́мо предста́вить: докуме́нт о сре́днем образова́нии (в по́длиннике), характери́стику, медици́нскую спра́вку (фо́рма 286), фотока́рточки (3×4) — 5 шт., вы́писку из трудово́й кни́жки, па́спорт, вое́нный биле́т или припи́сное свиде́тельство.
Вступи́тельные экза́мены по матема́тике (письменно и устно), физике (устно), русскому языку́ и литерату́ре (письменно)
прово́дятся:
на обуче́ние с отры́вом от произво́дства — с 1 по 20 а́вгуста.
на обуче́ние без отры́ва от произво́дства — с 11 а́вгуста
по 10 сентября́.
Адрес институ́та: Б. Ву́зовский пер., 3/12.
Прое́зд: метро́ ст. «Ки́ровская» или «Новокузне́цкая»; трамв.: «А», 3, 39 до ост. «Казарменный пер.»; тролл. 25, 41, 45; авт. 3 до ост. «Покро́вские воро́та».

latter (often those in a science) are even harder to get in to than the universities.

Once in the university (or institute), the course of study usually lasts about five years (though medicine takes six). Some students do fail, but generally it is considered to be the instructor's responsibility to keep his students there and working "at level."

Having finished his college work and received his (first) degree диплóм, the graduate дипломник, выпускник is assigned a place to work where he must stay from one to three years. Extenuating circumstances are allowed to temper this work rule, however. Husbands are not separated from wives, nor are children from sick parents, for example. This work period is used to supply trained manpower to areas that are generally unpopular.

THE STUDENT STIPEND — **СТУДÉНЧЕСКАЯ СТИПÉНДИЯ**

Most full-time students at the college level are paid to go to school, but the amounts they receive depend on five criteria: (1) the field chosen —historians are not so valuable as physicists; (2) year of study—fifth-year students get more than first-year students; (3) academic progress успевáемость—good students get more money; (4) attendance посещáемость—a student стáроста кýрса is elected and has among his duties the checking of attendance at lectures or classes; and (5) the parents' income and responsibilities —parents well able to support their child in college must do so. There are also some special larger stipends именнýе стипéндии, which carry the name of some well-known person and are granted to those who are both academically very talented and especially active in "social life" (party life) учáстие в общéственной жúзни. These grants, therefore, encourage active participation in Komsomol activities.

The higher stipends (mostly for science or technical majors) of seventy rubles are quite reasonable for student support, but thirty-five rubles (mostly for humanities or social science majors) must usually be supplemented by moonlighting or parental generosity.

Graduate work
Аспирантýра

Graduate work usually does not begin until after the hopeful student has worked for a few years. He then applies and takes yet another examination.

Graduate work in the USSR enjoys a different status than it does here. In the first place, fewer are chosen for the honor, and, perhaps as a concomitant, the honor is vastly greater. Graduate work is not only more honorable but also relatively well paid, so that it is not automatically associated with penury.

All Soviet graduate degrees must have the approval of the Higher Qualification Commission Вы́сшая Аттестацио́нная Коми́ссия (ВАК) of the Ministry of Higher and Secondary Specialized Education.

Both graduate degrees, the candidate degree and the doctor's degree, require the writing and public defense of a thesis диссертáция.

The dissertations are so publicly defended that announcements of the defense appear in the local newspaper:

ЦЕНТРАЛЬНЫЙ ОРДЕНА ЛЕНИНА ИНСТИТУТ УСОВЕРШЕНСТВОВАНИЯ ВРАЧЕЙ
(пл. Восстания, 1/2)
Терапевтический совет
17/VI—69 г.:
1. В 13 час. на соискание ученой степени доктора медицинских наук ЧЕЧУЛИНЫМ Ю. С. на тему: «Ультраструктурная организация, метаболизм и сократительная функция поврежденного сердца (экспериментальное исследование)».
2. В 15 час. на соискание ученой степени кандидата медицинских наук ВДОВИЧЕНКО А. С. на тему: «Клиника, диагностика и лечение хромосомных болезней человека (синдром Шерешевского — Тернера, мужской синдром Тернера, синдром Клайнфельтера)».
(Баррикадная ул., 8)
Хирургический совет
17/VI—69 г., в 13 час., на соискание ученой степени кандидата медицинских наук:
1. ГАЛКИНЫМ В. В. на тему: «Диагностика тромбоэмболии легочной артерии в хирургической клинике».
2. ГЛУЩЕНКО Э. В. на тему: «Влияние характера оперативного вмешательства и анестетиков на активность сывороточной аспартат- и аланинаминотрансферазы».

THE CANDIDATE DEGREE	КАНДИДА́ТСКАЯ СТЕ́ПЕНЬ

This first graduate degree is also called сте́-пень кандида́та. (In a Soviet university, only graduate degrees are called "degree" сте́пень.) The one doing the work is аспира́нт and his graduate study is аспиранту́ра.

Graduate students аспира́нты earning their first degree normally spend three years doing so. In the course of the first one and a half to two years, they must pass three tests, which together are called кандида́тский ми́нимум. One test is in a foreign language, another in philosophy, including general philosophy and Marxism and Leninism; either of these may or may not re-quire course work. A third test is in one's specialty for which there is no course work. These tests are not looked upon as a major bar-rier by students and once they have been com-pleted, thesis work is begun.

Though кандида́тская сте́пень is the lesser of the two Soviet higher degrees, it probably comes close to our Ph.D. degree.[6] (As an example, the student is expected to have published a few articles even before he gets his degree.) The re-cipient is given the title зва́ние of кандида́т нау́к (кандида́т педагоги́ческих нау́к, кандида́т медици́нских нау́к и т.д.).

THE DOCTORATE	ДО́КТОРСКАЯ СТЕ́ПЕНЬ

This degree is the highest attainable. It often, though not necessarily, takes many years to achieve and is awarded only to those who have done really significant work in their field.

For the до́кторская сте́пень no course work is required for the applicant доктора́нт. The degree must be applied for, however, and the dissertation до́кторская диссерта́ция must be a really major contribution to one's field. Up to one year is given with full pay тво́рческий о́тпуск for writing the doctoral thesis, and the "student" доктора́нт normally has to advise and supervise candidate degree applicants work-ing under his direction. The recipient of this degree has the title до́ктор нау́к.

Academy of Sciences of the USSR
Акаде́мия нау́к СССР

The highest position of scholarship is occu-pied by the academician акаде́мик, one among some 245 (active) members of the Academy of Sciences USSR. This institution is very presti-gious and powerful, and its members are not only honored and influential but also financially

6 Not everyone agrees. See *USSR, A Guide to the Academic Placement of Students from the USSR in Educational Institu-tions in the US*, World Education Series (Washington, D.C.: American Association of Collegiate Registrars and Admis-sions Officers, 1966).

very secure. Members, who live in special apartment buildings, have a large monthly stipend, the use of a country house **да́ча**, not to mention a chauffered car, special bookstores, and restaurants. There are two levels of membership in the academy—the active member **действи́тельный член** and the corresponding member **член-корреспонде́нт**, the latter with less prestige, power, and remuneration than the former. Among its functions, the academy has many research institutes under its direction (many of which grant graduate degrees), it advises the government on the direction research should take, and it maintains contacts with foreign scholars via meetings, conferences, and through some seventy publications. The initials АН СССР are familiar to and respected by almost any foreign (that is, non-Soviet) scholar who uses Soviet sources, materials, or reports in doing his own work. The Russian (and, in general, European) regard for the scholar has no parallel in the United States. Our National Academy of Sciences is prestigious, perhaps, but only in that small circle occupied by the academics themselves.

It should be noted that the Soviet Academy of Sciences includes not just the pure and applied sciences (as does ours) but also history, law, economics, literature, and linguistics. There are other specialized academies of science such as:

> Акаде́мия строи́тельных нау́к
> Акаде́мия педагоги́ческих нау́к
> Акаде́мия медици́нских нау́к

In addition there are smaller academies of science in many of the republics that concentrate on problems peculiar to their area. These include:

> Акаде́мия нау́к Украи́нской ССР
>   (АН УССР)
> Акаде́мия нау́к Грузи́нской ССР
>   (АН ГрузССР)
> Акаде́мия нау́к Латви́йской ССР
>   (АН ЛатССР)

Curriculum
Учёбный план

In grade and high schools
В сре́дних шко́лах

The curriculum chart given here is the standard one for the RSFSR (the Russian republic). It is modified for special circumstances, however. For instance, a special school **спецшко́ла**, that is, one that gives special emphasis to a particular subject, will give more and earlier attention to that subject. Special schools may concentrate on mathematics and physics or on ballet or music; more commonly, the specialization is in a foreign language. These schools are relatively few and are mostly confined to the major centers of population. (In 1968–69 there were 266 special [language] schools in the RSFSR.)

The other major deviation from the standard curriculum shown here occurs among the many different language groups within the USSR. All those major non-Russian language groups have schools that are conducted in their own languages.[7] In such a school Russian is taught as an additional subject. In some areas the additional time required is taken from such courses as physical education and work training; in other areas another year of study is added to make up the difference.

In spite of these variations, the Soviet curriculum is a radical change for the American who at home is used to as many curricula as there are school systems, most of which seem to be ignored as often as there are teachers. The Soviet curriculum can be considered essentially the same for the whole country.

Standardization extends to the text **уче́бник** as well as the course. As previously mentioned, parents buy books and other school materials. Textbook prices are even lower than standard

---

[7] People living in these regions also (technically) have the option of sending their children to a school conducted in Russian; knowing Russian is an advantage to those that aspire.

Учебные предмéты	Количество часóв в недéлю в клáссе (Class hours per week)										Subjects
Grade level	I	II	III	IV	V	VI	VII	VIII	IX	X	
Рýсский язы́к	12	11	12	7	6	5	3	2	—	1	Russian language
Литератýра	—	—	—	2	2	2	2	3	4	3	Literature
Математика¹	6	6	6	7	6	6	6	5	6	6	Mathematics
Истóрия	—	—	—	2	2	2	2	3	4	3	History
Обществовéдение	—	—	—	—	—	—	—	—	—	2	(Social studies²)
Природовéдение	—	1	—	1	—	—	—	—	—	—	Nature study
Геогрáфия	—	—	—	—	2	3	2	3	2	—	Geography
Биолóгия	—	—	—	—	2	2	2	2	1	2	Biology
Фи́зика	—	—	—	—	—	2	2	3	5	5	Physics
Астронóмия	—	—	—	—	—	—	—	—	—	1	Astronomy
Черчéние	—	—	—	—	—	—	1	2	—	—	(Technical) drawing
Хи́мия	—	—	—	—	—	—	2	2	3	3	Chemistry
Иностра́нный язы́к³	—	—	—	—	4	3	3	2	2	2	Foreign language
Изобрази́тельное искýсство	1	1	1	1	1	1	—	—	—	—	Art
Мýзыка	1	1	1	1	1	1	1	—	—	—	Music
Физи́ческая культýра⁴	2	2	2	2	2	2	2	2	2	2	Physical education
Трудовóе обучéние⁵	2	2	2	2	2	2	2	2	2	2	Work training
Начáльная воéнная подготóвка	—	—	—	—	—	—	—	—	2	2	Beginning military training
Всегó	24	24	24	25	30	31	30	31	33	34	Total
Прáктика⁶ (в днях)	—	—	—	—	6	6	12	—	24	—	Practice (in days)
Факультати́вные заня́тия	—	—	—	—	—	—	1	2	4	4	Elective courses

¹ At different stages, this subject goes under various titles: **арифмéтика, áлгебра, геомéтрия, тригономéтрия, и т.д.**

² "Social studies" should be taken in the Marxist sense, not really comparable to our meaning.

³ The most popular language is English, which almost half the students study. Thereafter the most common languages are French, German, and Spanish.

⁴ This is commonly referred to as **физкультýра**.

⁵ The word is often shortened to **трýд**. The subject deals with using common tools, growing a vegetable garden, keeping house, sewing, and cooking.

⁶ This usually refers to summer field work in agriculture, such as pulling weeds.

book prices (though the amount is not insignificant for a family receiving a minimum wage).

The uniformity of Soviet education is guaranteed, finally, by standardization of lesson plans. Teachers are expected to have their classes at about the same place in the plan as all other teachers in the subject at the same level.

A SAMPLE CURRICULUM

ПРИМÉРНАЯ УЧÉБНАЯ ПРОГРÁММА

School curricula are printed by subject and are on sale in school supply stores in the USSR.

The sample below shows the topics to be discussed in ninth-grade literature courses. Each topic is followed by a suggested number of class hours that might be devoted to the subject, though the teacher can change those amounts according to local conditions.

IX КЛАСС (140 час.)

Литератýра вторóй половины XIX в. (обзóр 4 часá)

А. Н. Острóвский, «Грозá» (9 час.)
И. С. Тургéнев, «Отцы́ и дéти» (12 час.)

Н. Г. Черныше́вский, «Что де́лать?» (8 час.)

Н. А. Некра́сов, «Размышле́ния у пара́дного подъе́зда», «Желе́зная доро́га», «Пуска́й нам говори́т изме́нчивая мо́да» (эле́гия), «Па́мяти Добролю́бова». Поэ́ма «Кому́ на Руси́ жить хорошо́» (14 час.)

М. Е. Салтыко́в-Щедри́н, «Исто́рия одного́ го́рода» (гла́вы по вы́бору учи́теля). Ска́зки «Медве́дь на воево́дстве», «Прему́дрый пес-ка́рь» (6 час.)

Ф. М. Достое́вский, «Преступле́ние и наказа́-ние» (12 час.)

Л. Н. Толсто́й, «Война́ и мир» (22 часа́)

А. П. Че́хов, «Вишнёвый сад», «Ио́ныч» (12 час.)

Из зарубе́жной литерату́ры

В. Шекспи́р, «Га́млет» (5 час.)
И. Гёте, «Фа́уст» (1-я часть) (4 часа́)
Стенда́ль, «Вани́на Вани́ни» (3 часа́)
О. Бальза́к, «Гобсе́к» (3 часа́)

Всего́: на изуче́ние произведе́ний—112 час.
   на бесе́ды по сове́тской литерату́ре—12 час.
   на рабо́ту по разви́тию ре́чи—16 час.

SAMPLE TEST   **ПРИМЕ́РНЫЙ ЭКЗА́МЕН**

In 1970 the high-school diploma examination for Russian literature was an oral examination. A list of thirty-two **«биле́ты»**, or test questions, was published, any of which the student should be able to discuss. For each **биле́т** one topic is on Soviet literature, a tenth-grade subject, and one topic is on nineteenth-century literature studied in the eighth and ninth grades. The following provide an example.

Биле́т № 5

- (1) Ра́нние революцио́нно-романти́ческие про-изведе́ния А. М. Го́рького, их иде́йная напра́вленность и худо́жественное своеоб-ра́зие.
- (2) Смысл назва́ния и осо́бенности компози́-ции рома́на И. С. Турге́нева «Отцы́ и де́ти». Отраже́ние в рома́не обще́ственно-полити́ческой борьбы́ 60-х годо́в XIX ве́ка.

Биле́т № 13

- (1) Поэ́ма А. А. Бло́ка « Двена́дцать». Иде́я. Компози́ция, ле́ксика и ри́тмика поэ́мы.
- (2) Гражда́нский по́двиг Н. Г. Черныше́вского.

Биле́т № 24

- (1) Изображе́ние красоты́ души́ и си́лы хара́к-тера сове́тского челове́ка—во́ина и тру́-женика в расска́зе М. А. Шо́лохова «Судьба́ челове́ка».
- (2) Иде́йная напра́вленность и худо́жественное своеобра́зие сати́ры М. Е. Салтыко́ва-Щедрина́. О́бразы Салтыко́ва-Щедрина́ в произведе́ниях В. И. Ле́нина.

Some further notion of what is expected of students can be gotten from the following example from the 1968 mathematics examina-tion, given to those who intended to major in physics at Moscow State University that year. This examination is more difficult than the usual high-school diploma tests since it represents the higher expectations of the better students in the country. This is the third part of a five-part examination reproduced in a *Guide for Appli-cants to Moscow State University*.[8]

- III. (1) Реши́ть нера́венство:

$$\log_5 \sin x > \log_{125} (3 \sin x - 2).$$

(2) Для ка́ждого действи́тельного числа́ a найти́ все действи́тельные реше́ния уравне́ния:

$$\sqrt{a(2^x - 2)} + 1 = 1 - 2^x.$$

(3) Покупа́тель купи́л не́сколько одина́ковых тетра́дей и одина́ковых книг, причём книг на 4 шту́ки бо́льше, чем тетра́дей. За все тетра́ди он заплати́л 72 коп., а за все кни́ги—6 руб. 60 коп. Е́сли бы тетра́дь сто́ила сто́лько, ско́лько сто́ит кни́га, а кни́га—сто́лько, ско́лько сто́ит тетра́дь, то покупа́тель истра́тил бы на по-ку́пку ме́ньше, чем 4 руб. 44 коп. Ско́лько ку́плено тетра́дей?

(4) В прямоуго́льной трапе́ции $ABCD$ углы́ A и D прямы́е, сторона́ AB паралле́льна стороне́ CD, дли́ны сторо́н таковы́: $AB = 1$, $CD = 4$, $AD = 5$. На стороне́ AD взята́ то́чка M так, что у́гол CMD вдво́е бо́льше угла́ BMA. В како́м отноше́нии то́чка M де́лит сто́рону AD?

(5) В прямо́й кругово́й ко́нус впи́сан шар. Отно-ше́ние объёмов ко́нуса и ша́ра равно́ двум. Найти́ отноше́ние по́лной пове́рхности ко́-нуса к пове́рхности ша́ра.

---

[8] *Спра́вочник для поступа́ющих в Моско́вский университе́т*, ред. В. И. Тропин (Москва́: Изда́тельство Моско́вского университе́та, 1969), стр. 159.

In vocational schools
В средних специальных учебных заведениях

For those attending a **техникум** or an **учи́лище**, the goals of attendance determine the curriculum. Part (about half) of the time is spent completing the academic requirements for a ten-year education, and the remaining time is spent, both in class and to a limited extent on the job, in training in the specific vocation. Those in the trade school **профессиона́льно-техни́ческое учи́лище (ПТУ)** spend almost all their time in on-the-job training. Only about 20 percent of their time is devoted to related academics and theory.

In college
В ву́зах

The most important thing to remember about the college curriculum in the USSR is that students essentially specialize upon entrance and their college courses are preselected for them. There is no confusion about whether to take History 101 or Anthro 104. They may take courses in addition to those that are part of their major field of study, but they do so on their own. Such courses are called "elective" **факульта́тивные ку́рсы**.

The usual college course takes five years to complete. Technically, the student may switch from, say, architecture to engineering, but to do so he must begin again at the bottom, losing credit thereby for the time he has already spent. There is no such thing as a pre-major (pre-law or pre-medicine); specialty training starts immediately.

Not only does specialty training start earlier, it is also more narrow in scope, especially in technical fields where the number of specialties seems close to endless. As a result, the majority of Soviet students tend to know more of their specialty and less about the rest of the world than do our students. (But this information must be tempered by what seem to be higher accomplishments at the secondary level.)

Research as part of one's undergraduate work is highly encouraged in the Soviet Union. Beginning in the second year of study, students can join a student research organization **Студе́нческое нау́чное о́бщество (СНО)** or **Студе́нческое констру́кторское бюро́ (СКБ)**. (The latter attempts to solve primarily technical problems that have arisen in industry.) These organizations meet regularly, research is conducted under the guidance of faculty members, and annual competitions are held. The best papers are published by the Academy of Sciences.

A research requirement in the major field is the writing of a diploma thesis **дипло́мная рабо́та** to show that the student has some understanding of a field and some control over its tools of investigation. This project is considered very important, and students are usually given their final semester to devote to their research and writing.

In addition to their specialty training, Soviet college students must also take courses in Communism: history of the Communist party, political economy, dialectical and historical materialism, scientific Communism—**исто́рия КПСС, полити́ческая эконо́мия, диалекти́ческий и истори́ческий материали́зм, нау́чный коммуни́зм**. These total approximately one semester of college work.

Also required of the student is study of a foreign language for two to three hours a week of the first two years. In his third year he must pass an examination on the foreign language.

Finally, most university students must take a few courses in pedagogy and do some practice teaching. Upon graduating, the student is eligible to teach in secondary schools, though there is no great rush to do so. Students whose specialty is not taught on a secondary level need not take such courses (those in law or medicine, for instance).

6

Месяц _сентябрь_

Дни и числа	Предметы	ЧТО ЗАДАНО	Оценка успеваемости	Подпись учителя
Понедельник 9	Русск. яз	§ 3. Упр. 18.		
	Физика	Задание в тетради.		
	Истор.	Параграф 2.		
	Математ	§ 41. 29.		
	Музыка	Принести нотную тетр		
Вторник	Geography	p. 179-180, 182; mark mineral	4	Голуб
	English	Read the second part Ret 1		
	English	Lear words, poem. Ex V p11		
	Труд	Переписать в тетрадь		
	Труд	классную запись, принести газету		
	Черчение	Принести принадлежности		
Среда 10	Истор.	Параграф 3.		
	Русск. яз	§ 1, 2, 3 Упр. № 21, 22		
	Математ	§ 25, 26. № 646, 677 (1,2), 650 (1), 657 (2)		
	Русск. яз	Прочит 5 глав Принести форму		
	Матем	Задание в тетради		
	Химия	Параграф 1.		

Пропуск уроков _____ из них по болезни _____

Количество опозданий на уроки _____

1/IX в 7 часов вечера состоится родительское

Месяц _сентябрь_

Дни и числа	Предметы	ЧТО ЗАДАНО	Оценка успеваемости	Подпись учителя
Четверг	Физика	§ 4. Стр. 184. № 1,2,3,4,5. 2 тетр		
	Алгебра	Задание		Иванова
	Алгебра	в тетради		
	English	Read and ret. the text Ex XII p6		
	Русский	Задание в тетради.		
	Пение	Принести нотную тетрадь		
Пятница	English	read to the end Ex 8 VII p.11		
	Geography	p. 183-184 mark blue pens		
	English	Learn dialogue Ret 2 parts		
	Литер.	пересказ близко к тексту		
	Геометр	Задание в тетради		
	Физкультура	Принести форму		
Суббота	Физ-ра	Принести форму		
	English	Задание в тетради		
	Химия	Задание в тетради		
	Биолог	Принести насекомых		

Классный руководитель _Иванова_

Подпись родителей _____

Grades
Отмéтки

In school
В шкóле

The school system uses five grades for distinguishing its pupils: **пятёрка** (5) **отлично** is excellent, **четвёрка** (4) **хорошó** is good, **трóйка** (3) **посрéдственно** is average, **двóйка** (2) **плóхо** is poor, and **едини́ца** (1) **óчень плóхо** is very poor. The last two grades are both failing, and, in fact, **едини́ца** is only very rarely used.

For grade school children, how and when those grades are given out is important (and drastically different from our practice). Every schoolchild has a booklet, in this case called **дневни́к** (also the word for a diary), which shows the assignment and grade for every subject on every day of the whole school year. The illustration shows a typical page with a week's assignments and grades.

The columns (from left to right) give the date, the subject, the assignment, the grade, and the teacher's initials. The relative infrequency of the initialed grades is typical. The children never know when they are to be called on. Once they are called on, their answers or lack of them supply their grades in the subject for that week (or whatever other period—some teachers obviously are more assiduous than others). Also note, at the bottom of the page, the signature of the homeroom teacher **кла́ссный руководи́тель** and the signature of the parent **пóдпись роди́телей** are required. Attendance figures on the

СВЕДЕНИЯ ОБ УСПЕВАЕМОСТИ И ПОВЕДЕНИИ УЧЕНИКА
за 19**69**./19**70** учебный год

НАЗВАНИЕ ПРЕДМЕТОВ	Оценки (отметки) успеваемости по четвертям				Годовая оценка (отметка)	Оценка (отметка), полученная на испытании (экзамене)	Итоговая оценка (отметка)
	I	II	III	IV			
Русский язык	4	4					
Литература	5	5					
Родной язык							
Родная литература							
Арифметика							
Алгебра	4	4					
Геометрия	5	4					
Биология	5						
История	5						
География	5	4					
Физика	4	5					
Химия	5	3					
Иностранный язык (какой)	5	4					
Рисование							
Пение	5						
Черчение	4	5					
Физическое воспитание	4	3					
Трудовое обучение	5	4					
Поведение	5						
Число уроков							
Из них пропущено							
Количество опозданий на уроки							
Подпись классного руководителя							
Подпись родителей							
ИТОГИ ГОДА: переведен в следующий класс, оставлен на второй год, исключен, выпущен и т. д.							

bottom left-hand side show the number of lessons lost because of absence and also any tardiness **опозда́ние** for the week.

The (proper) use of this **дневни́к** should (and probably does) have some outstanding advantages: the student is kept aware of how well he is doing, and, perforce, so are his homeroom teacher and his parents, every week! The latter also have specific information on the homework required of the child and are thereby able to carry out their responsibilities in seeing that it is done.

Other grades are regularly given; the school year is divided into quarters **че́тверти**. At the end of each quarter, every child receives a grade in each subject.

Notice that a grade is given for conduct **поведе́ние**. Any grade less than (5) in conduct is actually a severe reprimand under the present system. There is some sentiment for changing the grading of conduct to merely satisfactory or unsatisfactory, however.

The booklet **дневни́к** also has a section at the back for quarterly reports on how well the child fulfills his obligations in keeping the classroom in order, or how well he contributes to group projects for the common good—socially useful work **Обще́ственно-поле́зный труд**. Still another page in the **дневни́к** shows how well the pupil is doing in fulfilling the physical fitness norms for young people: **Но́рмы БГТО (бэгэтэ-о́).** ("**Будь гото́в к труду́ и оборо́не!**"— "Be prepared for work and defense!") A doctor's approval must be obtained to take these tests, and the children get a medal **значо́к**[9] for passing them.

[9] See "Medals" in Chapter 1.

A student can legally quit school at the end of his eight-year school training **восьмилётка, непóлная срéдняя шкóла** or at the end of the school year in which he reaches the age of sixteen. A pupil who fails at one year's work must take the course over and becomes a repeater **второгóдник**.

In college
В вýзах

Once at the college level, grades are given in the various subjects from time to time—for essays, homework, laboratory work and the like—so the student has a general idea of how well he is doing. However, the final grades for subjects are given only at the end of the semester and on the basis of final examinations. It is quite possible, though presumably infrequent, to do passing work all along and then fail the final exam and the course.

Some college grades come in four levels: **отлично, хорошó, посрéдственно,** and **плóхо.** The last one is a failing grade. Other courses at the university level use only two grades—**зачёт** satisfactory, and **незачёт** unsatisfactory.

The diploma **диплóм** is usually given after five years of college courses. Extraordinary students get a diploma "with distinction" **диплóм с отлúчием,** but most diplomas simply testify to the student's having taken and passed a course of study with a certain major. However, in addi-

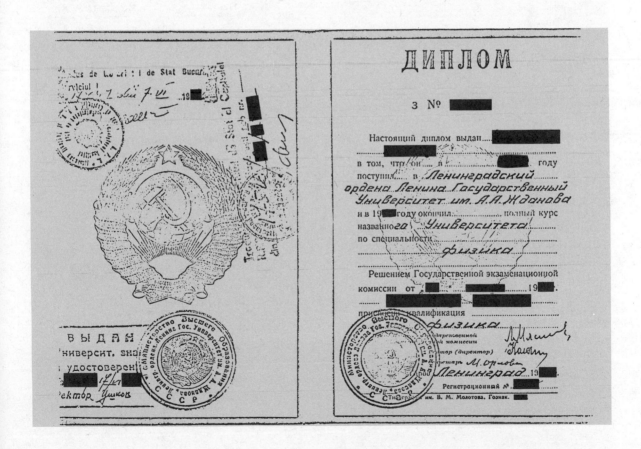

Приложение к дипломом № ██████

ВЫПИСКА ИЗ ЗАЧЕТНОЙ ВЕДОМОСТИ

(без диплома не действительна)

███████ ██████

за время пребывания в Ленинградском ордена Ленина Государственном университете им А. А. Жданова

с 19██ г. по 19██ г.

СДАЛ СЛЕДУЮЩИЕ ДИСЦИПЛИНЫ:

1. Основы марксизма-ленинизма . . . . . —зачет
2. Политическая экономия . . . . —отлично
3. Диалектический и исторический материализм . . . . —отлично
4. Иностранный язык . . . . —хорошо
5. История физики . . . . —отлично
6. Общая химия . . . . —хорошо
7. Черчение . . . . —зачет
8. Высшая математика . . . . —хорошо
9. Методы математической физики . . . —отлично
10. Общая физика . . . . —хорошо
11. Атомная физика . . . . —отлично

12. Теоретическая механика . . . . . . —хорошо
13. Термодинамика и статистическая физика . . . —зачет
14. Электродинамика . . . . —зачет
15. Квантовая механика . . . . —хорошо
16. Основы электрорадиотехники . . . . —отлично
17. Дифференциальные уравнения —хорошо
18. Теория относительности —зачет
19. Дополнительные главы механики и математической физики—зачет
20. Уравнения в частных производных —отлично
21. Квантовая теория много-электронных систем— —отлично
22. Квантовая теория столкновений— —зачет
23. Теория ядра . . . . —хорошо
24. Квантовая теория поля —зачет
25. Спецсеминар по теории поля —зачет
26. Физическое воспитание и спорт . . . . —отлично
27. Общий физический практикум . . . . —зачет
28. Специальный физический практикум . . —отлично
29. Лаборатория по специальности . . . . —хорошо
30. Химическая лаборатория . . . . . . —отлично
31. Курсовая работа . . . . —хорошо
32. Производственная практика . . . . . —зачет

Сдал ████ государственные экзамены по следующим дисциплинам:

1. Основы марксизма-ленинизма . . . . . —отлично
2. Физика . . . . —отлично

Защитил ████████ дипломную работу с оценкой
—хорошо.

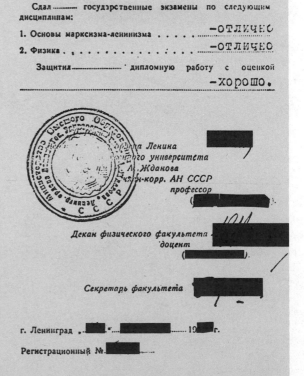

████████ ордена Ленина
████████ого университета
████ А. Жданова
████и-корр. АН СССР
профессор
(████████)

Декан физического факультета ████████
доцент
(████████)

Секретарь факультета ████████

г. Ленинград ████████ 19██ г.

Регистрационный № ████████

tion to a diploma, the student also gets a kind of transcript (here called **вы́писка**), which, though not as detailed as ours, still gives an idea of the major courses the student took and how well he did in them.

Administration
Администра́ция

The people that work in education in the USSR do so under fairly tight supervision so that extremes either in teaching method or goal tend to be eliminated. At the secondary level, therefore, especially imaginative teachers have less scope than ours, but poor teaching gets quicker and surer correction. At the college level, there is less confusion about course content but some dissatisfaction with restrictions on methods and goals of research. Throughout, one works for the betterment of the group **коллекти́в**.

At school
В шко́ле

THE TEACHER   **УЧИ́ТЕЛЬ**

Soviet schoolteachers **учи́тель**, **учи́тельница** come in two major categories: those who teach in elementary school **нача́льная шко́ла** (grades one to three), and those who teach in the upper grades **сре́дняя шко́ла**. The primary teacher is in charge of the same group of children all day, every day, in every subject (sometimes excepting music, drawing, and physical education). Her contact-hour (or lesson) load is, therefore, twenty-four hours a week (four lessons a day, six days a week). She usually has received her (three- to four-year) training at a primary teachers' school **педагоги́ческое учи́лище**. The secondary school teachers are trained as subject specialists, most of them at a pedagogical institute **педагоги́ческий институ́т**. Training there takes four to five years and includes one or two major subjects of specialization. Sometimes these secondary schoolteachers come straight from the universities, where everyone with an appropriate major is required to take a course in how to teach his subject. The secondary schoolteachers have a minimum of eighteen class hours a week, but most earn more money by teaching more.

Contrary to American habit, the teacher is free to go when she has no scheduled classes. (She is not required to stay at school until thirty minutes after the final bell rings.) She does have other obligations to tend to, however: visiting pupils' homes is the rule, not the exception; there are numerous teacher and parent-teacher meetings to attend; and teachers are often expected to lead an interest group **кружо́к** during the after-school hours. Perhaps as a reflection of the moral leadership the teacher is to display, about 20 percent of schoolteachers are party members (compared to 9 percent in the total adult population).

The social status that Soviet teachers enjoy is hard to establish, though evidence (often consisting only of innuendo) would suggest that they fare somewhat better than do teachers in the United States. As for the desirability of the profession, teacher training institutes **педагоги́ческие институ́ты** can accept only one-third of those that apply, but, on the other hand, it is sometimes very difficult even to force university graduates into teaching. A major problem is that wages are comparatively low—about 120 rubles a month for a beginning teacher.

Teachers, as well as professors, belong to a trade union **Профсою́з рабо́тников просвеще́ния, вы́сшей шко́лы и нау́чных учрежде́ний СССР**. Though not resembling an American trade union, the Soviet teachers' trade union does act as a sounding board (through the newspaper **Учи́тельская газе́та**) for teachers with problems presented by students, parents, or administrators.

The institution of the substitute teacher is not used in the USSR. Other teachers (or even the principal) cover for the absent one or else classes are doubled up.

Akin to our practice of having a homeroom teacher, the Russians have a **кла́ссный руководи́тель** who is charged with many of the same duties—the progress, conduct, health, parent relations, and so forth of the student. But there is one very major difference: the Soviet **кла́ссный руководи́тель**, though a subject teacher for the class, also fulfills the duties of homeroom teacher not just for one semester (as is usually the case here) but for the whole secondary school period. This system encourages the development of much closer ties between the pupil and at least one member of the establishment.

THE VICE-PRINCIPAL   ЗА́ВУЧ

There are at least two vice-principals in a school, each with differing responsibilities. (The title itself, **за́вуч**, is an abbreviation of the phrase **заве́дующий уче́бной ча́стью**, which is no longer used. The title now is officially **заме́ститель дире́ктора**, but **за́вуч** remains in normal conversation.) One vice-principal, **за́вуч (заме́ститель дире́ктора) по уче́бной ча́сти**, is mainly responsible for assuring that the curriculum is being followed, while the other, **за́вуч по внекла́ссной рабо́те**, organizes extracurricular activities. Special schools often have a vice-principal in charge of the school's specialty. For example, **за́вуч по англи́йскому языку́**. Vice-principals also teach, but their class load is much less than that of a regular teacher.

THE PRINCIPAL   ДИРЕ́КТОР

The head of the school is the **дире́ктор**, who, often as not, is a woman.[10] The Soviet school principal has a somewhat different role to play than does ours. For one thing, the principal usually is responsible for some teaching, though not more than twelve hours a week. For another thing, she is also expected to be a "master

teacher," able to do what she talks about. She also tends to keep a much tighter rein on what goes on in the school—regularly sitting in on classes, taking notes on the conduct of the class and the course, and reporting on this to the authorities—**ГорОНО́**, **РОНО́**, **ОблОНО́** (see "Letter abbreviations" in Chapter 12). Though a **дире́ктор** may criticize and reprimand, her opinions are still subject to the collective wisdom of the teachers among whom she works, usually expressed in a teachers' council **учи́тельский сове́т**, **педсове́т**.

The principal is also responsible for making arrangements for class trips, visitors to the school, equipment, supplies, and the care and treatment of recalcitrant children (or even parents). In rural areas, she has some status as a sort of village elder, so that she is often perforce involved in assorted community problems in addition to her own as principal.

OTHERS AT SCHOOL   ДРУГИ́Е В ШКО́ЛЕ

Others besides the pupils and teachers also are involved with school life. The equivalent of our custodian or janitor is **убо́рщица**, whose duties are the upkeep of the school. She is also sometimes in charge of the cloakroom when such an attendant is considered necessary. To aid her, the children themselves are called upon regularly to perform some small maintenance and cleanup work. They must help tape the (double) windows at the onslaught of winter, for instance; at lunch time, the pupils take turns in arranging the distribution of food, china, and cutlery; and occasional cleanup projects are organized. For all these efforts, the children are given a grade each quarter for the above-mentioned socially useful work **обще́ственно-поле́зный труд**.

Each school also has a nurse **медсестра́** on duty and a doctor on call.

At the college level
В ву́зах

The **ре́ктор** is in charge of a university or institute, and the **проре́ктор** is his vice-president.

---

[10] World War II, known as the Great Patriotic War **Вели́кая Оте́чественная война́**, was responsible for considerable decimation, especially of men. As a result, it has been discovered in the USSR that women can also do the work formerly relegated to men.

To aid and advise him in his deliberations, he has an academic council **учёный совет** consisting of all the deans and some professors plus representatives of the Ministry of Higher Education **Министе́рство вы́сшего образова́ния**, the trade union **профсою́з**, and representatives of the Communist party and the Komsomol.

The **вуз** is divided into departments **факульте́ты**,[11] which are headed by a dean **дека́н**. Typical departments are **истори́ческий факульте́т (истфа́к)**, **хими́ческий факульте́т (химфа́к)**, **филологи́ческий факульте́т (филфа́к)**. (Moscow University has fourteen such departments.) The **факульте́т** is also equipped with an **учёный совет** of its own.

Each department is further divided into two or more subspecialties **ка́федра** (*sg.*) with a chief **заве́дующий ка́федрой**. He is usually a professor in rank, though he need not be. (Moscow State University has 240 such subspecialties.)

THE ACADEMIC RANKS   АКАДЕМИ́ЧЕСКИЕ РА́НГИ

On the top of the ladder is the professor **профе́ссор**.[12] He usually has a doctor's degree **до́кторская сте́пень** and its title **до́ктор нау́к**. Just below him is the **доце́нт**, who normally has the **кандида́тская сте́пень** and the title **кандида́т нау́к**. (**Нау́ка**, the word for science, is used as freely in Russian as philosophy is in English.) The more important teaching problems, such as major lectures to larger classes, are assigned to teachers from these two ranks.

The lowest level of the regular faculty belongs to the **ассисте́нт**, who has lesser teaching responsibilities, laboratory courses, quiz sections, occasional substitution for a senior faculty member, and so forth. The title "instructor" **преподава́тель** is used for those who do not have their candidate degree but who teach quiz sections or ancillary courses—foreign

languages, for instance; the rank is not usually considered to be á step on the academic ladder.

Universities and institutes are expected to do research as well as teach; therefore, most also have research ranks, beginning with **лабора́нт**, then **мла́дший нау́чный сотру́дник**, and **ста́рший нау́чный сотру́дник**.

For vocational schools, the chief in charge is the **дире́ктор**, but the teaching staff does not go beyond the **преподава́тель** level.

In and out of school
Внутри́ и вне шко́лы

The school building
Шко́льное зда́ние

The school building itself naturally varies from small (300 to 500 pupils in rural communities) to large (800 to 1000 pupils in a large city school). Standard titles for rooms in a school include:

класс, кла́ссная ко́мната, кабине́т a classroom

коридо́р a hall

учи́тельская the teachers' room

столо́вая the lunchroom, if whole meals are served (**буфе́т** if snacks alone are served)

медпу́нкт the nurse's room or office

кабине́т дире́ктора the principal's office

физкульту́рный зал, спорти́вный зал the gymnasium

раздева́лка the cloakroom, invariably near the entrance to the school

а́ктовый зал the room for assemblies, school parties, and other functions

The names for some of these types of rooms change at the university level. A class is most often held in a large, tiered lecture room **аудито́рия**, while assemblies, meetings, or ceremonial affairs take place in an auditorium **а́ктовый зал**. At the entrance to the building one usually must show his pass **про́пуск** and then check his coat at the cloakroom **гардеро́б** (a more elegant term

---

[11] Soviet universities are not divided into colleges in the same way universities in the United States are. **Факульте́т** is translated here as "department," the closest approximation possible.

[12] The Academician **акаде́мик** is an award and a title bestowed for outstanding research. It is not a teaching rank, but its status is higher than that of a professor.

than **раздева́лка**), receiving in exchange for the coat a chit **номеро́к, би́рка**. The administrative division most affecting the student is the department **факульте́т**, and the name both for this administration and for the offices it occupies is **декана́т**.

Classroom furnishings
Ме́бель в кла́ссе

The Soviet classroom has school desks **па́рта** (*sg.*), which seat two pupils side by side. There is room underneath the desk lid **кры́шка** for the numerous items each child possesses. On the outside, on both sides, is a hook that holds the briefcase **портфе́ль** each child carries. (Small children carry satchels **ра́нец** (*sg.*) on their backs.) The seat **сиде́ние** is essentially a bench that extends from the desk of the pupils in the seat behind. The teacher's desk **пи́сьменный стол** is in the front of the room. The blackboard **доска́** is often smaller than what we are used to, and the remaining walls are often decorated with pupils' art work, school rules, and pictures of revolutionary heroes. Another device, the bulletin board **стенгазе́та (стенна́я газе́та)**, is also maintained for and by the pupils, under direct supervision. The Russian obsession with potted plants also extends to the classroom. Other basic equipment includes chalk **мел** and rags **тря́пки** for erasing.

The front flap on the lid of Soviet school desks allows children to stand up to answer a question without sliding into the aisle first.

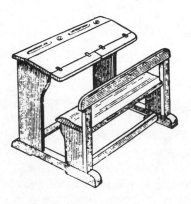

Dress-up uniforms are used for the first day of school.

School uniforms
Шко́льная фо́рма

School uniforms are discussed in Chapter 3. The strictness of uniform wearing varies. For one thing, the farther away from a big city, the more likely it is that uniforms will be worn by fewer children. For another, any reasonable excuse for not wearing a uniform is often accepted by the authorities. A sort of *sub rosa* battle begins when children who don't like uniforms try to escape wearing them. The same sort of fate often befalls the Pioneer ties. They are eagerly worn by the younger Pioneers and tend often to be avoided by older members.

Hair styles are similar to ours except that long hair is almost always restrained in some way. Long hair for boys is not acceptable.

Classroom organization
Поря́док в кла́ссе

Pupils are organized in several ways for several purposes. The student duty officer for the day **дежу́рный, дежу́рная** has among his obligations keeping the room in good order. He is in charge of opening and closing windows, keeping the rags used for erasing the blackboard both clean and wet, and other such functions. Other obligations of pupils include taking charge of the lunch table—setting the table, serving the food, making sure the cutlery and plates are removed when all is done. This job **дежу́рство** is arranged by rotation among the class members. Two are on duty at any time.

Communist party work at school
Обще́ственная жизнь шко́лы

The Communist party is quite attentive to the moral and political (often called social **обще́ственный**) upbringing of Soviet children. Here only the school organization of party work will be described, but keep in mind that party philosophy emerges in every aspect of school work, from textbooks to teachers and beyond. Lenin is ever present—in pictures, statues, and quotations.

In vocabulary, school party organization has a military cast to it, using terms that correspond somewhat to our "regiment," "brigade," and "platoon." (The military atmosphere, however, does not exceed that of our Boy Scouts.) The Pioneer-age pupils of a school, taken as a party unit, are called **дружи́на** (vaguely, a regiment), the pupils of a class are a brigade **отря́д**, and each class has four to five platoons **зве́нья** (*sg.* **звено́**).

The schoolchildren are divided into three age groups. All the pupils in grades one to three are "Little Octobrists" **октября́та** (*sg.* **октябрёнок**).

They have an official initiation ceremony, when they receive their pins **звёздочки** (in a star shape with a baby picture of Lenin in the center). Membership is all-inclusive and not a very serious affair, mostly a preparation for Pioneer activities.

The next age group, and the major party organization at school, is the Pioneers **пионе́ры**, who are from ten to fourteen years old. Here, membership takes on much greater significance. During the first year of eligibility perhaps half the pupils will be chosen as Pioneers. The next year more will be taken in until finally almost all children become Pioneers. Membership is held out as desirable and quite attainable, but requiring some commitment.

Finally, the oldest party group in the school is for those from fifteen to twenty-seven years old. Members are called Komsomols **комсомо́льцы**, an acronym formed from **Коммунисти́ческий сою́з молодёжи** (the same thing as **ВЛКСМ**). This group, though active in the school, does not have its major focus of interest there (as the Pioneers do). Instead, Komsomol work is closer to serious preparation for full Communist party membership later on. Membership is restricted and indicates both commitment and achievement.

A college student is usually in charge of the Pioneer work at schools. Often a student teacher, he is also a Komsomol member and his title is **(ста́рший) пионервожа́тый**. Individual Komsomol members from the senior classes (ninth and tenth grades) in a school are appointed leaders for individual classes at lower levels; their title is **пионервожа́тый**.

The school atmosphere
Атмосфе́ра в шко́ле

The atmosphere in a Soviet classroom tends to be both strict and friendly. It is strict in the sense that some rules are observed that we think of as formal. The pupils all rise when the teacher enters the room and seat themselves only when so instructed. They rise when they are called upon to answer a question and generally do not speak at all without permission. They are (overtly at least) respectful to their teacher, as a matter of course greeting him in a chance meeting in the hall, for instance. (Keep in mind, however, that schools do vary—some are more lax than others.) On the other hand, the teacher's attitude toward the children, especially outside the classroom, is not one of severity and repression but rather that of a loving and benevolent dictator. As mentioned above, the homeroom teacher system used in the secondary schools tends to build a close association between at least one teacher and a group of students. (Class size is usually about thirty-five to forty pupils, sometimes more, rarely less.)

Law and order
Зако́н и поря́док

Law and order is not maintained by threat of bodily punishment, which is officially outlawed. Other, often more powerful devices are used.

One such device is the use of the group: antisocial behavior and poor grades are equivalent to letting the team down. The "team" here can mean any of a number of groups, including the family group. Part of this group syndrome is the great dislike a tattletale **я́беда** often arouses. (The taunt is **"я́беда-беда́!"**) The pupils support each other, and they consider telling on someone sinful. There are two sides to the problem: the philosophy of mutual support and helpfulness in problems or projects whose goals the teacher finds desirable is described as **"Оди́н за всех, все за одного́."** Naturally, all-for-one and one-for-all is a Good Thing. The other side is when the children hang together against the establishment, that is, the teacher. This is called **кругова́я пору́ка**, that is, collusion, and is obviously the bane of the teacher's existence.

The teacher is far from alone in her efforts at maintaining law and order and keeping the academic backsliders from falling over the edge. After she has tried to use the class groups first to aid positively, next perhaps to ridicule, then she can use school honor (or ridicule) to make her point. Honor boards **до́ски почёта** regularly display pictures of students of merit in any of a number of endeavors. Students who are doing poorly also have their names publicly posted. The teacher can also report to the parents and enlist their cooperation. Most recalcitrants are taken care of by using one of these means. In an extreme case, the student can be expelled from school. (Severe discipline problems are sometimes handled at boarding schools.) The academic nonachiever must be sent back to take a course over again. In maintaining academic achievement, however, the teacher is also held responsible. If a teacher has too many repeaters, the conclusion is that she is not doing her work well.

The PTA meeting
Роди́тельское собра́ние

About once every two months, or at least once a quarter, there is an evening meeting of teachers and parents. Here, any discipline or academic problems are discussed, and parents are expected to help resolve these problems. If some children have been regularly misbehaving in the halls, for instance, a parent patrol might be set up. School or class projects and academic successes are also discussed. Attendance at these meetings is just short of obligatory.

Self-criticism
Самокри́тика

Another element, perhaps part of the group syndrome, is a general Soviet phenomenon of **самокри́тика**. Since it is the group, not the individual, that counts, criticism for the betterment of the group is actively indulged in. Thus, at their meetings, teachers openly criticize each other's work, the principal openly criticizes the teachers, and the teachers and parents openly charge each other. As a concomitant, all are also expected to discuss their own failures. In class, students are not given their grades with a silent notation in the grade book. Instead, Johnny is told publicly how well he did. One would expect that both students and teachers must develop very thick skins in order to survive.

Homework
Домáшние задáния

One tenet of Soviet pedagogy would seem to be that the busy child is doubly blessed; he can use his time for good in studying or practicing, and the time so devoted cannot therefore be spent on unproductive mischief. In the first grade the Soviet pupil is expected to spend about two hours after school every day doing his homework. In the later grades more and more is expected. The only relief in this schedule comes on weekends (Saturday afternoon and Sunday) when, at least officially, no homework is assigned. (Note the terminology: задáча is a particular problem or task; задáние is an assignment, in school or otherwise.)

Extracurricular activities
Внеклáссные занятия

The school also has much to do with activities not directly related to academic schoolwork. The homeroom teacher is often expected to take occasional small expeditions (for example, to a museum) with the class in her charge. The Pioneer leader organizes and superintends school Pioneer meetings. Their content is much the same as our Boy Scout meetings, with student council activities (political work) in addition. Finally, the vice-principal in charge of extracurricular activities is in charge of the many interest groups ("circles" кружки) that meet regularly to explore the joys of chess, puppetry, biology, chemistry, dancing, singing, and other special interests.

The time spent at school
Врéмя в шкóле

The most common type of secondary school срéдняя шкóла begins at about half past eight in the morning and ends at about two in the afternoon. The younger pupils at the primary level начáльная шкóла get out at about noon. Class periods last forty-five minutes and there is a ten minute break переры́в between classes. One or two of these breaks are lengthened to twenty minutes to allow the pupils time enough to have a brief lunch or a snack зáвтрак. (Food is not free, though it is subsidized for some pupils.) The children usually go home after school to eat their major meal of the day, but they can get it at school if they want.

Different types of schools
Рáзные шкóлы

Prolonged day school
Шкóла (и́ли грýппа) продлённого дня

There are two other types of schools, both of which handle a sizable fraction of students. One is the шкóла продлённого дня, where the children remain at school all day. Their after-school activities, including homework and play, are supervised; they are fed dinner обéд (the major meal) and then return home after supper ýжин about seven o'clock in the evening or whenever a parent picks them up. This type of facility is becoming popular, though most often it involves a group within a school грýппа продлённого дня rather than an entire school. In most families, both parents work, but not all have grandmothers who can care for the children during the day. This way the children are cared for but still live at home.

Boarding school
Шкóла-интернáт

Another type of school is the шкóла-интернáт, where pupils reside. Often special schools (described in the next section) are of this type. But there are also many boarding schools that have a totally regular curriculum. These schools are required, for instance, to care for orphans; they also have children who for some reason cannot be adequately cared for at home, through parental illness or neglect; and they frequently take children who have become a discipline problem. These schools should not be thought of as solely devoted to children with problems, however. Many children are in boarding schools simply because of the enormous convenience, not such a crass notion if one considers the extent of the housing problem. Contacts with home and the outside world are maintained as much as possible: those children who can, spend their Sundays at home, and frequent trips to museums, factories, or soccer games are made to remind the children of the world around them. The boarding school employs not only teachers **учи́тельницы** but "upbringers" **воспита́тели**, who concern themselves with the physical and moral progress of the children in their care.

Special schools
Спецшко́лы

These are schools whose emphasis is on developing special abilities, correcting or coping with special inabilities, or dealing with special situations. When at all possible, the regular curriculum is followed, except in those fields dealt with specifically in the specializations.

The Russian language student in the United States has probably heard of the language schools, for instance. These schools introduce a foreign language in the second grade (for three lessons a week) and then continue it all the way through school. In later grades, even other subjects (frequently geography and literature) are taught in the foreign language. There are about seventy such schools in Moscow alone. English (not American) is the most popular language, replacing French (of the nineteenth century) as the language of style. These are popular schools with parents because the quality of instruction is thought to be high and there are restrictions on who may attend: no child with hearing difficulties is accepted, and a child who seems to have less than average general ability is often not accepted. Special schools are not devoted solely to foreign languages; special mathematics schools, for example, are also fairly common.

Almost in a class by themselves are a relatively few but famous special talent schools. Those students who display considerable abilities in the arts are sent to schools that train musicians, ballet dancers, and artists. They are often boarding schools. A (largely experimental) school in Академгородо́к near Новосиби́рск has been established for those who show considerable abilities in the sciences, especially mathematics and physics.

And there are two types of schools for training future army and navy officers: Суво́ровское учи́лище for the army (named after Алекса́ндр Васи́льевич Суво́ров, 1730–1800, who commanded Russian troops against the Turks at Rymnik and Izmail and against the French in the Italian and Swiss campaigns), and Нахи́мовское учи́лище for the navy (named for Па́вел Степа́нович Нахи́мов, 1802–55, an admiral especially famous for his defense against the Turks in the Crimean War). These, too, are boarding schools. Preference is given to the orphaned children of army and navy personnel, but otherwise entrance is by competitive examination. As usual, the curriculum is the same as for the rest of the country, but also includes some military and naval studies.

6

Holidays
Пра́здники

The adoption of Christianity in the West has shown how easily pagan rites and customs (Yule logs, Easter eggs) could be incorporated into Christian celebrations. The Soviet experience shows how religion may come and religion may go, but holidays go on forever.

In this chapter holiday traditions before the Revolution will first be described, and then holidays as they are celebrated now. The reader should keep in mind, however, that many of the prerevolutionary holiday traditions are no longer common knowledge to all contemporary Soviet Russians. Easter and Christmas are foggy in the urban Soviet memory: one comes in the winter sometime, and the other in the spring. (Older people know more details.) Such information is given here so that the American student can understand his world, which includes emigré Russians who celebrate the traditional holidays, and which also includes passages in literature that can remain incomprehensible without explanation. Many contemporary Soviet holidays, however, do borrow heavily from their predecessors, and it is also true that many prerevolutionary holidays are still quite persistent in rural Soviet Union.

The chapter, therefore, is divided into sections on official church holidays, popular religious and secular holidays before the Revolution, and contemporary holidays.

The church holidays
Церко́вные пра́здники

The official church holidays were numerous and of varying importance. Easter **Па́сха**, the holiest of days, was in a class by itself and above all the others. Then there were the "twelve" holidays **двунадеся́тые пра́здники** deemed of special significance by the church and to be observed by all. And finally, the "altar" holidays **престо́льные пра́здники** were those celebrated in each locality on the name day of the church or monastery in that locality. (Except for its date, Easter is discussed separately under "Popular holidays before the Revolution.")

The "twelve" holidays
Двунадеся́тые пра́здники

The Russian Orthodox Church **Правосла́вная це́рковь** required observance of these especially

Числó по ст. ст.[1]	Назвáния двунадесятых прáздников	Перевóд на англи́йский
6 января	Крещéние (Госпóдне), Богоявлéние	Epiphany or Twelfth Day
2 февраля	Срéтение (Госпóдне)	Presentation of Christ in the Temple[5]
25 мáрта	Благовéщение (Пресвятóй Богорóдицы)	Annunciation
———[2]	Вéрбное воскресéнье, Вход Госпóдень в Иерусали́м	Palm Sunday
———[3]	Вознесéние (Госпóдне)	Ascension
———[4]	Трóица, День Святóй Трóицы, Пятидеся́тница	Pentecost, Whitsunday
6 áвгуста	Преображéние (Госпóдне)	Transfiguration
15 áвгуста	Успéние (Пресвятóй Богорóдицы)	Assumption
8 сентября	Рождествó Пресвятóй Богорóдицы	Birthday of Our Lady
14 сентября	Воздви́жение (Крестá Госпóдня)	Elevation of the Holy Cross, Exaltation of the Cross
21 ноября	Введéние во храм (Пресвятóй Богорóдицы)	Presentation of the Virgin Mary
25 декабря	Рождествó (Христóво)	Christmas

[1] по стáрому сти́лю Old Style.
[2] Always the Sunday before (Russian) Easter. Perhaps due to an absence of palms, this day is literally called Pussy Willow Sunday.
[3] Always on Thursday, the fortieth day after (Russian) Easter.
[4] Always on Sunday, ten days after (Russian) Ascension.
[5] The Roman Catholic and Episcopal churches refer to this same day as the Feast of the Purification of the Virgin, or Candlemas. Still others are familiar with it under the title of Groundhog Day.

important holidays.[1] Because the church has yet to recognize the Gregorian calendar, dates for these holidays follow the Julian calendar, also known as Old Style, which has been thirteen days later than the Gregorian calendar since 1900.[2] All dates here are Old Style. When there are several titles for the holiday, the most commonly used title has been underlined.

This list of the "twelve" holidays is of special interest to foreigners since many Russian surnames derive from these events, like the poets Рождéственский or Вознесéнский, as do the names of many churches, streets, cities, and towns.

When is Easter?
Когдá Пáсха?

Three of the "twelve" holidays depend on when Easter is celebrated. The date for Russian Orthodox Easter is not simply the two week difference between the two calendars. The popular formula sets Easter **Пáсха** as the first Sunday after the first full moon **полнолýние** following the vernal equinox **весéннее равнодéнствие**. The day so chosen must follow Jewish Passover (also called **Пáсха**), and if it does not, then Easter is celebrated the following Sunday. As a result, Russian Easter falls between March 22 and April 25 Old Style (between April 4 and May 8 New Style) and might or might not be celebrated on the same Sunday as Western Easter.

The "altar" holidays
Престóльные прáздники

Престóльные прáздники were holidays that had many of the features we associate with country fairs. They were local celebrations, occurring on the name day of the local church or monastery: **Трóицкая цéрковь** would have its celebration on Pentecost, **цéрковь Святóго Михаи́ла** celebrated on one of the St. Michael's days, and so on. On this day the local inhabit-

[1] Eight of them celebrate events of religious significance in Christ's life and four have to do with Mary.
[2] The difference is getting greater all the time. This is discussed in "Time" in Chapter 11.

ants and those from neighboring villages would attend church services and then gather in the local square, either near the church itself or on the edge of town. Here traders would have small booths selling foods, sweets, inexpensive decorations, and the like. In addition, the larger villages might have extensive fairgrounds with swings **качéли** and/or merry-go-rounds **карусéли**. Some of the fairs **я́рмарка** (*sg.*) at monasteries became famous and would draw people from a great distance. Eating and drinking, singing and dancing were naturally a part of these country holidays. Not so obviously, but very traditionally, semiorganized brawls between the young males of two or more villages were often a culmination to the joys of rural holidays. An entire story, "Обúда" by Солоýхин, describes what happened to an unwilling contestant in one such fight. The first line of the story sets the scene:

● Черкýтино бы́ло ра́ньше больши́м торгóвым селóм, кудá на я́рмарку ли в петрóв день, на ма́сленицу ли съезжа́лись крестья́не из окре́стных деревéнь.

Other saints' days
Другúе церкóвные пра́здники

Less official "church" holidays were various saints' days that from one association or another were familiar to the peasants. Especially in the country, it was (and still is) common to refer, not to a date, but to a specific saint's day. In "Матрёнин двор" by Солжени́цын, Матрёна says,

● По-быва́лошному кипéли с сéном в межéнь, с Петрóва до Ильина́.

Some of the more frequently encountered days were:

Петрóв день[3]   June 29
Ильúн день   July 20
Егóров день or **Ю́рьев день**   April 23

[3] Whether or not God, saints' days, or specific religious holidays are capitalized depends on where the material is printed. Outside the USSR such words are capitalized; in the USSR, those holidays based on a saint's name are usually but not always capitalized, while the purely religious holidays **покрóв день** and God **бог** are not capitalized.

Покрóв день   October 1 (**Покрóв Пресвятóй Богорóдицы** Protection of the Holy Theotokos)
Никóлин день
   Никóла вéшний   May 9
   Никóла зи́мний   December 6

The fasts
Посты́

To some extent, holidays can be defined by their opposite—the fasts. The Russian Orthodox fast was notable in that those who observed it ate no meat and also no eggs, milk, cheese, or butter. Some people even refused white (refined) sugar since bone ash was used in the refining process; brown sugar **пóстный са́хар** was used instead. What remained to be eaten was fish, vegetables, and bread; vegetable oil was used for fat. Food was not the only deprivation called for during the fasts: marriages were not performed while they were in effect.

There were four major fast periods in a year:

Вели́кий пост   the seven weeks before Easter
Фили́пповский (или Рождéственский) пост   the six weeks before Christmas
Петрóв пост (петрóвки)   from May 31 to June 29
Успéнский пост   from August 1 to August 15

Only Lent **Вели́кий пост** was regularly observed by most people, but the very devout could deprive themselves even further since Wednesdays and Fridays were also days of fasting. Such devotion could considerably lower the egg and meat bill, since over half the days in the year were officially days of denial.

Popular holidays before the Revolution
Нарóдные пра́здники до револю́ции
The Christmas holidays
Свя́тки

The Christmas holiday season (December 24–January 6) was especially gay, and not unlike our Christmas; the gaiety was due more to the pagan celebrations than the religious ones. The holiday began on Christmas Eve **сочéльник**, and continued until Epiphany **Крещéние**. The entire two week period **свя́тки** was a time for parties, including the usual singing and dancing **хорово́ды и пля́ски**, and also special celebrations usually reserved for this time of year—**ря́женье**, **гадáние**, **колядовáние**—each of which will be discussed.

CHRISTMAS EVE СОЧÉЛЬНИК

The Christian feature of this day was church attendance.

Christian festivals, as everywhere else, did not fill a vacuum but, rather, overlay a set of pagan beliefs and customs. Most of these had to do with ensuring and celebrating a good harvest and were often therefore in some relation to the seasons—the winter and summer solstices, the coming of spring, and so on. The festival of the god **коляда́ (бес Коляда́)** was celebrated with songs on December 24, strangely coincident with **сочéльник**. The songs **коля́дки** were sung at **колядовáние**, when children and young people would go from house to house, singing their wishes for wealth and a good harvest. The singers expected small gifts of food or money in return for their efforts. Here is one example of a **коля́дка**:

> ● Коляда́, коляда́
> Отворя́й ворота́,
> Снéги на зéмлю па́дали,
> Перепа́дывали.
> Как пришло́ рождество́
> К господи́ну под окно́.
> Ты встава́й, господи́н,
> Разбужа́й госпожу́.
> Хлéбом-со́лью нас корми́,
> Путь-доро́жку укажи́.
> Как у на́шей-то ма́тки
> Теля́тки-то гла́дки,
> Ска́чут чéрез гря́дку
> Копы́тцами щёлкают,
> Зéмлю не хвата́ют.
> Што у на́шей-то хозя́йки
> Усто́и-те то́лсты,
> Смета́ны-те гу́сты,
> Ма́сла-те жёлты . . .

Мы берём не рупь, не полти́ну,
Одну́ четверти́ну,
Пиро́г да ша́ньгу,
Зо́лоту дéньгу . . .[4]

As the connection with Christ's birth became stronger (very late in some places), the ritual took on some Christian symbols—the singing group carried a large star (of Bethlehem) at the end of a stick, and instead of singing **коля́дки** they sang religious songs "in praise of Christ" **Христа́ сла́вить**. Typical of the evening meal was a dish called **кутья́**[5] consisting of steamed wheat (or other grain), raisins, honey, and nuts, and served as dessert.

CHRISTMAS РОЖДЕСТВО́

The major feature of Christmas day was food. Among the peasants the day provided the most lavish meal of the year: if possible a suckling pig was served. (The lavishness was one of the remnants of a pagan custom to assure a good harvest.)

THE CHRISTMAS TREE РОЖДÉСТВЕНСКАЯ ЁЛКА

The **Рождéственская ёлка** was an innovation of Peter the Great. It became a part of the city Christmas celebration fairly soon but was not so common in the peasant hut until much later. As a matter of fact, it was not uncommon for the "noblesse" to "oblige" the common folk by allowing them to come in and see the Christmas tree. Tree decorations were not basically different from those in the West, often including such things as cookies, gilt nuts, small animal figures, or dolls. Gifts for children were put under the tree, but this was not a time for extensive gift giving. A child might expect a small toy; adults received nothing.

MUMMERY РЯ́ЖЕНЬЕ

A major feature of the Christmas holidays was **ря́женье**, when people, especially children,

[4] Н. Колпако́ва, *Кни́га о ру́сском фолькло́ре* (Ленингра́д: Учпедги́з, 1948), стр. 30.
[5] Also a specialty at funerals **поми́нки**.

would put on costumes and disguises, most often in animal shapes, and go from house to house, again receiving small gifts for their trouble. The Soviet motion picture *War and Peace* had one small scene showing such a group. This is how the book itself describes the event:

● Наря́женные дворо́вые: медве́ди, ту́рки, трак-ти́рщики, ба́рыни, стра́шные и смешны́е, принеся́ с собо́ю хо́лод и весе́лье, снача́ла ро́бко жа́лись в пере́дней; пото́м, пря́чась оди́н за друго́го, вы́-тесни́лись в за́лу; и снача́ла засте́нчиво, а пото́м все веселе́е и дружне́е начали́сь пе́сни, пля́ски, хорово́ды и свя́точные и́гры. Графи́ня, узна́в лица́ и посмея́вшись на наря́женных, ушла́ в го-сти́ную. Граф Илья́ Андре́ич с сия́ющею улы́бкой сиде́л в за́ле, одобря́я игра́ющих. Молодёжь ис-че́зла куда́-то.

Че́рез полчаса́ в за́ле ме́жду други́ми ря́же-ными появи́лась ещё ста́рая ба́рыня в фи́жмах —это был Никола́й. Турча́нка был Пе́тя. Пая́с—это был Ди́ммлер, гуса́р—Ната́ша и черке́с—Со́ня, с нарисо́ванными про́бочными уса́ми и бровя́ми.[6]

This custom, though especially associated with the Christmas holidays, also occurred during **ма́сленица**. The custom has not died out yet, but it probably is most often observed in the country rather than the city. The following passage describes the event as it was celebrated in the village of Кли́мово, Го́рьковская о́бласть, in 1960:

● В дни свя́ток и ма́сленицы ря́женые обхо́дят дома́ и на со́бранные проду́кты и де́ньги устра́и-вают вечери́нку. Так, в дни свя́ток зимо́й 1960 г. в Кли́мове по дере́вне ходи́ли же́нщины, ря́же-ные "кула́шниками," медве́дем с поводырём, бе́гали ребяти́шки, подро́стки в костю́мах цыга́нят.

. . . Бы́ло уже́ часо́в пять. Вдруг разда́лся стук в дверь, смех, то́пот на крыльце́. В избу́ ввали́-лись цыганя́та. Их бы́ло тро́е. Де́вочка лет десяти́—двена́дцати, наря́женная в моде́льный сарафа́н, шаль, изма́занная са́жей, с кото́мкой в рука́х, де́вочка поме́ньше и ма́льчик, тоже пере-ма́занные, в рванье́. Они хихи́кали, смуща́лись и подта́лкивали друг дру́га.

—Ну, что же вы, проси́те!—понука́ла их хозя́йка.

6 Л. Н. Толсто́й, *Война́ и мир*, том II, часть 4, гл. 10.

—Да́йте-пода́йте, тётя, пода́й с комари́ную но́жку мя́ска.

Мы одели́ли ребя́т конфе́тами.

Ра́ньше ряди́лись бо́льше—заме́тила А́нна Ива́новна—ни́щими, цыга́нами, Сме́ртью.[7]

FORTUNETELLING ГАДА́НЬЕ

The translation of **гада́нье** as "fortunetell-ing" is poor, since it actually relates only to the prediction of when and whom a girl might marry. It was therefore engaged in only by the unmarried girls of the village. All sorts of props were used: the number of grains of wheat a rooster consumed indicated how many months until the wedding took place; shoes thrown over the fence would indicate the direction from which the beloved would come; if one stared in a mir-ror just the right way, one could see the image of the future husband; and so on. In Tolstoy's *War and Peace* an old maid describes an incident that reportedly took place when one young lady awaited signs of her future husband in the bath-house.

● . . . в ба́не гада́ть, вот э́то стра́шно!—говори́ла за у́жином ста́рая де́вушка, жи́вшая у Мелюко́-вых.

. . . вот ка́к-то пошла́ одна́ ба́рышня,—сказа́ла ста́рая де́вушка,—взяла́ петуха́, два прибо́ра—как сле́дует се́ла. Посиде́ла, то́лько слы́шит, вдруг е́дет . . . с колоко́льцами, с бубенца́ми, подъе́хали са́ни; слы́шит, идёт. Вхо́дит совсе́м в о́бразе челове́ческом, как есть офице́р, пришёл и сел с ней за прибо́р.

—А! А! . . .—закрича́ла Ната́ша, с у́жасом вы-ка́тывая глаза́.

—Да как же он, так и говори́т?

—Да, как челове́к, всё как должно́ быть, и стал, и стал угова́ривать, а ей бы на́до заня́ть его́ раз-гово́ром до петухо́в; а она́ заробе́ла; то́лько заробе́ла и закры́лась рука́ми. Он ее и подхвати́л. Хорошо́, что тут де́вушки прибежа́ли. . . .

—Ну, что пуга́ть их!—сказа́ла Пелаге́я Дани́-ловна.

—Ма́маша, ведь вы са́ми гада́ли . . .—сказа́ла дочь.

—А ка́к э́то в амба́ре гада́ют?—спроси́ла Со́ня.

—Да вот хоть бы тепе́рь, пойду́т к амба́ру, да и слу́шают. Что услы́шите: закола́чивает, стучи́т—

7 *Совреме́нный ру́сский фолькло́р*, ред. Э. В. Помера́нцева (Москва́: Нау́ка, 1966), стр. 70–71.

ду́рно, а пересыпа́ет хлеб—это к добру́; а то быва́ет. . . .[8]

And this first stanza of the poem "Светла́на" by Жуко́вский is familiar to (if not actually memorized by) most Russians. Almost every line lists one more method or device for describing a future husband or the date of the wedding. Though гада́нье could be engaged in almost any evening during the Christmas holidays, it was especially popular on New Year's night and on Epiphany eve **Креще́нский ве́чер**.

> ● Раз в Креще́нский вечеро́к
> Де́вушки гада́ли:
> За воро́та башмачо́к,
> Сняв с ноги́, броса́ли;
> Снег поло́ли; под окно́м
> Слу́шали; корми́ли
> Счётным ку́рицу зерно́м;
> Я́рый воск топи́ли;
> В ча́шу с чи́стою водо́й
> Кла́ли пе́рстень золото́й,
> Се́рьги изумру́дны;
> Расстила́ли бе́лый плат
> И над ча́шей пе́ли в лад
> Пе́сенки подблю́дны.

EPIPHANY   КРЕЩЕ́НИЕ

The last day of **свя́тки** and one of the major church holidays is **Креще́ние**—in celebration of Christ's baptism (**крести́ть** to baptize). On that day (January 6), after the church ceremony, the priest led the flock to the local river (or lake) where a hole was broken in the ice. The priest blessed the water and then some of the especially faithful would take a dip.

> ● Свя́тки ока́нчивались на креще́ние. В э́тот день кре́стный ход шёл на Иорда́нь—к про́руби в реке́; по́сле «освяще́ния» воды́ не́которые купа́лись в про́руби.[9]

January brings the coldest frosts, and the term **креще́нские моро́зы** remains to denote them, while **Креще́ние** itself is fading from the popular memory.

8 Л. Н. Толсто́й, *Война́ и мир*, том II, часть 4, гл. 11.
9 Алекса́ндров, *Наро́ды европе́йской ча́сти СССР*, стр. 414.

The coming of spring
Жа́воронки

Traditionally, the skylarks arrived on March 9 announcing spring. Special rolls were baked on that day in the shape of these birds and were called **жа́воронки**. They are still baked and even called by that name, but the exact date of and reason for them are all but forgotten. The seasons were of considerable importance to agriculture, and in ancient times the children or young girls would go out in the fields on March 9 and welcome spring by throwing bread to the birds and shouting a call of welcome to spring.

Week-long Mardi Gras
Ма́сленица

Ма́сленица was the week just preceding Lent **Вели́кий пост**. Though the date for **ма́сленица** was dependent on when Easter was celebrated, **ма́сленица** itself was strictly a pagan holiday, a salute to the sun whose warmth made the grain grow high. It was a week of joy that gave special sanction to arsonists, gluttons, and wild drivers, since its major features were bonfires, pancakes **блины́** in huge quantities, and sleigh rides.

Fire of some sort was almost always part of the celebration. In the north, children would gather combustibles into a great pile on a hilltop for a week. The pile was set on fire at night and so arranged that the flaming mass went crashing down the hillside. In other places, burning wheels of straw drenched in pitch were carried in a procession; and in still others, mere bonfires were sufficient.

Large quantities of food were consumed during this week, enough so that one way to describe living high off the hog is **"не житьё, а ма́сленица."** (The restrictions of Lent that followed were severe enough to make up for this week of gluttony.) Specifically, the food to be consumed was **блины́**, raised dough pancakes, their shape in two dimensions rendering that of the sun in three.

And always associated with **ма́сленица** were

sleigh rides, with a troika if possible, but in any case using horses bedecked with gaily colored ribbons and quantities of sleigh bells. Some said the sleigh was to ride in great semicircles to commemorate the path of the sun through the sky.

Fun and games continued for the whole week. By ancient tradition this was the time of year that the Russian swings каче́ли were first used. In many places a snow city сне́жный городо́к was built, the young people divided into two groups, and a snow fight ensued that always ended in the fall of the snow city. Dressing up in costumes ря́женье occurred during ма́сленица almost as frequently as at Christmas time. The general merriment intensified toward the end of the week широ́кая ма́сленица, and in some places on the night before the beginning of Lent the stuffed effigy of ма́сленица, often in the shape of a country woman, was burned in yet another fire and buried until the next year.

The Easter season
Пасха́льный сезо́н

PALM SUNDAY   **ВЕ́РБНОЕ ВОСКРЕСЕ́НЬЕ**

The Sunday before Easter, Palm Sunday, was called Pussy Willow Sunday **Ве́рбное воскресе́нье**. Pussy willow branches were taken to church, blessed, and then taken home to be propped up behind the icon. On this day, Moscow had a **Ве́рбный база́р** in Red Square where tradesmen sold all kinds of toys and sweets and where the well-to-do came to show off their clothes, carriages, and girlfriends.

The week between Palm Sunday and Easter is called **Страстна́я Неде́ля** and each day of this week is called **вели́кий**: **Вели́кий Понеде́льник, Вели́кий Вто́рник, и т.д.** For the week after Easter, each day is **све́тлый**: **Све́тлый Понеде́льник ... Све́тлая Суббо́та.**

EASTER   **ПА́СХА**

Russian Easter starts the night before, not including the cooking that has to be done in pre-

paration. The faithful arrive at church in the late evening bringing with them their traditional Easter dessert **па́сха**[10] and Easter sweet bread **кули́ч** and some Easter eggs to be blessed. Church attendance at this ceremony is, as elsewhere, at its highest, leaving many people outside the church. (This is especially true in the West, where, on this night, many people can be seen standing outside the front doors of Orthodox churches, candle in hand.) Near midnight the priest opens the doors to the church and leads a procession of deacons, altar boys, the choir, and any parishioners wishing to join. The procession is called a **кре́стный ход**, which in this case symbolizes the search for Jesus's body by Mary Magdalene and others (see Mark 16), and the subsequent discovery that Christ is risen. The procession circles the church three times, its members singing as they go. The church doors represent the sepulchre, and when they are opened the priest announces several times that Christ is risen: **"Христо́с Воскре́се!"** The audience each time answers, "Truly He is risen!"—**"Вои́стину Воскре́се!"** Directly after this ceremony and for several days thereafter, a delightful ritual takes place, usually between friends but not necessarily so. One person goes to another and says: **"Христо́с Воскре́се!"** The other answers, **"Вои́стину Воскре́се!"** and then they kiss three times on alternate cheeks. (The verb for this procedure is **христо́соваться**.) Directly after church that night, the first meal with eggs, butter, and meat is eaten. Participation at this meal is called **ро́зговенье** (to participate **разговля́ться**). This can be a small family group eating a snack after the long church ceremony, or it can be a long night of eating and drinking.

Easter eggs **кра́шеные я́йца** (in Ukrainian, **пи́санки**) loomed as large in Russian Easter as in ours, although no Easter bunny was given credit for bringing them. The eggs were dyed and often

[10] For recipes and pictures of па́сха, кули́ч, блины́ see *Gourmet Cookbook*, Vol. II (New York: Gourmet Distributing Corporation, 1957); and Helen and George Papashvily, *Russian Cooking*, Foods of the World Series (New York: Time–Life Books, 1969).

had gaily painted designs. Some were taken to church and blessed—these were later either eaten or placed on the shelf with the icon; those not blessed could be used for games. **Катáть я́йца** was an egg-rolling contest where eggs were laid in a line; each contestant could keep the eggs hit out of that line when he rolled his own egg. **Бить я́йца** was played by two people holding eggs who would bang them into one another, the one holding the unbroken egg would win.

Easter was also a time for general merriment:

● На пáсху гуля́ли по у́лице, качáлись на качéлях, катáли крáшеные я́йца; молоды́е мужчи́ны игрáли в городки́, лапту́, бáбки, и други́е и́гры.... Одно́й из основны́х частéй весéнней обря́дности считáлись хорово́ды. Они́ бы́ли развлечéнием молодёжи. Води́ли хорово́ды обы́чно за дерéвней. Начинáлся хорово́д пéснями, приглашáющими прийти́ повесели́ться. Пото́м слéдовали рáзные хорово́дные и игровы́е пéсни, в большинствé те же, что и на свя́точных и́грищах; закáнчивался хорово́д пéснями, гласи́вшими, что порá расходи́ться по домáм.[11]

PENTECOST, WHITSUNDAY ТРО́ИЦА

This feast coincided with a pagan holiday whose main feature was spring greenery, especially birch **берёза**. Its adaptation to Christian rites involved bringing flowers and greenery to bedeck the church. For the religious, this holiday affirmed the trinity (**Тро́ица**) of God and also signaled the end of the Easter holiday cycle.

John the Baptist's Day
День Ивáна Купáлы

День Ивáна Купáлы (June 24) was actually a rather thin veneer of Christian ritual overlaying the pagan holiday of the summer solstice. John the Baptist (officially **Иоáнн Крести́тель**) became connected with this pagan festival because of his association with water. The day in pre-Christian mythology was associated with **Купáла** (or **Купáло**), a god that had to do with water (**купáться** to swim, bathe). On John the

Baptist's Day one could expect either a dunking from a pail of water or perhaps a less ceremonious push into the river. The night before, **Ивáнова ночь,** had some magical qualities: it was believed that the fern **пáпоротник** blossomed on this night, and anyone who could pick the flower would find all the buried treasure in the surrounding countryside. Bonfires were lit and jumped over,[12] and this was also a time for fortunetelling.

The harvest celebration
Дожи́нки

Дожи́нки was a harvest celebration that occurred especially in grain-producing areas on the last day of the harvest. When the last stalks of grain had been gathered, the harvesters lay down on the ground and rolled around, thinking that the earth would give back some of the strength it had taken away. Then ribbons were tied around a handful of stalks, which was paraded around the village and finally put to rest in the **крáсный у́гол** (see "Traditional peasant housing" in Chapter 4) of the person from whose field it came.

Contemporary holidays
Совремéнные прáздники

The first twenty years of the Soviet regime were a rejection of the old ways, which, indeed, one might expect. But the baby went out with the bath. Not only was the birth of Jesus rejected, but the Christmas tree, too; not only was the Resurrection denied, but so was **кули́ч**. Privately, individual families often continued to celebrate holidays as best they could, but not without discomfort. The generation gap created by the teachings at school found "principled" children rejecting their parents' holiday foods as symbols of a superstitious and ignorant past. Both religion and superstition were rejected.·

---

[11] Алексáндров, *Наро́ды европéйской чáсти СССР*, стр. 415.

[12] From pictures of the event, this is probably the day **Снегу́рочка** came to her sad end.

Масленица had never been a religious holiday, but the **блины** associated with it were not part of restaurant menus in the springtime until the 1950's. Life, however, was gray enough without the grim overlay of no holidays. So, as time went on, new holidays were borrowed from the old, and others developed some romance of their own.

Legal holidays
Дни праздников

1 января́	Но́вый год
8 ма́рта	Междунаро́дный же́нский день (Пра́здник Восьмо́го ма́рта, Же́нский день)
1 и 2 ма́я	День междунаро́дной солида́рности трудя́щихся (Пе́рвое ма́я)
9 ма́я	День побе́ды над фаши́стской Герма́нией (Пра́здник Побе́ды, День Побе́ды)
7 и 8 ноября́	Годовщи́на Вели́кой Октя́брьской социалисти́ческой револю́ции (Пра́здник Октября́)
5 декабря́	День Конститу́ции СССР

The New Year
Но́вый год

Generally speaking, the festivities formerly attached to Christmas made a short jump and combined with New Year. The basic ingredients are **Дед Моро́з**, **Снегу́рочка**, and **ёлка**.

GRANDFATHER FROST — ДЕД МОРО́З, ДЕ́ДУШКА МОРО́З

Дед Моро́з is reported to bring gifts for children during the night of December 31–January 1. The children actually see him only at children's parties **у́тренники**. The popular portrayal features a generally taller and thinner personality than our Santa Claus. **Дед Моро́з** also has more options on clothes: he can be dressed in red with white trimming, blue with white, or even white with white. (**Моро́з** was

originally, in folk stories, the personification of winter cold and had nothing to do with Christmas.) The idea of Grandfather Frost seems to be a relatively new one, probably not much more than 100 years old. It is as if, having the Christmas tree thrust upon them from the West, the Russians looked around and discovered they also needed a counterpart to Santa Claus (and also to Black Peter of the Dutch legend; the latter transformation was perhaps the most startling—to **Снегу́рочка**).

THE SNOW MAIDEN — СНЕГУ́РОЧКА

Снегу́рочка occupies two places in popular legend. She is (and was originally) the subject of a folk story that told how an old, lonesome, and childless couple made the figure of a young girl out of snow. The girl came to life and became a wonderful companion to her makers, only to melt away when enticed outside to play with her friends in the warmer weather. As Saint Nicholas's (**Дед Моро́з**) helper, she more resembles a fairy, regularly accompanying him and helping to distribute gifts to small children.

THE NEW YEAR'S TREE — (НОВОГО́ДНЯЯ) ЁЛКА

The Christmas tree, introduced by Peter the Great, is now a New Year's tree and universally a part of that day's celebration. Every home that can manage one does so, and the trees also appear in Pioneer clubs, stores, and public squares. The decorations resemble ours in overall impression, though the Russian tree is more often decorated with small edibles, and small animals seem to preponderate in the ornaments **украше́ния**. Often a red star decorates the top of public Christmas trees, and though Christians might like to think of it as the Star of Bethlehem, Soviet users probably have something else in mind.

THE NEW YEAR'S CHILDREN'S PARTY — (НОВОГО́ДНИЙ) У́ТРЕННИК

У́тренник is a children's party (from the hour it is given, **у́тро** morning): "**У нас бу́дет у́тренник.**" The party at this time of year might also

Дед Моро́з на Кали́нинском проспе́кте

be called ёлка since it centers on having a tree, dancing around it, and so on: "**Приходи́ к нам на ёлку.**" The party might be given at school (just before the New Year's school vacation, January 1–10), at a Pioneer club, or at home. The requirements for a **нового́дний у́тренник** are all of the aforementioned: **Дед Моро́з, Снегу́рочка, ёлка,** not to mention the children.

The basic ceremonies involved in this party are not complicated, but they are quite regular: at one point, the children join hands and walk around the tree (**де́ти хо́дят хорово́дом вокру́г ёлки**) singing songs. This one is common:

Ёлочка

Сне́гом укра́шена
Ёлочка зимо́й.
Йз лесу ёлочку
Взя́ли мы домо́й.

Бу́сы пове́сили,
Ста́ли в хорово́д.
Ве́село, ве́село
Встре́тим Но́вый год![13]

[13] These lyrics by З. Алекса́ндрова appeared in *Малю́тка*, ред. А. Чу́хин, 10ое изд. (Симферо́поль: Крымизда́т, 1964), стр. 156. Another (and longer) song with the same title by Р. Кудашёва is also universally popular.

Usually some entertainment is planned for these parties. In schools and clubs a program of some sort is arranged: some children might recite poetry, or a magician appears. At many of these parties you will see children around the tree, often dressed in costumes, as animals— rabbits, hedgehogs, wolves, hawks—as fairies, Grandfather Frost, the New Year, princesses, monsters, the evil **Кощей бессме́ртный** (a Russian warlock, skinny and old), or in any national costume—Scottish, Norwegian, and so on. These costumes are a remnant of **ря́женье** described earlier, though the children themselves may not be aware of the fact.

Sometime during the festivities, **Дед Моро́з** and **Снегу́рочка** appear with a large bag of many small gifts for the children.

When the party is given at home, there is not necessarily room enough to dance around the tree; instead the children have their own party at a table and **Дед Моро́з**, though he might not have **Снегу́рочка** with him, must appear. He is often required to supply the entertainment (in addition to small gifts).

THE NEW YEAR'S PARTY　　НОВОГО́ДНИЙ ВÉЧЕР

The New Year's party for adults is the brightest of the year—the atmosphere of our New Year's parties, combined with the gluttonous tendencies we reserve for Thanksgiving—and all of this with a Christmas tree in the background.

The party often begins in the early evening. Unlike New Year's parties in the United States, the celebration centers on especially elaborate food (and drink). The guests arrive and immediately seat themselves at a table crammed with plates of hors d'oeuvres **закýски** and bottles of wine, champagne, and vodka. Some form of **закýски** usually remains on the table throughout the meal to be eaten with the many toasts to be drunk in the course of the night. These hors d'oeuvres, however, are just the beginning of the meal. They are followed by a main dish—perhaps a goose with apples or a roast chicken. The meal naturally concludes with a dessert and tea (or, especially in large cities, coffee).

Several things have been happening in the course of the meal, however. The action at the table includes many toasts, and the table is also the center of the midnight ritual: just before midnight, the champagne is uncorked, Radio Moscow is turned on, and at the stroke of midnight one hears the Kremlin bells **бой Кремлёвских курáнтов**; everybody rises, raises his glass in a toast to the New Year, says **"С Нóвым гóдом!"** and clicks glasses with the others at the table, takes his first gulp of champagne, and settles down at the table again.

The New Year's dinner commonly is subject to other interruptions: dancing and singing are often as basic to the party as is the food. The time for the beginning and the end of the party and the time for serving the various courses (except the first one) are quite variable. It is not at all unusual that the party lasts all night.

GIFTS　　ПОДÁРКИ

The emphasis at this time of year is on merrymaking, not on gifts. Gifts are exchanged, but they are not so numerous or lavish as is the custom in the United States. The major problem at this time of year is not how to pay for gifts for the children but rather how to obtain refreshments for the New Year's party. Gifts are usually wrapped, but not in the ornate manner so obligatory in the United States.

Any dinner guests normally bring gifts of flowers, food, or drink to the host and hostess.

NEW YEAR'S CARDS　　НОВОГÓДНИЕ ОТКРЫ́ТКИ

New Year's postcards are regularly used but not to the same extent as are Christmas cards in the United States. The Russian tends to confine his list to friends living out of town. The usual greetings are **"С Нóвым гóдом!" "С нóвым счáстьем!"** or perhaps **"С прáздником!"** or **"С Новогóдним прáздником!"** Telegrams to send these messages are also very widely used, even within the same city, since they are relatively cheap and a special rate is offered for holiday greetings.

Women's Day (March 8)
Прáздник Восьмóго мáрта

American readers should be on guard: this holiday is not equivalent to Mother's Day. In the first place, it is an official day off for everyone, and secondly, it is a salute to all females, not just mothers. For this day, the boys in grade school will get a gift for their teacher (if she is a woman, of course), and they will also offer best wishes or a small gift to the girls in their classes. (On Army and Navy Day **День Совéтской Áрмии и Воéнно-Морскóго Флóта, 23 февраля́**, schoolgirls sometimes return the compliment.) University students (males) might throw a party for their female classmates, and women who have been especially successful at their jobs are given awards at work, or they might be mentioned in the newspaper.

Special women in one's life get special treatment, wives from husbands and mothers from children. The small ones might try making dinner, though more often a gift of some sort is

Пе́рвое ма́я

proffered. Though almost any gift is appropriate, flowers are especially popular: "В Москве́ айсо́ры продаю́т мимо́зу к пра́зднику Восьмо́го ма́рта." (Айсо́ры, ассири́йцы is a very small nationality group who live mainly in Transcaucasia and consider themselves descendants of the ancient Assyrians.)

It is also a custom to send Women's Day postcards поздрави́тельные откры́тки on this day; thus, the women who work will often get a card from their office, workshop, or ministry, as well as from friends.

The standard greeting is "Поздравля́ю с пра́здником Восьмо́го ма́рта." ("Я купи́л откры́тки к Восьмо́му ма́рта"—"I bought some Women's Day cards.")

The First of May
Пе́рвое ма́я

Soviet Russians celebrate May Day as Labor Day, as do the French, for instance. (The Second Socialist International in 1889 designated May 1 as the holiday for radical labor.)

The official celebrations for this holiday include a large public gathering, at least in major cities. This often is a type of parade called демонстра́ция, a parade without soldiers or military display. The participants consist, instead, of people in their usual dress marching or walking down the street in various degrees of organization. (The other word for parade пара́д refers to a parade of military troops and weapons unless otherwise specified, for example, **пара́д физкульту́рников**.)

The atmosphere of this holiday is one of gaiety compared with the more solemn and significant November 7. May Day combines a spring festival with Labor Day. Since it is considered a spring holiday **пра́здник весны́**, and since the dates sometimes coincide, there are those who make **па́сха**, the traditional Easter dessert, at this time. At home, parties are in order, but they are far from obligatory and take no special form. The next day is also a day off work.

Victory Day (May 9)
День Побе́ды

This day commemorates victory over Nazi Germany and is the time to visit the graves of or honor those millions who died during World War II **Вели́кая Оте́чественная война́**. For some years after the war, this was a day for parades, but now there are memorial meetings and a recounting of war stories. It must be noted that World War II still looms large in the Russian mind. (By comparison, we have forgotten.)

October Revolution Day (November 7–8)
Пра́здник Октября́

This October Revolution Day occurs in November because of the difference in the Julian and Gregorian calendars, the latter put into use only after the Revolution. The holiday is the one most associated with the founding of the Soviet regime and the most important of all the holidays introduced by the Soviets.

The major feature is naturally a parade (**пара́д**, **демонстра́ция**) for watching or joining in, but parties are also in order since there are two days of vacation. Cards **поздрави́тельные откры́тки** are also sent on this occasion; the written greeting is usually, **"С Пра́здником Октября́,"** and orally it is **"С Пра́здником!"**

Constitution Day (December 5)
День Конститу́ции

Constitution Day is a pleasant respite, a welcome time to start preparation for New Year's and not much else. Stalin was originally given credit for the Constitution, so that older people still think of this holiday as **День Ста́линской Конститу́ции**.

The old and the new
Ста́рое вме́сте с но́вым

Many features of the older holidays remain in some localities, both in an official and unofficial way. In villages (far from the cities, that is), the pagan rites continue alongside the newer "traditions." Children get dressed in costumes **ря́женье**; they also go from door to door singing songs **коля́дки** whose contents now wish a happy New Year. The unmarried girls, now mostly younger ones, still engage in **гада́нье** for the fun of it. The **престо́льные пра́здники** are still often celebrated, especially far from major cities, but this type of celebration is officially frowned upon as an unhappy survival of the past:

● Се́льская обще́ственность прово́дит акти́вную борьбу́ с э́тим вре́дным пережи́тком про́шлого. Внедре́ние но́вых обы́чаев в быт спосо́бствует отхо́ду населе́ния от пра́зднования «престо́льных дней».[14]

In other ways, the traditional celebrations have been incorporated into new (local, rather than national) festivals. Thus **Пра́здник урожа́я** formerly **дожи́нки** comes at the end of the harvest season and often features a parade with stalks of grain held high—in addition to plan fulfillment awards and the like. You are more likely to hear about **Пра́здник ру́сской зимы́**, however, which incorporates the joys of **ма́сленица** into other entertainments—dances and

[14] Алекса́ндров, *Наро́ды европе́йской ча́сти СССР*, стр. 452.

concerts, for instance. Local festivals of dance, music, and sports are also often arranged, but these can no longer be called holidays in our sense of the word.

April Fool's Day **Пе́рвое апре́ля** is celebrated exactly as is ours, though there is no particular association with fools: **"Пе́рвый апре́ль, нико́му не верь!"**—"On the first of April, don't believe anybody!"

There are, however, many officially designated days devoted most often to various professions or interests. They are not holidays except perhaps to some of the people directly involved in them: **День шахтёра, День физкульту́рника,** and many others. Some of these days have become of sufficient national interest as to border on real holidays:

21 января́ 1924 го́да у́мер Влади́мир Ильи́ч Ле́нин   Anniversary of Lenin's death

23 февраля́   День Сове́тской Армии и Военно-Морско́го Фло́та   Army and Navy Day

18 ма́рта   День Пари́жской Комму́ны   Day of the Paris Commune

12 апре́ля   День космона́втики   Cosmonautics Day

22 апре́ля   День па́мяти В. И. Ле́нина   Lenin's Birthday (он роди́лся в 1870 году́)

5 ма́я   День печа́ти   Press Day

7 ма́я   День ра́дио   Radio Day

28 ию́ля   День Военно-Морско́го Фло́та СССР   Navy Day or Sailor's Day

18 а́вгуста   День Возду́шного Фло́та СССР   Air Force Day

Пра́здник Октября́

7

Transportation
Tра́нспорт

It might be thought that the vastness of the Soviet Union, or Russia before it, would tend to immobilize the people living there. But, on the contrary, Russians are a traveling people and huge distances do not seem to be an unsurmountable obstacle. To the peasant it seems natural to go several hundred miles to a large city for major shopping. Contrast this with the stereotype of the Englishman quite content to spend his entire life in a small town. (Perhaps such opposite habits account for the wide variety of very strong English accents compared to the relative uniformity of Russian speech.)

In the USSR almost all transportation is accomplished via public means—trolleys, buses, trains, taxis, and airplanes. The most common form of private transportation seems to be the motorcycle, usually with a sidecar attached. The bicycle, so prevalent in much of Western Europe, seems conspicuous by its (relative) absence. Private cars exist, but the ratio of private car ownership to public transportation is very small. The construction of a factory by the Fiat company promises to change that frequency somewhat. Major terminology for parts of automobiles has been included here, although the car and its workings are much more a part of life in the United States.

A section on traditional ways of getting around has been included for two reasons: (1) you will (if you have not already) come across many references in literature to various kinds of sleighs, carts, and carriages, not to mention the unique system the Russian has for hitching a horse to the vehicle it is pulling; and (2) though the section on traditional transportation describes practices that were common before industrialization, almost all the devices shown here are still being made and used currently in the USSR, if only in the countryside. The pictures *are* contemporary.

Most of the chapter is devoted to contemporary means of transportation, including discussions of public urban transportation, the automobile, and other means for long-distance travel—trains, ships, and airplanes. The much briefer section on traditional means of transportation follows.

Public transportation
Общéственный трáнспорт

Public transportation in and between major cities of the USSR can seem to Americans a major improvement over what they have at home. In Moscow it is quite common, during the daytime especially, to just miss one bus, trolley, or trackless trolley and yet be able to see the next one coming a block away. This amount of public transportation seems very large to us, but it is still inadequate during rush-hour traffic **в часы́ пик**. The following is a paragraph from an article by Гр. Гóрин in *Литератýрная газéта*, 15 октября́ 1969 г, making fun of the pushing and shoving required in boarding and riding:

● А котóрые говоря́т, что в гóроде кругóм дáвки да óчереди, так те—не гуманúсты. Я, напримéр, многолю́дье люблю́.... Я в пустóй трамвáй и не ся́ду. Что в пустóм éхать-то? Уж лýчше в таксú. Там хоть с шофёром поговорúшь за свой же дéньги. А вот по утрáм я на трáнспорте éздить люблю́.... Там тебя́ сожмýт, стúснут, сдáвят.... Всё, дýмаешь, конéц!... Ан нет! Вы́кинут тебя́ на остановке, распрáвишь ты грудь, чýвствуешь—жив! И такáя рáдость на тебя́ нахóдит, такóе воодушевлéние.... Чýвствуешь, что гóры своротúть мóжешь!... Садúшься на трамвáй и éдешь в другýю стóрону.

Like everywhere else, however, the further you are from major population centers, the harder it is to get from one place to another. Roads are frequently in poor condition, buses are obviously infrequent, and the train station can be miles away. Generally speaking, much greater use is made in the USSR of trains, both suburban and interurban. It should be further noted that public transportation is considerably less expensive for everyday trips and for long-distance travel as well.

Going places in the USSR offers special problems: you will find that those whose official job it is to inform or direct you tend to be rude and close to surly.[1] (This is partially because the American thinks that a smile is part of any exchange or greeting. The Russian reserves his smile to express real pleasure and wonders why the American seems to have that incessant grin.) This unpleasantness is more than counterbalanced by the readiness of people around you to help. Feel free to ask anyone who looks as if he knows his way around how to get to your destination, where schedules are, and so on. Have the place you are going written out in case your Russian fails you, and then just ask. "**Язы́к до Кúева доведёт**"—"You can find your way to Kiev by asking."

Here are some phrases you must have:

Как доéхать до ——? How does one get to ——?

Какáя слéдующая остановка? What's the next stop?

Вы сейчáс выхóдите? Are you getting out now?

Разрешúте пройтú. May I get by, please.

The streetcar, trackless trolley, bus
Трамвáй, троллéйбус, автóбус

When using public transportation in large cities, it is wise not to walk out of the hotel without quantities of small kopeck pieces on you. (Hotels have cashiers as do subway stations.) You need three kopecks to ride a streetcar **трамвáй**, four kopecks for a trackless trolley **троллéйбус**, and five kopecks for a bus **автóбус** or for the subway **метрó**.

Maps showing central routes and stops are published for tourists. (There are more detailed maps for natives, but these are not always available.) Routes **маршрýты** are identified by numbers, but, more important, the stop **остановка** has a name, often the name of a cross street or a landmark, and also a sign indicating what vehicles stop there and how frequently they stop. Take into consideration that these stops are considerably farther apart (three to four Russian blocks) than what you are probably used to. Some conveyances have only a driver **водú-**

---

[1] This comment does not usually hold true for Intourist employees.

тель, шофёр while some also have a conductor кондукторша (in feminine form here since most are women). In the latter case you pay the conductor and keep the receipt, which is occasionally checked by an inspector контролёр. When there is no conductor, which is the case most of the time, there will be a receptacle касса toward the front and back of the conveyance where you can put your money and then take a receipt билет from the dispenser nearby. It is also possible to buy tickets from the driver if exact change escapes you, but your life will be less complicated if you come prepared. Often buses and trolleys will be quite crowded, and it will be impossible in actual practice to pay. Here the accepted thing is to pass the money forward: "Опустите, пожалуйста"—"Drop it in, please"; or "Передайте, пожалуйста"—"Pass it on, please." With time and luck on your side, the receipt will be returned to you. (Though it is not accepted behavior, students especially tend to think of riding without paying as a minor sport: "Он проехал зайцем"—"He didn't pay for a ticket." Some buses used to have signs with pictures and cartoons of people caught not paying.)

The driver announces the names of the stops, but the likelihood that you will be able both to hear and understand is small enough that you should always be prepared to ask somebody for directions.

The subway[2]
Метро

Entrance to the метро is gained by a five-kopeck piece in the turnstile турникет at the entrance. Getting around on the subway is less complicated than the above-ground methods because the system itself is simpler and maps are easily obtainable. The major thing to remember

[2] In referring to American subways and the English underground, the Russians will often use the word подземка instead of метро. Even сабвей is sometimes applied to the American subway!

is the name of the stop where you want to get off, since each stop is listed on the direction signs as you walk through the marble halls. (The Moscow subway is as much a monument as it is a means of transportation. Leningrad, Kiev, and Tbilisi also have a subway system, with others planned or under construction in Baku and Khar'kov.)

Taxis, minibuses
Такси, маршрутки

Taxis are, of course, a great convenience and also relatively inexpensive—ten kopecks to start the meter plus ten kopecks per kilometer. They have a major drawback, however. Although easily obtainable from your hotel, where they can be ordered, they are not so readily available once you are stranded in the street somewhere. The problem is that there are just not enough of them. Identifiable by a black and white checkerboard pattern on the front doors, they can be hailed once found and unoccupied, but you would do well not to be in a hurry and totally dependent on a taxi. The taxi stand стоянка такси exists, but it is not at all uncommon to see a line of people waiting there.

There is still another way to get around the largest cities: маршрутное такси (маршрутка) is a sort of personalized bus-taxi service using minibuses микроавтобусы. They generally concentrate on a certain area, picking up people from a subway station or bus stop and then delivering them to their door. The fee is higher (ten kopecks) than for regular buses but lower than for taxis.

Automobiles
Автомобили

The formal term is легковой автомобиль but the word in standard speech is машина. Because the supply of cars is not great, those available are both wildly expensive and require several years of waiting after an order is placed. As a result, the streets in major cities seem much less crowded than ours do, and there are many more buses, trolleys, trucks, and also many more two-wheeled forms of transportation.

мотоци́кл   a motorcycle

мотоци́кл с коля́ской, мотоколя́ска   a motorcycle with a sidecar

мопе́д (педа́льный мотоци́кл)   a motorcycle that can be pedaled

моторо́ллер   a motor scooter

Those who do own automobiles tend to use them differently. Especially if they live in a large city, Russians will often reserve the car for summer excursions rather than for driving to work; it will be left in a parking lot during the winter. Cars are hard to start at 20° C. below anyway.

Various makes **ма́рки** of cars, in varying degrees of elegance, are made in the USSR. In ascending order there are:

Запоро́жец   a very small car, resembling a Fiat, made in the Ukraine

Москви́ч   the most common private passenger car

Жигули́   a new car produced at the Fiat factory at Togliatti **Толья́тти**

Побе́да   a medium-size car, no longer in production

Во́лга   a bigger, roomier model, often used as a taxi

Ча́йка   a seven passenger car that is elegant but newer than the **ЗИЛ**

ЗИЛ   a large model and the ultimate in respectability and elegance

All of them also have model numbers that might be familiar to small boys and professional drivers: **Во́лга 21Г, Москви́ч 407**.

Especially in the countryside, road conditions during the spring and fall require vehicles that can manage essentially without roads. This place is filled by the **га́зик** (built by **Го́рьковский автомоби́льный заво́д**), which strongly resembles what we call a jeep.

Parts of the automobile
Ча́сти автомоби́ля

OUTSIDE THE AUTOMOBILE   АВТОМОБИ́ЛЬ СНАРУ́ЖИ

крыло́   fender
капо́т   hood
ба́мпер, бу́фер   bumper
облицо́вка   grill
фа́ра   headlight
указа́тель поворо́та   turn signal
две́рца   door
окно́, стекло́   window
ветрово́е стекло́   windshield
стеклоочисти́тель   windshield wiper (*informal* **дво́рник**)
фо́рточка   wing window
кры́ша   roof
колесо́   wheel
ши́на, автопокры́шка   tire
о́бод   rim (of tire) (*pl.* **обо́дья**)
ка́мера   inner tube
номерно́й знак   license plate
но́мер (автомоби́ля)   license number

INSIDE THE AUTOMOBILE   ВНУТРИ́ АВТОМОБИ́ЛЯ

дви́гатель   engine
по́ршень   piston
кла́пан   valve
цили́ндр   cylinder
  блок цили́ндров   cylinder block
  голо́вка цили́ндров   cylinder head
карбюра́тор   carburetor
аккумуля́тор, батаре́я   battery
распредели́тель   distributor
переда́ча   transmission
карда́нный вал   drive shaft
ось   axle
дифференциа́л   differential
радиа́тор   radiator
вентиля́тор   fan
  реме́нь вентиля́тора   fan belt
глуши́тель   muffler
выхлопна́я труба́   exhaust (pipe)
амортиза́тор   shock absorber
бензоба́к   gas tank

бензи́н gasoline
ма́сло oil
то́рмоз brake
 тормозно́й бараба́н brake drum
 тормозна́я жи́дкость brake fluid
запа́льная свеча́ spark plug

замо́к зажига́ния ignition
спидо́метр speedometer
указа́тель давле́ния ма́сла oil gauge
термо́метр систе́мы охлажде́ния temperature
 gauge
переключа́тель све́та headlight switch
включа́тель стеклоочисти́теля windshield
 wiper switch
кно́пка возду́шной засло́нки карбюра́тора
 choke
контро́льная ла́мпочка генера́тора generator
 indicator light
переключа́тель освеще́ния каби́ны inside light
 switch
бага́жник, вещево́й я́щик glove compartment
указа́тель у́ровня бензи́на gas indicator

ручно́й то́рмоз emergency or hand brake
акселера́тор accelerator
руль steering wheel
рулева́я коло́нка steering column
кно́пка, кольцо́ (звуково́го) сигна́ла horn
рыча́г переме́ны скоросте́й, переключа́тель
 скоросте́й gearshift
педа́ль сцепле́ния clutch
педа́ль (гидравли́ческого) то́рмоза foot brake
сиде́нье seat
бага́жник trunk

Once any original equipment on a car requires replacement, the owner is in for trouble. Spare parts **запасны́е ча́сти** are often not readily available, a situation that has given rise both to minor thievery and a flourishing black market.

Trucks
Грузовы́е автомоби́ли

In everyday speech a truck is a **грузови́к**; in official language it is a **грузово́й автомоби́ль**. Trucks are distinguished (usually among specialists) by the factory that makes them and a model number: **ГАЗ-56, ЗИЛ-157 (Заво́д и́мени Лихаче́ва), УАЗ-450 (Улья́новский автомоби́льный заво́д)**. The same is true for buses.

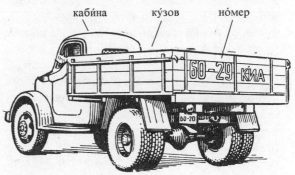

Грузови́к

Truck parts include a cab **каби́на** and load carrier **ку́зов**. Trucks and buses have their license number painted in very large figures across the back of the vehicle.

Among the several kinds of trucks, trailers, and tractors are:

самосва́л a dump truck
автопо́езд a truck with additional trailers
прице́п a trailer
тяга́ч a tractor used on highways with trailers
тяга́ч с полуприце́пом a tractor-trailer
тра́ктор a tractor, used mostly for pulling
 farm equipment
колёсный тра́ктор a tractor with wheels
гу́сеничный тра́ктор a caterpillar tractor

Soviet teamsters follow an interesting practice. For the safety gained in numbers, it is common practice to transport goods in a caravan **эшело́н** of trucks. These can be a challenge to the lone driver, especially when roads are mainly two-way, two-lane affairs.

For drivers and pedestrians
Для води́телей и пешехо́дов

Different countries and sometimes different cities within countries (compare New York City and Washington, D.C.) have varying driving styles. Here the concern is not so much the rules and regulations that are imposed from above. (For those, if you are planning to drive in the USSR, you should find out which apply at the time you are going. The rules change somewhat from time to time.) Driving "style" in this discussion means how the people choose to obey or, to some extent, disobey those rules and regulations. In London one finds amazingly considerate driving. In Paris driving is a sport and bluffing is the major play. In Moscow, however, driving is less formal than a sport and more a game. The cars are toys, while pedestrians and other cars are not necessarily obstacles: timid drivers should stay home. Making a mistake and hitting something is a very serious affair, however, and Soviet laws and their penalties are very much harsher than are ours. Here the penalties are listed in ascending order.

● К числу́ администрати́вных взыска́ний в зави́симости от хара́ктера наруше́ния и его́ после́дствий отно́сится:
(1) у́стное предупрежде́ние;
(2) штраф;
(3) просе́чка тало́на предупрежде́ний;
(4) вре́менное лише́ние прав управле́ния тра́нспортными сре́дствами;
(5) в слу́чаях, когда́ наруше́ние пра́вил движе́ния повлекло́ за собо́й нае́зд или ава́рию, свя́занную с нанесе́нием теле́сных поврежде́ний челове́ку и поврежде́нием госуда́рственного и ли́чного иму́щества, вино́вные привлека́ются к уголо́вной отве́тственности.[3]

The foreign driver must therefore drive with considerable caution.

● Иностра́нцы, прибы́вшие на террито́рию СССР на свои́х автомоби́лях (мотоци́клах), обя́заны име́ть:
(1) докуме́нты на автомоби́ль (мотоци́кл);

(2) междунаро́дное разреше́ние на управле́ние тра́нспортным сре́дством и́ли вкла́дыш к национа́льному води́тельскому удостовере́нию;
(3) национа́льный регистрацио́нный номерно́й знак и отличи́тельный знак страны́ вы́езда, присво́енный согла́сно Междунаро́дной конве́нции.[4]

This description of driving suggests something to tourist-pedestrians. Until you are used to when traffic will stop, which it does, you must assume that cars always have the right of way. This may seem an exaggeration, but it is not. You should act as if it were true especially when you are alone on a street corner waiting to cross or when you are the front runner in a group. As a pedestrian **пешехо́д** you do have some advantages: downtown Soviet sidewalks are often very crowded—and there is some protection in numbers. Another advantage built into the system is the underpass **перехо́д** for pedestrian use. (**Перехо́д** is also equivalent to our "Cross here" signs.) Sometimes these are so located as to be obvious, even unavoidable, but they are also often built as part of subway entrances and exits so that their existence is far less obvious. As a general rule, on a busy downtown street, do not try crossing unless you see other people going the same way you are.

The confusion about traffic in the foreign pedestrian's mind is only partially due to what he regards as wild driving. Also responsible is the way native Russian pedestrians cope with traffic. They seem to follow two principles: (1) every man for himself, and (2) go across if you can get across. There are occasional exceptions to these rules, making the pattern difficult for the foreigner to perceive.

In cities, drivers at night use only parking lights, turning on the regular headlights only as a final warning in place of a horn signal, which is illegal except in emergencies.

Driving outside major cities has other problems. Only certain roads may be used by foreign

---

[3] А. И. Манзо́н и Г. Е. Нагу́ла, *Посо́бие по пра́вилам движе́ния* (Ки́ев: "Техніка," 1967), стр. 11.

[4] Манзо́н и Нагу́ла, *Посо́бие по пра́вилам движе́ния*, стр. 10.

drivers between major cities (an Intourist[5] map will show them). In addition you may not investigate the world that extends beyond the city limits of those cities you are allowed to visit (except Moscow), and you must specify before you get your visa which places (selected from the special list) you will visit and on which days. Another problem is that you must take care to have enough gas to get to the next gas station since they are few and far between. Finally, roads in the Soviet Union are not well marked: at a junction you must often choose the largest, widest paved road as the most likely one.

Gas stations
Бензоколо́нка, запра́вочная ста́нция

Gas is obtained from a gas pump **бензоколо́нка** located at a gas "station" **запра́вочная ста́нция**. These two terms are used interchangeably since gasoline (and perhaps water) is all that is available. Repair facilities **ста́нции техни́ческого обслу́живания** exist, but they are much less frequent than are the gas stations, and the Russian car-owner tends to avoid them by doing the repairs himself or by consulting a knowledgeable friend.

Getting gasoline **бензи́н** is not an easy affair; the rule book for drivers has specific instructions on how one is to line up for gas: trucks three meters apart, cars one meter apart. The gas stations themselves are infrequent enough to force planning on the most improvident driver. A much lower octane gas is used by Soviet cars, so tourists with Western cars are given special coupons that allow them the privilege of buying higher octane gas at certain gas stations. You pay for your gas first, then pump it yourself.

You may find the following terminology useful.

Газу́й!   Step on it!
Запра́вьте маши́ну бензи́ном!   Fill 'er up!
Мне на́до запра́виться.   I need to get some gas.

---

[5] **Интури́ст**—Всесою́зное акционе́рное о́бщество по иностра́нному тури́зму в СССР.

Hitchhiking
«Голосова́ние», автосто́п

Hitching a ride is a fairly common practice, especially outside cities where public transportation is inadequate (though it is also practiced to some extent within cities). The process merely requires standing at the side of the road with an arm raised above the head, whence the name **голосова́ть** to "vote." (Compare, too, **голосова́ть** to try to catch a ride with **проголосова́ть** to catch a ride.) "Нахо́дка" by В. Тендряко́в contains the following passage: "**Трофи́м проголосова́л и прое́хал по большаку́ до поворо́та на Копно́вку, а там—руко́й пода́ть.**"—"Trofim caught a ride along the main road as far as the turn to Kopnovka. From there it was just a short distance."

Hitchhiking is not reserved for the young and the poor; it is used by anyone in need of a ride. The driver usually expects payment. **Автосто́п** is an official (governmental) effort to formalize the payment practices. The prospective rider buys tickets **тало́ны** ahead of time, dispensing them to drivers according to the distance traveled.

Road signs
Доро́жные зна́ки

The Russians use the same system for traffic signs as is used in Western Europe, so that little or no Russian (French or German) is required to be able to "read" them. Of considerable help in distinguishing these signs are the different shapes and colors used for different categories of signs. The illustration shows the types and numbers of signs referred to here.

Warning signs **Предупрежда́ющие зна́ки** are triangular with an orange red border, yellow background, and black figures. They indicate conditions the driver should watch out for: slippery roads, railroad crossings, two-way streets, children playing, road repair work in progress, and so on.

Prohibiting signs **Запреща́ющие зна́ки** are round, and most of them use the same colors as

Железнодоро́жный перее́зд без шлагба́ума (1)

Железнодоро́жный перее́зд со шлагба́умом (2)

Перекрёсток (3)

Пересече́ние со второстепе́нной доро́гой (4)

Пересече́ние с гла́вной у́лицей или доро́гой (5)

Регули́руемый перекрёсток (уча́сток доро́ги) (6)

Поворо́т напра́во (7а)

Поворо́т нале́во (7б)

Изви́листая доро́га (8)

Круто́й спуск (9)

Неро́вная доро́га (10)

Ско́льзкая доро́га (11)

Суже́ние доро́ги (12)

Разводно́й мост (13)

Двухсторо́ннее движе́ние (14)

Пешехо́ды (15)

Де́ти (16)

Ремо́нтные рабо́ты (17)

Живо́тные на доро́ге (18)

Про́чие опа́сности (19)

Въе́зд запрещён (1)

Движе́ние запрещено́ (2)

Автомоби́льное движе́ние запрещено́ (3)

Грузово́е движе́ние запрещено́ (4)

Мотоцикле́тное движе́ние запрещено́ (5)

Гужево́е движе́ние запрещено́ (6)

Движе́ние тра́кторов запрещено́ (7)

Велосипе́дное движе́ние запрещено́ (8)

Ограниче́ние ве́са (9)

Ограниче́ние нагру́зки на ось (10)

Ограниче́ние габари́тной высоты́ (11)

Ограниче́ние габари́тной ширины́ (12)

Прое́зд без остано́вки запрещён (13)

Поворо́т нале́во запрещён (14а)

Поворо́т напра́во запрещён (14 б)

Разворо́т запрещён (15)

Обго́н запрещён (16)

Обго́н грузовы́м автомоби́лям запрещён (17)

Ограниче́ние ско́рости (18)

Пода́ча звуково́го сигна́ла запрещена́ (19)

Остано́вка запрещена́ (20)

Стоя́нка запрещена́ (21)

Коне́ц ограниче́ний (22)

● Доро́жные зна́ки

the warning signs. As their title implies, these signs describe what one cannot do. The most vital ones are the "Stop" sign (II-13) and the "Do not enter" sign (II-1). Notice also that a prohibition is often indicated by a diagonal slash through the sign; thus, II-21 means "No parking."

Limiting signs **Предпи́сывающие зна́ки** have blue backgrounds and white figures. They describe the *only* way something can be done: the first sign in III-1 says that you must turn right, while the second says you must turn left; sign III-7 permits only bicycle traffic and III-5 only truck traffic.

Informational signs **Указа́тельные зна́ки** are square with a blue background; they let you know what you can do or what facilities are available: IV-1 is "Park here," IV-2 says "U-turn is allowed here," IV-7 is "Public telephone," and so on.

ПРЕДПИ́СЫВАЮЩИЕ ЗНА́КИ (III)

Разрешённое направление движения (1)

Направление объе́зда препя́тствия (2)

Кругово́е движе́ние (3)

Движе́ние легковы́х автомоби́лей (4)

Движе́ние грузовы́х автомоби́лей (5)

Мотоцикле́тное движе́ние (6)

Велосипе́дное движе́ние (7)

УКАЗА́ТЕЛЬНЫЕ ЗНА́КИ (IV)

Ме́сто стоя́нки (1)

Ме́сто разворо́та (2)

Ла́герь автотури́стов (3)

Пу́нкт пита́ния (4)

Пу́нкт медици́нской по́мощи (5)

Пу́нкт техни́ческого обслу́живания (6)

Телефо́н (7)

Автозапра́вочная ста́нция (8)

Гла́вная у́лица и́ли доро́га (9)

Коне́ц гла́вной у́лицы и́ли доро́ги (10)

ДОПОЛНИ́ТЕЛЬНЫЕ ТАБЛИ́ЧКИ К ЗНА́КАМ (V)

Зо́на де́йствия зна́ка (1)

Расстоя́ние до объе́кта (2)

Вре́мя де́йствия зна́ка (3)

Направле́ние объе́зда (4)

Ви́д тра́нспортных сре́дств (5)

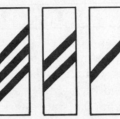

Опа́сный железнодоро́жный перее́зд (6)

Указа́тель "Береги́сь по́езда" (7)

ДОРО́ЖНЫЕ УКАЗА́ТЕЛИ (VI)

Указа́тель наименова́ний (1)

Указа́тель направле́ний (2)

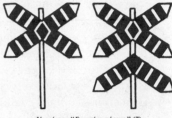

Предвари́тельный указа́тель направле́ний (4)

Указа́тель расстоя́ний (3)

Маршру́тная ма́рка (5)

Километро́вый указа́тель (6)

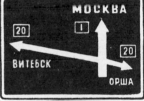

Other signs can also accompany those that have been discussed; they are **Дополни́тельные табли́чки к зна́кам.** Thus V-1 describes how far the sign to which it is attached is in effect, and V-3 indicates the specific hours that the sign is in effect.

The signs given under the heading **Доро́жные указа́тели** simply tell you where you are, how to get somewhere, or how far it is until you get there.

Trains
Поезда́

The train **по́езд** is the most common method for traveling between cities **междугоро́дный по́езд**. Buses make such trips, but they are less often resorted to because of poor road conditions, especially in the spring and fall. Suburban trains **при́городные поезда́** are also widely used.

TRAINS   119

Suburban trains
Пригородные «электрички»

Major cities usually are the center of a network of suburban trains **пригородные поезда** (called **электричка** in everyday life). They emanate from a terminal **вокзал** in a city, stopping at stations **станции** on their way. Access to them is relatively simple. Usually, there is only one class of tickets, the so-called hard class **жёсткие** (**сидения**), here meaning wooden seats. Tickets **билеты** are obtained either from a cashier **в кассе** or from a slot machine **автомат**, where care must be taken to put in the right amount of money for the length of trip you are taking. A schedule **расписание** is posted (though they are sometimes out of date), and the only other worry is to ascertain what track the train leaves from. (Tracks are **рельсы**, except that in Russian one worries about which platform **платформа** or **перрон** to stand on, not what track the train leaves from: "**От какой платформы отходит поезд?**" "**С какого пути отходит поезд?**") Tickets are not taken at the gate or door; in fact they are often not checked at all. You had better have your ticket with you when the ticket checker **контролёр** does come around, however.

Long-distance trains
Междугородные поезда

More forethought and preparation is required for longer trips. Tickets can often be bought not only at the terminal but also at downtown central ticket offices. There are two basic kinds of passenger space on a Russian train, coach and compartment, and there are dining facilities as well. It is possible to check one's baggage **багаж** (to go in the baggage car) but the Russians avoid doing so.

COACH CARS   В ОБЩЕМ ВАГОНЕ

The least expensive seats are those left unreserved in this type of car. The seats may be hard, unpadded **общий жёсткий вагон** or they may be padded **общий мягкий вагон**. Seating may be arranged in several ways, usually depending on the age of the car. Newer cars are more likely to have an aisle down the middle with seats on both sides all facing one direction, or they might be facing each other. For a reserved place in such a car one buys a **плацкартный билет**.

COMPARTMENTS   КУПЕ

Very long-distance travel, on the Trans-Siberian **Сибирская железная дорога**, is more often accomplished in these four-person compartments **купе**. (Two-place compartments **двухместные купе** are also available on some trains.) On these, seats are reserved and again come in two degrees of luxury: **жёсткий вагон** the hard car where one rents bedding—**матрас, одеяло, две простыни, подушка**—from the conductor **проводница**; and **мягкий вагон** the soft car, with more built-in plushness. In the compartments, beds are made of the two seats (which accommodate four in the daytime) and two more are formed from "shelves" **полки** that fold down for the night. To the delight of some Americans and to the dismay of others, the Russians make no attempt to separate the sexes in these compartments.

EATING ON TRAINS   ПИТАНИЕ В ПОЕЗДЕ

For eating while traveling, you may take advantage of the dining car **вагон-ресторан** or a sort of snack bar **буфет** (candy, sandwiches, wines). Tea also is generally made available from a hot-water heater **титан** attended to by the **проводница**. You pay, not for the tea, but for the sugar or lemon in the tea. But you will find that most people eat what they have brought along with them for the trip. (Food on trains is expensive all over the world.) When their own provisions give out, they buy food (meat pies, cucumbers, berries, and so on) at the train stops along the way. As a result, when a long-distance train stops for only a short while at a station, a crush of people develops—first trying to get off to be the first in line to buy food, and then again scrambling to get on the train before it leaves the station.

You should also expect trains to be relatively slow though usually on time.

On long-distance trains you might notice a wooden barrier **щиты** or tree plantings **лесны́е поса́дки** that parallel the railroad tracks for many miles. Their purpose is to keep wind-driven winter snow from banking on the tracks.

Ships
Суда́

A respectable Russian geography book will tell you what is done on water now. Inland, the canals uniting various river systems, often with locks **шлю́зы**, are among the marvels that have consumed quantities of ink in the Soviet press.

● Беломо́рско-Балти́йский кана́л, Во́лго-Балти́йский во́дный путь им. В. И. Ле́нина, кана́л им. Москвы́ и Во́лго-Донско́й судохо́дный кана́л им. В. И. Ле́нина, соедини́в ме́жду собо́й пять море́й, образова́ли еди́ную глубоково́дную систе́му европе́йской ча́сти СССР.

Equal amounts of ink are spent in describing the dams **плоти́ны** that are significant in making rivers navigable, not to mention the hydroelectric power they provide: **Бра́тская ГЭС (Ги́дроэлектроста́нция), Во́лжская ГЭС, Цимля́нская ГЭС.**

The river fleet
Речно́й флот

The rivers freeze over during the winter, but during the summer they form an avenue for vacations. A major boat passenger terminal is a **речно́й вокза́л.**

● Мно́гие тури́стские маршру́ты начина́ются от Москвы́—от речно́го вокза́ла Хи́мки. Но́вые речны́е вокза́лы в Го́рьком, Каза́ни, Улья́новске и Осетро́ве. Ме́жду Москво́й и А́страханью пла́вает трёхпа́лубный ди́зель-электрохо́д «Ле́нин» —флагма́н речно́го фло́та, кото́рый рассчи́тан на перево́зку 439 пассажи́ров.

Kinds of ships
Ви́ды судо́в

Perhaps the most common word for ship is **парохо́д**, which technically refers to a ship with a steam engine; **теплохо́д** (technically, a ship with an internal-combustion engine) is used almost interchangeably. Less frequent by far is the **электрохо́д**, a ship powered by electricity. Of considerable popularity on inland waterways is the hydrofoil **раке́та**: "**Раке́та—это теплохо́д (и́ли су́дно) на подво́дных кры́льях.**"

The names for kinds of ships are often acronyms.

линко́р (лине́йный кора́бль) battleship
авиано́сец airplane carrier
миноно́сец torpedo boat
эсми́нец (эска́дренный миноно́сец) destroyer
ка́тер cutter
подло́дка (подво́дная ло́дка) submarine
кре́йсер cruiser (**Кре́йсер «Авро́ра»**)
паро́м ferry, raft

Besides the general term for ship, there are others: businesslike and very common is **су́дно** (*pl.* **суда́**), often applied but not limited to ships that operate on the open sea; **грузово́е су́дно** is a freighter; **кора́бль** is a somewhat more high-flown, even poetic, term and is often applied to large naval vessels.

● «Ива́н Франко́»—оди́н из се́рии пассажи́рских ла́йнеров торго́вого фло́та СССР. На нём бо́лее 300 каю́т для 750 пассажи́ров. Ско́рость хо́да ла́йнера—20 узло́в.[6]

Other ships are frequently mentioned in the Soviet press: **та́нкер** and **пассажи́рский ла́йнер** are obvious; an icebreaker **ледоко́л** is required to keep the northern passage (north of Siberia) open as long as possible; **букси́р** is a tugboat (also, less frequently, **толка́ч**, when it pushes instead of pulls).

---

[6] The quotations in Russian on ships were chosen from *Тра́нспорт* СССР, общ. ред. А. Л. Голова́нова (Москва́: Тра́нспорт, 1967).

Ви́ды судо́в

морско́й букси́р

пассажи́рское су́дно

грузово́е су́дно

нефтеналивно́е су́дно

паро́м для перево́зки
железнодоро́жных соста́вов
и пассажи́ров

речно́е су́дно «Раке́та»
на подво́дных кры́льях

тра́улер

а́томный ледоко́л «Ле́нин»

ЛЕНИН

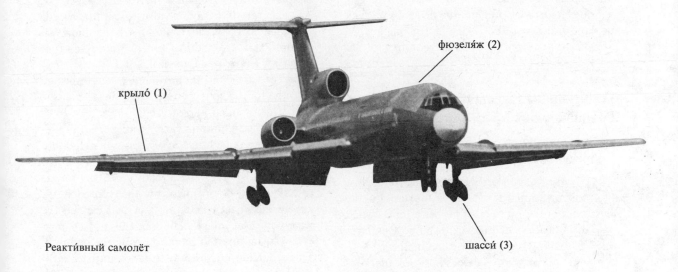

крылó (1)

фюзеля́ж (2)

шасси́ (3)

Реакти́вный самолёт

Boats
Ло́дки

Smaller boats **ло́дки** are available usually through a club or a resort. Those who live near or work on the water, of course, also require boats. Among the types of smaller craft are the rowboat **гребна́я ло́дка**, sailboat **па́русная ло́дка**, and motorboat **мото́рная ло́дка**. There are various kinds of boats that can be rowed and sailed, however.

Boats using oars **вёсла** (*sg.* **весло́**) include a rubber raft **рези́новая (надувна́я) ло́дка**, a kayak **байда́рка**, and a canoe **кано́э**. **Чёлн** was originally a small dugout (not necessarily in the shape of a canoe) used mostly for hunting and fishing; **ял, я́лик** is a wide, large rowboat with one to three pairs of oars; a lifeboat **спаса́тельная ло́дка** would be a kind of **ял**. **Шлю́пка** is a small boat that can be rowed or sailed, but the common pleasure sailboat is a **я́хта**. Those who sail in the winter (on ice) use an iceboat **бу́ер**. **Мото́рная ло́дка** can be any small boat with a motor attached, but **ка́тер** is in the shape of our motorboat.

Airplanes
Самолёты

(1) wing
(2) fuselage
(3) landing gear

also: **возду́шный винт** (propeller)

Civil aviation is controlled and accomplished by **Аэрофло́т** (**Гла́вное управле́ние гражда́нского возду́шного фло́та**). That agency flies airplanes **самолёты**, also obsoletely referred to as **аэропла́ны**, and poetically described as **возду́шные корабли́**. (A jet airplane is a **реакти́вный самолёт**; a helicopter is a **вертолёт**.) Airplanes land and take off from a landing field **аэродро́м** and are stored in **анга́ры**, both of which would be located at an airport **аэропо́рт**. They are flown by **лётчики**, and passengers **пассажи́ры** are attended by a **стюарде́сса, бортпроводни́ца**.

Airplanes are named after their principal designer (see "'Letter' abbreviations" in Chapter 12), the most famous of whom is **Ту́полев**. He has been given credit for the **ТУ-104, ТУ-114,**

ТУ-124, and most recently the supersonic **ТУ-144**. The other designers, **Илью́шин** and **Анто́нов**, were almost as productive of airplane names.

Travelers may appreciate the news that Soviet airplane rides cost about one-half what they do elsewhere. Accommodations are comfortable, if not luxurious.

Traditional transportation
Традицио́нный тра́нспорт

Hitching a horse
Упря́жка ло́шади

The horse was formerly responsible for almost all transportation. (It was so important to the Russian that the number of horses a man owned was an indication of his wealth.) The Russian's way of hitching his horse was distinctive.

The horse collar **хому́т** does not look markedly different from ours, but it was connected to the **дуга́**—that arched piece of wood rising over the horse's shoulders found in any picture of a Russian horse pulling something. Its official purpose was to form a link between the collar **хому́т** and the shafts **огло́бли**. But the **дуга́** was also decorative in that it was often gaily painted and trimmed with bells **колоко́льчики**. The

collar, arch, and shafts were all connected by a loop **гуж** attached to the collar, and it is this loop that has supplied the name for horse- (or animal-) drawn vehicles—**гужево́й тра́нспорт**. A very familiar saying also uses the word: **"Взя́лся за гуж, не говори́, что не дюж"**—"Don't start something unless you intend to finish it" (**дюж** = **си́льный**).

At the other end the **огло́бли** were connected directly to the axle **ось** so that, in effect, the shafts both pulled and steered.[7]

The most common arrangement of horses **упря́жка** was one horse to a wagon or sleigh, but the most popular was the troika **тро́йка**, three horses side by side. The direction the wagon was to take was determined by the center horse **коренни́к**, since it was this one that carried the **хому́т-дуга́-огло́бли**. The outside horses **пристяжны́е**, connected by straps, only helped pull. These outside horses had to work under conditions that we would consider somewhat inhumane. Almost any picture of a troika in action will show them with their heads turned to the side. This occurred because, in addition to the

[7] Another way of hitching horses, **дышлова́я упря́жка**, is now commonly used when two horses side by side are needed. This method, of Ukrainian rather than Russian origin, involves a single shaft **ды́шло** that goes between the two horses. No arch is used.

The horse collar хому́т *has a leather strap* гу́ж *on both sides, which connects both the arch* дуга́ *and the shafts* огло́бли.

Са́ни-дро́вни, дро́вни

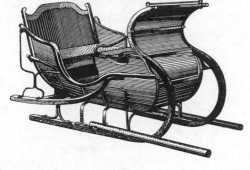

Са́ни легковы́е одноко́нные
This is a contemporary sleigh very similar to the most common sleigh for travel вы́ездны́е са́ни *that was used both in and between cities.*

Ро́звальни *is a traditional type of sleigh still widely used.*

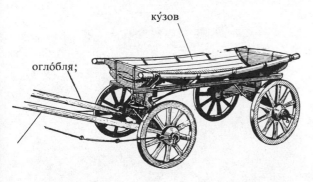

ку́зов

огло́бля;

Теле́га

Дро́жки

two reins **во́жжи** attached to the center horse, there was a single rein on each side connected to the other horses' bits on the outside; the driver pulled on these outside reins, forcing the two horses to turn their heads as they ran. This was done because the Russians thought the horses looked elegant running that way. (They still think so.)

Wagons and sleighs
Пово́зки и са́ни

The horses pulled several kinds of devices. When poor road conditions prevailed, either on mountainous paths or during the spring and fall "roadlessness" **бездоро́жье**, the horses themselves might carry the load: **вью́чный** тра́нспорт, вью́чная ло́шадь. Волоку́ша, the simplest device to be pulled, consisted merely of огло́бли to which a load was attached toward the bottom end with the ends of the shafts dragging along the ground. (This arrangement is similar to the travois used by American Plains Indians.)

Sleighs са́ни supplied transportation for much of the year. The simplest kind of sleigh, the дро́вни, consisted of nothing but a long, narrow skeleton platform on runners поло́зья and served principally for hauling wood. (Gathering wood was a major winter occupation for the Russian peasant.) Another traditional peasant type of sleigh, the ро́звальни, is still in use today and is even described as the most convenient type of sleigh. The side rails гря́дки of this sleigh are much closer to each other at the front end than they are at the back end. They serve not only to help form the top rim but also to keep the sleigh from turning over in going around corners. (A fast turn is especially subject to spills.) Many Russian sleighs have similar rails for just that purpose.

A child's sled is now best translated as са́нки; сала́зки also refers to this, but the term is now obsolete.

The general term for a vehicle for carrying either goods or people is пово́зка. Теле́га refers especially to peasant carts to accomplish this purpose. The two-wheeled cart двуко́лка was used as a last resort when the spring and fall "roadlessness" set in.

There were many varieties of light, four-wheel carriages экипа́жи, principally for carrying two to four people, including the таранта́с, про-лётка, and дро́жки.

The каре́та was a type of экипа́ж completely enclosed and essentially reserved, for economic reasons, for those both highborn and rich. Киби́тка was any covered пово́зка, strongly resembling our covered wagon, though often much smaller and consisting of leather or cloth stretched over a frame.

THE DRIVERS КУ́ЧЕР, ИЗВО́ЗЧИК, ЯМЩИ́К

The people whose lives were principally involved in driving these vehicles had various titles: ку́чер, изво́зчик, ямщи́к. The ку́чер was hired for his services as a driver, while the изво́зчик was hired both for his services and for those of his vehicle. The ямщи́к was one who drove on a regular route тракт between two places that were part of a nationwide stage system. This ямщи́к was the driver who has been immortalized in countless songs and poems. Here are four verses of a very famous poem, "Зи́мняя доро́га," by Пу́шкин:

● Сквозь волни́стые тума́ны
Пробира́ется луна́,
На печа́льные поля́ны
Льёт печа́льный свет она́.

По доро́ге зи́мней, ску́чной
Тро́йка бо́рзая бежи́т,
Колоко́льчик однозву́чный
Утоми́тельно греми́т.

Что́-то слы́шится родно́е
В до́лгих пе́снях ямщика́
То разгу́лье удало́е,
То серде́чная тоска́. . . .

Ни огня́, ни чёрной ха́ты,
Глушь и снег. . . . Навстре́чу мне
То́лько вёрсты полоса́ты
Попада́ются одне́.

Riding on water
Речно́й тра́нспорт

Долблёная ло́дка

Плоскодо́нка

The earlier (before 1850) Russian small boat **ло́дка** was a dugout **долблёная ло́дка** formed from a single log. Later, when whole logs were less accessible, the boats were made from boards and more variety in shape appeared: **плоско-до́нка** was a flat-bottom boat. Traditionally, these small boats were pointed at both ends.

Russia's immense spaces required the full use of all routes of transportation, including the major rivers for shipping. Peter the Great saw the problem and started the building of canals to unite major riverways flowing north and south, but it was not until after he died that a connection between the **Нева́** in the north and the **Во́лга** in the south was made. Before the advent of the steamboat, sails **паруса́** supplied some of the power, but the Volga boatmen are more familiar to us as the Russian contribution to river transport. Men who could find no other work became "boatmen" **бурлаки́**—those who pulled the barges **ба́ржи** and ships **суда́** upstream from towpaths along the shore.

These men inspired a very famous painting by Repin entitled "Бурлаки́"; they also supplied the world with the "Volga Boat Song."

Volga "boatmen" бурлаки́ *were not romantic figures, nor were they on boats.*

● Эй, у́хнем! Эй, у́хнем!
Ещё ра́зик, ещё раз!
Разовьём мы березу́,
Разовьём мы кудряву́,
Ай да, да, ай да,
Ай да, да, ай да,
Разовьём мы кудряву́.

8

Play
Óтдых

This chapter provides a view of the Russian's free time, how he uses it, and especially the terminology he applies to it. Because the scope of such a project is close to overwhelming, the space devoted to a topic does not necessarily reflect its importance or popularity. Rather, the activity's popularity is described, while space is given over to the accompanying language that is less familiar to the American. The subject is divided into discussions of:

The time to play
Annual vacations
Short trips
Leisure time
Official sports
Children's play
Traditional amusements

The time to play
Свобóдное врéмя

For children
У детéй

Free time is naturally limited by certain fixed obligations. For children this means that schools are in operation six days a week, even though most adult occupations are now on a five-day week. Therefore only one full free day a week remains. But, except for those attending two-shift schools, children also have much of the afternoon off, attending school only during a rather long morning. For younger pupils this school day is shorter (four forty-five-minute classes a day) than for older pupils (who attend for five or more hours a day). It would be a mistake to say that the time away from classes is really "free time," however, since a major component of education is homework. The academic requirements of the school are such that the time that might be used for youthful digressions and aggressions is very limited. And another major component of education is attendance at various organized activity groups (such as photography "circles" кружки́, chess clubs, and biology clubs) often connected with the schools or with "Pioneer" clubs. The attitude toward these кружки́ is similar to what an American's might be toward the Boy Scouts: for some, the clubs serve to interest, amuse, and develop; for others, they are paramilitary Mickey Mouse.

Attendance at clubs is strongly encouraged by the authorities but limited to not more than two clubs per pupil at any one time.

Annual vacations from school include the fall holidays **осе́нние кани́кулы**, which just precede and include November 7 (the anniversary of the Revolution); the ten days after the New Year **нового́дние кани́кулы**; a spring vacation **весе́нние кани́кулы**, a week at the end of March; and a summer vacation **ле́тние кани́кулы**, which begins at the end of May and continues until September 1, when school starts again.

University students, however, have significantly less free time than American students. Except for some very good students **отли́чники**, who can work out their own study schedule on approval, class attendance is generally compulsory, and many more subjects are required than in the United States; also, course reading lists are immense, and classes are held six days a week. Some time is allowed to prepare for exams or to write dissertations, but, again, it would be difficult to call this free time. Annual vacations include two weeks at the end of January **зи́мние кани́кулы** and the summer vacation **ле́тние кани́кулы** for the months of July and August.

Rather than waiting on tables in summer resorts, the popular Russian student summer work is to join a student construction brigade **студе́нческий строи́тельный отря́д (ССО)**. The work is paid for, often involves fairly distant and rudimentary construction projects, and frequently has the atmosphere of a work party. These work brigades are not the only possibility, of course. Some students do summer work in their own field of study—on an anthropological field trip, an archaeological dig, and so on.

For adults
У взро́слых

The working adult, no less than the schoolchild and the university student, is hard pressed for time. The eight-hour day is standard enough, but time is consumed in many other ways that subtract heavily from what might otherwise be free time. Many people, for instance, take evening and correspondence courses—a popular way to a better job. Though attendance at various meetings is less obligatory than it used to be, parents must go to PTA meetings, workers are urged to attend trade-union meetings, party members are likely to have to go to get-out-the-vote rallies, and so forth. To this must be added the time necessary to support life: standing in line to buy things, for instance, is a major occupation in what often seems to be an anticonsumer-oriented selling process.

A paid annual vacation **о́тпуск** for adults varies from two weeks to a month. Though longer vacations are more common, their length depends on place of work, position occupied, and length of service.

Annual vacations
Ежего́дные отпуска́

The summer vacation comes in two varieties depending on whether or not one can get a **путёвка**, in this case, a reservation at one of the following: (1) a sanatorium **санато́рий**, (2) a "resort" **дом о́тдыха**, (3) a headquarters for hikers **турба́за**, or (4) a small hotel or boardinghouse **пансиона́т**. (Each of these will be discussed.) The **путёвка** gives the right to go to such places at varying rates—sometimes totally free, more often at a reduced rate, or also at the full price. The **путёвка** is a way of distributing still limited resort facilities to the deserving and is usually handled by a trade union or employer. In the general population it is easier for a production worker to get a **путёвка** than it is for a nonproduction worker (a teacher, for instance).

A sanatorium **санато́рий** is closest to what we would call a rest home. People go there for reasons of health more than for recreation—for mud baths, mineral waters, and the like. Those who literally require special medical care are also sent to a sanatorium, usually for no less than twenty-six days.

The **дом о́тдыха** (literally, house of rest) is not what we mean by a rest home nor is it really comparable to our resort. One goes there not for reasons of health but as a reward for having worked well. But it differs from a resort because of the considerable regulation of activities there: morning exercises, meals at a certain time, and rest at a specified hour. A **дом о́тдыха** is usually attended for twelve or twenty-four days.

The **дом о́тдыха** or **санато́рий** is often located at a spa **куро́рт**—any region where the climate, beaches, mineral waters, or any physical aspect of the area is thought to be conducive to good health.

Since these resorts are a reward for good work, it is quite common for one spouse to attend one while the other stays home or finds some other way to amuse himself. For that matter, it is fairly common for Russian couples to vacation separately by choice. This joke appeared in *Вече́рняя Москва́*:

● — Я сказа́ла му́жу, что, е́сли не бу́ду от него́ ежедне́вно получа́ть по письму́, неме́дленно верну́сь с куро́рта домо́й.
— И что же он?
— Пи́шет два ра́за в день!

The **турба́за** (**тури́стская ба́за**) is a sort of hiking headquarters. Some, for older people, are set up as a base for shorter hikes, and others, for younger people, are the starting points for much longer hikes. The length of stay at the **турба́за** varies.

The small hotel or boardinghouse **пансиона́т**, also available through a **путёвка**, has rooms and a dining hall or cooking facilities. The **пансиона́т** is attended by whole families and is in a location conducive to rest and recreation, often with equipment (such as rowboats) for rent **обору́дование на прока́т**.

For those who do not have a **путёвка**, there are still a number of vacation possibilities open. One possibility is renting a room or two in a house in the country **да́ча**. The word **да́ча** describes more the use to which a house is put

rather than what the house looks like. It can range from a peasant hut **изба́** to a rather large affair, some even tinged with former elegance. It is always thought of as being in the country (often with an orchard nearby), but it is usually not far from a large city. The advantages of peace and quiet, country air, and unhurried living must be balanced against the disadvantages inherent in the lack of "conveniences"—plumbing, stores, supplies. Dacha living may be thought of as a kind of "covered" camping with the concomitant pleasures and displeasures; it is usually a vacation device of the urban middle classes.

Long trips are quite common, the country is large, and people do not use space as a barrier. Summer vacations, therefore, often involve long trips. If grandparents or similar relations have a house in the country, then they might become the object of a summer vacation.

Another vacation possibility is renting a room in a resort area, for instance, somewhere along the Black Sea coast. Finding a room to rent is not easy. Such information is either passed from friend to friend, or reservations are arranged by oneself on a previous visit to the area. A local housing bureau **кварти́рное бюро́** located in the municipal services center **исполко́м** at the destination may also be of help. There, one should be able to arrange and find lodging for a ruble a night. To go on such a long trip to a general destination without a **путёвка** is е́хать **дикарём**: "Мы е́здили **дикаря́ми**" (**дика́рь** savage).

For those with cars, there are some camping areas **кэ́мпинг** (*sg.*) with tents **пала́тки** or cabins **до́мики** and cooking and recreational equipment for rent.

Children often accompany their parents in the summer, and many also attend a Pioneer camp **пионе́рский ла́герь**. There is a wide network of such camps, which operate on a schedule of three shifts **сме́на** (*sg.*) per summer, each lasting twenty-six days. The atmosphere is similar to our Boy and Girl Scout camps (taken together, for they are coeducational).

Short trips
За́городные экску́рсии

Perhaps more peculiarly Russian is the short (day or so) trip. For most city dwellers, a short train trip is usually necessary to reach the goal—the real object of this discussion.

The goal of the trip is berries **я́годы** and mushrooms **грибы́** hunted for in the summer and fall. (Mushrooms require some warmth and considerable water. One way of describing a light warm rain is "mushroom rain" **грибно́й дождь**.) This recreation is a major theme in Russian[1] life and lore. You will come across berry picking and mushroom hunting as a national tradition in fairy tales ("Ма́ша пошла́ в лес по грибы́ . . .") and in classic Russian literature; you will also find them a contemporary recreation for Russians high and low. You may properly doubt the "Russianness" of someone unable to distinguish a bolete from a gill mushroom.

Mushrooms and berries are not the only reasons for a short trip: swimming, volleyball, or fishing and a picnic **пикни́к** are often among the goals. A short train trip and perhaps a long walk are often required to reach these objectives, but the walking itself is rarely a goal.

These trips are often made in small groups of six to ten people—Russians like togetherness. (The exception is the hunter and fisherman, who often go alone or in the company of one.) Typically, a lunch is packed, often including such things as sausage **колбаса́** (or **соси́ски**, small sausages reminiscent of frankfurters), bread **хлеб**, cucumbers **огурцы́**, tomatoes **помидо́ры** in season, herring **селёдка**, eggs **я́йца**, and often vodka or wine. If berries and mushrooms are to be collected, then baskets **корзи́нки** for them must also be brought. Trains coming in from the suburbs on summer evenings are often crowded with people carrying baskets covered with leaves to protect the delicate contents.

In winter the short trip is almost as frequent

---

[1] It is not, of course, confined to Russians. In the fall, our woods are combed by Italians, Poles, Chinese, and Japanese —all looking for their favorite mushrooms.

as in the summer, but at this time of year the point of the trip is skiing through winter forests. When a Russian says he is going skiing, by the way, he means cross-country skiing. Skiing is a way to get somewhere, not a slide down a hill.

These short trips for skiing, berry and mushroom collecting, swimming, or just picnicking must be considered the favorite basic delights of the Russians, approached only by perhaps chess and reading.

Leisure time
Досу́г

Reading
Чте́ние

Russians are very avid readers and what is written and by whom it is written is of far greater concern both to the Soviet government and to the people than in the United States. The awe and reverence that an author of good literary fiction or poetry commands make him something of a national monument. The building up or tearing down of these monuments is of much greater concern than the comings and goings of the corresponding (essentially) academic architecture in the United States. Imagine, if you can, a poetry reading that fills a football stadium.

THE LIBRARY   БИБЛИОТЕ́КА

Libraries reflect both the policies and problems of the state. Reading and library use is encouraged, while the contents are limited by current political acceptability and, to some extent, by sheer availability. Many books of foreign publication are kept in special collections open only to authorized scholars.

A library can range from the reading room set aside in a peasant house **изба́-чита́льня** to the massive Lenin Library **Библиоте́ка и́мени Ле́нина** in Moscow. Libraries distribute books in two ways—via reading rooms or through lending libraries.

Books may be checked out for reading on the

A book request form is needed in a reading room.

premises in a reading room **читáльный зал**; this method is most common at the large university or research library. Here one gains entrance with a reader's card **читáтельский билéт**, looks up necessary information about a book in a catalog **катáлог**, fills out a request form **трéбование**, and then gives it to a librarian **библиотéкарь**. Reading rooms at large libraries always seem to be filled because living quarters for students are crowded enough to make home study and reading difficult.

The use of many public and specialized lending libraries is very much encouraged. Here, a library card **библиотéчный абонемéнт** is needed to check out books. ("He is a subscriber to the library" is either **"Он запúсан в библиотéку"** or **"Он абонéнт библиотéки."**)

The Russian librarians' role seems more re-

strictive than that of their American counterparts. Open stacks are much less frequently encountered. For instance, children in school libraries may not just pull a book down from the shelf and start reading. The books are kept behind the librarian's desk or under lock and key and must be checked out before being released to a pupil. The librarian seems primarily a guardian of the storehouse and only secondarily a distributor of the wealth therein.

Theater, concerts, ballet, circus
Теáтр, концéрт, балéт, цирк

Attendance at any of a number of types of spectacles is also perhaps more commonly desired in the USSR, if not more commonly achieved. The problem in almost all cases is getting tickets since the common demand is greater than the supply. Theatergoers approaching the entrance to the theater will often be asked, **"Нет ли у вас лúшних билéтов?"** (**лúшний** extra) To go to a movie in the large cities you must usually buy your tickets in advance. The demand is greatest, of course, on weekends and for better movies. (The general ticket problem will not affect you as a tourist, for tickets are available at the Service Bureau **Бюрó обслýживания** of the hotels.) Ticket prices are much lower than ours for almost all spectacles, but the demand for them is large enough sometimes to turn a ticket into a prize; tickets to the theater or ballet serve, therefore, as a very nice gift.

Tickets are often bought at centrally located ticket offices **театрáльные кáссы**. Not all productions are equally popular, however. If the ticket sales for one show are lagging, then the ticket seller **кассúрша** might insist that you buy a ticket to another less popular performance in addition to the one you want; in this case the latter is called **"билéт с нагрýзкой"**—"a ticket with a load." Devious, effective, common, and illegal.

Applause very frequently takes the form of clapping in rhythm, and Russian performers also have the delightful custom of clapping while their audiences are clapping for them. Americans should note the now ambiguous significance of whistling. It used to be a sign of audience disapproval, as it is elsewhere in Europe, but its meaning depends on the type of performance. Thus, whistling at a ballet still indicates disapproval (and is, in fact, quite rare), while it is not uncommon to hear whistling as approval at popular music events.

Another special feature of any theater (ballet, circus, or the like) is the cloakroom **гардероб**. There is a rule, if not actually a law, that you must remove your overcoat, hat, and rubber overshoes **галоши, боты**. (Exceptions are movies and sports events.) Upon entering, you will see racks of coats, usually behind a waist-high counter, and on the other side of the counter will be the coat checkers **гардеробщик, гардеробщица**, who will give you a coat check **номерок**. (Coats are not hung on a hanger **плечики, вешалка**, but on hooks via a loop **вешалка** at the back of the neck. If you go to the USSR, make sure yours is in good working order or checkers will use a buttonhole for the purpose.) Checking does serve the useful function of limiting applause after a performance; the rush to be first in line to retrieve belongings can seem like a charge of the Light Brigade. There is a way to get ahead in the coat line without actually waiting. The trick is to rent a pair of binoculars from the coat checkers before the performance. Those who have done so will get their coats first. The checkers will say something like **"С биноклями вперёд"** or **"С биноклями без очереди."** The problem of tips is a difficult one: you will officially be told not to tip, but tipping is regularly practiced if there has been a special service. ("I gave him a tip"—**"Я дал ему на чай"**; **"Я дал ему чаевые."**)

Once you have rid yourself of your outer wear, proceed to your seat. Ushers **билетёр** (*sg.*) are stationed at the entrances to concert or theater halls rather than in them. They may be asked which aisle **проход** or stairway **лестница** must be used, but you are expected to find the correct row **ряд** and seat **место**.

Tickets to Soviet theatrical events look as if they have been torn out of a book because they have been.

The theaters built in the old-fashioned opera house arrangement have seating areas designated as follows, starting at the bottom:

партер   the orchestra seats
бенуар   the seats around and behind the orchestra seats and on the same level
бельэтаж   the dress circle, the tier just above the **бенуар**
ярус   any of the tiers above the **бельэтаж**
галерея, галёрка   the topmost balcony
ложа   a box

A newer concert hall will still have the front, main floor seats labeled **партер**, but the section behind them is called **амфитеатр**, while the balcony above will be **балкон**. A program **программа** is usually available for a nominal fee—two to ten kopecks.

As you go from the aisle to your seat, and there are people already seated, face those people even if it seems awkward. If you pass them with your derrière in their direction, they will think you rude.

Hobbies
Хо́бби

There are many other amusements that can take up smaller packages of time. The word **хо́бби** has recently crept into the language. Collecting things is a fairly common hobby: "**Он коллекциони́рует солда́тики[2] ра́зных стран, а моё хо́бби—коллекциони́рование ма́рок**" (**ма́рка** stamp). The larger activities, those requiring considerable tools, equipment, or space, must usually be indulged in via a club, and many others are also considered a sport.

Song and dances
Пе́ние и та́нцы

Both singing and dancing are normal concomitants of any party, especially one that includes food and drink and especially when any type of celebration is involved. Russians seem to know countless songs, and many are able to sing in harmony. If the songs are accompanied, the instrument will most likely be a guitar **гита́ра**, not a balalaika **балала́йка**. The latter is now restricted mostly to professional folk song troupes or to amateur folk song groups formed in and associated with the countryside. Dancing, however, will take many forms, from the traditional Russian folk dances to the relatively sedate ballroom varieties, from the Hebrew Havah Nagilah to versions of what is sometimes called dancing in this country, even including the Charleston **ча́рльстон**. The term **ро́к-н-ро́лл** is part of Russian vocabulary as **джаз** has long been.

Modern popular music, some rock and hard rock, for instance, is officially regarded as decadent and its dissemination is discouraged. So,

[2] The use of the nominative-accusative rather than the genitive plural is apparently justifiable on the grounds that toy soldiers are not alive, nor were they ever.

homemade tapes are frequently made from Western records (even blank recording tape makes a good gift) and Western records themselves are valuable on the black market that has grown to meet the demand.

The museum
Музе́й

When one visits a major museum in the USSR it is more like paying tribute to one's national heritage than attention to self-edification and "culture." (Art is not for art's sake in the USSR.) For one thing the museum building itself is often a major part of the exhibit, if not the entire exhibit, for this is the way the major old churches, cathedrals, and palaces have generally been preserved or even rebuilt. As just one example, the Winter Palace **Зи́мний Дворе́ц** is now an extension of the Hermitage **Эрмита́ж**, one of the most famous art museums in the world. Museum visitors are often asked to don slippers **та́почки** over their shoes to protect that part of the exhibit they will be walking on. Museums often require a small entrance fee, and, as usual, you deposit your overcoat and hat at the cloakroom.

The "club"
Клуб

The club is the major official outlet for authorized and organized activities. It can range from an edifice as grand as a Palace of Culture **Дворе́ц Культу́ры** down to the **изба́-чита́льня** set aside in a small country house. Often it is neither of these, but a medium-sized building whose most common facility is an auditorium **зри́тельный зал** and whatever smaller rooms are necessary or possible.

The club is most often attached to one's place of work and the building itself is often called **дом** or **клуб**: "**Клуб железнодоро́жников, Дом писа́телей, Дом Сове́тский А́рмии**" (**желе́зная доро́га** railroad). The club can also be maintained by sports or scientific organizations, however. For the young set there is the Pioneer Palace **Дворе́ц пионе́ров** or Pioneer House **Дом пионе́ров**. In the big cities the former are often so imposing that they are regularly shown to tourists.

For most people, and especially those in smaller communities in the countryside, the **клуб** is the center of social life. Dances are held there or movies shown. A rather frequent amusement is the amateur hour **ве́чер худо́жественной самоде́ятельности**, a function not confined to country life. The following are fragments from a passage of the book *Колле́ги* by В. Аксёнов that shows what went on in at least one such event (however fictional) that took place in a small club in the country. The hero **Зеле́нин** is talking to his bride **Йнна Зеле́нина**.

● В воскресе́нье Зеле́нин потащи́л Йнну в клуб.
—А что́ там за де́йство сего́дня?
—Снача́ла бу́дет ле́кция об уме́нии краси́во одева́ться. . . . Ле́кция интере́сная, чехослова́цкие мо́ды че́рез прое́ктор бу́дем пока́зывать. . . . Мы и реши́ли вести́ войну́ за хоро́ший вкус.
—Кто это "мы"?
—Правле́ние клу́ба.

. . .

По́сле ле́кции начался́ конце́рт. Зеле́нин то и де́ло появля́лся на сце́не, уча́ствовал в конфера́нсе, прилепи́в боро́дку, игра́л в ске́тче роль профе́ссора, отца́ беспу́тного сы́на, со́льным но́мером чита́л стихи́. . . .
Зеле́нин чита́л стихи́, Тимофе́й игра́л на бая́не заду́мчивые ва́льсы, Да́ша пе́ла часту́шки, Бори́с с како́й-то то́ненькой де́вочкой, о кото́рой сза́ди сказа́ли, что она́ бето́нщица, пока́зывали акроба́тический этю́д. Вдруг Зеле́нин подошёл к кра́ю эстра́ды и гро́мко сказа́л:
—Сле́дующий но́мер—ноктю́рн Шопе́на . . . исполня́ет Йнна Зеле́нина.

Besides providing such social or cultural events, the club is also the place where any of a variety of special interest groups can engage in their special interests. Thus a club might have a billiard or ping-pong table, maintain a supply of skis for lending, house an amateur radio station or reading room, or organize a wide range of sports, cultural, or interest groups.

Playing cards
Игра́льные ка́рты

There are no card games of major national interest as bridge is in the United States. But cards are far from unheard of. Children do play equivalents of hearts, rummy, old maid, and the like: "**Де́ти игра́ют в просто́го дурака́ (в подкидно́го дурака́, в аку́льку, и т. д.).**" The favorite gambling game **аза́ртная игра́** is twenty-one **два́дцать одно́** (though gambling is illegal). Solitaire **пасья́нс** is looked upon as both old fashioned and bourgeois. (To play solitaire is **раскла́дывать пасья́нс.**) **Префера́нс**, a relative of whist, is also played sometimes. In any case, everybody knows the names for cards.

A deck **коло́да** of cards has four suits **четы́ре ма́сти**: spades **пи́ки** (also **ви́ни**), clubs **тре́фы** (also **кре́сти**), diamonds **бу́бны**, and hearts **че́рви**, **че́рвы**. And each suit has **дво́йка, тро́йка, четвёрка, пятёрка, шестёрка, семёрка, восьмёрка, девя́тка, деся́тка, вале́т, да́ма, коро́ль**, and **туз**.

пи́ковая тро́йка, тро́йка пик the three of spades
черво́нный вале́т, вале́т черве́й the jack of hearts
бубно́вая деся́тка, деся́тка бу́бен the ten of diamonds
трефо́вый туз, туз треф, туз крестей́ the ace of clubs

Read the original version of "The Queen of Spades" ("**Пи́ковая да́ма**") by Pushkin. The opera by Tchaikovsky, "The Queen of Spades," based on Pushkin's story, is perhaps even better known to Russians.

Dice and dominoes
Ко́сти и домино́

For gambling purposes dice **ко́сти** (literally, bones) are used, but the usage is perhaps even more limited than it is in the United States, because it is even more lacking in respectability.

However, the word **ко́сти** is also used to denote domino pieces, and the game of dominoes **доминó** is both quite respectable and very popular.

Official sports
Прúзнанные вúды спóрта

Below is a list of the sixty-one sports officially recognized (in 1964) by the Presidium of the Central Council of the Union of Sport Societies and Organizations of the USSR.[3]

For each sport the various norms of achievement required to reach a certain level of proficiency are established. The following are titles bestowed upon those who fulfill the norms:

Спортúвные звáния-разря́ды: (**звáние** title; **разря́д** rank, grade)
Мáстер спóрта СССР междунарóдного клáсса (**междунарóдный** international)
Мáстер спóрта СССР
Спортúвные разря́ды:
Спортсмéн I (пéрвого) разря́да
Спортсмéн II разря́да
Спортсмéн III разря́да
Спортсмéн I ю́ношеского разря́да (**ю́ноша** a youth)
Спортсмéн II ю́ношеского разря́да
Спортсмéн III ю́ношеского разря́да

Not all sports use all the categories (for one reason, because not all sports are played outside the USSR). In chess the title **Гроссмéйстер СССР** replaces **Мáстер спóрта СССР междунарóдного клáсса**.

Each of the ranks has a medal **значóк**, which can be, and often is, worn by those who attain the requirements for that rank. This is just one of the ways of encouraging wide participation in these sports.

The list contains a large number of popular amusements (model airplane and car racing, for instance) and also a large number of paramilitary endeavors—ham radio operation, parachuting, and even fire-fighting exercises. Many

[3] *Едúная всесою́зная спортúвная классификáция на 1965–1968 гг.*, 2ое изд. (Москвá: "Физкульту́ра и спорт," 1967).

of the latter have norms established by the Armed Forces or their auxiliaries, **ДОСААФ** (see " 'Letter' abbreviations" in Chapter 12). Naturally, the list gives the whole range of official possibilities—popularity is something else again. Those sports that are especially popular in the USSR for either participants or spectators are starred. Sports with two, three, five, or many aspects of the general sport under discussion or that are comparable to the collection of sports we call the pentathlon or decathlon are designated by a dagger. The basic minimum equipment for engaging in the sports has been noted in parentheses after each sport, with translations when they were considered necessary.

авиамодéльный спорт   model airplane racing
автомобúльный спорт   automobile racing
автомодéльный спорт   model car racing
акробáтика   acrobatics
альпинúзм   mountain climbing, mostly practiced in the Caucasus and points south since the Urals are not very high (**рюкзáк** knapsack; **спáльный мешóк** sleeping bag; **палáтка** tent; **верёвка** rope; **ледору́б** ice axe; **скáльный молотóк** piton hammer; **топóр** axe)
бадминтóн   badminton (**ракéтка**; **волáн** shuttlecock; **сéтка** net)
баскетбóл*   basketball (**баскетбóльный мяч**; **корзúна** basket)
бокс   boxing. You probably recognize **нокаутúровать, хук, апперкóт.** (**боксёрские перчáтки** gloves; **ринг**; **гонг**)
борьбá вóльная, классúческая, и сáмбо (**самозащúта без ору́жия**) freestyle, Greco-Roman, and judolike wrestling (**мат**)
велосипéдный спорт—гóнки на трéке   bicycle racing on a track (**велосипéд**)
велосипéдный спорт—гóнки на шоссé и кросс   bicycle racing on roads and cross-country
вертолётный спорт   helicopter piloting (**вертолёт**)
вóдное пóло   water polo (**бассéйн**; **мяч**; **ворóта с сéткой**)
вóдно-лы́жный спорт   water skiing (**вóдные лы́жи**; **мотолóдка**)

во́дно-мото́рный спорт motorboat racing (**мотоло́дка**)

вое́нно-прикладны́е ви́ды спо́рта и упражне́ния aspects of sports and exercises that have military applications

волейбо́л* volleyball (**волейбо́льный мяч; се́тка**)

гимна́стика спорти́вная* gymnastics (**бру́сья гимнасти́ческие** parallel bars; **перекла́дина гимнасти́ческая, турни́к** a horizontal bar; **кана́т** a rope; **конь** a side horse or a long horse; **козёл** a (short) horse; **трампли́н** a springboard, not a trampoline; **ко́льца гимнасти́ческие** rings; **шве́дская сте́нка** a stall ladder)

гимна́стика худо́жественная a combination of ballet and gymnastics for women only

городки́ "gorodki," a Russian game described in some detail later (**бита́; городки́**)

гре́бля академи́ческая rowing, as we think of it (**ло́дка** boat; **вёсла** oars)

гре́бля на байда́рках и кано́э kayak and canoe rowing (**байда́рка; кано́э**)

гре́бля на я́лах и наро́дных ло́дках Russian yawl and rowboat rowing (**ял** a small boat; **наро́дная ло́дка** Russian rowboat)

ко́нный спорт horseback riding (**ло́шадь; седло́** saddle)

конькобе́жный спорт* ice skate racing (**коньки́**)

лёгкая атле́тика* track and field (**барье́р** hurdle; **диск** discus; **копьё** javelin; **мо́лот** hammer; **шест** high jump pole; **ядро́** shot)

лы́жный спорт—го́нки, совреме́нное зи́мнее двоебо́рье† и многобо́рье† шко́льников* cross-country ski racing (**лы́жи; лы́жные па́лки**)

лы́жный спорт—го́рные ви́ды downhill skiing

лы́жный спорт—прыжки́ на лы́жах с трампли́на ski jumping (**лы́жи; трампли́н** ski jump)

морско́е многобо́рье† events including swimming, shooting, rowing, sailing, and cross-country running

мотобо́л soccer on a motorcycle (**мотоци́кл; мяч**)

мотоцикле́тный спорт motorcycle racing

ориенти́рование на ме́стности pathfinding, "orienteering" (**ка́рта; ко́мпас**)

парашю́тный спорт parachute jumping (**парашю́т; самолёт**)

па́русный и бу́ерный спорт sailing and iceboat sailing (**па́русная ло́дка** sailboat; **бу́ер** iceboat)

пла́вание swimming (**пла́вательный бассе́йн** swimming pool)

планёрный спорт glider piloting (**планёр**)

подво́дный спорт underwater swimming (**ла́сты** fins; **аквала́нг**)

пожа́рно-прикладно́й спорт aspects of sport applicable to fire-fighting

прыжки́ в во́ду diving (**бассе́йн; трампли́н**)

радиоспо́рт ham radio operating (**переда́тчик** transmitter; **приёмник** receiver)

ре́гби rugby (**мяч**)

ручно́й мяч 7:7 (семь-семь) team handball, played like both soccer and basketball, and especially popular in the Ukraine. The "7" refers to the number of people on the team. (**мяч; се́тка**)

самолётный спорт airplane piloting (**самолёт**)

совреме́нное пятибо́рье,† троебо́рье,† и многобо́рье† ГТО:

пятибо́рье horseback riding, fencing, shooting, swimming, running

троебо́рье shooting, swimming, running

многобо́рье ГТО swimming, shooting, chinning oneself, grenade throwing, cross-country bicycle racing, broad jumping, cross-country running (**ГТО** is a physical fitness slogan, "**Гото́в к труду́ и оборо́не**," and also a set of fitness standards.)

спорти́вное рыболо́вство sport fishing (**у́дочка** pole, hook, line, sinker)

сте́ндовая стрельба́ trap and skeet shooting (**винто́вка** rifle; **мише́ни** targets)

стрелко́вый спорт rifle and target shooting (**винто́вка** rifle; **пистоле́т; револьве́р; мише́нь** target)

стрельба́ из лу́ка archery (**лук** bow; **стрела́** arrow; **мише́нь**) судомоде́льный спорт   model boat racing

те́ннис   tennis (те́ннисный мяч; раке́тка; се́т-
ка; корт)

те́ннис насто́льный (пинг-понг)   table tennis
(мяч целлуло́идный; раке́тка; насто́льная
се́тка; стол)

тури́зм*   hiking, not tourism here (рюкза́к)

тяжёлая атле́тика   weight lifting (шта́нга с
ди́сками barbell; ги́ря a weight; ганте́ли
dumbbells)

фехтова́ние   fencing (рапи́ра foil; шпа́га epee;
эспадро́н saber; ма́ска фехтова́льная)

фигу́рное ката́ние на конька́х*   figure skating
(коньки́)

футбо́л*   soccer (футбо́льный мяч; се́тка;
по́ле field)

хокке́й, хокке́й с ша́йбой, кана́дский хокке́й*
ice hockey (клю́шка hockey stick; ша́йба
puck; коньки́; воро́та хокке́йные goals;
като́к skating rink)

хокке́й с мячо́м, ру́сский хокке́й   a kind of ice
hockey using a ball, not a puck (клю́шка;
мяч; коньки́)

ша́хматы и ша́хматная компози́ция*   chess
and chess problems. It is so universally played
that it will be described in detail separately.
(ша́хматная доска́; фигу́ры; пе́шки)

ша́шки и ша́шечная компози́ция   checkers and
checkers problems (ша́шечная доска́; ша́шки)

Soccer
Футбо́л

Soccer means almost more to the Russian
than baseball does to the American. Huge sta-
diums are regularly filled with eager fans
боле́льщики: "I'm rooting for 'Spartak'"—
"Я боле́ю за Спарта́к." Moreover, almost
every little boy learns to play soccer. Soccer
teams are at least as famous as our baseball
teams and a correspondence to the World
Series can be found in play for the USSR Cup
Ку́бок СССР, not to mention world, European,
and USSR championships—пе́рвенство ми́ра,
пе́рвенство Евро́пы, пе́рвенство СССР, чем-
пиона́т СССР—and the Olympic games олим-
пи́йские и́гры. The most commonly used team
names are Спарта́к, Дина́мо, and Торпе́до, all
of which may be from any city or organization,
although the best known are the Moscow teams.
Sometimes the team name gives a clue to who is
represented: Локомоти́в designates the railroad
workers and Кры́лья Сове́тов the airplane
makers. Others simply announce who they are:
ЦДСА (цэдэса́) Центра́льный дом Сове́тской
А́рмии, ВВС (вэвээ́с) Военновозду́шные си́лы.

The foreign (namely, English) origin of the
game is reflected in some of the terminology that
seems to leap from a page of otherwise impene-
trable prose: the game is played in two halves,
пе́рвый тайм and второ́й тайм, both of which
last forty-five minutes with a ten- or fifteen-

В - *ворота* (goal)
Б - *площадь ворот* (goal area)
А - *точка 11-метрового удара* (penalty spot)
Все размеры в метрах (all measurements are in meters)

Площа́дка для игры́ (по́ле)   *A soccer field*

minute break **переры́в**. The game is played by two teams **кома́нды** of eleven members, who can have the following positions:

Футбо́льная кома́нда:

оди́н врата́рь (*formerly* **голки́пер**)
три полузащи́тника (*formerly* **ха́вбек**)
два защи́тника (*formerly* **бек**)
пять напада́ющих (*formerly* **фо́рвард**)

Actually, terminology using the Russian roots is more commonly used now, but the eradica-

tion of foreign roots is far from complete: **ко́рнер** is also **угловой уда́р**, and **áут** is **мяч вы́шел за боковую черту́**; **офса́йд** and **гол** remain the same except that "He made (kicked) a goal" can be either "**Он заби́л мяч**" or "**Он заби́л гол**"; a penalty (kick) is **одиннадцатиметро́вый штрафно́й уда́р** or **пена́льти**, and a referee is **судья́** or **ре́фери́**; **помо́щник судьи́** is a linesman.

To express displeasure with a referee, or, for that matter, with the players, a common entreaty is: "**На мы́ло!**"—"Make soap out of him!"

The following is an account of a game between an all-star **сбо́рная** team from the USSR playing a similar team from (and in) the German Democratic Republic (East Germany):

СПОРТ

А ПОБЕДА БЫЛА БЛИЗКА

ОЧЕНЬ поздно закончился товарищеский футбольный матч между сборными Германской Демократической Республики и Советского Союза, проходивший в Лейпциге.

Сборная СССР вышла на поле в составе: Рудаков, Пономарев, Шестернев, Капличный, Хурцилава, Ловчев, Мунтян, Еськов, Пузач, Хусаинов и Хмельницкий. В составе команды ГДР — игроки девяти клубов.

Интересно отметить, что за последние шесть лет немецкая сборная на своем поле проигрывала всего лишь два раза. Вот и вчера хозяева начали матч весьма активно, и уже на шестой минуте 23-летний Леве великолепным ударом открыл счет. Лишь на 35-й минуте Пузач провел не менее красивую «сольную» атаку и забил ответный гол.

Во втором тайме наши футболисты действовали более активно. Блестящим ударом Хмельницкий на 14-й минуте забил второй гол в сетку ворот хозяев поля. Но, к сожалению, гости не смогли удержать победный счет. За две минуты до конца Френцель, игрок олимпийской сборной ГДР, завоевавшей в 1964 году бронзовые медали, сквитал счет. В итоге ничья — 2 : 2.

Chess[4]
Ша́хматы

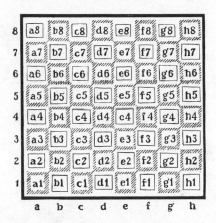

Ша́хматная доска́

Chess is doubtless the most popular table game in the Soviet Union. Apparently, it is played by everyone, from the youngest to the oldest, and is, as mentioned, one of the country's officially recognized "sports." Here the major Russian terminology used in playing is presented, including the Russian (European) notational system. You must learn to play chess from some other source, however, for its intricacy defies elucidation here. For those to whom chess is a way of life, all Soviet rules and regulations appear in *Ша́хматный ко́декс СССР.*

The chessboard is **ша́хматная доска́**, a black square is **чёрное по́ле**, and a white square is **бе́лое по́ле**. The European notational system is used, as shown in the illustration. Notice that the letters are in Latin script. They are pronounced in Russian as: **"а," "бэ," "цэ," "дэ," "е," "эф," "же," "аш."**

For Russians there are two kinds of chessmen —the pawn **пе́шка** and all the remaining chess pieces **фигу́ры**. There are names, both formal and colloquial, for the individual pieces and standard notation for them in Russian, as is shown in the following table:

English	Formal Russian	Conversa-tional Russian	English abbrevia-tion	Russian abbrevia-tion
pawn	пе́шка	пе́шка	P	п[2] (*pl.* пп)
rook or castle	ладья́	тура́	R	Л
knight	конь	конь	Kt	К
bishop[1]	слон	офице́р	B	С
queen[3]	ферзь	короле́ва	Q	Ф
king	коро́ль	коро́ль	K	Кр

[1] One wonders how "elephant," "officer," and "bishop" all came to signify this piece.
[2] In describing the plays the Russian abbreviation for pawn is usually not written at all.
[3] Promotion or queening is **пе́шку прово́дят в ферзи́**.

A turn, move, or play **ход** may be specified further as Black's turn **ход чёрных, ход—чёр-ным**; or White's turn **ход бе́лых, ход—бе́лым**. There are also varying ways of writing down what happened in a chess game.

Event		Notation	
English	Russian	English	Russian
check	шах	ch × †	+
checkmate	мат	× × ††	×
capture	взя́тие	×	:
double check	двойно́й шах	dbl ch	+ +
castling on king's side	коро́ткая рокиро́вка	0–0	0–0
castling on queen's side	дли́нная рокиро́вка	0–0–0	0–0–0

In discussions and comments on games, the same notations are used, though perhaps the Russians use more of them, as shown here:

~   любо́й ход
!   хоро́ший, си́льный ход
!! прекра́сный, блестя́щий ход
?   плохо́й ход, оши́бка
?? гру́бая оши́бка

[4] The name of the game is not without interest: **шах** in Persian means king, as in the *Shah* of Iran. (This root as used in chess is also the origin of our word "check," both the financial and political kind.) **Мат** in Arabic means dead: **шах + мат**—checkmate—the king is dead.

!?	ход, приводя́щий к нея́сным осложне́-ниям
=	ша́нсы сторо́н приме́рно равны́
±	положе́ние бе́лых лу́чше
±	у бе́лых преиму́щество
∓	положе́ние чёрных лу́чше
∓	у чёрных преиму́щество

There are also two different ways for writing down the progression of moves; the full notation **по́лная нота́ция** is used when games are officially being described, while the short notation **коро́ткая нота́ция** will often be used in the commentator's notes.

По́лная нота́ция	Кра́ткая нота́ция
Kgl-f3	Kf3 (1)
e2-e4	e4
Cc1-e3 Kg4:e3	Ce3 K:e3
d7-d8Ф	d8Ф
e2-e4 e7-e5	e4 e5
d2-d4 e5:d4	d4 ed (2)
Фd1:d4 Kb8-c6	Ф:d4 Kc6
Фd4-e3 Kg8-f6	Фe3 Kf6
Фd3-h7+?	Фh7+?

- (1) ука́зывается то́лько по́ле, куда́ ста́вится фигу́ра и́ли пе́шка;
- (2) при взя́тии пе́шкой пи́шется вертика́ль, на кото́рой она́ стоя́ла, и вертика́ль, на кото́рую перешла́ в результа́те взя́тия.

The game is traditionally divided into three sections: the opening **дебю́т**, which might involve a gambit **гамби́т**; the mid-game **ми́ттельшпиль**; and the end game **э́ндшпиль**. In the course of the game, various plays **комбина́ции** might be used. If no win is possible, then the game is a draw **ничья́**: "**Па́ртия зака́нчивается вничью́**"; "**Па́ртия счита́ется ничье́й.**" A drawn game may result from a stalemate **пат**.

In describing the game it is interesting to note that the two sides, **чёрные** and **бе́лые**, are often referred to in the plural: "**Бе́лые проведу́т одну́ из свои́х пе́шек в ферзи́ и даду́т мат.**"

"Gorodki"
Городки́

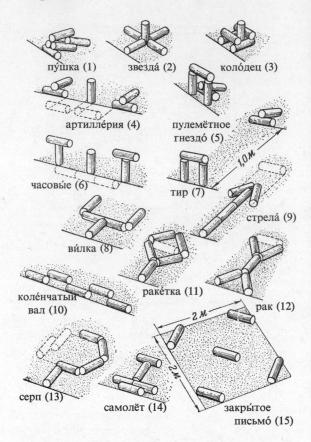

пу́шка (1)   звезда́ (2)   коло́дец (3)
артилле́рия (4)   пулемётное гнездо́ (5)
часовы́е (6)   тир (7)
стрела́ (9)
ви́лка (8)
коле́нчатый вал (10)   раке́тка (11)   рак (12)
серп (13)   самолёт (14)   закры́тое письмо́ (15)

Городо́шные фигу́ры. *Only the first few figures should be thought of as generally familiar to Russians. The remaining ones are shown here to give some idea of the extent of the game.*

(1) Cannon	(9) Arrow
(2) Star	(10) Crankshaft
(3) Well	(11) Racket
(4) Artillery	(12) Crayfish
(5) Machine gun nest	(13) Sickle
(6) Sentries	(14) Airplane
(7) Shooting range	(15) Sealed (closed)
(8) Fork	letter

This game, like **лапта́**, which is described in the discussion on children's games, is a traditional Russian game both in origin and development, but unlike **лапта́** it has gained the superior status of an officially recognized sport. As a result the equipment for the game is regularly manufactured and generally standardized now (though this was not true until the Soviet period). The game is relatively simple and anyone can play, regardless of age or size. It consists of throwing a long (one meter) stick **бита́** at a set of small cylindrical (two by eight inch) sticks **городки́**, thereby removing the small set of sticks from the target area **го́род**. Though presumably any even number of people can play, an official team **кома́нда** consists of five players. (A player at **городки́** is a **городо́шник**.) Each team has a target area two meters square, in the front line **кон** of which the **городки́** are arranged.

Each team has its own target area **го́род**, and each player in turn has two throws of the **бита́** to try to knock the five small sticks out of place. The first figure must be disarranged at a distance of thirteen meters **броски́ с ко́на**, but the remaining figures, except the last one, are thrown at from a distance of six and one-half meters **броски́ с полуко́на**.

Бросо́к биты́

"Лобово́й" уда́р

The technique of the game involves throwing the **бита́** sideways, not end over end, so that it hits the center of the stack of **городки́** broadside **лобово́й уда́р** (literally, frontal attack).

Since **городки́** is an officially recognized sport, there are requirements for official recognition as "Master of Sport" and other titles, which included, for the years 1965–68, the following:

● Ма́стер спо́рта—затра́тить не бо́лее 156 бит на 90 фигу́р и вы́полнить да́нную но́рму в тече́ние го́да два́жды: оди́н раз на соревнова́ниях не ни́же городско́го масшта́ба при усло́вии уча́стия в них не ме́нее трёх спорти́вных организа́ций разли́чных ве́домств и ДСО; второ́й раз на пе́рвенстве СССР, пе́рвенствах и зона́льных соревнова́ниях сою́зных респу́блик, Москвы́ и Ленингра́да, всесою́зных пе́рвенствах ве́домств, пе́рвенствах центра́льных и республика́нских сове́тов ДСО,

и л и

установи́ть реко́рд СССР в коли́честве затра́ченных бит на 15, 30, 45, 60, 90 фигу́р на ли́чных и́ли кома́ндных соревнова́ниях.

I разря́д—затра́тить не бо́лее 165 бит на 90 фигу́р.

II разря́д—затра́тить не бо́лее 140 бит на 60 фигу́р и́ли 216 бит на 90 фигу́р.

III разря́д—затра́тить не бо́лее 165 бит на 60 фигу́р и́ли 90 бит на 30 фигу́р.

I ю́ношеский разря́д (16–18 лет)—затра́тить не бо́лее 175 бит на 60 фигу́р и́ли 85 бит на 30 фигу́р с расстоя́ния 13 м.

II ю́ношеский разря́д (до 16 лет)—затра́тить не бо́лее 105 бит на 30 фигу́р и́ли 50 бит на 15 фигу́р с расстоя́ния 10 м.

The score
Счёт

Though both words have other uses, **счёт** is the score and **очко́** means a point. The Soviet sports fan uses the following terminology to keep track of who is winning:

Како́й счёт?   What is the score?
  Семь пять. (7:5)   Seven to five.
Ско́лько очко́в он набра́л?   How many points did he make?
  Три очка́.   Three points.
  То́лько одно́.   Only one.

Сухóй счёт.[5] No score (made by one side). (*literally* dry score)

Онú сыгрáли всухýю.[5] They didn't score once.

Он размочúл счёт.[5] He made the first score (for his team). (*literally* "He got the score wet.")

сквитáть счёт, сравнять счёт to even the score

ничья́ a tie

Матч закóнчился вничью. The game ended in a tie.

Two sets of words are commonly used for winning and losing:

вы́игрыш a win	**прóигрыш** a loss
Кто вы́играл?	**Кто проигрáл?**
Who won?	Who lost?
побéда a victory	**пораже́ние** a defeat
Кто победúл? Who won (beat)?	

Children's play
Дéтские úгры

Toys
Игрýшки

There is a universality about toys. Babies start out with a rattle **погремýшка** and from there graduate to various stuffed toys **набивны́е игрýшки,** such as a doll **кýкла (быва́ют и говоря́щие и шага́ющие кýклы)** or a teddy bear **мúшка (медвéдь = Мúша).** Later on, dolls become more sophisticated in a childish way when they are often made to represent characters in children's fairy tales, both modern and ancient: **Дóктор Айболúт** (from Chukovsky's rendition of Dr. Doolittle), or **Буратúно** (Pinocchio), and many others that can be identified only through familiarity with the stories themselves. **Кýкла** is used for puppets also. Puppetry is a commonly enjoyed recreation which has been elevated by the now world-famous puppet theater of V. Obraztsov: **"Дава́й игра́ть в кýкольный теа́тр"** —"Let's play (with) puppets."

5 These terms are used in soccer scores.

The classic figure in a puppet show was and is **Петрýшка.** He is represented as a peasant/clown who by wile and wit is able to do in his adversaries, the latter often being those of considerably higher status in society than he. (**Петрýшка** is also used to denote this puppetry as a whole, and, by association, has become a pejorative slang expression for something or someone who is stupid, funny, awkward, or strange: **"Вот кака́я петрýшка получúлась!"**)

Children must also have their blocks **кýбики**; **чýрки, чýрочки** are a variation of blocks in that, though they serve the same general purpose, their shapes include pyramids, sticks, cones, discs, and so on. Blocks are also often made specifically to form a traditional shape: the Savior's Tower **Спáсская бáшня** (the major entrance to the Kremlin from Red Square) is one such favorite subject.

A cross between dolls and blocks is achieved with the ubiquitous **матрёшка,** a gaily painted and stylized figurine of a peasant woman. Many pull apart to reveal a smaller edition of the same figure inside, which also pulls apart, and so on. This same motif is taken up by **шар с яйцами,** a simple wooden ball that pulls apart and contains many more little balls inside.

Another fairly common Russian toy is a figurine or doll so constructed that it will always right itself. **Вáнька-встáнька** is one name for such a device, especially if the figure is a male; **неваля́шка** is another name applied to the female counterpart.

Other common and universal toys are:

мяч ball (**"Малышú игра́ют в мя́чик."**)

скака́лка a jump rope (*less common* **пры́галка**)

воздýшный шар a balloon

юла́, волчóк a top

свистýлька a whistle (**свистéть** to whistle)

змей a kite

бараба́н a drum

бирю́льки pickup sticks, played like jackstraws except that any large collection of small objects may be used and these objects must be picked up with a small hooked stick

калейдоскóп   a kaleidoscope
катáлка   a pull toy
телéжка   a wagon
заводнáя игрýшка   a windup toy
óбруч   a hoop ("Пéтька óбруч гоня́ет.")
лошáдка, конь на пáлочке   a toy horse

Many toys are simply reductions of things children might have to deal with in the future: a small car **машúнка**, a truck **грузовúк**, a crane **подъёмный кран**, a sailboat **корáблик**, not to mention tools of all shapes and sizes.

Organized play areas, those connected to nurseries or kindergartens, often have larger pieces of equipment. A sandbox **песóчница** (**песóк** sand) requires a small bucket **ведёрко**, a shovel **лопáтка** or **совóк**, perhaps a rake **грáбли**, and a wheelbarrow **тáчка** for making mud pies **пирожкú, кулúчики**, or for building a fort **крéпость** (not a castle, as in English). These play areas also might have a swing **качéли** and a seesaw, also called **качéли**. Russian swings, by the way, are likely to hold more than one person and hang from two to four long steel bars or pipes rather than chains as do ours. (Originally they were long wooden poles suspended from the limb of a tree.) Another piece of playground equipment resembles a rocking chair, except that there are two seats facing each other, both mounted on the same rockers. This is a **качáлка**. The very well equipped play area might even have a small rendition of a merry-go-round **карусéль**. And in the winter a common sight is an "ice mountain" for sliding **ледянáя горá, ледянáя дорóжка**.

Some children's toys also go under the heading of sports equipment. Winter weekends are often spent skiing **катáться на лы́жах**, so that skis **лы́жи** are very commonly owned or easily accessible. Since Russians ski cross-country, their skis are narrower than ours. For children the bindings are vastly less complicated and are strapped onto regular boots; adults often use ski boots, reserving safety bindings for mountain skiing, a far less popular kind of skiing. Winter also requires skates **конькú** and a myriad of

sleds **сáнки** (**салáзки**, a somewhat old-fashioned term); the latter are used both for grandmother's convenience (hauling water or grandchildren) and children's fun.

Toys and play equipment are also often homemade. For instance, stilts **ходýли** ("Он идёт на ходýлях"), a kite **змей** ("Дéти запускáли змéя"), a whistle **свистýлька,** a scooter **самокáт**, and the inevitable slingshot **рогáтка** are often of the homemade variety.

Russian toy collections tend to be relatively small. This is so not for lack of parental regard or even money but because storage space is limited. Actually, most of the usual games that children play require a minimal amount of equipment anyway.

Games outside
Ѝгры на ýлице

Winter and snow bring all sorts of possibilities for play. One can throw snowballs **игрáть в снежкú**, build and use a fort **игрáть в крéпость**, slide down a hill on a sled **сáнки**, and build a snowman **лепúть снéжную бáбу** (literally, snowwoman). Children almost always learn to ice skate **катáться на конькáх**, and also to ski **катáться на лы́жах**.

In the summer, children, girls especially, play hopscotch **игрáть в клáссы** according to the same principles that ours do. Boys play a game with knives **игрáть в нóжички**, which requires them to gain a specified territory ("давáй зéмлю делúть"), throwing a knife into the ground a certain way. Marbles are nonexistent.

Кýча-малá falls somewhat short of being a game. The setting requires a group of children playing outdoors (and sometimes indoors, too). For one reason or another, one of them falls. Suddenly one or several others yell "кýчамалá!" whereupon all the children race to pile on top of the one who fell. In some places the point is to avoid being the last one to join the pile, for he is the fool **дурáк**.

Горéлки is a traditional game still often

played, in Pioneer camps, for instance. The children line up in pairs with one child left over; he is "it," **горе́лка** in this case. The first pair, holding hands, starts running while the rest of the children chant

● Гори́, гори́ я́сно,
Чтобы не пога́сло.
Глянь на не́бо,
Пти́чки летя́т,
Колоко́льчики звеня́т!
Раз, два, не воро́нь!
Беги́, как ого́нь!

The moment the chanting is finished, the **горе́лка** races to catch the pair that had started running. If he catches either of them, he then takes the other as partner and the one who was tagged becomes the **горе́лка** for the next turn.

Russians have many of the group chasing games we do. A parallel to playing cowboys and Indians is **игра́ть в «казаки́-разбо́йники»**. Russian cops and robbers **сы́щики и во́ры** often consists of more than two groups of children chasing one another. Roles in the game are assigned by drawing lots **выбира́ют по жре́бию**. Depending on the number of children, there might be two detectives **два сы́щика**, two thieves **два во́ра**, one judge **оди́н судья́**, and two policemen **дво́е полице́йских**, for instance.

Playing hide-and-seek **игра́ть в пря́тки, пря́танки** is as common as it is here and uses the same ground rules: the person who is "it" hides his head and counts up to any agreed upon number (**раз, два, три, . . .**) while the other children run and hide; when he is done he yells, **"Я иду́ иска́ть!"**—"Here I come, ready or not!" In the variation **па́лочки-стука́лочки**, a stick is left at home base and those who have hidden must get back to there and bang with the stick before they are found (**"Я тебя́ ви́жу"**) by the one who is "it."

Playing tag is **игра́ть в догоня́лки** or **игра́ть в са́лки**. The person who is "it" is the **са́лка** (**са́ло** fat, lard), who must run and tag another who then becomes the **са́лка**: **"Са́лка, са́лка, дай колба́ски!"**—"Neah, neah, can't catch me!" Another form of tag is **пятна́шки**, where

пятна́шка, the one who is "it," must either throw a ball and hit or tag by hand one of the other players in order to catch him.

Perhaps leapfrog **игра́ть в чехарду́** falls short of being a game, yet children play it. And races are run everywhere:

На старт! On your mark!
Внима́ние! Get set!
Марш! Go!
Раз, два, три . . . Марш! One, two, three . . . Go!

Totally unfamiliar to us, however, is a traditional Russian game **лапта́**. The formal requirements of the game are minimal and vary according to what is locally available. A ball about the size of a tennis ball or perhaps smaller and a bat **лапта́**, which may be a stick, are required. The official bat is no more than 1.2 meters long with a diameter up to 5 centimeters. The playing field should be about seventy to eighty meters long and thirty to forty meters wide. (A scrub version, **кругова́я лапта́**, requires less space and is therefore popular in cities.) The players divide into two teams of five to fifteen players each. One team **бью́щая кома́нда, го́род** is at bat, and the other **водя́щая кома́нда, по́ле** is in the field. Someone from the field team pitches **подаёт мяч** to an opponent at bat, who tries to hit the ball as hard and as far as possible. If someone in the field catches a fly ball, then the teams change places **"го́род про́дан," горожа́не иду́т в по́ле**; otherwise the batter runs to the other end of the field (a line previously established among the players) and then back again. In this run he must avoid being hit with the ball or being tagged by someone with the ball, since that will also result in an "out" **"го́род взят,"** and the teams will change places. A run is one point **одно́ очко́**. (You are much more likely to read about **лапта́** than to see it. Though officially Russians are supposed to take pride in the game, contemporary children prefer to play soccer if they possibly can.)

Games inside
Игры в доме

The games **каравай** and **кошки-мышки** are played by smaller children. For **каравай** (literally, a large round loaf of bread) one child is chosen to be in the center of a circle formed by the other children holding hands. The game begins when the children circle to the left and sing (about the child in the center, here called **Алёша**), "**Как на Алёшины именины, испекли мы каравай.**" Then the children in the circle raise their (joined) hands high and say, "**Вот такой вышины,**" lower them to the floor and sing, "**Вот такой нижины,**" spread out as far as possible singing, "**Вот такой ширины,**" and rush to the center and sing, "**Вот такой ужины.**" Next they begin circling again, this time chanting, "**Каравай каравай, кого любишь, выбирай,**" until the child in the center has chosen the next one to stand in the center. The cat and mouse game **игра в кошки-мышки** requires one child as the mouse and one as the cat. The other children join hands in a circle and try to keep the cat from catching the mouse by letting the mouse in and out of the circle freely while making it difficult for the cat.

Blindman's buff is a common childhood game: **Дети играют в жмурки** (**жмуриться** to squint or close eyes). The principle is the same as always: the child who is "it" is blindfolded and spun around while the other children question him: "**Где стоишь?—На мосту**"; "**Что продаёшь?— Квас.**" Then they issue the challenge: "**Ищи три года нас!**" Rules vary; sometimes the blindman has only to catch one of the other children, but sometimes he must also identify his prey. In a variation the "blindman" is called the cat **кот** and the other children give themselves bird names—**галка, синица,** or **воробей,** for instance. The **кот** must identify the bird before his duties are discharged.

Horses and riders **лошади и всадники** is a more boisterous game and can occur when the teacher is absent from class. The children form pairs of "horses" carrying their riders piggyback; the point is to force the other riders to fall off or lose balance without doing so oneself.

Another common childish occupation is to play **масло жать** (literally, oil or fat squeezing). This often occurs when any group of children is standing lined up or seated in a row on a bench. The point is to squeeze as many people out of line as possible while remaining in line oneself.

Игра в фанты is basically similar to charades, except that the charade **фант** is often a request to do something silly, tending to make a fool of the one who must fulfill the request. Much depends on who is playing the game, of course: "**Кому какой фант выпал?**"—"Who has to do which (trick)?"

Another game **играть в фантики** involves a carefully folded candy wrapper **фантик.** The object is to make one's **фантик** go farther when it is thrown in a certain way.

Russian children also play a version of "telephone" **Играют в глухой телефон, испорченный телефон.** The children line up, a leader thinks of a word, whispers it to the first one in line, who whispers it to the next, and so on. At the end the last person says out loud what the word was. If there is a change, then there is a search made for the person who first misunderstood the word. That person is the next one to be "it."

A relative of bingo is **лото,** requiring a leader to call numbers and players with cards to be filled up, five in a row or the like. It is frequently encountered as a teaching toy, where numbers are replaced, for instance, by pictures of objects that the children must understand before they can fill out their cards.

You may also play tick-tack-toe in the USSR: **Дети играют в крестики-нолики.** (х—**крестик,** о—**нолик.**)

Who is "it"?
Чья очередь?

Rather inconveniently, the Russians have no one word like "it" to denote the person playing the main role in children's games. Russian equivalents can vary according to the game it-self. Thus, if they are playing **горе́лки** then **горе́лка** is "it"; if **са́лки**, then **са́лка**; if **пятна́шки**, then **пятна́шка** is "it"; if **жму́рки**, then **кот**; and so on. Another practice, though a formal one, is to refer to "it" as **води́тель, вожа́к, водя́щий**. A common solution to the problem is just to say "Whose turn is it?"—"**Чья о́чередь?**" or "**Кому́ води́ть?**" or "**Кто во́дит?**"

Determining the first person to be "it" is commonly done in either of two ways—by using a counting rhyme **счита́лка** or by drawing lots **выбира́ть по жре́бию, по жеребьёвке**.

The counting rhymes referred to here (for there are many others) are those used as we use "eenie, meenie... "; the problem is that there does not seem to be one generally recognized equivalent rhyme for choosing who is to be "it." The following are examples of **счита́лки** and the first two are especially popular:

> Э́ники, бе́ники
> Е́ли варе́ники,
> Э́ники, бе́ники
> Клёц.

> ● На злато́м крыльце́ сиде́ли
> Царь, царе́вич, коро́ль, короле́вич,
> Сапо́жник, портно́й.
> Отвеча́й, кто ты тако́й.

> Э́кета пэ́кета цу́кота мэ́,
> А́бель фа́бель до́минэ,
> Йки пи́ки граммати́ки,
> Он-зос-пёс.

> ● В э́той ма́ленькой корзи́нке
> Есть пома́да и духи́,
> Ле́нты, кру́жево, боти́нки,
> Всё, что ну́жно для души́.

Traditional amusements
Традицио́нные развлече́ния

The amusements and delights of the former upper classes will not be considered here: these were often an attempt to do what was thought to be done in the "sophisticated" West, and most of the forms are therefore familiar to us.

For the Russian peasants, however, things were different. All of life was a do-it-yourself affair—including recreation. Unable to read, they told stories instead; singing and dancing were very popular; and toys were made from available materials.

Many of the country joys were connected with the holidays (see Chapter 6) or with the various turning points of life—births, weddings, and funerals. Singing and dancing were major accompaniments to these celebrations, and their songs and dances **обря́довые пе́сни и хорово́ды** are the oldest; the songs we think of as Russian folk songs are of more recent origin. Traditional dancing most often took the form of a **хорово́д**, which was essentially any kind of group dance in a circle. (Even children holding hands and skipping around a Christmas tree is therefore a **хорово́д**.)

Children played a game called **ба́бки**, which required a set of cattle knucklebones. One piece **свинча́тка** was made heavier by stuffing it with lead **свине́ц**; the other pieces **ба́бка, ба́бки** were lined up in a row, and the object was to use the heavy piece to knock the others out of place. You could keep the ones you knocked out. (The closest American equivalent is surely marbles.)

Children were not the only ones who played on swings **каче́ли** suspended by two long poles hung from a tree. Traditionally, the **каче́ли** did not make their appearance until **ма́сленица**.

A kind of Russian baseball **лапта́**, though very traditional, is discussed under contemporary games children play because they still do. Another very Russian game is **городки́**, now an officially recognized sport and therefore described in that section.

The sewing bee
Посиде́лки (*pl. only*)

The Russian stove **ру́сская печь** (see Chapter 4) was a very creditable solution to the problem of winter cold. The **посиде́лки** was the Russian peasant answer to long winter evenings. The (usually unmarried) girls of the village would congregate at a house **изба́**, often one rented for the purpose. They brought some handwork to do—spinning, sewing, and so on. The girls were joined at these affairs by the young men of the village. In some places it was customary for the men to supply the necessary food or libation, and in others the men were guests. The evening was spent mostly in singing, sometimes in dancing, and frequently in playing games; often singing games or contests were the vehicle for merriment. You might also assume that these evenings were enlivened by some flirtation.

The **посиде́лки** has not yet been completely eliminated from rural life, but its existence does not seem to meet with official approval:

● Посиде́лки встреча́ются гла́вным о́бразом там, где ещё ма́ло культу́рных учрежде́ний и́ли где они́ недоста́точно хорошо́ рабо́тают.[6]

6 Алекса́ндров, *Наро́ды европе́йской ча́сти СССР*, стр. 452.

9

Speech
Речь

This chapter deals with some major and minor aspects of speech and language that are not usually discussed in language texts. It is important to be able to recognize northern and southern Russian accents or "illiterate" speech (if such is possible) and to know some of the common expletives. Russian pig Latin is included just for fun. The major topics discussed here are:

Speech and society
Some special concerns of Russian speech
"Sudden" words and "semiwords"
Terms of rejection and endearment
Expletives
Unprintable words

Speech and society
Речь и общество

Styles of speech
Стили речи

Style is just the way somebody goes about saying or writing something. As with many things in life, it is exactly this, the way something is done, that is so very important. For all its importance, however, style is a difficult thing to describe accurately. The language in a scientific article is different from the language in an historical treatise, which is, in turn, different from journalese or standard colloquial speech or the language of peasants, and so on. And all of these different forms change with time.

The differences exist, and with time and considerable practice you will begin to notice them. Try reading many newspapers at once, and then read many children's stories at once. Don't bother to look up all the words you don't know, but notice how many words and phrases are repeated again and again. Observe how some characters in modern writing tend to use phrases you learned in school and how others seem not to have heard of your school texts. Notations in dictionaries that indicate style or obsolescence are helpful; for example: **книжн.(ое слово)** literary or pedantic, **прост.(оречие)** informal or slang, **устар.(елое)** obsolete, **обл.(астное)** regional, **брáн.(ное)** abusive or swear word, **разг.(оворное)** informal, **стар.(инное)** archaic. But you must pay attention to the publication date of the dictionary. The most recent should surely indicate current usage, and a thirty-year-old dictionary is by that much out of date.

For guides to various levels of speech or styles in writing, there are many books available with **культу́ра ре́чи** or **стили́стика** in the title. One very good, relatively short text by L. A. Kiselyova and others, *A Practical Handbook of Russian Style* (Moscow: Progress Publishers, no date), deals especially with styles in Russian for speakers of English and includes a key to the exercises. And Корне́й Чуко́вский, *Живо́й как жизнь* (Москва́: Изд. "Де́тская литерату́ра," 1966) gives a clever and delightful presentation of one man's view of Russian, how it has changed in his lifetime, what trends he thinks are unhappy, which are unavoidable, and which are to be relished.

For those Americans interested in contemporary colloquial Russian usages, especially recommended are Soviet sources, including publications of the Center for Russian Language Studies of Moscow University (Нау́чно-методи́ческий центр ру́сского языка́ при МГУ). Teachers of Russian would profit from the center's magazine *Ру́сский язы́к за рубежо́м*, which often contains articles describing current styles and levels—what greetings are used and when, how to phrase requests, and so forth. Both Moscow and Leningrad universities have published a number of very good texts for developing conversational Russian (with titles such as *Посо́бие по разви́тию ре́чи*). Their only drawback is that they are frequently out of print.

Such publications are useful because usages change, and the spoken language reflects those changes more quickly than the written language. For example, a formalist of English in the 1920's could insist on "It is I." To do so now, however, is quaint at best and ridiculous most of the time. Russian has undergone similar changes in the USSR. A **фуфа́йка** is no longer normally a sweater, and **"Как вы поживаете?"** is not an equivalent for the English greeting "How are you?" (Use instead **"Как живёте?** or **"Как дела́?"** or **"Что но́вого?"**)

To enumerate the world of Russian slang is a larger task than there is space for here.[1] For the foreigner slang in another language can often be identified by the appearance of an unusual or unfamiliar word or expression in place of the expected one. Here are some examples from *Живо́й как жизнь*, by Чуко́вский:

хорошо́!—блеск! си́ла! мирово́! мирове́цки!
напи́ться допьяна́—накиря́ться
пойдём обе́дать—пошли́ руба́ть
мне э́то неинтере́сно—а мне до ла́мпочки
спать—кима́рить, заземли́ться
расска́зывать анекдо́ты—трави́ть анекдо́ты

The foreigner is better off making it a rule never to use either slang or the expression labeled **простра́чие** in the dictionary. **Простора́чие** seems to cover a nebulous area of speech that ranges from slang to colloquial.[2] The reason for this ban is simply that the foreigner is rarely aware of the appropriateness, strength, and limitations of these expressions. The label **простора́чие** does not really separate the unacceptable from the merely informal. The reason for this prohibition will perhaps be clearer in an example in English. Imagine that you are talking, in English, to a Russian teacher of English. He regularly refers to his pupils as **"кидз."** A normal colloquialism? Yes, but even if you are not a schoolteacher, this **"кидз"** sounds very strange. Even if said with a strong accent, "children" would have been better. Other examples of the same phenomenon often occur in the magazine *Soviet Life* where too much slang is used inappropriately in the effort to be informal, even folksy.

Speech and education
Речь и образова́ние

● Пусть ко мне́ в ко́мнату войдёт незнако́мец, и я по его́ ре́чи в пе́рвые же де́сять мину́т определю́

[1] A short but useful list of Soviet student slang can be found in Nils Åke Nilsson, "Soviet Student Slang," *Scando-Slavica*, Vol. VI (1960), pp. 116–23.

[2] For purposes of this discussion "slang" will be defined as nonstandard and unacceptable usage; "colloquial" here refers to a perfectly acceptable but conversational use of language.

духо́вную его́ биогра́фию и уви́жу, начи́танный ли он челове́к, враща́ется ли он в культу́рной среде́ и́ли он забулды́га, водя́щий компа́нию с неве́ждами.[3]

Distinguishing educated speech is an easy enough task for the native speaker. In English one double negative or an incorrect third person singular verb is all that is necessary to make an initial assumption about the speaker. "He don't do nothing" is a fine example. Leaving the *g* off the -*ing* makes it even worse. The less educated Russian makes mistakes too.

As a nonnative speaker of Russian you may at first think it difficult to characterize the speech of the uneducated Russian when you are not really clear about what constitutes educated speech. However, if you have been studying Russian using a system that stresses hearing and speaking, you have been learning the accepted educated forms. It follows, therefore, that consistent or frequent lapses (by the native speaker) from those patterns or forms often indicates uneducated (or careless) speech. Misplaced stress is one such lapse.

Incorrect	Correct
зво́нит	звони́т
ква́ртал	кварта́л
мага́зин	магази́н
мо́лодежь	молодёжь
по́ртфель	портфе́ль
хозяева́	хозя́ева

Even for the beginning student of Russian many of these words have been repeated correctly so often that the incorrect stress sounds wrong. The limits of acceptability do change with time, however, even though grammars and dictionaries slow down the process. Russian stress references tend to be conservative so that advanced students of Russian will notice that a few words will carry a stress among contemporary educated Russians that stress dictionaries disallow. For example, buttonhole or loop **пе́тля** will often be heard as **петля́**, salmon **ло-**

[3] К. Чуко́вский, *Живо́й как жизнь*, стр. 38.

сось as **лосо́сь**; and the dictionary gives "Whoops!" as "**Оп-пля́!**" but people say "**О́п-пля!**"

Grammatical forms are also a problem, even for the native speaker. Here are some of the more common mistakes:

Incorrect	Correct
бежа́т	бегу́т
да́дено	дано́
мно́го де́лов	мно́го дел
е́хай	поезжа́й
пекёт	печёт
ско́лько вре́мя[4]	кото́рый час
ско́лько разо́в	ско́лько раз
место́в нет	нет мест
моё фами́лие	моя́ фами́лия
хуже́е	ху́же
чего́ ты де́лаешь?	что ты де́лаешь?

It is almost comforting for the foreigner to see that even the natives have trouble with Russian grammar and stress. You must temper such feelings with the foreknowledge that what is gained in comfort is lost to literacy.

Overcompensations and the attempt at snobbery
Языково́й сноби́зм

There seem to be misguided people in all countries who try to impress you with their erudition, refinement, and sensibility. Too often they bend over so far backward that they fall flat. How might a Russian be snobbish in speech? Snobbery is suggested when a Russian speaker takes a foreign word and tries to pronounce it as he thinks it is pronounced in its language of origin. For instance, he will say "**Викто́р Юго́**" instead of the accepted "**Ви́ктор Гюго́.**" Or he will try to replace е with э in any foreign word: "**милиционэ́р**" instead of "**милиционе́р**"; "**музэ́й**" instead of "**музе́й.**"

[4] But "**Ско́лько вре́мя?**" is now becoming an acceptable expression for "What time is it?" "**Ско́лько вре́мени?**" is a standard expression for either "What time is it?" or "How long?"

Beyond this grayish area of poor taste is the no man's land of bad grammar and incorrect usage. "**Я кýшаю**" is used by the pretentious ignoramus. **Кýшать** is a verb suggesting considerable refinement: dining, rather than eating: "**Бáрин кýшает, а корóва éст.**" Its use in the first person singular arrogates to the speaker a *delicatesse* that is so out of place when referring to oneself that it is wrong. On the other hand, the imperative "**кýшайте**" is polite and more formal than "**éшьте.**" Using words of foreign origin, often with the stress moved to the last syllable (reminiscent of French), is also a sign of affectation. By analogy, perhaps, with **докумéнт, аргумéнт, инструмéнт**, the would-be man of culture will say "**фундамéнт**" (which is incorrect) instead of "**фундáмент**" (the correct form).

Regional accents
Мéстные гóворы

The English have quite a rigid system for establishing social status: either one speaks upper-class (Oxford) English or one has a regional and lower-class accent. In the United States we can try to detect generally where the man is from and whether or not he is or pretends to be educated. However, we Americans can be far less secure than the English can in our conclusions about speech and social status. The Russian is in about the same predicament. In the USSR, esteem is gained by education and then success in certain fields, especially in the fine arts and the sciences. Thus, conformity to the standard (**литератýрный язы́к**) phraseology, stress, and grammar is more important than ridding oneself of a local accent. This is true, of course, only if the accent is a slight **óканье** or **áканье**, which will be described. The other characteristics of northern and southern accents are thought of as peculiar to peasant/lower-class/uneducated speech. Upon hearing a northern accent, the Russian will perhaps smile and note where the speaker is from, but the speaker will not usually be looked down upon until the rules of accept-

able grammar, stress, and usage are regularly breached.

There are three major accent areas in spoken Russian—northern, southern, and central.[5] The major distinguishing feature of the northern Russian accent is **óканье**—the clear enunciation of all *o*'s as *o*: **водá, хорошó, золотóй**. This is the feature you are most likely to hear and recognize. (Recordings by **Урáльский нарóдный хор** supply examples.)

There are less vital and sometimes less common features of the northern accent, however, such as:

(1) Pronunciation of unstressed *e* as *ё* at the end of a word or in front of hard consonants: **женá—жёнá, селó—сёлó, велá—вёлá, плáтье—плáтьё**

(2) Pronunciation of the old *ять* as *и* (as in Ukrainian): **хлеб—хлиб, песня—писня, место—мисто**

(3) When stressed, pronunciation of *я* as *е*: **зять—зеть, взять—взеть, грязь—грезь**

(4) The yod (*й*) between vowels sometimes disappears: **бывáет—бывáт, дýмает—дýмат**

(5) Pronunciation of the singular genitive adjectival endings as *во* rather than *го*: **дóброго—дóброво, сńнего—сńн(ё)во, тогó—товó**

The major feature of the southern Russian accent is **áканье** or **яканье**, the pronunciation of unstressed *o* as *a* or *ъ*: either **харашó** or **хърашó** is heard. The *o* is heard only when stressed: **мой дом, óкна**. Other southern peculiarities are that sometimes:

(1) Unstressed *e* sounds like *и* or *я*: **рекá—рикá/рякá, несý—нисý/нясý, перó—пирó/пярó**

(2) The *г* sounds more like *х*: **Бог—Бох, Гóс-поди—Хóсподи** (these two examples, however, are standard pronunciation)

(3) Third person singular and plural verb forms are pronounced as if there were a soft sign

[5] These classifications and examples of accent areas are cited in А. М. Фńнкель и Н. М. Бажéнов, *Курс совремéнного рýсского языкá*, 2ое изд. (Кńев: Издáтельство "Радя́нска шкóла," 1965), стр. 17–19.

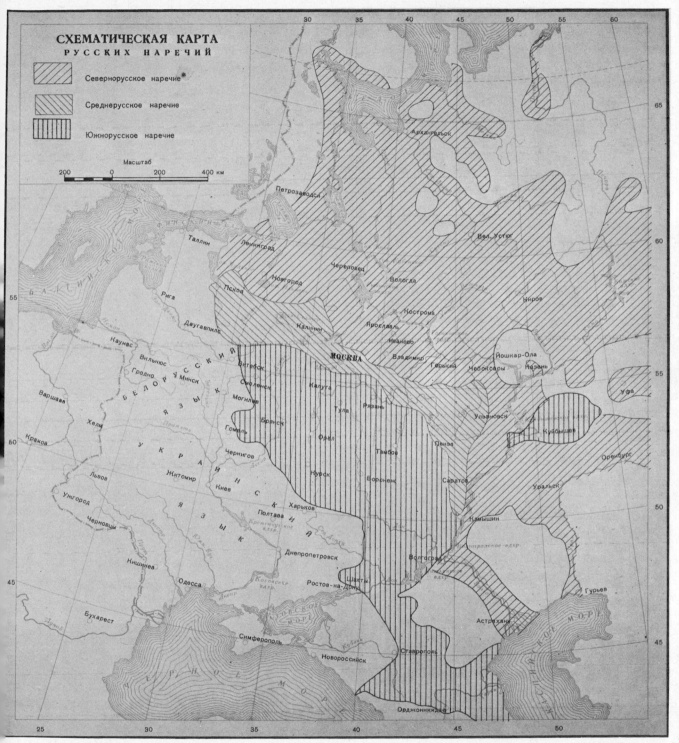

СХЕМАТИЧЕСКАЯ КАРТА
РУССКИХ НАРЕЧИЙ

Севернорусское наречие*

Среднерусское наречие

Южнорусское наречие

Масштаб
200   0   200   400 км

*наре́чие dialect

on the end: **несёт—н(и)сёт***ь*, **пойдёт—
п(а)йдет***ь*, **берут—б(и)рут***ь*

(4) Adjectival genitive singular masculine endings are pronounced as *го* rather than *во*: **доброго—добр(а)го**, **того—т(а)го**, **пятого—пят(а)го**

(5) Pronunciation of accusative-genitive cases of personal and reflexive pronouns use *е* in place of the *я*: **тебя—т(и)бе**, **меня—м(и)не**, **себя—с(и)бе**

The central Russian (Moscow) accent found itself in the relatively small no man's land between the northern and southern accents and took the democratic way out. It pronounces vowels as the southerners do and consonants as the northerners, except for the southern replacement of *е* for *я* in pronouns.

Though there are these differences in the northern and southern accents in Russian, what is truly amazing and quite satisfying for the student of Russian is the relative uniformity of the language for speakers from one end of the huge country to the other. The differences described are really quite small and rarely halt understanding; rather, they indicate that the speaker does not know or care to hide his regional accent. Most Russians you are likely to meet will speak the standard Moscow version. You will come across the accents in literature, however.

Some special concerns of Russian speech
Некоторые особенности русской речи

The use of ты and вы
Употребление ты и вы

By now, you are aware that there are two ways to say "you" in Russian: the formal **вы** and the familiar **ты**. Of course, the problem of choosing **ты** or **вы** arises only in the singular since the plural "you" must be **вы** no matter how near and dear the referents might be.

The **ты** form (what used to be "thou" in English) is widely used especially by children in talking to other children and by adults in talking to children. Except for parents or other close relatives, the children always refer to their elders as **вы**. Beginning in early adolescence and thenceforth the use of **ты** is reserved for family and close friends. Often the older one gets, the more circumspect one is about using it.

Schoolmates and students regularly use **ты** with one another well after adolescence, but once they have started to work they will be more selective.

Part of the trouble with circumscribing the use of **ты** is determining what constitutes a close friend. That depends very much on the individuals involved and the practices observed in the (speech) community from which each came. For instance, northern Russians are reputed to be somewhat more reserved in using it than are southern Russians. In the nineteenth century it was common for all the peasants of one village to use **ты** with one another. Indeed, according to an authority the use of **вы** to refer to just one person was a borrowing from the French (tu/vous), unknown in Russia until about 1700.

Вы is used when the people or the situation require politeness, respect, or some formality, and when you are addressing two or more people. It is quite possible, therefore, that privately two people would use **ты** with each other but in front of others revert to the **вы** form. For instance, two saleswomen who use **ты** would switch to **вы** in front of customers, outsiders, or perhaps their employer. Always remember, however, that this usage is highly dependent on the people and the situation.

Since **вы** is a term of respect and **ты** one of

familiarity, both have a certain area of appropriateness. When they are used out of place, either of them can be insulting or at least an expression of anger and displeasure. An angry spouse might well call his mate **вы** (among other things); a subordinate who calls his boss **ты** (when usually he had used **вы**) is trying to insult him. The boss can use **ты** with more impunity when speaking to his subordinates: the more he wants to exert authority, the more likely he is to insist on the submission of his workers by using **ты**.

For the English speaker learning Russian, the problem is not so much when to use **ты** (use it with all children and with those Russians who refer to you that way) as becoming aware of it and recognizing it when it is used by Russians. Since there is no such distinction in English, our minds tend to exclude the possibility that we might make one.[6]

The Russian "lisp"
Картáвость

Two sounds seem to be especially difficult for a few (native) Russian speakers to make, the *r* and the hard *l*. The standard mispronunciation of either or both of these sounds is a kind of lisp called **картáвость**[7] (**картáвить** to lisp this way): "**Он картáвит на эр (и́ли на эл).**" This particular lisp consists of a uvular *r* as in French or German and/or pronouncing the hard *l* as *u*. Thus a Russian can sound like a Frenchman when saying "**кукурýза**"; and "**салáт**" becomes "**сауáт**." A famous example of this kind of lisp can be heard on records of Lenin's speeches: "**Лéнин картáвил на эр.**"

This lapse in pronunciation is frequent enough to suggest that there are cultural as well as physical reasons for its persistence. In the past, when French (and earlier, German) was the language of culture itself, the French *r* was something to be cultivated, not made fun of. There is even another verb to denote the use of the uvular (French) *r*—**грасси́ровать**: "**Онá говори́ла, кокéтливо грасси́руя.**"

Nowadays, this **картáвость** is not encouraged,[8] and indeed it seems to be much less frequent among younger Russians.

The use of diminutives
Употреблéние уменьши́тельных форм

Conversational Russian makes a very wide use of diminutive forms. Most of the time, these forms are used to indicate the speaker's attitude toward the subject. Any time the speaker thinks of something as cute, charming, small, lovable, or the like, he will use a diminutive: **ёж—ёжик, стол—стóлик**, for example.

The speaker who wants something will often lace at least part of his request with diminutives, thereby either expressing the smallness of his request or describing how nice the person might be who is to fulfill it: "**чайкý, пожáлуйста**" is vastly more pleasant than "**чáю, пожáлуйста**"; and **немнóжко** sounds like less but probably amounts to the same as **немнóго**.

Diminutives are also frequently found in use by or in reference to women and their belongings: **шля́па—шля́пка, кóфта—кóфточка**. And women will almost invariably refer to their children with a more lavish use of diminutives.

Пáпа	Мáма
Андрю́ша	Андрю́шенька
Пéтя	Пéтенька
Жéня	Жéнечка

---

[6] Highly recommended for those reading Russian literature in the original is Paul Friedrich, "Structural Implications of Russian Pronominal Usage," *Sociolinguistics*, ed. William Bright, Janua linguarum, Series maior 20 (The Hague: Mouton, 1966), pp. 215–59. Despite the verbiage, many examples and much background information are there. For those who expect to work (not just tread on) the soil of Academe, the discussion at the end supplies fine examples of academic one-upmanship and a few delightful anecdotes.

[7] Speech defects caused by a physical deformation such as a cleft palate are referred to as **косноязы́чие**.

[8] It is often attributed to Jews, for instance. Lenin's enemies used this lisp in their arguments to suggest that he was at least part Jewish.

These are some of the frequent but optional uses of diminutives. There is an occasion, however, when their use is obligatory. In discussing babies, their attributes, parts, and possessions, diminutives are always used. A red-haired baby is **ры́женький**, never **ры́жий**—a red-haired adult· For babies: **штаны́—штани́шки, руба́шка— руба́шечка, рука́—ру́чка, но́ги—но́жки**. And babies are: **краси́венькие, хоро́шенькие, гря́зненькие, чи́стенькие**, and so forth.

Since these distinctions are not found in English, the American student must make a special effort first to recognize diminutives and later to use them himself. A warning, however, must be inserted here, especially applicable to reading: not all the words that look like diminutives are diminutives. **Воро́нка** is not a small crow or raven but a funnel; a Christmas tree must be **ёлка** while **ель** is a spruce tree; **рука́** is a hand, but **ру́чка** can be, besides a small hand, a handle or a pen. In addition, **ла́мпа** is a lamp, but **ла́мпочка** is a light bulb; **кры́ша** is a roof, but **кры́шка** is a lid.

The excessive use of diminutives can indicate rather low social status, limited education, or just poor taste.[9]

Russians and their alphabet
Ру́сская а́збука
Ру́сский алфави́т

Essentially every English-speaking child learns his ABC's, that is, how to say his alphabet and what order to follow. The Russians seem to have a problem with their alphabet. Neither the pronunciation of the letters in the alphabet nor the order in which they appear are of great concern to them. If you ask a Russian to recite the alphabet, you are most likely to hear a jumble of sounds that amount to what the letters sound like to him rather than a formal recital of the

names of the letters. And toward the end of the alphabet, order is also usually lost.

Evidence of this phenomenon appears in the common pronunciation of letter abbreviations (see Chapter 12). Some letters can be pronounced two ways: "**эр**" or "**рэ**," "**эс**" or "**сэ**," "**эф**" or "**фэ**," "**ка**" or "**кэ**," for instance. Although both dictionaries and school texts have tables showing the proper pronunciation of the letters of the alphabet, even they disagree!

This version appears in a first-grade text and is probably the most common:

Аа	Бб	Вв	Гг	Дд	Ее	Ёё
а	бэ	вэ	гэ	дэ	е	ё
Жж	Зз	Ии	Йй	Кк	Лл	Мм
жэ	зэ	и	(и кра́ткое)	ка	эль	эм
Нн	Оо	Пп	Рр	Сс	Тт	Уу
эн	о	пэ	эр	эс	тэ	у
Фф	Хх	Цц	Чч	Шш	Щщ	Ъъ
эф	ха	це	че	ша	ща	твёрдый знак
Ыы	Ьь	Ээ	Юю	Яя		
ы	мя́гкий знак	э	ю	я		

The student of Russian should learn both the order and the pronunciation of Russian letters for his own convenience. Russian vocabulary learning is such that those who know the order of the letters will find their words fastest.

The Russian pronunciation of Latin and Greek letters, so commonly used in mathematics, will be found in Chapter 12. And the occasional use of letters in chemical formulas is described in the Appendix, as are the Morse code and the Braille alphabet in Russian.

Russian pig Latin
"Фуфа́йский язы́к"

Russian unfortunately does not have a single child's language that corresponds in its universality to our pig Latin. Instead there are a

[9] For more details on the formation and use of diminutives, see B. V. Bratus, *The Formation and Expressive Use of Diminutives, Studies in the Modern Russian Language*, No. 6, ed. Dennis Ward (New York: Cambridge University Press, 1969).

variety, if not a welter, of similar possibilities. One, for instance, is to take the last syllable of a word and put it at the beginning: сюда́—дасю́. Other varieties introduce nonsense syllables: я хочу́ пить—я́хонцы хочу́хонцы пи́тьхонцы. The form cited in the heading, фуфа́йский язы́к, places фа or фу before each syllable. Thus ничего́ becomes фани-фаче́-фаго́ or фуни-фуче́-фуго́. Other syllables—по, ка, and so on—are used in the same way. Thus the phenomenon of children's languages exists, but there is no real substitute for pig Latin.

"Sudden" words and "semiwords"
Восклица́ния

Interjections
Междоме́тия

Expressions used almost unconsciously or involuntarily for expressing agreement, warning, pain, and the like are called междоме́тия. They are used constantly in daily speech but are not often granted the status of "word," and some are not even capable of standard transcription. Careful attention should be paid to them, however, since it is easy to misinterpret some of the most common ones.

The list below gives a few of the common expressions of this sort. The Russian equivalents of the American "uh-huh" (assent) and "huh-uh" (dissent) require a somewhat fuller explanation. When an American says "uh-huh" he is saying "yes" or at least admitting agreement with whoever is talking. The Russian makes the same sound, but it is just a supportive sound to indicate that he is listening. It does not necessarily mean that he agrees with what is being said (although it *can* mean agreement), nor even that he has understood what has been said (although it can mean that, too). Since both Russians and Americans use this expression almost unconsciously, it is very easy to misinterpret it. The Russian sound is often written as Угу́ or Ага́ but is pronounced as "аха́" (with the mouth open more broadly than in English).

If a Russian is understanding you *and* wishes to express his agreement, he might say "так, так," often drawing out the vowel: "та-а-ак." The Russian expression "ни-ни́" is equivalent to "ника́к нельзя́" (total denial), and "не-е-е" is often a request meaning, "Thanks, don't bother. . . . I'd rather not."

Other interjections that you might come across include:

Уф! Phew! (I'm tired.)

Ай! Ай-ай! Ой! Ой-ой! Ouch! (It hurts.)

Фу! Фу-фу́! Pee-you! (It stinks.)
(Фу! is also used for mild disappointment.)

Тс-с-с! Ш-ш-ш! (not voiced), Ша! (loudly and voiced) Sh-h-h! (Be quiet!)

Тс-с-с! Psst! (Listen to this.)

Чхи! Ап-чхи́! Ah-choo!

Оп-пля! Whoops! Oops! Alley-oop! (Up you go!)
(It can also be used for dogs doing tricks, as can Гоп! pronounced "Хоп.")

Ой! Oh! (surprise, combined with fright)

Ах! Oh! (surprise, delight, or fright)

Ну! Да ну́! Well! (surprise and some disbelief)

Ох! Oh! (dismay, sadness, pain)

Эй! Hey! (You, there!)

М-м-м, Э-э-э Uh-h, ah-h . . . (hesitation, when rendered in print, though the actual sound, made with the mouth shut, is not much different from ours)

М-м-да́. Well, yes. (doubtful agreement)

Ау́! Halloo! (a signal for "Where are you?" commonly used among Russians, who are out together hunting mushrooms or gathering berries, in order not to lose one another. It can also be used in answer to any loud call.[10])

Ай-ай! Ой-ой! Oh, oh! (disappointment or dismay)

Ай-ай-ай! (*pronounced* "айяя́й") Tsk-tsk! (Shame on you!)
(The English clicking sound "tsk-tsk" in Russian is used to call small animals.)

[10] "Как ау́кнется, так и откли́кнется"—"Treat her like a lady and she'll act like one."

Тьфу! (strong disgust or disappointment: the American might say anything from "Nuts!" to "Damn it!" as an equivalent. The Russian sound resembles spitting, and is easily achieved by starting out with your tongue between your teeth.)

Бр-р! Br-r! (It's cold!)

Чу! (old-fashioned term for "Listen!" or "Look!")

Чур! (originally, a warning of a limit in a child's game; now, a general warning: "Watch out!")

Чур меня! (Don't touch me! Stay away! I don't want to play.)

Айда! (used mostly among country children for "C'mon!" or "Let's go!")

Warnings and alarms
Предостережения и тревога

If you will come to serious harm if you continue to do what you are doing, the Russian will yell **"Берегись!"** or **"Стоп!"** (**Стоп** is also commonly used as part of the set of traffic signals.) If he wishes to turn your attention to a possible danger, he will say **"Смотри!"** or, more formally, **"Осторожно!"** Among children, the whispered shout **"Атас!"** is a warning of approaching authority (teachers, grown-ups, and others).

When you have already come to grief, the cry is **"Помогите!"** with especially long stress on the **и**. To summon the aid of others (either as an observer or as a victim), **"На помощь!"** or **"На подмогу!"** can be used.

If you need police assistance, yell **"Караул!"** This call is also a request for personal aid, so that it can mean "Help!" in addition to "Police!" For fire, the scream is **"Пожар!"**

Terms of rejection and endearment
Бранные и ласковые обращения

Technically, the list of names people call each other is almost endless and most can be found in dictionaries. The foreigner cannot spend forever in a dictionary, however, nor will the dictionary tell him how strong a word is or how commonly he will encounter it. Compiled here is a very select list of the most commonly used terms of rejection and endearment. Modern literature can supply dozens more. Any of these words can be used alone, but they are also often modified for added strength. **"Скотина безрогая!"** ("Hornless cattle!") is somehow worse than just **"Скотина!"** And **"Душенька моя!"** seems just a little stronger than **"Душенька!"**

Name-calling
Бранные обращения

The strength or seriousness of name-calling is often quite dependent on situation. As in *The Virginian*, if one smiles when saying it, the intent can be just the opposite of the literal meaning of the words used: **паршивый поросёнок**, translated, means "mangy little pig," but it is used often as a term of endearment, especially toward small children.

Most of the words listed below, however, are usually used in their pejorative sense and were chosen for their frequency. They are divided into two sets, the general and the specialized. The general words might be compared to calling someone a "dirty bum" in American English, even when the name-caller is quite well aware that the object of his derision is in fact neither dirty nor a bum. Though they are used in a general sense, they usually refer to a specific vice or fault. Words referring specifically to men (M) or women (F) and especially mild or strong words are noted.

General pejorative terms include:

балда (M, F) stupidity (*from* the thick end or stump of a stick)

болван (M) stupidity/laziness (*from* an idol, a roughly hewn log, or a stone)

гад (M), **гадина** (M, F) vileness (**гадюка** the common poisonous snake of Russia; **гадость** something revolting, disgusting) (*very strong*) дура́к, ду́рень (М), ду́ра (F) stupidity (M: *weak*; F: *fairly strong*)

идио́т (М), идио́тка (F) stupidity

мерза́вец (М), мерза́вка (F) vileness (ме́рзость something revolting, sickening, disgusting) (*strong*)

наха́л (М), наха́лка (F) brazenness

негодя́й (М), негодя́йка (F) worthlessness and nastiness (никуда́ не годи́тся good for nothing)

осёл (М) stupidity, stubbornness

па́костник (М), па́костница (F) defilement or contamination, often with deception involved (па́кость something dirty/revolting) (*strong*)

парази́т (М), парази́тка (F) parasitism

паску́да (М, F) vileness (паску́дить = де́лать га́дости) (*very strong and crude*)

подле́ц (М), по́длая (F) dishonesty/lowness (*from* bottom, base; под hearth; подо́шва sole)

свинья́ (М, F) crudeness/vileness (*from* swine, hog)

сво́лочь (М, F) filthiness (*strong*)

скоти́на (М, F) crudeness/stupidity (*from* cattle) (*strong*)

сте́рва (М, F) lowness (*from* carrion) (*strong*)

су́ка (М, F) promiscuousness (*from* bitch) (*strong*)

су́кин сын (М) general lowness (son of a bitch) (*strong*)

хам (М), ха́мка (F) rudeness (*from the Biblical character* Ham)

холе́ра (М, F) general nastiness (*from* cholera)

хулига́н (М), хулига́нка (F) rascality exceeding mischievousness (*from* hooligan)

Among the words for specific offensiveness are:

ба́ба a peasant wife or woman (*mild when applied to women who are not peasants*; *stronger when applied to men with traits of weakness, indecision*)

безде́льник (М), безде́льница (F) a shiftless, lazy person (без де́ла)

ве́дьма (F) a mean, bad-tempered woman; a witch

дармое́д (М), дармое́дка (F) a freeloader (да́ром ест)

моше́нник (М), моше́нница (F) a swindler, cheater (*from* мошна́ purse)

недоно́сок (М) a prematurely born person; therefore, one thought to be weak and poorly put together, mentally and physically

пижо́н (М), пижо́нка (F) an overly well dressed and rude individual

потаску́ха (F) a whore

проститу́тка (F) (Some people consider this word so awful that they supply another: "Прости́ Го́споди!")

проходи́мец (М), проходи́мка (F, *rarely used*) a person capable of doing almost anything dishonest, especially by wile

разгильдя́й (М), разгильдя́йка (F) someone who pays no attention to appearance or business affairs; a slob

растя́па (М, F) a careless, awkward, and stupid individual

ста́рая карга́ (F) a mean old woman; a witch

ста́рый хрен (М) an "old man," implying impotence

стиля́га (М, F) earlier, someone who wore unusual clothes; now, someone who overdresses

фра́йер (М) a clotheshorse; a generally untrustworthy person

холу́й (М) a slovenly and subservient man

шалопа́й (М) a purposeless and uninterested person, often applied to a teenager

шлю́ха (F) a streetwalker, prostitute (*strong*)

Terms of endearment
Ла́сковые обраще́ния

It is perhaps a sad comment on humanity that it is much easier to think of commonly used bad names for people than good ones. Here are some good ones, with the major forms in which they appear, their meaning, and special notes, when applicable, on frequency and strength:

голу́бчик (*from* го́лубь pigeon) (*very common*) голу́бушка голу́бка

дорого́й (-а́я)   dear (mild and most common)
  дорогу́ша (bordering on the saccharine)
  дорогу́ля
душа́ (моя́)   soul (old fashioned)
  ду́шечка
  ду́шенька
золото́й (-а́я) ты мо́й   gold
  ты моё зо́лото
  зо́лотце моё
краса́вец, краса́вица   beautiful
ла́ска ты моя́   (from ласка́ть to pet, caress)
  (strong and rare)
любо́вь моя́   love
  люби́мый (-ая)
  лю́ба моя́
ми́лый (-ая) мой   darling (very frequent)
  ми́лочка
  ми́ленький (-ая)
ненагля́дный (-ая) мо́й   I-can't-get-enough-of-
  looking-at-you (very strong and less frequent)
родно́й (-а́я) мо́й   birth, family, kin, country
  (common)
се́рдце моё   heart
  серде́чко моё
со́лнышко моё   My sunshine! (especially endearing, considering the climate) (very common)

Expletives
Во́згласы

The use of expletives in the United States and
Soviet Union makes an interesting contrast. For
us, "God!" is "taking the name of the Lord in
vain," while for the Russian **"Бо́же!"** and
"Го́споди!" are used without any hint of poor
taste and without offense to anyone. The following are other expletives used in the USSR,
whether or not the speaker has any religious
convictions:

Бо́же мо́й!   Good heavens! (common and used
  in surprise, dismay, and disbelief; **Бо́же** is a
  remnant of the vocative case for **Бог** God)
Го́споди!   Good Lord! (an equivalent in intent

and prevalence to **"Бо́же мо́й,"** also in the
vocative case)
Ра́ди Бо́га!   For heaven's sakes! (often part of
  a plea: **"Ради Бо́га, не ходи́ туда́ опя́ть!"**—
  "For heaven's sake, don't go there again!")
Не да́й Бог! Упаси́ Бог! Бо́же упаси́!   Heaven
  forbid!
Сла́ва Бо́гу!   Thank heaven!

There are many other such locutions, sometimes filling several pages in a Russian dictionary (under **бог**). These are the most common,
however. (Notice that the Soviets are careful not
to capitalize God.)

Though God is called upon frequently and
almost with impunity, the Devil cannot be referred to so easily. The problem for the foreigner
is to know when he can use "the Devil" expressions. They are sufficiently strong that most
people are offended by their use. The prohibition
against the Devil is particularly rooted in the
superstition that calling upon him is likely to
make him appear, and this explains the many
substitutes for devil **чёрт**: **шут, пёс, нелёгкая
(си́ла), бес, ле́ший**. On the other hand, these expressions are not so offensive, generally speaking, as "Not bloody likely" was to Liza in
Pygmalion. The degree of offense taken by the
use of these words is highly dependent on who
uses them and under what conditions. They are
stronger when specifically directed against other
people; thus, **"Иди́ к чёрту!"** can equal "Go to
hell!" while **"Чёрт возьми́!"** can mean only
"Darn it!" **"Чёрт!" "К чёрту!" "Чёрт по-
бери́ (подери́, возьми́)!"** and **"К чёртовой
ма́тери!"** are the most commonly used expressions, but there are many others in circulation.
Soldiers doubtless use these expressions for any
mild offense. They are sufficiently strong that
they are not recommended for use by foreigners.
Again, the dictionary is the best source for the
complete list.

There does not seem to be a large variety of
usable (inoffensive) words to express anger, disgust, and the like. The following can be used for
the purpose:

Фу! Фу-фу́! Фу́-ты! (relatively mild dismay, disgust) (*very common*)

Тьфу! (strong rejection, disgust, dismay)

Ёлки-па́лки! (fairly strong surprise and dismay)

Ерунда́! (Каки́е) глу́пости! Вздор! Nonsense! That's silly! Hogwash! Balderdash!

Пустяки́! It's nothing. It's trivial. (dismissal of importance, also used as an answer to "thank you")

Unprintable words
Непеча́тные слова́

Russian abounds with taboo words and expressions, most of which are based on six or seven root words that refer to what such words usually refer. The total assemblage of four-letter or taboo words in Russian is called **мат** (from the most common of such expressions, which includes the word "mother"): **"Он руга́ется ма́том"**—"He uses dirty words." Even **мат** is too strong for some people who will instead euphemistically say, **"Он выража́ется трёхэта́жными слова́ми"**—*literally*, "He uses three-storied words." (Swearing or a swear word is **ру́гань, руга́тельство** and may or may not include the aforementioned taboo words: **"Он его́ вы́ругал"**—"He cussed him out." **Брань, бра́нные слова́** are also swear words but the connotation is not so strong.)

Though it is true that millions of people use four-letter words, they still remain publicly unprintable in Russian. For the Russian these terms are even stronger than their English equivalents are for us. If you manage to find out what these words are, under no circumstances should you use them. These words for you as a foreigner are mere collections of letters or sounds devoid of the redolent connotations they have for the native speaker. Even though you might know the literal translation of such a term, you cannot know its full strength. Using an obscenity in another language is like shooting a gun without knowing where the bullet comes out.[11]

[11] Specialists may want to refer to *A Short Dictionary of Russian Obscenities*, compiled by D. A. Drummond and G. Perkins (El Cerrito, California: Berkeley Slavic Specialties, 1971); or to *Soviet Prison Camp Speech*, compiled by Meyer Galler and Harlan E. Marquess (Madison: University of Wisconsin Press, 1972).

10

Animals
Живóтные

Animals are a problem for the Russian language student for several reasons. One is that he seldom appreciates the extent to which animals and notions about them are part of his own language. (Humans so often see some of their humanity in animals—in the hen, weasel, fox, or bear, for example.) Another reason is that he is likely to assume that the Russian animal is to the Russian what the American animal is to the American. This chapter is long partially because that is not true. Animals (and nature in general) are closer to the Russian and therefore play a larger part in the Russian view of things. That statement will be reiterated in several ways in this chapter because understanding it is so much a part of mastering the language.

The distinctions a Russian makes and what he stresses will be kept to. Not much space is given to domestic animals, therefore. Livestock breeding was traditionally not a highly developed art. A good cow was one that was even-tempered, could eat as little as possible and still stay alive to produce a calf and a little milk for the family. A good dog was one that kept the wolves from the sheep.

Wild animals present another problem. Sometimes translations come up against differences in types: the common squirrel in the United States is gray; the common Russian squirrel is usually red (in the summer) and has tufted ears. Sometimes there simply are no equivalents for the Russian animal: the Russian's beloved hedgehog does not live in the Western Hemisphere. Occasionally British usage is different from the American; our common dictionaries are translations into British, not American, usage: the British "elk" is an American "moose." And the chances are that "capercaillie" means absolutely nothing to the American reader who has just looked up **глухáрь** in the dictionary.

Domestic animals—pets, farm animals, and zoo animals—will be dealt with first, and, just for fun, how to talk with those animals and what they "say" will be touched on. The discussion of wild animals that follows is divided along traditional lines of classification for the animal kingdom.

Man and his animals
Человек и его животные

Pets
Домашние и комнатные животные

The word "pet" is untranslatable; **домашние животные** are those animals raised for man's pleasure or profit and therefore include cats, dogs, cows, sheep, rabbits, and so on. **Комнатные животные** are those animals that can consider the inside of a house to be home. Most dogs, however, spend their time outside or in the barn, not in the house (doghouse **конура**). Cats, birds, and hedgehogs can live inside. Pet stores **зоомагазины** sell birds, hedgehogs, turtles, guinea pigs, goldfish, and white mice, but they do not sell cats and dogs.

DOGS	СОБАКИ

Dogs occupy a much different position in the USSR than they do here. For one thing there is much less attention paid to purebred dogs, although people with a special interest occasionally keep them or know something about them. Until recently dogs were almost always kept for their real usefulness, either as watchdogs or as hunting dogs. Now their use approaches ours, though not so commonly. And finally dogs are thought of as being much less tame. A Russian will be much more careful about patting a strange dog than we will, and many dogs are fitted with muzzles **намордники**. In the large cities apartment size is also a reason that dogs are much less frequently a part of family life. (Instead birds are quite popular as pets, especi-

ally the **чиж**, **щегол** (see Appendix) and the parakeet **попугайчик**.)

When a dog is kept as a pet, it is likely to be a dog "of mixed parentage" **дворняжка** or **дворняга** (**двор** a court or yard). In fact they constitute about 95 percent of all dogs. Most of these dogs usually resemble the Russian breed **лайка**.

By far the best known breed of dog **порода собак** is the German shepherd **немецкая овчарка** or just **овчарка** (**овца** sheep). In this country they are thought of as police dogs or guide dogs for the blind, but for Russians they are more often used as border guard dogs. There are other Russian shepherd breeds, such as **южнорусская овчарка**, which strongly resembles the English sheepdog; of course, **шотландская овчарка— колли**.

There are two major breeds of Russian origin, **борзая** and **лайка**; only the first (borzoi[1] or Russian wolfhound) is familiar in the United States. The borzoi is a very large, graceful dog originally developed to run down wolves for the hunting nobility. The other major Russian breed, **лайка**, is not so elegant in appearance, nor so large, but much more useful. It is a hunting dog developed in the north for chasing and treeing game, howling or barking (**лайка-лаять** to bark) until the hunter comes. There are four kinds of **лайка**; only one of them, the all-white Samoyed, is known commonly outside of the USSR. More common in the USSR is (**русская**) **лайка**, which resembles the Samoyed in shape though its fur is less fluffy and its coloring varies,

[1] The English transliteration probably refers to **борзой пёс**.

Дог

Боксёр

Пекинес

Борзая

Пудель

usually black and white with various gradations in between. (**Ла́йка** can also be any dog's name, especially a noisy one.)

The nobility also hunted using a class of medium-sized dogs, **лега́вые**, for stalking and pointing game birds. This group includes **по́йнтер** and **се́ттер**. (**Лега́вые** also became a pejorative slang word for the police.) Russian breeds in the hound family **го́нчие соба́ки** are the **ру́сская го́нчая** and the **ру́сская пе́гая го́нчая**; they most resemble a large beagle, but their fur is less smooth.

Other Russian breeds do exist, but the ones most people recognize have been described. Common Russian breeds include many that are familiar to us: **пу́дель**, **боксёр**, **сенберна́р**, **спаниель**, **бульдо́г**, **фокстерье́р**, **тойтерье́р**, **эрдельтерье́р**, **до́берман-пи́нчер**. **Та́кса** is a variety of dachshund; **ище́йка** (**иска́ть** to search for) is a bloodhound (or, sometimes, a German shepherd), and, of all things, **дог** is a Great Dane.

CATS КО́ШКИ

If little attention is paid to breeds of dogs, then even less is paid to those of cats. There are longhaired varieties—**сиби́рские**, **перси́дские**, **буха́рские коты́**; and **сиа́мские коты́** are fairly rare except in cities. This does not mean that cats themselves are a rarity. Their small space requirements commend them for life in the city, and their habit of keeping the mouse population under control commends them for life in the country.

Domestic animals (nomenclature)   Дома́шние живо́тные

Russian[1]	Meat	Young	Male	Notes	English
ло́шадь (лоша́дка)	кони́на[2]	жеребёнок, жеребя́та	жеребе́ц	кобы́ла—mare ме́рин—gelding	horse
коро́ва (коро́вушка)	говя́дина		бык (бычо́к)	вол—ox, steer	cow
	теля́тина	телёнок, теля́та			calf
овца́ (ове́чка)	бара́нина	ягнёнок, ягня́та	бара́н (бара́шек)		sheep
коза́ (ко́зочка)	козля́тина	козлёнок, козля́та	козёл (ко́злик)		goat
свинья́	свини́на	поросёнок, порося́та	каба́н	бо́ров—barrow	pig
ку́рица	ку́рица, ку́ра	цыплёнок, цыпля́та	пету́х	(*pl.* ку́ры)	chicken
гусь	гуся́тина	гусёнок, гуся́та	гуса́к	(*female* гусы́ня)	goose
у́тка	у́тка	утёнок, утя́та	се́лезень		duck
индю́шка, инде́йка	инде́йка	индюшо́нок, индюша́та	индю́к		turkey
кро́лик	кро́лик	крольчо́нок, крольча́та		(*female* крольчи́ха)	rabbit
соба́ка[3]		щено́к, щеня́та	кобе́ль	су́ка—bitch	dog
ко́шка (ко́шечка)		котёнок, котя́та	кот (ко́тик)		cat

[1] The general term for the type of animal is given; it sometimes also refers to the female of the species. Common diminutives are in parentheses.   [2] The name for horse meat comes from the now poetic (and sometimes military) word for horse **конь** (**конёк**): "**Тата́ры едя́т кони́ну**"—"Tartars eat horse meat."   [3] **Пёс** is frequently encountered. It is old fashioned and familiar, much as hound is used in English when not applied to a specific breed or type of dog.

Animal husbandry
Животноводство

Animal husbandry has never been the major concern of the Russian farmer; his crops were his problem. This does not mean that he did not have animals, for even the poorest probably had at least one goat. Of all the animals he might have, however, the most important one to him was a horse **лóшадь**. It was only with the horse that he could plough the land or get his crops to market. Perhaps it was that very importance of the horse that led to the interesting division of labor on the farm: the men took care of the horses (or oxen **волы́**, used among the Ukrainians and Don cossacks for plowing), and the women tended all the rest of the animals.

Cows were the next most valuable animal, kept for their milk and manure. A peasant household would also keep two to three sheep, **óвцы**, rarely more, for their wool and their meat. Goats **кóзы** were also commonly raised, both for their hair[2] and for their milk. Among the poorer peasants the goat took the place of a cow.

In the far north and in Siberia cattle were allowed to roam within a pasture area during the summer, but in most areas of Russia, the village hired a shepherd **пасту́х** whose job it was to tend cattle for the entire summer. This job was the least prestigious in the entire village; only orphans or the poorest boys without prospects would take it on as an occupation. The whole village paid him a salary for the summer, either in kind or in money, and village families would take turns feeding and housing him. This arrangement is still sometimes used for the care of privately owned cattle in the country; otherwise their owners take turns at the job. The process is described in "Матрёнин двор" by Солженицын:

---

[2] A famous Russian scarf, **Оренбу́ргский плато́к**, made from the finer hair **пух** of a special longhaired goat, was very light, very large, very expensive (and still is).

● Ещё суета́ больша́я выпада́ла Матрёне, когда́ подходи́ла её óчередь корми́ть кóзьих пастухо́в: одного́—здорове́нного, немоглухо́го, и второ́го —мальчи́шку с постоя́нной слюня́вой цига́ркой в зуба́х. Óчередь эта была́ в полтора́ ме́сяца раз, но вгоня́ла Матрёну в большо́й расхо́д. Она́ шла в сельпó, покупа́ла ры́бные консе́рвы, расста́рывалась и са́хару и ма́сла, чего́ не е́ла сама́. Ока́зывается, хозя́йки выкла́дывались друг пе́ред дру́гом, стара́ясь накорми́ть пастухо́в полу́чше.

The cattle also had their church calendar days. On April 23, St. George's Day **Егóрьев день**, when the cattle were sent out to pasture for the first time that year, they were specially blessed by the village priest. **Вла́сий** was also considered a protector of cattle; and on July 20, **Ильи́н день**, some animals were sacrificed, blessed, cooked, and eaten to give thanks to St. Ilya for preserving the cattle.

The animals were not especially well fed. Hay was not sown for them; instead, one of the regular summer jobs was to mow the grasses in the meadows and along the roadside to provide animal feed. Slaughtering was mostly done in the late fall so that the animals did not have to be fed over the winter, and the Russian winter was a very convenient freezer.

Pigs **сви́ньи** were also common farm animals; it is interesting to note that the Ukrainians raised them for their fat, while the Russians raised them for their meat. In other respects, pigs have the same reputation in Russia that they have here.

Chickens **ку́ры**, geese **гу́си**, and ducks **у́тки**, in that order, were raised almost everywhere, but turkeys **индю́шки** were very rare. Chickens and geese also had their church calendar days, but for them the date was the end, not a beginning. Chickens were traditionally slaughtered on November 1, **день Кузьмы́ и Демья́на**, while geese came to the same end on September 15, **день Ники́ты гуся́тника**.

Beekeeping **пчелово́дство** was also quite common, hives being maintained in hollowed-out logs especially set up for the purpose. Honey, along with berries and mushrooms, was also often the object of searches in the wilds.

Most of the cattle raising, milk production, and the like now takes place on a state farm, called a "sovkhoz" (**совхо́з** = **сове́тское хозя́йство**), or on a smaller collective farm, the "kolkhoz" (**колхо́з** = **коллекти́вное хозя́йство**). A kolkhoz is a group of farmers working together who share the produce of the farm according to the number of workdays each has contributed. A sovkhoz is a farm operated as an industrial enterprise, that is, one with salaried employees. The trend now is toward more of the latter.[3] However, the small private plots allotted to each household produce a very significant portion of the meat, milk, and eggs for the entire country.

The Soviet Union has had an almost remarkable lack of success in meat and egg production: less was produced in 1940 than in 1913.[4] Perhaps one reason for this failure is that cattle raising and the like were traditionally not specialties but rather small and integral parts of each farm household. Obviously such an arrangement is much harder to collectivize since each peasant could see a significant part of his livelihood disappear. As late as 1966, 40 percent of the meat and milk and almost two-thirds of the eggs in the USSR came from the small private plots allowed to each peasant household, only 3 percent of the total sown area.

The farmer's problem now is not so much to try to produce everything he needs from his private plot. Now he will try to supply his own meat, milk, and eggs and sell the remainder at the peasant markets. Nor is the economy any longer dependent on horses for major transportation and ploughing, though they certainly have not disappeared from the rural scene. Further, today's peasant will often keep only a goat for his own milk supply because, as the state farms become more efficient, it is less worth the farmer's while to maintain a cow. He is also likely to raise pigs (and sometimes chickens and rabbits) to enhance the meat supply and keep ducks and geese if there is a pond.

---

[3] See Paul Lydolph, *Geography of the USSR*, 2nd ed. (New York: John Wiley & Sons, 1970).

[4] *СССР в ци́фрах в 1966 году́* (Москва́: Стати́стика, 1967), стр. 92–93.

What do the animals say?   Как «говоря́т» живо́тные?

Как говори́т живо́тное	Звук	Значе́ние
ло́шадь ржёт	и-го-го́	a horse neighs
коро́ва мычи́т	му, му	a cow moos
овца́ бле́ет	бэ-бэ, бе-бе	a sheep bleats
свинья́ хрю́кает	хрю, хрю	a pig oinks
соба́ка ла́ет	гав-гав, ав-ав	a dog barks
щено́к, ма́ленькая соба́ка тя́вкает	тяв-тяв	a pup or small dog yips
ко́шка мяу́кает	мя́у	a cat mews
ко́шка мурлы́кает	мур, мур	a cat purrs
ку́рица куда́хчет (куда́хтать)	куд-куд-куда́х, куда́х-куда́х	a chicken clucks
пету́х кукаре́кает	кукареку́	a rooster crows
у́тка кря́кает	кря-кря	a duck quacks
гусь гого́чет (гогота́ть)	га-га-га́	a goose honks
воробе́й чири́кает[1]	чик-чири́к	a sparrow chirps
куку́шка куку́ет (кукова́ть)	ку-ку́, ку-ку́	a cuckoo cuckoos
лягу́шка ква́кает	квак, квак	a frog croaks
пчёлы, му́хи жужжа́т	ж-ж-ж	bees and flies buzz

---

[1] Не все пти́цы чири́кают: наприме́р, жа́воронки и соловьи́ пою́т (sing), иногда́ и́волга звени́т (rings), воро́на ка́ркает и го́лубь ворку́ет. Не́которые ма́ленькие пти́цы щебе́чут (twitter).

Talking to animals
"Обраще́ния" к живо́тным

The sound made to start a horse out involves puckering your lips and sucking in air or clicking your tongue. Another alternative is to shout **"Но-о-о"** (in Russian). Saying **"пру"** or **"тпру"** loudly, as if trying to pronounce all the letters at once, will stop the horse. ("Giddy-up" and "whoa," unfortunately, will not work.)

To call a cat, the sound to make is **"кс-кс,"** **"кис-кис,"** or **"кы́ська,"** all with a high-pitched voice. To make it go away, the usual sound is an unvoiced **"кш, кш."** An equivalent for "scat" is **"брысь,"** though the Russian word is somewhat more formal than ours.

Chickens and ducks are called by saying **"цып, цып, цып"** in a high-pitched voice, while geese can be called with **"те́ги, те́ги"** or **"те́га, те́га."** **"Тря, тря"** will summon sheep or goats, though perhaps more frequently sheep are called by **"бара́шки"** and cows will be called by name—**"Краса́вка!"**

Zoo animals
Живо́тные в зоопа́рке

Zoo animals, that is, nonnative animals, also supply some imagery to language and life. For those lucky enough to visit the Soviet Union, a trip to the Moscow Zoo **зоопа́рк** is highly recommended. You will find it more interesting than many other officially "cultural" events that often occupy the tourist's time.

The animals listed below are those that will rarely be seen outside a zoo. Terminology is stressed, plus any attributed qualities that are not commonly ascribed in English. You should recognize the untranslated names.

млекопита́ющие mammals
  слон elephant
  жира́ф(а)
  верблю́д camel (**одного́рбый верблю́д, двуго́рбый верблю́д**)
  гиппопота́м, бегемо́т hippopotamus (behemoth)

носоро́г rhinoceros (*from* nose + horn)
зе́бра
тигр
лев lion
осёл donkey, ass (reputation for stupidity, but also for stubbornness: **"упря́мый, как осёл"**—"stubborn as a mule")
мул
гие́на
муравье́д anteater (**мураве́й** ant)
лени́вец sloth (**лени́вый** lazy)
обезья́ны monkeys and apes (also a pejorative for someone who imitates)
  марты́шка a small monkey, technically a macaque
  орангута́нг
  гори́лла (also anyone who is very large, strong, and unattractive)
  бабуи́н
  шимпанзе́
  мака́ка
пти́цы birds
  стра́ус ostrich
  попуга́й parrot (**попуга́йчик** parakeet)
  пингви́н
зме́и snakes
  пито́н
  уда́в boa constrictor (**дави́ть** to press, squeeze)
морски́е живо́тные aquatic animals
  кит whale
  дельфи́н dolphin
  морска́я свинья́ porpoise (**морска́я сви́нка** guinea pig)
  аку́ла shark
  морж walrus
  меду́за jellyfish

Animals in nature
Живо́тные в приро́де

Worms
Че́рви

The general word for worm is **червя́к, червь**: **"Ма́льчики иска́ли черве́й для ры́бной ло́вли."**

The term for larva, grub, or maggot is **личи́нка**; therefore, **гу́сеница—личи́нка ба́бочки**.

Глисты́ is the general word for intestinal worms: **"Не ешь сыро́е мя́со, полу́чишь глисты́"**—"Don't eat raw meat or you'll get worms." Common types of parasitic worms are: **солите́р**, **солитёр** the tapeworm, **аскари́да** a roundworm, and **остри́ца** the pinworm.

LEECHES   ПИЯ́ВКИ

Пия́вки are found in still-water ditches or ponds. For medicinal purposes they are still sometimes used when bloodletting is thought to be an appropriate treatment, for example, in thrombophlebitis, some types of hypertension, miocardial infarction, and so on.

● В СССР пия́вок медици́нских ло́вят преиму́щественно в Краснода́рском кра́е, Молда́вской, Укра́инской, Грузи́нской, и Азербайджа́нской ССР, а та́кже разво́дят в лаборато́рных усло́виях.[5]

Insects and the like
Насеко́мые и други́е

The lists that follow name insects that every Russian schoolchild recognizes; almost all of these names appear in beginning school readers. Some general vocabulary first will serve to introduce the subject.

There are two very useful words in Russian that can be used to denote almost any insect too small or insignificant for more accurate identification—**бука́шка** and **козя́вка**. Anything even vaguely resembling a beetle can be **жук**. And any very small animal with an unusually large number of legs is **сороконо́жка** or **многоно́жка** (sometimes applied to a caterpillar **гу́сеница**).

When the Russian wants to identify a particular kind of insect (or bird or mammal, for that matter), he often uses two nouns: **жук-навозник** a dung beetle, **пау́к-челно́к** a "shuttle" spider, **жук-плавуне́ц** a water beetle, and so on. Especially in poetry these nouns are combined just for the sake of alliteration: **жучо́к-светля-**

[5] А. Н. Ба́кулев и Ф. Н. Петро́в, *Популя́рная медици́нская энциклопе́дия* (Москва́: Изда́тельство "Сове́тская энциклопе́дия," 1966), стр. 679.

чо́к, **бука́шка-тарака́шка**, **бло́шки-бука́шки**, **жучки́-тарака́шки**.

Historically, if not currently, those insects that relate so well to people have been the bane of the Russian's existence. This is true of the flea **блоха́**, louse **вошь**, bedbug **клоп**, and cockroach **тарака́н**, especially the latter two. Modern insecticides have been of major importance in reducing such infestations.

As a final general word, note that moths and butterflies are divided into different categories in Russian. **Мотылёк** is a kind of small moth known for flying in swarms at night; **моль** is the small moth whose larvae eat clothes or infest granaries. All the rest to a Russian are **ба́бочки**.

●USEFUL OR HARMLESS   ПОЛЕ́ЗНЫЕ ИЛИ
INSECTS   БЕЗВРЕ́ДНЫЕ НАСЕКО́МЫЕ

ба́бочка butterfly, moth
Мно́гие коллекциони́руют ба́бочек.
В жи́зни ба́бочки есть четы́ре эта́па: (1) яйцо́, (2) гу́сеница, (3) ку́колка, (4) ба́бочка.

бо́жья коро́вка ladybug
    Бо́жья коро́вка, улети́ на не́бо.
    Там твои́ де́тки ку́шают котле́тки.
    (Улети́ на не́бо, принеси́ нам хле́ба.)

жук beetle
Жук—это вся́кое насеко́мое с твёрдыми кры́льями.

мотылёк moth
То́ же, что ба́бочка, но ча́сто появля́ется на у́лицах но́чью. Мотылёк порха́ет.

мо́шка gnat (**мошкара́** swarm of gnats)
Мошкара́ появля́ется гла́вным о́бразом ве́чером при захо́де со́лнца.

мураве́й ant
Мураве́й рабо́тает день и ночь, он си́мвол трудолю́бия. Муравьи́ живу́т в мураве́йнике.

пау́к spider
Пау́к плетёт паути́ну.

оса́ wasp
Не тронь оси́ное гнездо́, беда́ бу́дет.

пчела́ bee
Пчёлы живу́т в у́льях. Ма́тка—са́мая больша́я пчела́; она́ кладёт я́йца. Рабо́чая пчела́ собира́ет мёд, а тру́тень не произво́дит никако́й рабо́ты. Рой сле́дует за ма́ткой.

сверчо́к cricket

Сверчки́ ча́сто живу́т в дома́х за пе́чкой; ра́ньше счита́лось, что они́ ча́сто разгова́ривают с домовы́м.[6] Иногда́ они́ отождествля́ются с сами́м домовы́м.

светля́к firefly

Светляки́ появля́ются но́чью.

стрекоза́ dragonfly

Чита́йте ба́сню Крыло́ва "Стрекоза́ и мураве́й."

шмель bumblebee

Шмели́ о́чень похо́жи на пчёл, но они́ бо́льше.

●INSECT PESTS   НАСЕКО́МЫЕ-ВРЕДИ́ТЕЛИ

капу́стница cabbage moth

Капу́стница (капу́стная ба́бочка) кладёт яи́чки в стебельки́ капу́сты, а пото́м личи́нки их поеда́ют.

клещ tick

Лесно́й клещ передаёт энцефали́т.

кома́р mosquito

"Че́шется. Кома́р укуси́л."

кузне́чик grasshopper

Зелёненький кузне́чик, коле́нками наза́д, волну́ется, стреко́чет, чему́-то о́чень рад.

ма́йский жук May beetle
(и́ли) хрущ

Ма́йский жук ест берёзу. Хрущ—вреди́тель се́льского хозя́йства.

мокри́ца sow bug, wood louse

Мокри́цы о́чень проти́вные; счита́ют, что они́ гря́зные.

моль moth

Про́тив мо́ли ну́жно употребля́ть нафтали́н.

му́ха fly

Обяза́тельно прочита́йте "Му́ху-цокоту́ху" Чуко́вского.

Что́бы изба́виться от мух, употребля́ют и мухобо́йки и ли́пкие ле́нты.

саранча́ locust

Они́ набро́сились на стол как саранча́. (Всё о́чень бы́стро съе́ли.)

тарака́н cockroach

Тарака́ны о́чень неприя́тные, и от них тру́дно изба́виться.

тля aphid

(Сло́во "тля" употребля́ется гла́вным о́бразом в

[6] See "The house 'spirit'" in Chapter 4.

еди́нственном числе́.) Тля появи́лась. Там тля по́лзает.

уховёртка earwig

Согла́сно суеве́рию, уховёртка проника́ет в у́хо и да́же в мозг.

●HUMAN INFESTATION   ПАРАЗИ́ТЫ ЧЕЛОВЕ́КА

блоха́ flea

"Что ты ска́чешь, как блоха́?"

вошь louse

Вши пита́ются то́лько кро́вью челове́ка и млекопита́ющих. На челове́ке парази́тируют три ви́да вшей: головна́я, платяна́я, и лобко́вая.

гни́да nit

Гни́да—э́то яи́чко вши. Они́ ме́лкие, бе́лые, и не дви́гаются.

клоп bedbug

Клопо́в боя́тся ме́ньше, чем вшей, так как они́ обы́чно живу́т на веща́х, а не на те́ле.

Ме́жду про́чим, дуст-ДДТ наибо́лее распространённое сре́дство по борьбе́ с дома́шними парази́тами. (ДДТ произно́сится дэ-дэ-тэ́.)

From mollusks to amphibians
От моллю́сков до земново́дных

Of the mollusks **моллю́ски**, the most familiar are the snail **ули́тка** and slug **слизня́к**. The oyster **у́стрица** has been heard of but is far from familiar, while clams have not even reached that status. The squid **кальма́р** is associated with Oriental cookery.

The most familiar of the crustaceans **ракообра́зные** is the crayfish **рак**, a popular accompaniment to beer. Crab **краб** is a highly regarded delicacy that is commonly exported and therefore hard to obtain in Soviet stores.

In the class of reptiles **пресмыка́ющиеся**, there are two kinds of native snakes **зме́и** that are commonly distinguished: **уж** is the common garden snake, useful at least for eliminating garden pests; **гадю́ка** is poisonous and immediately distinguishable from the nonpoisonous snakes by a triangular-shaped head noticeably separate from its body: "**У гадю́ки ядови́тый зуб.**" (Клык fang is not used in referring to snakes; only dogs and wolves have fangs: "**Вы** читáли «Бéлый клы́к» Джéка Лóндона?'') The lizard **я́щерица** and turtle **черепáха** are common and retain their reputations:

● В слýчае опáсности, я́щерицы спасáются "теря́я" хвосты́.
Он ползёт, как черепáха. (Он óчень мéдленно идёт.)

The amphibians **земновóдные** include the frog **лягýшка** (**головáстик** tadpole) and the toad **жáба**, a common animal that has retained its reputation:

● Соглáсно суевéрию, у людéй от жаб появля́ются бородáвки.

Fish
Ры́ба

● —А какáя у вас ры́ба?
—Ры́ба-то? Ры́ба вся́кая.... И караси́ на плёсах есть, щýка, ну, потóм э́ти ... óкунь, плотвá, лещ ... Ещё линь. Знáешь линя́? Как поросёнок. Тó-олстый! Я сам пéрвый раз поймáл—рот рази́нул.[7]

Fish supply a major source of protein in the Russian's diet; they are comparatively plentiful and relatively cheap. That is why a Russian will distinguish many different kinds of fish, while it is much less likely that he will also be familiar with the difference between a chuck roast and a rump roast.

The criterion for elegance is the fat content of the fish—the more fat, the better. Especially good fish are: **все осетрóвые и лососёвые, а тáкже щýка, сом, ýгорь и нали́м**. Especially inexpensive fish are: **кáмбалá** (**атланти́ческая**), **сельдь, салáка, ёрш**.

The preserving of fish is both a science and an art, with such varieties as canned "bullheads in tomato sauce," smoked salmon (or sturgeon), and many kinds of salted, dried, and pickled fish. Of course, fish are also sold fresh, frozen, and live. The most common fish to be sold live are: **карп, карáсь, сазáн, стéрлядь, форéль, щýка, лещ**.

[7] Ю́рий Казакóв, "Ти́хое ýтро," *На полустáнке: расскáзы* (Москвá: Совéтский писáтель, 1959), стр. 8.

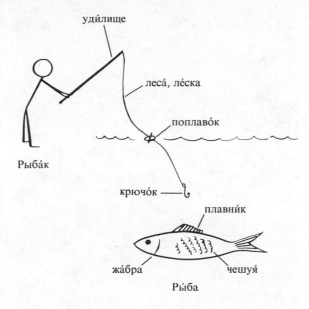

ýдочка = уди́лище + лесá + крючóк

уди́лище

лесá, лéска

поплавóк

Рыбáк

крючóк

плавни́к

жáбра

чешуя́

Ры́ба

The traditional Russian fish were freshwater fish. They are the ones you are most likely to encounter in Russian literature, and in the discussions that follow they are marked with an asterisk.[8]

STURGEON FAMILY **СЕМÉЙСТВО ОСЕТРÓВЫХ**

The USSR accounts for 90 percent of the world's supply of sturgeon, an elegant, expensive, and very traditional fish because of its rich meat and even richer roe (caviar). The sturgeon are called "red" fish **крáсная ры́ба** even though the meat is white, just as the main square in Moscow is called "Red" Square; the word was formerly equivalent to "good" and "beautiful." Except for **стéрлядь**, most sturgeon is sold frozen or smoked.

осётр* Russian sturgeon, *Acipenser güldenstädti* (commonly weighs 30 to 40 pounds)

[8] Fishermen may be interested in *Russian-English Glossary of Names of Aquatic Organisms and Other Biological and Related Terms*, Circular No. 65, compiled by W. E. Ricker (Nanaimo, B.C.: Fisheries Research Board of Canada, 1962).

The beluga белу́га *is the giant of the sturgeon family. This one weighed 635 kilograms.*

севрю́га stellate sturgeon, *Acipenser stellatus* (weighs between 14 and 64 pounds and is especially highly valued for its meat)

белу́га beluga, *Huso huso* (the largest, commonly 70 to 140 pounds, but some grow to be huge)

сте́рлядь* sterlet, *Acipenser ruthenus* (the smallest, usually from 6 to 12 pounds, but its meat is supposed to be the best of all)

Други́е осетро́вые ры́бы: **шип, калу́га.**

CAVIAR ИКРА́

Caviar comes from two major sources: salmon from the Far Eastern rivers supply red caviar **кра́сная и́ли ке́то́вая икра́**, and black caviar **чёрная икра́** is supplied by the sturgeon family.

Red caviar is generally considered to be the less desirable of the two. The smaller and lighter colored roe (from **горбу́ша** the humpback salmon) are thought to be the best.

Black caviar **чёрная икра́**, however, dominates the scene; here the larger-sized and lighter-colored roe are preferred. One way of describing caviar is to name the fish that supplied it: **"Белу́жья зерни́стая икра́ счита́ется са́мой лу́чшей, за не́й идёт осетро́вая икра́, на тре́тьем ме́сте севрю́жья икра́."**

There are two major ways of preparing black caviar. In the first, **зерни́стая икра́**, the individual eggs are clearly distinct from one another. Caviar prepared this way can be bought fresh (presumably the best), but it does not keep well. More commonly, it is pasteurized in little glass jars. It is in this form that most Americans come across caviar. **Па́юсная икра́**, the second kind of preparation, is pressed caviar, where the individual eggs are not distinct and the resultant mass vaguely resembles a thick gray blackberry jam. Pressed caviar will keep longer than **зерни́стая икра́**: **"Наилу́чшая па́юсная икра́— севрю́жья."**

SALMON FAMILY СЕМЕ́ЙСТВО ЛОСОСЁВЫХ

The Russian salmon family is both elegant and large, including not only Atlantic and Pacific salmon, but also some trout, inconnu, and whitefish which have white meat (**сиг, о́муль, не́льма, белоры́бица**) and are often therefore referred to as **бе́лая ры́ба**, not to be confused with the white-meated **кра́сная ры́ба** of the sturgeon family. Salmon is currently available canned, smoked, or salted.

The fish that we usually think of as salmon (and therefore not including trout, whitefish, and so forth) comes in two major categories: Atlantic salmon and Pacific salmon. All salmon can be referred to as **лосо́сь**, but that word perhaps more often identifies the Atlantic salmon, the specific word for which is **сёмга**. The meat of the Atlantic salmon is held in higher regard than the Pacific salmon probably because of its higher fat content; it is often smoked or air-dried.

For very large-scale commercial fishing, however, the Pacific (Far Eastern) salmon takes first place by far. Of the six fish in this family, three are of major economic importance in the Soviet Union. First comes the humpback or pink salmon **горбу́ша**, then the chum or dog salmon **кéта́**, and finally the sockeye or red salmon **нéрка**. The chum salmon **кéта́** has given its name to red salmon caviar **кéто́вая икра́** and to Pacific salmon in general: **"Кéта́ идёт"**—"The salmon are running."

Of the smaller fish in the salmon family, **форéль** refers to any of the salmon trout; it is often raised in ponds and is highly regarded. The char **голéц** is less well known but of major economic importance to Arctic fishermen.

PERCH FAMILY · СЕМÉЙСТВО О́КУНЕВЫХ

Famous for their spiny fins, these fish can also be distinguished by dark horizontal stripes. In this family, only the **суда́к** is commonly and joyfully eaten. The other two are most frequently come upon by the amateur fisherman who is more interested in going fishing than in catching anything.

о́кунь* perch, *Perca fluviatilis* (small, rarely on sale, but commonly caught and made into fish soup)

ёрш* ruff, *Acerina cernua* (very small, bony, and famous both for its belligerence and bony spines: **"Он всегда́ ершится"**—"He always has his back up.")

суда́к* pikeperch, *Lucioperca lucioperca* (highly regarded, averaging from two to five pounds, and often especially raised in reservoirs)

Други́е о́куневые ры́бы: **берш, морско́й суда́к.**

COD FAMILY · СЕМÉЙСТВО ТРЕСКО́ВЫХ

The cod family, most of whose members are saltwater fish, is of great economic significance. In 1969 cods, hakes, and haddock amounted to 40 percent of the total fish catch. Leningraders and Archangelites especially are supposed to appreciate the glories of this category.

треска́ cod (caught in the northern seas, relatively bony, but of significant economic interest; the liver is canned separately and sold as a delicacy)

нали́м* burbot (predatory, long, narrow, and without scales; considered to be very good; the only freshwater fish in this category)

нава́га *Eleginus spp.* (very small, bony, but especially tasty and caught in the northern seas: **беломо́рская нава́га**)

пи́кша haddock (very much like **треска́**, but somewhat smaller)

хэк, хек European hake, *Merluccinus sp.*, or Pacific hake **тихоокеа́нский хэк** (both fished commercially in large numbers and commonly sold frozen in the markets)

CARP FAMILY · СЕМÉЙСТВО КА́РПОВЫХ

Carp is a very common type, usually cheap, and quite bony. Some kinds (**карп, лещ**) are very commonly raised in ponds or reservoirs since they adapt quickly and grow very fast. Many of them are sold live.

карп carp (at their best at three to four pounds; often specially raised in ponds)

саза́н* (the same fish as **карп**, except they are wild and thought of as much bigger)

песка́рь* gudgeon (very small, only weighing a few grams, and caught for fun and fish soup)

лещ bream, *Abramis brama* (usually from six to fourteen inches long; the largest are the best)

кара́сь* crucian carp, *Carassius carassius* (small, often sold live, fished for fun, or raised where no other fish will grow)

во́бла Caspian roach, *Rutilus rutilus caspicus* (relatively cheap and common: **вя́леная во́бла**—air-dried Caspian roach; **"Она́ худа́я (и́ли суха́я) как во́бла"**—"She's as thin (dry) as a Caspian roach.")

плотва́ roach, *Rutilus rutilus*

тара́нь Azov roach, *Rutilus rutilus heckeli*

Други́е ка́рповые ры́бы: **линь, шемая́, рыбе́ц, куту́м, жéрех, толстоло́б, бéлый аму́р, язь.**

бычо́к goby, sculpin, bullhead, *Gobiidae* (like our tuna fish in that they are cheap and always sold canned: **бычки́ в тома́те** bullheads in tomato sauce)

кефа́ль gray mullet (small, caught in the Black Sea and the Mediterranean, commonly canned: **кефа́ль в тома́те**, dried or smoked, and also eaten fresh; prized for its high fat content)

ка́мбала́ flounder, sole, or any flatfish (taken commercially in large numbers and frozen; not very highly regarded, principally because of its "fishy" taste)

морско́й о́кунь redfish or ocean perch (usually sold frozen; smaller ones weighing up to four pounds are considered the best)

ску́мбрия, макре́ль mackerel (small, relatively fatty, often smoked or canned)

нототе́ния *Nototheniidae* (newcomer to Soviet markets and an example of how far Soviet commercial fishing is willing to go: the fish is found in deep waters of the Antarctic)

селёдка (salt) herring (abundant, accounting for almost 20 percent of the total commercial catch in 1969, and universally available with smoking, drying, and soaking techniques used for preserving, though it can also be bought fresh; *formal* **сельдь**)

сала́ка Baltic herring (popular, and sold salted, smoked, and fresh)

шпрот, ки́лька sprat (usually sold smoked and considered to be very elegant)

сом* sheatfish, Danube catfish (easily distinguished from other fish by its "whiskers" **у́сики** and lack of scales; very large, up to five meters long, though only the smaller ones are considered the best eating and often are sold live)

у́горь eel (large, with a high fat content, and therefore often smoked and considered a delicacy: **"Кру́пные угри́ горя́чего копче́ния осо́бенно це́нятся потреби́телями"**—"Consumers especially like large hot-smoked eel.")

щу́ка* pike (relatively large, predatory, and a freshwater variety, often considered at its best when stuffed; for its traditional place in Russian lore, read the fairy tale "По щу́чьему веле́нью")

CURING FISH   СОЛЕ́НИЕ И КОПЧЕ́НИЕ РЫ́БЫ

Ice and rapid transportation have made fresh (or frozen) fish available in addition to what can be caught in the local pond or river. But Russians preserve fish in many ways for later consumption, usually as hors d'oeuvres **заку́ски**.

The first step in curing fish is always to salt it, applying either salt in solution or dry salt for varying lengths of time depending on the kind of fish and its further treatment. To make salt fish **солёная ры́ба**, the process could stop at this stage. The fish must then be soaked and cooked before being eaten. Pickled fish **марино́ванная ры́ба** is simply wet-salted fish with vinegar and spices. Especially fatty fishes require more than salting: smoking or drying under certain conditions is used to preserve what the salting cannot.

Вя́леная ры́ба is fish that has been salted, washed, drained, and then hung on special frames and dried either by air or a combination of air and sun for seven to thirty days: **"В вя́леном ви́де гото́вятся во́бла, саза́н, шемая́, рыбе́ц, тара́нь."** **Балы́к** is the boneless, thick top part of sturgeon (either **осётр** or **севрю́га**) and whitefish (**белоры́бица, не́льма**, or **о́муль**) prepared this way. As a delicacy **балы́к** is outranked only by caviar.

Ры́ба горя́чего копче́ния is fish that has been salted, washed, and then smoked for three to four hours at 80° to 140°C. Often used for carp, sturgeon, salmon, eel, and many others, this method produces a delicious result; but fish so prepared does not keep well and must be eaten within a few days. Fish that has been salted, washed, drained, and then cold-smoked (at 28° to 32°C) for two to four days is **ры́ба холо́дного копче́ния**. This method is used when fish must keep for a long time. Almost all fish can be preserved this way.

Finally, **сушёная ры́ба** denotes dried fish, with or without a foretreatment of salt. This method can be used for a low fat content fish and requires that the fish be cooked before it is eaten.

Birds
Пти́цы

Осень.

Ла́сточки пропа́ли,
а вчера́ зарёй
всё грачи́ лета́ли
да как сеть мелька́ли
вон над той горо́й.
С ве́чера всё спи́тся,
на дворе́ темно́,
лист сухо́й вали́тся,
но́чью ве́тер зли́тся
да стучи́т в окно́...
Лу́чше б снег да вью́гу
встре́тить гру́дью рад!
Сло́вно как с испу́гу
раскрича́вшись, к ю́гу
журавли́ летя́т.

А. Фет

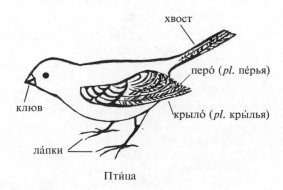

Пти́ца

● К кру́пной ди́чи отно́сят куропа́тку, ря́бчика, те́терева, глухаря́, фаза́на, ди́кого гу́ся и у́тку; к ме́лкой—пе́репела, бека́са, ду́пеля, ва́льдшнепа.[9]

The dictionary is of very little use to language students on the topic of birds. Rarely are birds

[9] Е. и М. Нико́льские, *Кни́га о культу́ре бы́та* (Москва́: Профизда́т, 1967), стр. 195.

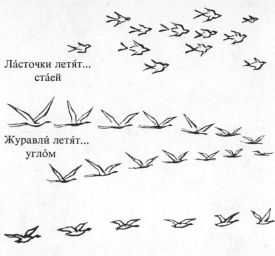

Ла́сточки летя́т...
ста́ей

Журавли́ летя́т...
угло́м

Гу́си летя́т...
верени́цей

important enough for a dictionary picture; the reputation of a particular kind is of no concern; the scientific name is rarely given; language dictionaries tend to translate to British, not American, usage; and finally, only a few birds are common to both the Soviet Union and the United States. These problems are compounded by the Russian's own real delight in his feathered friends; Russians are countryfolk, though they may not like that description. Even now only half the population lives in cities, and most of those people were not born there. The countryside and the nature lore that goes with it are part of a Russian's heritage.

For example, to us the starling **скворе́ц** is such a pest that thousands of dollars have been spent trying to eliminate or at least banish it. The Russian orchardist might be unhappy that starlings like cherries, but the bird is still highly regarded both for its capacity for insects and also just because it is always around. The word for birdhouse is "starling house" **скворе́чник, скворе́чня**. Some time in March, Russian children run home to mother with the delighted cry, **"Скворцы́ прилете́ли! Скворцы́ прилете́ли!"** (It seems that many birds are harbingers of

Сорóка
Ворóна
Воробéй
Снеги́рь
Сини́ца

spring, especially starlings and larks.) Conversely, the Russian does not share our affection for hummingbirds **коли́бри**. He has none.

The following are birds particularly noticeable in Russian life and literature. All, in addition to the starling, are familiar to Soviet preschoolers. A section on birds in the Appendix gives scientific names, sizes, color descriptions, and comments on most birds that any eight-year-old Russian knows.

снеги́рь bullfinch (small, gray and red in color, and well liked for its prettiness and the fact that it arrives and stays throughout the winter when most other birds have left; it spends its summers deep in northern forests far from the common view)

воробéй sparrow (very common and renowned for its quarrelsomeness, thievery, and the fact that it doesn't fly south for the winter)

соловéй eastern nightingale (noted for a gay, proud song in contrast to that of the sad western nightingale familiar to West Europeans; its gray feathers are as plain as its song is brilliant)

This is the way Prof. Kaygorodov reports the nightingale's song:

Проф. Д. Н. Кайгорóдову удалóсь все стрóфы пéния соловья́ изобрази́ть на человéческом языкé. Это вы́глядит приблизи́тельно так:

(1) Фи-тчурр, фи-тчурр, вад-вад-вад-вад-ции!
(2) Тю-лит, тю-лит, тю-лит.
(3) Клю-клю-клю-клю.
(4) Юу-лит, юу-лит.
(5) Ци-фи, ци-фи, ци-фи.
(6) Пью, пью, пью, пью.
(7) Ци-фи, ци-фи, чочочочочочо—вит!
(8) Цици-вит, тю-вит, тю-вит.
(9) Юу-лит, чочочочо-тррр-ц!
(10) Пи-пи-пи-пи, клю-клю-клю-клю.
(11) Чричи-чу; чричи-чу, чричи-чу.
(12) Ци-вит (тихо), клюи (громко), клюи (очень громко).[10]

сини́ца titmouse (related to the chickadee and known as a sociable busybody; it seeks populated places for food in the winter)

сорóка magpie (medium-sized, black and white, a very long tail, and almost always pictured with its bill open—not for food, but to

[10] Ф. Ф. Остáпов, *Пéвчие пти́цы нáшей рóдины* (Москвá: Акадéмия наýк СССР, 1960), стр. 140.

complain; it is famous both for an unpleasant squawk and a tendency to take anything: **соро́ка-воро́вка** thieving magpie)

воро́на crow (mostly gray with black patches and thought of as a not very bright pest: "**Воро́на—рази́ня**"—"A crow is a gawk." It is distinguished from the **соро́ка** by the mnemonic: "**Все соро́ки белобо́ки, все воро́ны чернобо́ки.**")

грач rook (all black in color and generally seen in great flocks whose appearance denotes the arrival of spring; a famous painting is "Грачи́ прилете́ли" by Савра́сов)

жа́воронок skylark (the preeminent harbinger of spring)

куку́шка cuckoo (noted for its nasty habit of depositing its eggs in the nests of other birds; when the egg hatches, the newborn cuckoo pushes any other egg out of the nest and the mother-hostess has the joy of raising the stranger)

жура́вль crane (often kept as a pet, relatively easily tamed, and well loved as evidenced by the number of stories about it; the children's name for it is **жу́рка**)

● —Вот они́, жу́рки! Ух, как бли́зко! Что́ за пти́цы удиви́тельные! А но́ги-то, но́ги—бу́дто дли́нные па́лки!
. . . Один жу́рка разбежа́лся.[11]

глуха́рь wood grouse (very large, black, quite popular, and noted for its deafness during its mating call when ear passages are blocked off: **глухо́й** deaf; the hunter runs up close while the call lasts and then freezes until the next call is under way)

те́терев black grouse (as a male, black, somewhat smaller than a chicken, and readily distinguishable by its rather large tail in the shape of an upside down lyre; as a female—**тете́рка**—brown and with a plain old tail; both find refuge from the winter's cold in snowbanks)

[11] Соловьёва, Щепето́ва, и Карпи́нская, *Родна́я речь: кни́га для чте́ния во* II *кла́ссе нача́льной шко́лы* (Москва: Учпедги́з, 1964), стр. 32.

Грач

Жа́воронок

Куку́шка

Жура́вль

Те́терев

Тете́рка

Russian mammals
Млекопитáющие

Млекопитáющие include the most familiar of all the animals and also the widest variety. Limitations imposed by space and reason have compressed the discussion to eleven that seem to have the most associations in Russian life and are familiar to Russian preschoolers. A more extensive listing of mammals familiar to Soviet third and fourth graders follows this discussion.

To us, the hamster **хомя́к**, *Cricetus cricetus*, is a cute children's pet or a laboratory animal. The Russian hamster, on the contrary, is a scourge to grain farming and the object of considerable efforts at eradication. Since the hamster likes ripened grain, it eats as much as it can hold and then carries off the rest in its cheek pouches to a hole in the ground. These grain depositories have been raided by starving peasants in times of famine.

Су́слик

Another major pest in grain fields is the suslik **су́слик**, *Citellus suslicus*, a ground squirrel that prefers unripened grain. The **су́слик** lives in large colonies and is famous for sitting on its hind feet and whistling loudly when alarmed. This animal devastates by biting off green stems and sucking the juice (whence its name— **су́слик**): **"Хомяки́, су́слики, полёвки, мы́ши— враги́ урожа́я. С ни́ми ведётся беспоща́дная**

Бе́лка

борьба́"—"Hamsters, susliks, field voles, and mice are enemies of the harvest. They are being fought without mercy."

The squirrel **бе́лка**, *Sciurus vulgaris*, there, as here, is thought of as a "little forest friend." The common squirrel is grayish red in summer and reddish gray in winter, and it always has tufted ears. Especially in Siberia, the squirrel is the object of commercial hunters' expeditions. Below is a description of one such sad end in a third-grade book. (Note that in northern dialect **ве́кша** is **бе́лка**.)

● На сле́дующий день Ники́фор с соба́кой отпра́вился на охо́ту.

Зала́яла соба́ка. Это был совсе́м осо́бенный лай, по кото́рому промысло́вый охо́тник сра́зу узнаёт, что соба́ка вы́следила бе́лку. Бе́лка ска́чет с де́рева на де́рево. Соба́ка бежи́т внизу́ и подла́ивает жа́лобно и нетерпели́во, и охо́тнику то́лько остаётся идти́ на лай.

Ско́ро на де́реве появи́лась се́ренькая ве́кша. Почти́ то́тчас же из кусто́в вы́скочила соба́ка, продолжа́я без у́стали тя́вкать. Ве́кша не испуга́лась соба́ки, враг на земле́ не стра́шен бе́лке, сидя́щей на де́реве. Она́ опусти́лась на ни́жнюю ве́тку и ста́ла фы́ркать на свою́ преследова́тельницу. Соба́ка пры́гала и топта́лась по́ снегу, а бе́лка серди́то ворча́ла и шипе́ла.

В э́то вре́мя из-за кусто́в показа́лся Ники́фор. Он, не спеша́, положи́л свою́ винто́вку на сучо́к ствола́ и стал це́литься в ве́кшу. Ве́кша не заме́тила охо́тника: её внима́ние бы́ло прико́вано к соба́ке.

Ники́фор вы́стрелил. Уби́тая бе́лка пови́сла на ве́тке, зацепи́вшись за неё когтя́ми. Охо́тник сбил бе́лку и то́тчас стал снима́ть с неё шку́рку. Он надре́зал её о́стрым ножо́м и стал сдира́ть бели́чью шу́бку, завора́чивая её так, как снима́ют чуло́к с ноги́.

Содра́в шку́рку, он бро́сил го́лую ту́шку ла́йке. Соба́ка съе́ла её с жа́дностью.

Четы́ре ме́сяца про́жили зверо́ловы в тайге́. Они́ уби́ли мно́го бе́лок.

В середи́не ма́рта Ники́фор со всей арте́лью верну́лся домо́й.[12]

Two major types of hare are relatively common and well known: (1) **за́яц-беля́к**, or just **беля́к**, *Lepus timidus*, turns white for the winter; and (2) **за́яц-руса́к**, or just **руса́к**, *Lepus europaeus*, keeps the same color, a light brown, all year. Hare is eaten only in very dire necessity, though it is hunted for its fur. (The hare has longer ears and hind legs than does the rabbit.) Properly, "rabbit" should be used only when applied to **кро́лик**, the domesticated rabbit of Russia, which is eaten and which also supplies fur.

Related to the shrew and mole is the hedgehog **ёж**,[13] *Erinaceus europaeus*. Though most

Ёж

Americans would associate bears and wolves with Russia, few would add the hedgehog to that list. The animal, close to beloved to a Russian, is thought of as cute, charming, and even useful. Sometimes hedgehogs are kept as pets and are traditional residents of basements where their duties are to eliminate mice, small snakes, and the like. Their nocturnal habits tend to keep them out of sight.

The European badger **барсу́к**, *Meles meles*, is omnivorous and is noted for digging up plants, often invading gardens and removing whole plants for winter storage. Its numbers are not large enough to constitute a real threat, however. The badger is featured in a short story by Konstantin Paustovskiy, "Барсу́чий нос," and Leonid Leonov's first novel is *Барсуки́*.

Барсу́к

The common fox **лиси́ца** or **лиса́**, *Vulpes vulpes*, is red with a white-tipped tail, but varieties of this species extend from almost all-black to all-white. The **чернобу́рая лиси́ца** is dark brown or black, rare, and therefore much more valuable. **Кресто́вка** and **сиводу́шка** are more like the red fox but have a significant amount of brown or black in their fur. Three kinds of silver fox are bred artificially and raised in captivity: **серебри́сто-чёрная**, **пла́тиновая**, and **белосне́жная лиси́ца**. The fox is, of course, one of the best known of all Russian animals. Stories about it abound in folk tales, not to mention Krylov's fables. **Лиси́ца** is the usual word for fox, while **лиса́** is somewhat more poetic (and also the term for fox fur).

The wolf **волк**, *Canis lupus*, is in the fore-

[12] Соловьёва, Щепето́ва, Карпи́нская, Волы́нская, и Кана́рская, *Родна́я речь: кни́га для чте́ния в* III *кла́ссе нача́льной шко́лы*, 20ое изд. (Москва́: Учпедги́з, 1964), стр. 207.

[13] In Europe, the hedgehog and the porcupine are two quite different animals. The only thing the two have in common is that they both can be unpleasant to the touch. The porcupine **дикобра́з** lives only in more remote southern areas of the USSR. Hedgehogs have spiny fur, not quills.

ground, not the background, of the Russian language. A predator on farm animals and formerly a threat to human life (especially in the hungry winter months), it is a standard figure in Russian stories and sayings. The wolf's number has dwindled now, but its reputation remains undimmed.

The deer family, which includes the moose and reindeer, has several well known representatives in the USSR, two of which run into serious trouble when they are dealt with by translators. The most common problem is that the moose **лось**, *Alces alces*, is often translated as "elk" since, as previously mentioned, elk is British English for moose. The moose, partly because of its size, is thought of as a benevolent king of the forest (**лесно́й царь—лось**), and since it is well protected by game laws, it is actually a fairly common sight in the taiga. The other major problem for careless translators is the "reindeer" versus "deer" confusion brought on by Russian usage. A reindeer (a very close relative of our caribou) is **се́верный оле́нь**, *Rangifer tarandus*, and should not be translated as "northern deer." The reindeer is domesticated and widely used for hides, food, and services in the far north.

Perhaps the most "Russian" animal is the (brown) bear (**бу́рый) медве́дь**, *Ursus arctos*. It is a close relative of the grizzly and the Alaskan brown bear: "**Медве́дь—хозя́ин ле́са.**" The bear is perhaps thought of as fearsome because of its size, but it is certainly not feared as the wolf is. The Russian thinks of the bear as very intelligent and even not without dignity. The children's story name for it is **Ми́ша**.

Below is a list of other mammals familiar to most Russians and found outside a zoo, pen, or laboratory. The star indicates those animals that supply fur.

байба́к *see* **суро́к**

барс snow leopard or ounce, *Uncia uncia* or *Felis uncia* (spotted, with a large fluffy tail; rare in reality but a symbol of size and strength in the cat family. The name "**Ба́рсик**" for a cat is equivalent to our "Tiger.")

бе́лый медве́дь polar bear, *Ursus maritimus*

бобр* (*technical*), **бобёр** (*colloquial*) beaver, *Castor fiber* (highly regarded for its industry and also thought of as good, even kind: "**Он добёр, как бобёр.**")

бурунду́к chipmunk, *Eutamis sibiricus*

вы́дра* otter, *Lutra lutra* (prized for its fur; the animal has given its name to any ugly and mean woman)

вы́хухоль* desman, *Desmana moschata* (large, shrewlike, prized for its fur; it lives near water)

горноста́й* ermine, *Mustela erminea* (white with a black-tipped tail in the winter: "**У царя́ была́ горноста́евая ма́нтия.**")

ди́кая ко́шка wildcat (of several varieties, not normally distinguished)

ено́т *Nyctereutes procyonoides* (of the canine family; its full name is **енотови́дная соба́ка** or **уссури́йский ено́т**, not to be confused with **ено́т-полоску́н**, which it resembles)

ено́т-полоску́н raccoon, *Procyon lotor* (**полоска́ть** to rinse! Native to North America but acclimatized in some areas of the USSR)

землеро́йка (*literally* earth-digger) shrew, *Sorex araneus* (without the unpleasant connotations of the English counterpart)

зубр bison, *Bison bonasus* (freely roamed the European plains in the past but now confined to preserves, e.g., **Belove̋жская пу́ща**)

бизо́н American plains buffalo, *Bison bison*

каба́н boar, wild pig, *Sus scrofa* (or uncastrated male pig)

кала́н *see* **морска́я вы́дра**

коза́ (**лесна́я, ди́кая**) *see* **косу́ля**

колоно́к* (Siberian) kolinsky, *Mustela sibirica* (in the weasel family; hunted for its cheaper fur)

корса́к* fox, *Vulpes korsac* (small and found in the Asian steppes)

косу́ля roe deer, *Capreolus capreolus* (very small and therefore also called **ди́кая (и́ли) лесна́я коза́**)

ко́тик *see* **морско́й ко́тик**

крот mole, *Talpa europaea* (noted for its blindness: **"Он слепо́й, как крот."**)

кры́са rat (notorious as here: **"Ух, кры́са!"**—"The dirty rat!")

куни́ца* marten, *Martes* (prized for its fur; in the weasel family and of the same genus as the sable: **"Осо́бенно це́нится мех лесно́й куни́цы."**—"The fur of the European pine marten is especially [highly] valued.")

ла́ска weasel, *Mustela nivalis* (smallest of the weasel family and famous for taking prey by pouncing and biting the back of the neck)

летя́га flying squirrel, *Pteromys volans*

морска́я вы́дра* sea otter, *Enhydra lutris* (historically famous for luring the Russians to Alaska for its fur; also called **кала́н, камча́тский бобр**)

морско́й ко́тик* northern fur seal, *Callorhinus ursinus* (prized for fur; also responsible for bringing the Russians to Alaska)

мышь mouse (characterized much as it is here; **летучая мышь** bat)

не́рпа* seal, family: *Phocidae* (several varieties of true seals, the best known of which is **байка́льская не́рпа**, a seal that lives over 1000 miles from salt water)

но́рка* mink, *Mustela lutreola* (well known for its fur)

ну́трия* coypu (imported from South America and acclimatized for fur)

оле́нь deer

    благоро́дный, настоя́щий оле́нь red deer, *Cervus elaphus*

    мара́л, изю́бр (subspecies of red deer, raised and hunted for their antlers, which supply a common tonic **пантокри́н**)

онда́тра* muskrat, *Ondatra zibethica* (native to North America but imported and acclimatized for fur)

песе́ц* polar fox, *Vulpes lagopus* (resembles a cross between a dog and a fox; prized for fur: **бе́лый песе́ц, голубо́й песе́ц**

росома́ха* wolverine, *Gulo gulo* (largest of the weasel family and predatory; because of its reputation as unkempt and dirty, it has given its name to women with disheveled hair)

рысь lynx, *Felis lynx* (fierce and fearless; **"У ры́си ки́сточки на уша́х."**—"The lynx have tufts on their ears.")

се́рна chamois or mountain goat, *Rupricapra rupricapra* (famous for beauty, grace, speed, and nervousness: **"Она́ пугли́вая, как се́рна."**—"She is very easily frightened.")

со́боль* sable, *Martes zibellina* (of the weasel family and noted for highly prized fur: **"На боя́рах бы́ли собо́льи шу́бы."**—"The boyars wore sable coats.")

суро́к woodchuck, marmot, *Marmota bobac* (famous for whistling: **"Суро́к свисти́т в степи́"**; and hibernating: **"Он спит как суро́к."**—"He sleeps like a log.")

тигр tiger, *Panthera tigris*

тюле́нь* (a general term) any seal (reputed to be pleasant but lazy and slow)

хорь, хорёк (European) polecat or fitch, *Mustela putorius* (of the weasel family; thought of as ugly and mean: **"Ах, ты хорёк воню́чий"**; not to be confused with the skunk **ску́нс, воню́чка**, a native of North and Central America)

шака́л jackal, *Canis aureus* (a symbol of nastiness, meanness)

RUSSIAN FURS   **РУ́ССКИЕ МЕХА́**

To Americans, furs are as Russian as troikas and samovars, and for very good reason. Cold Siberian weather and immense forest land combine to afford the thickest, most luxuriant pelts. Many animals are also raised in captivity for their fur, but the very best skins still are from the wild animals of the northern taiga **тайга́** where weather forces a warmer coat. Professional hunters bring in the harvest. Capitalizing on what it does well, the USSR has imported and acclimatized fur bearers from the Western Hemisphere, including our raccoon **ено́т (-поло́скун)**, the muskrat **онда́тра**, and the coypu **ну́трия**. For animals best known for their fur, check those starred in the preceding list.

Fur comes from the domestic animals, too. **Кара́куль** comes from black baby karakul lambs not over three days old: **каракульча́** comes from the same animal but it is obtained before the animal has had time to be born. This is a very elegant fur and one of the largest branches of the fur industry. Considerably less elegant, perhaps, is calf fur **опо́ек** and pony fur **жеребо́к**.

Of course it would be close to impossible to read a Russian novel that did not include references to coats made of sheepskin **овчи́на**, especially the **тулу́п** (an extra long coat of sheepskin, fur side in) and the **шу́ба** (not so long and somewhat more elegant). Technically, **шу́ба** is a fur coat with the fur side *inside*, and the correct way to denote what we call a "fur coat" is **мехово́е пальто́** (a mink coat **пальто́ из но́рки**). However, popular usage often includes **шу́ба** to mean any fur coat no matter where the fur is.

Before you buy your fur coat, you ought to consult the table to find out which fur will last the longest. The otter and the sea otter will last the longest, while the water rat (or water vole) is hardly worth bothering with.

Сравни́тельная износосто́йкость мехо́в[1]

Назва́ние ви́да	Износо- сто́йкость (в %)
Вы́дра, морско́й ко́тик	100
Росома́ха, бобр речно́й	90
Со́боль	80
Но́рка	70
Белёк	70
Жеребо́к	64
Опо́ек	62
Кара́куль	60
Куни́ца мя́гкая	60
Куни́ца го́рская	55
Тюле́нь	55
Лиси́ца	50
Корса́к	45
Песе́ц	45
Рысь	40
Хорь тёмный	35
Бе́лка	30
Суро́к	27
Колоно́к	25
Горноста́й	25
Песча́ник	22
Ко́шка	17
Кро́лик	12
Крот, су́слик	10
Бурунду́к	8
Хомя́к	6
За́яц	5
Кры́са водяна́я	3

[1] *Това́рный слова́рь*, Том VII, стр. 471–72.

11

Numbers
Числа

It is said that mathematics is a language. Perhaps, but our mental pictures of 30 pounds, 60 miles per hour, 4 yards, 36–26–36, or 212° F. must be translated to scales used in Russian before they can have meaning for a Russian. (Even then we cannot assume that 36-26-36 is as much a Russian ideal as it is an American one.)

There are also special locutions used in Russian to express the same systems we use: latitude and longitude; $2 \times 4 = 8$. Those locutions are rarely mere translations of the words we use, but that is the stuff of language books like this one.

This chapter, of course, cannot cover all of the language of this vast field. Most of the discussion centers on the most basic arithmetic and geometric terminology and its practical applications, though there are a few specialized sections of interest to the student in mathematics, engineering, or the sciences. The topics to be covered include:

Numbers and their names
Reading and writing numbers
Declining numbers in spoken Russian
Arithmetic operations
Common geometric figures
Reading mathematical expressions
Measures

Numbers and their forms
Числа и их названия

The numbers
Числа

For your convenience, a table of numbers in units, tens, hundreds, thousands, and so on up to the billions is given.

When Russians are counting, however, they do not usually say **"один, два, три, ..."** but rather, **"раз, два, три, ..."** ("**Один раз**" is understood.) On the other hand, a few fussy people do insist on observing a rule to the effect that in counting (to count **считать**) objects one starts with **один** but in counting actions (such as keeping time to music) one may start with **раз**. The Russian equivalent for "One, two, three, go!" is **"Раз, два, три, вперёд!"**

Just for exercise:

Считайте по́ два до 20 (двадцати). (2, 4, 6. 8, ...)
Считайте по́ три до 30 (тридцати). (3, 6, 9, 12, ...)

Числа[1]

Едини́цы	Деся́тки	Со́тни	Ты́сячи
0—нуль, ноль[2]	10—де́сять	100—сто	1000—ты́сяча
1—оди́н, одна́, одно́	11—оди́ннадцать	200—две́сти	2000—две ты́сячи
2—два, две	12—двена́дцать	300—три́ста	3000—три ты́сячи
3—три	13—трина́дцать	400—четы́реста	4000—четы́ре ты́сячи
4—четы́ре	14—четы́рнадцать	500—пятьсо́т	5000—пять ты́сяч
5—пять	15—пятна́дцать	600—шестьсо́т	6000—шесть ты́сяч
6—шесть	16—шестна́дцать	700—семьсо́т	7000—семь ты́сяч
7—семь	17—семна́дцать	800—восемьсо́т	8000—во́семь ты́сяч
8—во́семь	18—восемна́дцать	900—девятьсо́т	9000—де́вять ты́сяч
9—де́вять	19—девятна́дцать		
	20—два́дцать		
	30—три́дцать		
	40—со́рок		
	50—пятьдеся́т		
	60—шестьдеся́т		
	70—се́мьдесят		
	80—во́семьдесят		
	90—девяно́сто		

деся́тки ты́сяч   10 000–90 000
со́тни ты́сяч   100 000–900 000
миллио́ны   1 000 000–9 000 000
деся́тки миллио́нов   10 000 000–90 000 000
со́тни миллио́нов   100 000 000–900 000 000
миллиа́рды   1 000 000 000–9 000 000 000

[1] For declensions of these numbers, and the formation of the ordinal numbers, consult your grammar book.
[2] Though both pronunciations are common, "нуль" seems to predominate in the oblique cases.

"Numerical nouns"
Имена́ числи́тельные коли́чественные

Russian has a set of "numerical nouns" in addition to the cardinals (оди́н, два, три, . . .), the ordinals (пе́рвый, второ́й, тре́тий, . . .), and the collectives (дво́е, тро́е, че́тверо, . . .) usually treated in grammar books. They are frequently encountered in everyday conversation and are usually limited to the numbers one to ten:

1—едини́ца	6—шестёрка
2—дво́йка	7—семёрка
3—тро́йка	8—восьмёрка
4—четвёрка	9—девя́тка
5—пятёрка	10—деся́тка

These numerical nouns are principally used two ways: (1) to title a sequence, or (2) to refer to objects containing the indicated number of units. The best example in English for the first case is the use of an article or the words "number" or "figure" before a cardinal number: *the* 4 четвёрка, *the figure* 8 восьмёрка, *the* 2 of spades дво́йка пик. Often, context must tell what the number relates to: "He came on *a No.* 7 bus" (that is, route no. 7)—**"Он прие́хал на семёрке"**; or *the number* 5 (ball, for example) **пятёрка**. A very frequently heard application of the numerical noun is in the form of school (and most university) grades, where "a five" **пятёрка** is an *A* grade, "a four" **четвёрка** is a *B*, and so on: **"Он получи́л дво́йку по арифме́тике."**

These numerical nouns are also used to refer to objects that contain the indicated number of units. Thus **тро́йка** can be a team of three horses, a three-man commission, or a man's three-piece suit (jacket, vest, and pants). **Пятёрка** can be a five-ruble and **десятка** a ten-ruble bill, or **двойка** can be a boat with two oars. This usage presents many problems for language students, however.[1] **Тройка** can be a team of three horses, but a team of two horses is **пара**. The five- and ten-ruble bills can be **пятёрка** and **десятка** but a one-ruble bill cannot be **единица**. (**Единица** is commonly used both in the singular and plural to mean units or ones. See the description of an abacus.)

Words derived from or containing numbers
Сло́жные слова́ с числи́тельным в ко́рне

Nouns, adjectives, and adverbs formed from the genitive case of the number itself are both very common and easy to recognize:

двугла́вый орёл a two-headed eagle
двухдне́вный срок a two-day period
треуго́льник a triangle
трёхколёсный велосипе́д a tricycle
пятиле́тка a five-year period (or plan)

Those formed from the collective numbers two, three, and four are just as easily recognizable:

двоежёнство bigamy
троекра́тно three times
четвероно́гий four-footed

Other sets of words have numbers as their base: **двойно́й** means double or twice as much ("**в двойно́м разме́ре**") and **тройно́й** means triple or three times as much. **Четверно́й, пятерно́й, шестерно́й, семерно́й, восьмерно́й, девятерно́й**, and **десятерно́й** are used in spoken Russian, and then only rarely.

Двойни́к and **тройни́к** are common, as in **двойни́к** your double or someone who looks just like you, and **тройни́к** a three-way plug or pipe. **Четвери́к, пятери́к, шестери́к, семери́к, восьмери́к, девятери́к**, and **десятери́к** can refer

---

[1] Imagine a comparable problem in the restricted usages of words in English whose root signifies "two": duo, duet, dual, deuce, double, twain, twice, and so on.

---

to measurements or objects containing the indicated number of units; for instance, **Упря́жка шестерико́м** is a team of six horses. But these words are rarely used.

In mathematics and electronics one often uses the binary system **двои́чная систе́ма счисле́ния** and the quinary system **пятери́чная систе́ма счисле́ния**; the decimal system is **десяти́чная систе́ма**.

Children born at the same time of the same mother are **близнецы́**, which naturally most often applies to twins. (It can also apply to look-alikes.) One can be specific about the number of children using the series **дво́йня, тро́йня, четверня́**, or (in conversation) **двойня́шки, тройня́шки**: "**Она́ родила́ тро́йню**"—"She had triplets." The concept of quadruplets and quintuplets is often paraphrased: "**Она́ родила́ сра́зу четверы́х дете́й**."

Reading and writing numbers
Чте́ние и написа́ние чи́сел

Writing whole numbers
Написа́ние це́лых чи́сел

Russians (like other Europeans) write numbers differently from the way we do:

$$1, 2, 3, 4, 5, 6, 7, 8, 9$$

Notice that the one often has a hook on the front of it; the two, six, and nine often are rounded when ours are not; and the seven almost always has a line drawn through it.

In writing large numbers, thousands are sometimes separated by periods: 24.432 (**два́дцать четы́ре ты́сячи четы́реста три́дцать два**); but almost more often the thousands are not separated at all: 60000 (**шестьдеся́т ты́сяч**). In printing, thousands are most often separated by a space and nothing else: 28 123 (**два́дцать во́семь ты́сяч сто два́дцать три**).

Writing and reading decimals
Написа́ние и чте́ние десяти́чных дробе́й

Russians indicate the decimal point with a comma **запята́я**, not with a period **то́чка**. In Russian, the period is used as we do the comma.

По-англи́йски	По-ру́сски
0.32	0,32
4,256.01	4.256,01

These examples show how decimals are read out loud:

0,0	ноль це́лых, ноль деся́тых
1,1	одна́ це́лая, одна́ деся́тая
2,2	две це́лых, две деся́тых
3,3	три це́лых, три деся́тых
20,01	два́дцать це́лых, одна́ со́тая
21,02	два́дцать одна́ це́лая, две со́тых
42,001	со́рок две це́лых, одна́ ты́сячная
546,438	пятьсо́т со́рок шесть це́лых, четы́реста три́дцать во́семь ты́сячных

Це́лая, це́лых is often omitted and replaced by **и**; for example, 43,5 can be read **"со́рок три и пять деся́тых."** To do so is less formal but quite common.

Russians do try, much harder than we, to report tenths, hundredths, thousandths, and so forth. But even they have their limits. When faced with decimals carried out to many places, they simply read the decimal point **запята́я** and then continue the list of numbers, breaking them up as they wish. Thus, 89,031824 can be read **"во́семьдесят де́вять запята́я ноль три́дцать оди́н во́семь два́дцать четы́ре."** The point at which one no longer bothers counting decimal places is also a matter of convenience and formality: 57,368 can be read as **"пятьдеся́т семь це́лых, три́ста шестьдеся́т во́семь ты́сячных"** or as **"пятьдеся́т семь запята́я три́ста шестьдеся́т во́семь."**

The adjectives used in reading decimals (**це́лая, це́лых, деся́тая, деся́тых, со́тая, со́тых, ты́сячная, ты́сячных, . . .**) are thought of as modifying **до́ля едини́цы** or **часть**.

Reading simple fractions
У́стное чте́ние просты́х дробе́й

The numerator of a fraction is **числи́тель**, and the denominator is **знамена́тель**.

$$\frac{48}{183} \quad \begin{array}{l} \text{числи́тель} \\ \text{знамена́тель} \end{array}$$

With one exception, the denominator is in the genitive plural.

$\frac{5}{8}$	пять восьмы́х
$\frac{18}{41}$	восемна́дцать со́рок пе́рвых
$\frac{135}{159}$	сто три́дцать пять сто пятьдеся́т девя́тых

That exception occurs when the last digit in the numerator is a "one" (excluding eleven); then the denominator is in the nominative singular feminine, since either the word **до́ля** or **часть** is understood to be modified.

$\frac{1}{2}$	одна́ втора́я[2]
$\frac{1}{3}$	одна́ тре́тья[2]
$\frac{1}{4}$	одна́ четвёртая[2]
$\frac{1}{5}$	одна́ пя́тая
$\frac{1}{61}$	одна́ шестьдеся́т пе́рвая
$\frac{41}{23}$	со́рок одна́ два́дцать тре́тья

Notice, too, that since either **до́ля** or **часть** is understood to be the word modified, both one and two in the numerator appear in the feminine.

$\frac{2}{3}$	две тре́тьих
$\frac{2}{5}$	две пя́тых
$\frac{22}{44}$	два́дцать две со́рок четвёртых

Mixed numbers
Сме́шанные чи́сла

Mixed numbers are sometimes read using **це́лая, це́лых**, but more commonly **и** is used instead:

$1\frac{2}{3}$	одна́ и две тре́тьих одна́ це́лая две тре́тьих
$48\frac{3}{8}$	со́рок во́семь и три восьмы́х со́рок во́семь це́лых три восьмы́х

[2] The forms (одна́) полови́на, треть, and че́тверть are perhaps more often used in daily life, while одна́ втора́я, тре́тья, and четвёртая are more common in arithmetic and mathematics.

Declining numbers in spoken Russian

Склоне́ние числи́тельных в разгово́рном языке́

You have perhaps seen the tables in your Russian grammar book giving the declensions of numbers. It is perhaps some consolation to know that Russians have a hard time with such intricacy too—so much so that for practical purposes, and with some exceptions, only two cases, the nominative and the genitive, are commonly used. If you are talking to a Russian and suddenly realize that you are supposed to decline a number but cannot remember how, go ahead and use the nominative, especially if you are dealing with numbers specifically, as in mathematics or statistical reports.

The Russian himself has devised circumlocutions to avoid declining numbers. For instance, the preposition **ме́жду** requires the instrumental case. But when asked to read **"Найти́ ра́зность ме́жду 341 820 и 239 619"** ("Find the difference between . . ."), the Russian will probably say, **"Найти́ ра́зность ме́жду чи́слами . . ."** ("Find the difference between the numbers . . ."), and then read off the numbers in the nominative. The words for equal(s) in Russian—**равно́**, **ра́вен**, **равна́**, **равны́**, or **равня́ется**—take the dative. Often the Russian ignores that fact altogether and uses the nominative instead, especially if the numbers are long or involved. Or he will often use other words instead that do not require the dative. For instance, **есть**, **бу́дет**, **э́то**, and **полу́чится** can all be interchanged with **равно́** yet do not require the dative. Sometimes no verb or substitute is used at all.

As a general guide, you may consider that the smaller the number, the more likely it is to be declined. Therefore, it is best to learn all the cases for 0, 1, 2, 3, and 4 and only the nominative and genitive for the rest. (Unless, of course, your teacher insists to the contrary. Not all the requirements of academe are based on reality, however.)

Arithmetic operations
Арифмети́ческие де́йствия

Addition
Сложе́ние

Some basic terminology in the operation of addition is given below. Notice in the example that the plus sign is placed higher than ours.

$$\begin{array}{r} \text{плюс} \longrightarrow \\ \text{(знак сложе́ния)} \end{array} \quad + \begin{array}{l} 14 \leftarrow \text{слага́емое} \\ 7 \leftarrow \text{слага́емое} \\ \hline 21 \leftarrow \text{су́мма (ито́г)} \end{array}$$

There are several ways of saying "seven and fourteen is twenty-one." The first one listed is both very common and the easiest for us to use.

Семь плюс четы́рнадцать бу́дет два́дцать оди́н.

Семь плюс четы́рнадцать равня́ется двадцати́ одному́.

К семи́ приба́вить четы́рнадцать, бу́дет два́дцать оди́н.

Éсли сложи́ть семь и четы́рнадцать, то полу́чится два́дцать оди́н.

Éсли сложи́ть семь с четы́рнадцатью, бу́дет два́дцать оди́н.

Су́мма семи́ и четы́рнадцати соста́вит два́дцать оди́н.

And in performing an addition problem, the Russian will say to himself (про себя́ говори́т):

$$+ \begin{array}{r} 57 \\ 42 \\ 96 \\ \hline 195 \end{array}$$

Семь плюс два—де́вять, плюс шесть—пятна́дцать.

Пять пи́шем, оди́н в уме́.

Пять и оди́н—шесть, плюс четы́ре—де́сять, плюс де́вять—девятна́дцать.

These are a few typical problems in addition (зада́чи по сложе́нию):[3]

[3] All of the problems in the arithmetic section have been taken from Soviet arithmetic books.

(1) Одно́ слага́емое 16 427, друго́е 8 697. Найти́ их су́мму.

(2) Пе́рвое слага́емое 9668, второ́е на 397 бо́льше пе́рвого, а тре́тье равно́ су́мме пе́рвых двух слага́емых. Чему́ равна́ су́мма трёх слага́емых?

(3) Су́мму двух чи́сел 13708 и 6075 увели́чить на 10970.

(4) Вы́полнить сложе́ние и сде́лать прове́рку:

$$30\ 478 + 137 + 590$$

(5) На уча́стке посади́ли в пе́рвый день 60 дере́вьев, а во второ́й день 80 дере́вьев. Ско́лько дере́вьев посади́ли за́ два дня?

(6) Найти́ неизве́стное слага́емое x (икс)

$$x + 625 = 1200$$

Отве́ты на зада́чи по сложе́нию: (1) 25 124; (2) 39 466;   (3) 30 753;   (4) 31 205;   (5) 140 дере́вьев;   (6) $x = 575$.

THE RUSSIAN ABACUS　　　　СЧЁТЫ

The Russian abacus can be seen in the Soviet Union almost anywhere money is to be paid. Cashiers and bookkeepers use them, and children are taught how to add and subtract on them, principally so that they may learn the relationship of units, tens, hundreds, and so on. Ele-mentary classrooms will often have a large abacus on a rack at the front of the class. Many people have one at home as well.

The illustration shows the regular version of the Russian abacus. The set of four beads is used either for separating kopecks from rubles or for computing one-quarter units. Japanese and Chinese abacuses are differently arranged.

HOW TO ADD ON THE RUSSIAN ABACUS　　　СЛОЖЕ́НИЕ НА СЧЁТАХ

(1) Add 23 and 45.   (Always start out with all the beads on the right side.) To set up the first number, move two beads from the second rank (tens) to the left side. Move three beads (three units) from the first rank to the left side. The second number is done the same way: move four beads from the second rank (tens) to the left and five beads from the first rank to the left. As a result the abacus has six beads on the second rank (tens) and eight beads (units) on the first rank. Therefore: 23 + 45 = 68.

(2) Add 52,314 and 5,362.   For the first number move five beads to the left in the fifth rank, two beads in the fourth rank, three beads in the third rank, one bead in the

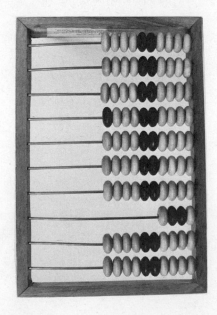

Счёты

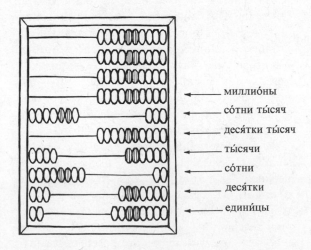

миллио́ны
со́тни ты́сяч
деся́тки ты́сяч
ты́сячи
со́тни
деся́тки
едини́цы

Вот 704 832 на счётах

second, and four beads in the first rank. For the second number move five beads to the left in the fourth rank, three in the third rank, six in the second rank, and two in the first rank. Result: 52,314 + 5,362 = 57,676.

(3) Add 156 and 278. Set up the number 156 on the left side just as you have done before. Now, for the second number move two beads (hundreds) to the left in the third rank. Since it is now impossible to move seven beads to the left in the second rank (tens), you must now move one more bead (hundred) to the left in the third rank and then three beads to the right in the second rank (100 − 70 = 30). For the units, since you cannot move eight beads to the left in the first rank, instead move one of the beads in the second rank to the left and then move two beads in the first rank to the right (10 − 8 = 2). The result: 156 + 278 = 434.

Subtraction
Вычита́ние

For subtraction, the minus sign is also placed higher than ours. The terminology applicable to the operation includes:

$$\text{ми́нус} \longrightarrow \begin{array}{r} - 35 \longleftarrow \text{уменьша́емое} \\ 4 \longleftarrow \text{вычита́емое} \\ \hline 31 \longleftarrow \text{ра́зность} \end{array}$$

(знак вычита́ния)

The following are common ways of saying "thirty-five minus four equals thirty-one." The first is the easiest and quite common.

Три́дцать пять ми́нус четы́ре бу́дет три́дцать оди́н.

Три́дцать пять ми́нус четы́ре равня́ется тридца́ти одному́.

Е́сли из тридцати́ пяти́ вы́честь четы́ре, полу́чится три́дцать оди́н.

От тридцати́ пяти́ отня́ть четы́ре, бу́дет три́дцать оди́н.

Ра́зность ме́жду тридцатью́ пятью́ и четырьмя́ соста́вит три́дцать оди́н.

Про себя́ говоря́т:

$$\begin{array}{r} - 698 \\ 489 \\ \hline 209 \end{array}$$

От восемна́дцати—де́вять, это бу́дет де́вять.
От восьми́—во́семь—ноль.
От шести́—четы́ре—два.

$$\begin{array}{r} - 35 \\ 4 \\ \hline 31 \end{array}$$

От пяти́—четы́ре—оди́н.
Три сно́сим, бу́дет три́дцать оди́н.

Зада́чи по вычита́нию:

(1) Уменьша́емое 1080, вычита́емое 675. Найти́ ра́зность.

(2) Ско́лько полу́чится, е́сли из 85 (восьми́десяти пяти́) вы́честь 25? 96 уме́ньшить на 24?

(3) На ско́лько 76 бо́льше 36 (тридцати́ шести́)? 17 ме́ньше 80 (восьми́десяти)?

(4) В библиоте́ке бы́ло 2 000 книг. 500 книг вы́дали. Ско́лько книг оста́лось?

(5) Река́ Ле́на длинне́е Днепра́ на 1979 км, Днепр коро́че Во́лги на 1403 км. Найти́ длину́ Во́лги и Днепра́, е́сли длина́ Ле́ны 4264 км.

Отве́ты на зада́чи по вычита́нию: (1) Ра́зность 405; (2) 60, 72; (3) На 40, на 63; (4) Оста́лось 1500 книг; (5) длина́ Во́лги 3688 км; длина́ Днепра́ 2285 км.

Multiplication
Умноже́ние

The terms applicable to the notation system for multiplication are:

косо́й
крест $\longrightarrow$ $\times$ $\begin{array}{r} 12 \longleftarrow \text{мно́жимое} \longleftarrow \text{сомно́-} \\ 5 \longleftarrow \text{мно́житель} \longleftarrow \text{жители} \end{array}$
(знак
умноже́ния) $\underline{60} \longleftarrow$ произведе́ние
то́чка (знак умноже́ния) 5 · 12 = 60

There are also several ways of saying "five times twelve is sixty."

Двена́дцать умно́жить на пять (бу́дет) шесть-
деся́т.

Е́сли двена́дцать умно́жить на пять, полу́чит-
ся шестьдеся́т.

Двена́дцать умно́женное на пять равня́ется
шести́десяти.

Произведе́ние двена́дцати и пяти́ соста́вит
шестьдеся́т.

Двена́дцать умно́жить в пять раз, (бу́дет)
шестьдеся́т.

The verb **помно́жить** is used as well as **ум-
но́жить**. A stress change occurs when multiply-
ing (or dividing) "by two" **на́ два**, "by three"
на́ три, and in the following cases, both ways:
на́ пя́ть, на́ ше́сть, на́ се́мь, на́ сто́. Thus:

12 × 5 = 60   Двена́дцать помно́жить на́
пя́ть (бу́дет, э́то) шестьдеся́т.

9 × 3 = 27   Де́вять помно́женное на́ три́—
два́дцать семь.

6 × 2 = 12   Шесть умно́женное на́ два́—
две́надцать.

2 × 2 × 4 × 3 × 6 = 288   Два умно́жить на́
два, на четы́ре, на́ три, на шесть бу́дет
две́сти во́семьдесят во́семь.

THE MULTIPLICATION TABLE	ТАБЛИ́ЦА УМНОЖЕ́НИЯ

Watch out for the stress changes in the numbers five through nine when they are multipliers.
In reciting the multiplication table, **бу́дет** is
almost always eliminated.

1 × 9 = 9   Оди́ножды де́вять (бу́дет, э́то)
де́вять.

2 × 4 = 8   Два́жды четы́ре—во́семь.

3 × 6 = 18   Три́жды шесть—восемна́дцать.

4 × 5 = 20   Четы́режды пять—два́дцать.

5 × 3 = 15   Пя́тью три—пятна́дцать.

6 × 2 = 12   Ше́стью два—двена́дцать.

7 × 4 = 28   Се́мью четы́ре—два́дцать во́-
семь.

8 × 6 = 48   Во́семью (или во́сьмью) шесть
—со́рок во́семь.

9 × 8 = 72   Де́вятью во́семь—се́мьдесят
два.

Про себя́ говоря́т:

$$\begin{array}{r} 755 \\ \times\ 36 \\ \hline 4530 \\ 2265 \\ \hline 27180 \end{array}$$

Пя́тью шесть—три́дцать. Ноль пи́шем, три в
уме́. Пя́тью шесть—три́дцать, да три в уме́—
три́дцать три, три пи́шем и три в уме́.
Ше́стью семь—со́рок два, да три́—со́рок
пять. Три́жды пять—пятна́дцать, оди́н в уме́.
Пятна́дцать да оди́н—шестна́дцать, оди́н в
уме́. Два́дцать оди́н да оди́н—два́дцать два.
Ноль, во́семь, оди́н, оди́н в уме́, шесть, семь,
два.

Два́дцать семь ты́сяч сто во́семьдесят.

Зада́чи по умноже́нию:

(1) Число́ 284 увели́чить в 36 раз.

(2) Записа́ть при по́мощи зна́ка де́йствия и
зна́ка ра́венства: число́ 280, умно́женное
на 6, даёт 1680.

(3) Мно́жимое 94, мно́житель 27. Вы́числить
произведе́ние.

(4) Оди́н из сомно́жителей 18, друго́й 15.
Найти́ произведе́ние.

(5) Вы́полнить умноже́ние и сде́лать про-
ве́рку:

86 × 28,   407 × 652

(6) Самолёт лети́т со ско́ростью 326 *км* в час.
Ско́лько киломе́тров пролети́т самолёт за
6 часо́в, е́сли бу́дет лете́ть с той же
ско́ростью?

Отве́ты на зада́чи по умноже́нию: (1)
10 224; (2) 280 × 6 = 1680; (3) 2538; (4)
270; (5) 2408, 265 364; (6) 1956 *км*.

Division
Деле́ние

At first, the Russian system of stating long
division problems seems quite different from
ours.

In Russian	In English

дели́мое ⟶ 200 |8 ⟵ дели́тель   8 ⟌ 200

       16 |25 ⟵ ча́стное

$$\begin{array}{r}
25 \\
8\overline{)\,200} \\
16 \\ \hline
40 \\
40 \\ \hline
0
\end{array}$$

As with the others, there are several ways of expressing the operation of division; take, for example, "twenty-seven divided by nine equals three":

Два́дцать семь раздели́ть на де́вять, бу́дет три.

Два́дцать семь делённое на де́вять равня́ется трём.

Éсли два́дцать семь раздели́ть на де́вять, полу́чится три.

Ча́стное от деле́ния двадцати́ семи́ на де́вять соста́вит три.

This is a long division problem and its answer:

$$\begin{array}{r|l}
1434 & 22 \\
132 & \overline{65} \\ \hline
114 \\
110 \\ \hline
4
\end{array}$$

1434:22 = 65 и 4 в оста́тке. (Ты́сяча четы́реста три́дцать четы́ре делённое на два́дцать два равно́ шести́десяти пяти́ и четы́ре в оста́тке.)

Про себя́ говоря́т:

Сто со́рок три (делённое) на два́дцать два бу́дет приме́рно шесть. (Двена́дцать, оди́н в уме́, двена́дцать да оди́н—трина́дцать. Оди́н, оди́н.) Сто четы́рнадцать (делённое) на два́дцать два, э́то бу́дет приме́рно пять. Сто де́сять и четы́ре. Полу́чится шестьдеся́т пять и четы́ре в оста́тке.

Зада́чи по деле́нию:

(1) Дели́мое 240, дели́тель 12. Найти́ ча́стное.

(2) Найти́ ча́стное от деле́ния 9600 на 10.

(3) Ско́лько полу́чится, е́сли 720 раздели́ть на 8 ра́вных часте́й? 640 уме́ньшить в 8 раз? взять восьму́ю часть от 560?

(4) Во ско́лько раз 480 бо́льше 8? Ско́лько раз 8 соде́ржится в 200?

(5) Вы́полнить деле́ние и результа́т прове́рить умноже́нием: 3216:48, 86904:284.

(6) По пла́ну заво́д до́лжен вы́пустить 3640 сельскохозя́йственных маши́н за 26 дней. Рабо́чие реши́ли вы́полнить план досро́чно и выпуска́ли в день на 42 маши́ны бо́льше, чем бы́ло наме́чено по пла́ну. На ско́лько дней ра́ньше сро́ка заво́д вы́полнил план?

(7) Из сле́дующих чи́сел: 56, 64, 78, 90, 96, 120, 140, 160, вы́писать те, кото́рые:
де́лятся на во́семь без оста́тка и
де́лятся на во́семь с оста́тком.

Отве́ты на зада́чи по деле́нию: (1) 20; (2) 960; (3) 90, 80, 70; (4) 60, 25; (5) 67, 306; (6) На шесть дней ра́ньше; (7) Без оста́тка: 56, 64, 96, 120, 160; с оста́тком: 78, 90, 140.

Common geometric figures
Обыкнове́нные геометри́ческие фигу́ры

Many words in geometry resemble ours: **диа́метр, ра́диус, хо́рда, перпендикуля́р, центр, трапе́ция, э́ллипс, фо́рмула, гипотену́за, пери́метр, ромб, куб, пирами́да, параллелепи́пед, цили́ндр, ко́нус, при́зма.** But note that sphere is **шар.**

Зада́чи по геоме́трии:

(1) Начерти́те прямоуго́льник длино́й 7 *см*, ширино́й 4 *см*. Вы́числите су́мму длин сторо́н прямоуго́льника.

(2) Найти́ пло́щадь по́лной пове́рхности ку́ба, ребро́ кото́рого равно́ 25 *см*.

(3) Два равнобе́дренных треуго́льника име́ют о́бщее основа́ние. Бокова́я сторона́ одного́ из них втро́е бо́льше боково́й стороны́

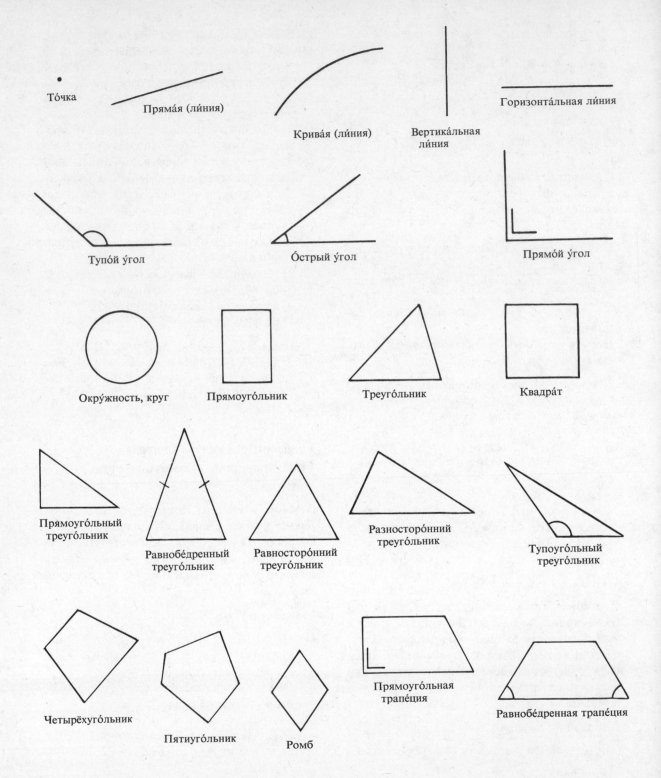

Точка

Пряма́я (ли́ния)

Крива́я (ли́ния)

Вертика́льная ли́ния

Горизонта́льная ли́ния

Тупо́й у́гол

О́стрый у́гол

Прямо́й у́гол

Окру́жность, круг

Прямоуго́льник

Треуго́льник

Квадра́т

Прямоуго́льный треуго́льник

Равнобе́дренный треуго́льник

Равносторо́нний треуго́льник

Разносторо́нний треуго́льник

Тупоуго́льный треуго́льник

Четырёхуго́льник

Пятиуго́льник

Ромб

Прямоуго́льная трапе́ция

Равнобе́дренная трапе́ция

другóго. Периметры треугóльников равны́ 28 и 68 *см*. Найти стóроны кáждого из треугóльников.

Ответы на задáчи: (1) 22; (2) 3750 *см²*; (3) основáние—8 *см*, однá сторонá—10 *см*, другáя сторонá—30 *см*.

Reading mathematical expressions
Чтéние математи́ческих выражéний

The symbols and letters used in mathematics are very similar to ours, but they sound quite different when a Russian is reading them. The general reader might be interested in seeing how Russians pronounce the Latin alphabet, how they read "squares, cubes, and roots," and what the common formulas are.

The pronunciation of the Greek alphabet and a few more technical expressions and terms are included here because they are very difficult to find elsewhere, yet are very important to the mathematician, physicist, or engineer who has occasion to talk to his Soviet colleagues. Therefore, in reading this section, if you don't understand the mathematics in English, don't let the Russian equivalent concern you.

For chemists, the Appendix includes the periodic table in Russian and instructions on how to read a few chemical formulas.

The alphabets
Алфави́ты

Equations and formulas used in mathematics look almost exactly the same as ours do. But when the Russian reads them out loud, the sounds he makes are quite different. Just as in English, unknowns are most frequently expressed as *a*, *b*, *c*, *n*, *x*, *y*, and *z*.

Mathematicians, physicists, and engineers must often call upon the Greek alphabet for use as symbols. In equations and formulas in Russian scientific works, you should assume that the letters that you are looking at are either Latin or Greek, but not Russian.

Pronunciation of the Latin alphabet

Бýква	Произношéние	Бýква	Произношéние
a	а	n	эн
b	бэ	o	о
c	цэ	p	пэ
d	дэ	q	ку, кю
e	е	r	эр
f	эф	s	эс
g	же	t	тэ
h	аш	u	у
i	и	v	фáу, вэ
j	йот	w	вэ, дубль вэ
k	ка	x	икс
l	эль	y	и́грек
m	эм	z	зет

Как и в английском, неизвéстные выражáются чáще всегó и́ксом, и́греком и зéтом.

Грéческий алфави́т

Бýква	Назвáние бýквы	Бýква	Назвáние бýквы
α	áльфа	ν	ню
β	бéта[1]	ξ	кси
γ	гáмма	о	о́микрон
δ	дéльта[1]	π	пи
ε	э́псилон	ρ	ро
ζ	зéта[1]	σ	си́гма
η	э́та	τ	тáу
θ	тэ́та	υ	и́псилон
ι	йóта	φ	фи
κ	кáппа	χ	хи
λ	лáмбда	ψ	пси
μ	мю	ω	омéга[1]

[1] бéта, дéльта, зéта, and омéга are usually pronounced as "бэ́та," "дэ́льта," "зэ́та," "омэ́га."

Squares, cubes, and roots
Стéпени и кóрни

Пи́шут		Говоря́т
3^2	три	квадрáт, в квадрáте, во второ́й стéпени
4^2	четы́ре	
8^2	вóсемь	
2^3	два	в кубе, в трéтьей стéпени
6^3	шесть	
10^3	дéсять	
5^4	пять в четвёртой стéпени	
10^{10}	дéсять в деся́той стéпени	
a^n	"а" в стéпени "эн," "а" в э́нной	
$\sqrt{-1}$	кóрень квадрáтный из ми́нус едини́цы	

$\sqrt{2}$	ко́рень квадра́тный из двух
$\sqrt{-2}$	ко́рень квадра́тный из ми́нус двух
$\sqrt{49}$	ко́рень квадра́тный из сорока́ девяти́
$\sqrt[3]{27}$	ко́рень куби́ческий из двадцати́ семи́
$\sqrt[4]{81}$	ко́рень четвёртой сте́пени из восьми́десяти одного́

Reading common formulas
Чте́ние основны́х фо́рмул

Some Latin letters are known to most schoolchildren in the USSR since many of the common formulas use them rather than the Russian equivalent: L = length, S = surface (area), V = volume, d = density, P = weight (poids), p = pressure, h = height, F = force, and so forth. The table below gives some common formulas with their pronunciation and equivalent in English. Notice that the Greek π is pronounced "**пи**," and that tangent is abbreviated as "tg" rather than "tan," as in English.

The official wording of the Pythagorean Theorem is, "**Квадра́т гипотену́зы ра́вен су́мме квадра́тов ка́тетов.**" But unofficially the children have reworded the expression, "**Пифаго́ровы штаны́ во все сто́роны равны́.**"

Common formulas: how they are read

Основны́е фо́рмулы: как их чита́ть

По-англи́йски	По-ру́сски	Произноше́ние
$C = 2\pi r$ Circumference of a circle	$L = 2\pi r$ Длина́ окру́жности	эль равно́ два пи эр
$A = \frac{1}{2}ab$ Area of a triangle	$S = \frac{1}{2}ah$ Пло́щадь треуго́льника	эс равно́ полови́на (одна́ втора́я) а на аш; (и́ли) эс равно́ полови́не (одно́й второ́й) а на аш
$A = \pi r^2$ Area of a circle	$S = \pi r^2$ Пло́щадь кру́га	эс равно́ пи эр квадра́т
$A = 4\pi r^2$ Area of a sphere	$S = 4\pi r^2$ Пло́щадь пове́рхности ша́ра	эс равно́ четы́ре пи эр квадра́т
$V = \frac{4}{3}\pi r^3$ Volume of a sphere	$V = \frac{4}{3}\pi r^3$ Объём ша́ра	вэ равно́ четы́ре тре́тьих пи эр куб
$a^2 + b^2 = c^2$ Pythagorean Theorem	$a^2 + b^2 = c^2$ Теоре́ма Пифаго́ра	а квадра́т плюс бэ квадра́т равня́ется цэ квадра́т
$\sin^2 \theta + \cos^2 \theta \equiv 1$ Trigonometric identity	$\sin^2 \theta + \cos^2 \theta \equiv 1$ Тригономи́ческое то́ждество	си́нус квадра́т тэ́та плюс ко́синус квадра́т тэ́та тожде́ственно равно́ едини́це
$\tan \theta = \dfrac{\sin \theta}{\cos \theta}$ Definition of a tangent	$\operatorname{tg} \theta = \dfrac{\sin \theta}{\cos \theta}$ То́ждество та́нгенса	та́нгенс тэ́та (есть) си́нус тэ́та делённое на ко́синус тэ́та

Other terminology
Други́е те́рмины

The following signs and terms are commonly used in algebra, geometry, and mathematics in general:[4]

[4] Information used here is taken from the booklet *Гото́вимся слу́шать ле́кции; вы́пуск* 1, ред. И. К. Га́почка (Москва́: Университе́т дру́жбы наро́дов и́мени Патри́са Луму́мбы, 1963), стр. 33–35.

$+2$	положи́тельное число́
-2	отрица́тельное число́
$\lvert 2 \rvert$	абсолю́тная величина́
$-a; +10; ab;$ $(a + b)\,c; \dfrac{a - b}{c}$	одночле́н
$(a + b)\,c + ab$	многочле́н
$6a^2b$	-6- коэффицие́нт
$x^2 + 2 = 3x$	уравне́ние

$3x - 3y = 21$ $2x - 3y = 3$ }	система уравне́ний	$\log_b$	логари́фм при основа́нии b
$x; y; z \ldots$	неизве́стные	lg	десяти́чный логари́фм $(2 = \lg 100)$
$=$	равно́ (ра́вен, равна́, равны́)	ln	нату́ра́льный логари́фм
$\equiv$	тожде́ственно равно́	(); []; {}	ско́бки кру́глые, квадра́тные, фигу́рные
$\neq$	не равно́	lim	преде́л
$<$	ме́ньше	$\to$	стреми́тся к . . .
$>$	бо́льше	∞	бесконе́чность
$\leqslant$	ме́ньше и́ли равно́ (но не бо́льше)	i	мни́мое число́ ($\sqrt{-1}$)
$\geqslant$	бо́льше и́ли равно́ (но не ме́ньше)	Δ	прираще́ние
		d	дифференциа́л
$\ll$	значи́тельно (и́ли мно́го) ме́ньше	$\int$	интегра́л
		$\perp$	перпендикуля́рно
$\gg$	значи́тельно (и́ли мно́го) бо́льше	$\parallel$	паралле́льно
		$\vec{d}$	ве́ктор d

Reading typical mathematical expressions

Чте́ние не́которых математи́ческих выраже́ний

Выраже́ние	Как оно́ чита́ется
$ax^2 + bx + c = 0$ (квадра́тное уравне́ние)	a икс квадра́т плюс *бэ* икс плюс *цэ* равня́ется нулю́.
$x_{1,2} = \dfrac{-b \pm \sqrt{b^2 - 4ac}}{2a}$ (ко́рни квадра́тного уравне́ния)	Икс оди́н, два равня́ется ми́нус *бэ* плюс-ми́нус ко́рень квадра́тный из *бэ* в квадра́те ми́нус четы́ре *a цэ* (делённое) на два *a*.
$\|2 - 4\| = 2$	Мо́дуль два ми́нус четы́ре равня́ется двум. (То́же мо́жно: абсолю́тное значе́ние чи́сла два ми́нус четы́ре равня́ется двум.)
$a^2 - b^2 = (a + b)(a - b)$	a квадра́т ми́нус *бэ* квадра́т есть a плюс *бэ* (помно́женное) на a ми́нус *бэ*.
$\sqrt{x} = x^{1/2}$	Ко́рень квадра́тный из икс есть икс в сте́пени одна́ втора́я.
$\ln a = (\ln 10) \log a$	Логари́фм нату́ра́льный a есть логари́фм нату́ра́льный десяти́ на логари́фм a при основа́нии де́сять.
$10^{10} \gg 1$	Де́сять в деся́той сте́пени мно́го бо́льше едини́цы.
$\lim\limits_{x \to 0} \left(\dfrac{\sin x}{x} \right) = 1$	Преде́л отноше́ния си́нус икс к икс при икс, стремя́щемся к нулю́, ра́вен едини́це.
$e^{ix} \equiv \cos x + i \sin x$	e в сте́пени *и* икс есть то́ждество ко́синус икс плюс *и* си́нус икс.
$\dfrac{dx}{dt} \equiv \lim\limits_{\Delta t \to 0} \left(\dfrac{\Delta x}{\Delta t} \right)$	Произво́дное *дэ* икс по *дэ* *тэ* э́то есть преде́л отноше́ния прираще́ния де́льта икс к де́льта *тэ* при де́льта *тэ*, стремя́щемся к нулю́.
$\int e^x \, dx = e^x + c$	Интегра́л от e в сте́пени икс *дэ* икс равня́ется e в сте́пени икс плюс *цэ*.
$y = f(x)$	И́грек равня́ется *эф* от икс.

Выражéние	Как онó читáется
$a^4 - b^4 \neq (a + b)^2 (a - b)^2$	*а* в четвёртой стéпени ми́нус *бэ* в четвёртой стéпени не равнó *а* плюс *бэ* в квадрáте на *а* ми́нус *бэ* в квадрáте.
$\measuredangle \; \theta < 90°$	Угол тэ́та мéньше девянóста грáдусов.
$[a(a^2 + b)(c - d)]^2 - 4d$	Откры́ть квадрáтную скóбку, *а* умнóжить, откры́ть кру́глую скóбку, *а* квадрáт плюс *бэ* закры́ть кру́глую скóбку, умнó-жить, откры́ть кру́глую скóбку, *цэ* ми́нус *дэ* закры́ть кру́-глую скóбку, закры́ть квадрáтную скóбку, всё в квадрáте, ми́нус 4 *дэ*.

For those who would like more practice with numbers, "Арифмéтика, áлгебра, черчéние,"[5] one of a series of booklets, is excellent. Though entirely in Russian, the material is presented in such a way that even the first-year student in Russian can comprehend most of it. There are many exercises with their answers.

Measures
Мéры

Length, area, and volume
Длинá, плóщадь и объём

Most people are aware that Russians use the metric system: the meter is the basic unit for measuring length, height, distance, and so on. A meter is approximately 39.37 inches. Multiples of the meter, 0.001 meter (a millimeter), 0.01 meter (a centimeter), 1000 meters (a kilo-

meter), are some of the larger or smaller common units of measure.

Getting a feel for these sizes is another matter. For everyday purposes a meter can be equated with a yard. But the centimeter is considerably shorter than our inch, and the kilometer is about five-eighths of a mile. To get a better feeling for the size of these measures, get a meter stick and actually measure objects. Calculate how far away you are from the center of your city or from some familiar but relatively distant point. You should not have to stop and think when a Russian tells you that a certain kolkhoz is only twenty kilometers away from another kolkhoz, or that a box is ten centimeters high, fifteen centimeters long, and five centimeters wide.

A table of units of measure and their abbreviations follows. The most common measures are marked with an asterisk.

Мéры длины́ (Линéйные мéры)

микрóн (0,000.001 *м*)	*мк*
миллимéтр* (0,001 *м*)	*мм*
сантимéтр* (0,01 *м*)	*см*
децимéтр (0,1 *м*)	*дм*
мéтр* (1 *м*)	*м*
декамéтр (10 *м*)	*дкм*
гектомéтр (100 *м*)	*гм*
киломéтр* (1.000 *м*)	*км*

Мéры плóщади (Квадрáтные мéры)

квадрáтный микрóн	*кв. мк*
квадрáтный миллимéтр*	*кв. мм*, *мм*^{2}
квадрáтный сантимéтр*	*кв. см*, *см*^{2}
квадрáтный децимéтр	*кв. дм*, *дм*^{2}
квадрáтный метр*	*кв. м*, *м*^{2}
ар	*а*
гектáр*	*га*
квадрáтный киломéтр*	*кв. км*, *км*^{2}

[5] Макáрова и други́е, "Арифмéтика, áлгебра, черчéние," *Пéрвый раз по-ру́сски* (Львов: Издáтельство Львóвского университета, 1966). Others in the series are entitled "Бо-тáника, зоолóгия, анатóмия"; "Хи́мия и фи́зика"; and "Геогрáфия и истóрия."

Ме́ры объёма (Куби́ческие ме́ры)

Liquids Жи́дкости (и сыпу́чие тела́)		Solids Твёрдые тела́	
миллили́тр (0,001 *л*)	*мл*	куби́ческий миллиме́тр куби́ческий сантиме́тр*	*куб. мм, мм³* *куб. см, см³*
литр* (1 *л*)	*л*	куби́ческий дециме́тр	*куб. дм, дм³*
гектоли́тр (100 *л*)	*гл*	куби́ческий метр*, кубоме́тр*	*куб. м, м³*

Объём ли́тра ра́вен куби́ческому дециме́тру.
Ты́сячная до́ля ли́тра называ́ется миллили́тр.
Объём миллили́тра ра́вен куби́ческому санти-ме́тру.
Оди́н куби́ческий метр соде́ржит ты́сячу ли́тров.

бо́чка равна́ 40 (сорока́) вёдрам—о́коло 480 *л*
ведро́ равно́ 20 (двадцати́) буты́лкам—о́коло 12 *л*
буты́лка—0,6 *л*

Other units of measure were in use before the Revolution; they come up constantly in literature and a few of them are still used by the older generation. Below is a listing of the most common such units of measure and their equivalents in the metric system.

Лине́йные ме́ры:

верста́ равна́ 500 (пятиста́м) саже́ням—1,067 *км*
са́жень равна́ 3 (трём) арши́нам—2,134 *м*
арши́н ра́вен 16 (шестна́дцати) вершка́м—0,711 *м*
вершо́к ра́вен—4,4 *см*

На фа́бриках употребля́ли сле́дуюшие ме́ры:

фут $\frac{1}{7}$ (одна́ седьма́я) саже́ни—30,5 *см*
дюйм $\frac{1}{12}$ (одна́ двена́дцатая) фу́та—о́коло 25 *мм*

Ме́ры пло́щади:

квадра́тные вершки́, арши́ны, са́же́ни и вёр-сты
десяти́на равна́ 2400 (двум ты́сячам четырём-стам) *кв. саж.* (квадра́тным саже́ням)—1,092 гекта́ра

Ме́ры объёма жи́дкостей:

HOUSING SPACE ЖИЛПЛО́ЩАДЬ

Different conditions influence what and how you measure. Thus, in the United States, when you are asked to describe the size of a house or apartment, it is expected that you will reply with the number of rooms. Though this is a possible answer in Russian—"**У меня́ двухко́м-натная кварти́ра**"—the same question in the USSR will often be phrased, "**Ско́лько у вас ме́тров?**" (**Жилпло́щади** is understood.) **Жи-ли́щная (и́ли жила́я) пло́щадь** is the number of square meters of living space (housing) not including kitchens, bathrooms, or hallways. In 1970 the per capita average of housing space was less than eight square meters; you may properly conclude that housing space is at a premium.

HOW TO ASK ABOUT DISTANCE, AREA, AND VOLUME КАК СПРОСИ́ТЬ О РАССТОЯ́НИИ, ПЛО́ЩАДИ И ОБЪЁМЕ

Since grammar books often omit a description of how to ask about length, height, and so on, some examples are included here. The Russian constructions for doing so do not parallel ours for the most part. You should examine all the questions first, and then all the answers.

Како́го он ро́ста? (**рост** growth, height)
Он ро́стом в оди́н метр 13 сантиме́тров.
(Его́ рост) оди́н метр 13 сантиме́тров.

Како́го разме́ра нам ну́жен ковёр? (**разме́р** size)

Како́й величины́ нам ну́жен ковёр? (**величина́** magnitude)

Ковёр разме́ром в 3 ме́тра ширино́й и 5 ме́тров длино́й.

Три ме́тра в ширину́, и 5 ме́тров в длину́.

Три на пять (3 × 5).

Како́й толщины́ э́та стена́? (**толщина́** thickness)

(Эта стена́) толщино́й в 10 сантиме́тров.

Де́сять сантиме́тров в толщину́.

Де́сять сантиме́тров.

Како́й высоты́ э́то де́рево? (**высота́** height)

(Это де́рево) высото́й в 10 ме́тров.

Де́сять ме́тров в высоту́.

Де́сять ме́тров.

Како́й длины́ э́та ко́мната? (**длина́** length)

(Эта ко́мната) 4 ме́тра в длину́.

Длино́й в 4 ме́тра.

Четы́ре ме́тра.

Како́го объёма э́тот я́щик? (**объём** volume)

(Этот я́щик) объёмом в 100 *куб. см* (сто куби́ческих сантиме́тров).

100 *куб. см.*

Како́й глубины́ э́то о́зеро? (**глубина́** depth)

Глубино́й в 3 ме́тра.

Три ме́тра в глубину́.

Три ме́тра.

На како́м расстоя́нии от земли́ нахо́дится са́мая бли́зкая звезда́? (**расстоя́ние** distance)

На расстоя́нии четырёх световы́х лет.

Четы́ре световы́х го́да.

(В кни́жном сти́ле пи́шут; Какова́ высота́ э́тих гор? Какова́ длина́ кла́сса?)

Weight
Вес

The metric standard also applies to measures of weight, where the gram is the basic unit; other measures of weight are merely multiples of the gram. A kilogram (1000 grams) is equivalent to about 2.2 pounds.

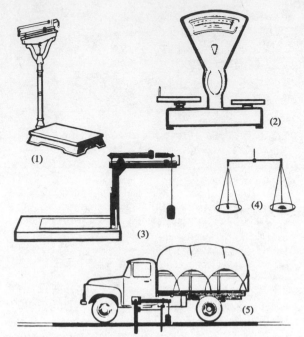

Ви́ды весо́в: (1) медици́нские весы́, (2) насто́льные торго́вые весы́, (3) десяти́чные весы́, (4) шко́льные весы́, (5) весы́ для взве́шивания автомаши́н

The weights in the metric system are given below.

Табли́ца мер ве́са

0,001 *г*—1 миллигра́мм (*мг*)

0,01 *г*—1 сантигра́мм (*сг*)

0,1 *г*—1 децигра́мм (*дг*)

1 *г*—1 грамм (*г*)

1.000 *г*—1 килогра́мм (*кг*)

100 *кг*—1 це́нтнер (*ц*)

1.000 *кг*—1 то́нна (*т*)

Ме́ры ве́са до введе́ния метри́ческих мер:

золотни́к—4,25 *г*

фунт ра́вен 96 золотника́м—409,5 *г*

пуд[6] ра́вен 40 фу́нтам—16,38 *кг*

It is useful to become familiar as well with the terminology for scales and the process of weighing. The illustration on this page covers the

[6] **Пуд** is still commonly used in reporting grain shipments and the like.

former; for the latter, the important words and phrases to know are:

вес weight
Сли́вы продаю́тся на вес.

ве́сить to weigh, have a certain weight
Я ве́шу 54 кило́.
Письмо́ ве́сит 25 гра́мм.[7]

взве́шивать, взве́сить to weigh something
Она́ сейча́с взве́шивает паке́т.

взве́шиваться, взве́ситься to weigh oneself
Они́ все взве́сились вчера́.[8]

В метри́ческой систе́ме мер за едини́цу ве́са при́нят *грамм* (сокращённо г или Г). Грамм—это вес одного́ куби́ческого сантиме́тра чи́стой воды́, взя́той при температу́ре 4° С. (Четы́ре гра́дуса по Це́льсию.) Килогра́мм (кг или кГ)—это вес 1 дм³ (одного́ куби́ческого дециме́тра) чи́стой воды́ при температу́ре 4° С.

Вес одного́ куби́ческого сантиме́тра вещества́ в гра́ммах называ́ется уде́льным ве́сом э́того вещества́.

Time
Вре́мя

Time, at least, does not involve a different system of measurement from ours for the most part. If you are not already familiar with them, you will recognize the time units mentioned in the following list by the numbers.

Столе́тие равно́ 100 (ста) года́м.
Век ра́вен 100 (ста) года́м.

Год ра́вен 12 (двена́дцати) ме́сяцам.
В просто́м году́ 365 дней.
В високо́сном году́ 366 дней.
Ме́сяц ра́вен 30 (три́дцати) дням и́ли 31 (три́дцати одному́) дню. В феврале́ 28 и́ли 29 дней.
Су́тки равны́ 24 (двадцати́ четырём) часа́м.[9]
Час ра́вен 60 (шести́десяти) мину́там.
Мину́та равна́ 60 (шести́десяти) секу́ндам.

CLOCKS AND WATCHES ЧАСЫ́

All instruments that tell time may be referred to as **часы́**, but if you want to be specific: wall clock **стенны́е часы́**, pocket watch **карма́нные часы́**, wristwatch **нару́чные часы́**, sundial **со́лнечные часы́**. Some timepieces, however, are not built on the word **часы́**. Thus, **хо́дики** is similar to our cuckoo clock (but the bird is optional); an alarm clock is **буди́льник** (**буди́ть** to awaken someone); and a stop watch is **секундо-ме́р** (**ме́рить** to measure). All clocks and watches have a dial or face **цифербла́т**, an hour hand **часова́я стре́лка** (**стрела́** arrow), and a minute hand **мину́тная стре́лка**.

Часы́ говоря́т, "тик-та́к, тик-та́к." Ти́канье—негро́мкий звук. Вы слы́шите, как ва́ши часы́ ти́кают?

Russian language texts usually attend to the problem of telling time in Russian. (**Вы ду́маете, что трёхле́тний ма́льчик зна́ет как определя́ть вре́мя?**) In writing down the time, however, notice that hours are separated from minutes by a period rather than a colon (as in continental Europe): "**Нача́ло сеа́нса в 18.30**"; "**По́езд при́был в 7.39 утра́.**"

For railroads, post offices, theaters, or wherever any official time is cited, the time almost in-

---

[7] The official genitive plural of **грамм** is **гра́ммов** but in colloquial (acceptable spoken) Russian **грамм** is used.

[8] A word of warning: "**Он пове́сился**" is "He hanged himself."

[9] In an interesting article, "Twelve Names for Twelve Things" *Ру́сский язы́к за рубежо́м*, No. 4 (1969), стр. 79–86, L. S. Barkhudarov points out that the Russian **су́тки**, a twenty-four-hour period, is divided into four parts: **у́тро**—from sunrise to about ten o'clock in the morning; **день**—from about ten or eleven o'clock in the morning to sunset; **ве́чер**—from sunset to ten or eleven at night; and **ночь**—from ten or eleven o'clock at night to sunrise. Thus, for example, the English phrase "two o'clock in the morning" should be "**два часа́ но́чи**" in Russian.

Сообщение СССР—Италия

МОСКВА — ВАРШАВА — ВЕНА — РИМ

№ поезда	Прибытие	Отправление	Км	Главнейшие железно-дорожные станции	Прибытие	Отправление	№ поезда
				Московское время			
21	—	23.55	0	**Москва-Белорусская**	9.50	—	
	5.18	5.31	419	Смоленск	4.21	4.31	
	9.27	9.37	750	Минск	0.11	0.21	
8802	13.07	14.45	1101	Брест	19.00	20.35	22
				Среднеевропейское время			
	13.05	13.40	1102	Тересполь	15.55	16.22	
3	17.27	19.08	1314	**Варшава Гд.**	11.09	12.05	8801
	23.13	23.19	1634	Катовице	6.48	6.57	
	0.20	0.41	1708	Зебжидовице . . .	5.15	5.40	
285	0.50	1.20	1711	Петровице у Карвине	4.24	5.06	4104
	1.35	1.44	1729	Новый Богумин . . .	4.05	4.09	
	3.00	3.15	1820	Пршеров	2.35	2.52	286
Ex42	4.38	5.45	1919	Бржецлав	23.40	1.10	
	6.03	6.33	1938	Хохенау	23.00	23.20	
509	7.35	12.25	2008	Вена	18.10	22.00	Ex41
	18.05	18.23	2375	Виллах	11.55	12.19	
				Восточноевропейское время			
							502
47	0.08	0.52	2635	Венеция	8.01	8.30	
	2.42	2.59	2795	Болонья	5.36	5.55	
	4.13	4.23	2892	Флоренция	4.11	4.21	
	8.20	—	3213	**Рим Термини**	—	0.37	44

(a) A Moscow-Rome train schedule

(b) Time zones

variably appears as somewhere on the twenty-four-hour scale (like ships' time). Therefore, one o'clock in the afternoon is thirteen o'clock, six o'clock in the evening is eighteen o'clock, and so forth.

TIME ZONES   **ЧАСОВЫЕ ПОЯСÁ**

It is perhaps easier to appreciate the size of the Soviet Union if you realize that it requires eleven time zones **часовóй пóяс** (*sg.*). Railroad

and airplane schedules between cities within the USSR are listed according to Moscow time in order to obviate the problems that can arise in a country with that number of time zones.

CALENDARS   **КАЛЕНДАРИ́**

Days are usually listed at the left rather than across the top, and the weeks start with Monday rather than Sunday.

Май

Пн.		6	13	20	27
Вт.		7	14	21	28
Ср.	1	8	15	22	29
Чт.	2	9	16	23	30
Пт.	3	10	17	24	31
Сб.	4	11	18	25	
Вс.	5	12	19	26	

Russians are very fond of the tear-off type of calendar **отрывно́й календа́рь**, one page for each day. Tear-off calendars are published for many "special interest" groups, such as school-children, women, members of the armed forces, and so on. The illustration shows a page from Календа́рь шко́льника на 1968.

Листо́к из отрывно́го календаря́

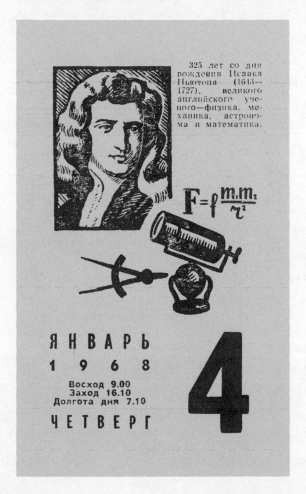

THE JULIAN AND GREGORIAN CALENDARS — СТА́РЫЙ СТИЛЬ И НО́ВЫЙ СТИЛЬ

Julius Caesar, on the advice of an astronomer, set up the Julian calendar (also now called Old Style, O.S. **Ста́рый стиль, ст.ст.**) with a year's length of 365 days, 6 hours, just a little longer than the solar year of 365 days, 5 hours, 48 minutes, 46 seconds. As the centuries went by, the discrepancy between the counting method and natural appearances widened by some ten days. So in 1582 Pope Gregory XIII introduced the calendar now in general use, the Gregorian calendar (also called New Style, N.S. **Но́вый стиль, н.с./нов.ст.**). The Roman Catholic countries quickly accepted the change, but England (and America therefore) did not change over until 1752; the USSR changed over in February, 1918. Much of the Eastern Orthodox Church continues to use the Old Style, Julian calendar.

Until February 28, 1700, the difference in calendars remained ten days and has increased by one day every one hundred years so that since 1900 the difference has been thirteen days. This explains why the Great October Revolution (October 25, O.S.) is celebrated on November 7, and why Orthodox Russians celebrate Christmas on January 7.

THE DATE — ЧИСЛО́

In conversation, the usual word for date is **число́**: "**Како́е сего́дня число́?**" When a document, letter, or something official is being referred to, then the word becomes **да́та**: "**Да́та почто́вого штемпеля.**"

When Russians write the date, there is a specific order in which it is done: the day, the month, then the year. The month is usually written as a Roman or an Arabic numeral: 30.6.73 or 30/VI-73 or 30.VI.

"**Тридца́тое шесто́го се́мьдесят тре́тьего**" is what is said; the complete expansion is, "**Тридца́тое число́, шесто́го ме́сяца, ты́сяча девятьсо́т се́мьдесят тре́тьего го́да.**"

A.D. and B.C. are expressed by **на́шей э́ры (н.э.)** and **до на́шей э́ры (до н.э.).**

Кали́гула у́мер в со́рок пе́рвом году́ на́шей э́ры. Архиме́д жил с две́сти во́семьдесят седьмо́го по две́сти двена́дцатый год до на́шей э́ры. (Йли: Архиме́д жил в две́сти во́семьдесят седьмо́м— две́сти двена́дцатом года́х до на́шей э́ры.)

Centuries are almost always expressed in Roman numerals: "Пу́шкин жил в нача́ле XIX ве́ка."

THE SEASONS   ВРЕМЕНА́ ГО́ДА

The year is divided into:

зи́мние ме́сяцы (зима́): декабрь, янва́рь, февра́ль
весе́нние ме́сяцы (весна́): март, апре́ль, май
ле́тние ме́сяцы (ле́то): ию́нь, ию́ль, а́вгуст
осе́нние ме́сяцы (о́сень): сентя́брь, октя́брь, ноя́брь

For the summer and winter solstices and the vernal and autumnal equinoxes, the dates and names are:

22 ию́ня   день ле́тнего солнцестоя́ния
22 декабря́   день зи́мнего солнцестоя́ния
21 ма́рта   день весе́ннего равноде́нствия
23 сентября́ день осе́ннего равноде́нствия

Notice the similarity between solstice and **солн- цестоя́ние**, equinox and **равноде́нствие**. The Russians do not consider that the seasons officially start on these days.

Temperature
Температу́ра

Someday, the United States will join the rest of the world, as indeed the Soviet Union has

Comparative Table of Temperatures

Centi-grade	Fahren-heit	Centi-grade	Fahren-heit	Centi-grade	Fahren-heit	Centi-grade	Fahren-heit	Centi-grade	Fahren-heit	Centi-grade	Fahren-heit
−50	−58	−9	15.8	3.3	38	16	60.8	28.9	84	42	107.6
−45	−49	−8.9	16	4	39.2	16.7	62	29	84.2	42.2	108
−40	−40	−8	17.6	4.4	40	17	62.6	30	86	43	109.4
−35	−31	−7.8	18	5	41	17.8	64	31	87.8	43.3	110
−34.4	−30	−7	19.4	5.6	42	18	64.4	31.1	88	44	111.2
−28.9	−20	−6.7	20	6	42.8	18.9	66	32	89.6	44.4	112
−25	−13	−6	21.2	6.7	44	19	66.2	32.2	90	45	113
−23.3	−10	−5.6	22	7	44.6	20	68	33	91.4	45.6	114
−17.8	0	−5	23	7.8	46	21	69.8	33.3	92	46	114.8
−17	1.4	−4.4	24	8	46.4	21.1	70	34	93.2	46.7	116
−16.7	2	−4	24.8	8.9	48	22	71.6	34.4	94	47	116.6
−16	3.2	−3.3	26	9	48.2	22.2	72	35	95	47.8	118
−15.6	4	−3	26.6	10	50	23	73.4	35.6	96	48	118.4
−15	5	−2.2	28	11	51.8	23.3	74	36	96.8	48.9	120
−14.4	6	−2	28.4	11.1	52	24	75.2	36.7	98	49	120.2
−14	6.8	−1.1	30	12	53.6	24.4	76	37	98.6	50	122
−13.3	8	−1	30.2	12.2	54	25	77	37.8	100	51	123.8
−13	8.6	0	32	13	55.4	25.6	78	38	100.4	52	125.6
−12.2	10	1	33.8	13.3	56	26	78.8	38.9	102	53	127.4
−12	10.4	1.1	34	14	57.2	26.7	80	39	102.2	54	129.2
−11.1	12	2	35.6	14.4	58	27	80.6	40	104	55	131
−11	12.2	2.2	36	15	59	27.8	82	41	105.8	100	212
−10	14	3	37.4	15.6	60	28	82.4	41.1	106		

already done, and it too will use the Celsius (centigrade) scale **шкала́ Це́льсия** rather than the Fahrenheit scale **шкала́ Фаренге́йта**. Until then we must learn what it means when a Russian says 10°. As you know, the centigrade scale puts the boiling point of water at 100° and freezing at 0°.

● Це́льсий—Термо́метр со шкало́й в 100 гра́дусов от то́чки та́яния льда до то́чки кипе́ния воды́. Замерза́ние воды́ происхо́дит при температу́ре 0° (ноль гра́дусов). Вода́ кипи́т при 100° (ста гра́дусов, ста гра́дусах) по Це́льсию.

To convert degrees Fahrenheit to centigrade and vice versa, use the formulas:

$$F° = (C° \times \tfrac{9}{5}) + 32°$$
$$C° = (F° - 32°) \times \tfrac{5}{9}$$

There are various ways of stating temperature, including:

10°	плюс де́сять гра́дусов
3°	три гра́дуса вы́ше нуля́
1°	оди́н гра́дус тепла́
0°	ноль гра́дусов
−2°	ми́нус два гра́дуса
−1°	оди́н гра́дус хо́лода (моро́за)
−20°	два́дцать гра́дусов ни́же нуля́

WEATHER AND TEMPERATURE — **ПОГО́ДА И ТЕМПЕРАТУ́РА**

You have a feeling for how hot or cold a certain number of degrees is in English. About 80° is where hot begins, and 90° is very hot. How cold " cold " is depends on where you live. The following are two weather forecasts from *Изве́стия* for midwinter and midsummer.

Прогно́з пого́ды на 15ᵒᵉ января́: В Москве́ и о́бласти 15 января́ ожида́ется холо́дная пого́да: температу́ра но́чью о́коло ми́нус 20, на се́вере о́бласти до ми́нус 25, днём ми́нус 16–17 гра́дусов. Небольша́я о́блачность, без оса́дков, ве́тер уме́ренный.

Прогно́з пого́ды на 11 ию́ля: В Москве́ и о́бласти 11 ию́ля ожида́ется переме́нная о́блачность, места́ми кратковре́менные дожди́ и гро́зы. Ве́тер за́падный, от сла́бого до уме́ренного, температу́ра о́коло 25 гра́дусов.

Жа́рко (28–33 гра́дуса) бу́дет в респу́бликах Закавка́зья. Здесь места́ми пройду́т дожди́ и гро́зы.

THERMOMETERS — **ТЕРМО́МЕТРЫ/ГРА́ДУСНИКИ**

There are two words for thermometer: **термо́метр** is usually used in either more formal or technical situations; what is found around the house is a **гра́дусник**.

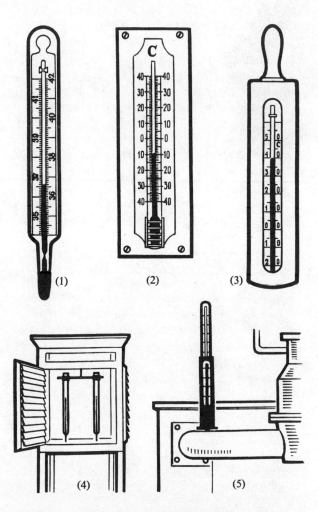

Ви́ды термо́метров: (1) медици́нский термо́метр, (2) нару́жный термо́метр, (3) термо́метр для измере́ния воды́, (4) термо́метры для метеорологи́ческой ста́нции, (5) термо́метр для измере́ния температу́ры жи́дкости в промы́шленных устано́вках

Обы́чные нару́жные термо́метры име́ют шкалу́ от −50° (ми́нус пяти́десяти гра́дусов) до +50° (плюс пяти́десяти гра́дусов).

There is also an indoor thermometer **ко́мнатный термо́метр** that registers from 0° C. to 50° C. The accepted indoor temperature is about 20° C.

The well-equipped household, especially one with children in it, also has a medical thermometer **медици́нский термо́метр, гра́дусник**. The scale is from about 34° to 42°. The construction of the Russian medical thermometer is different from ours; it is much less breakable and much bigger. Russians take temperatures by putting the thermometer in an armpit and leaving it there for ten minutes. (If you put a Russian thermometer in your mouth, the Russians would know you were sick.) A normal temperature is 36.6° (**говоря́т: три́дцать шесть и шесть**).[10] A reading of 37.5° (**три́дцать семь и пять**) indicates that something is wrong, and if it goes up to 40°, the patient is very sick.

A water thermometer is also a fairly common device, often used for determining the temperature of a baby's bath.

Temperature regulators on ovens **регуля́торы для духо́вок** are relatively new devices so that you will find the great majority of recipes do not mention heat, though they usually do indicate how long the item is to be cooked. (If you are following a Russian recipe at home and no indication of temperature is given, use 350° F. and hope.) Newer ovens do have them, and the range is from 50° to 350° C.

Pressure
Давле́ние

The usual unit of pressure encountered in everyday life is grams or kilograms per square centimeter.

$$1\,\frac{\text{г}}{\text{см}^2} \quad \text{и́ли} \quad 1\,\frac{\text{кг}}{\text{см}^2}$$

---

[10] Notice that our normal body temperature, 98.6° F., actually converts to 37° C. (not 36.6). Absolutely speaking, the oral thermometer is more accurate, but practically speaking, relative temperature is the concern in fever.

Children in school learn the formula: $p = \dfrac{F}{S}$

$$\text{Давле́ние } (p) = \frac{\text{си́ла давле́ния } (F)}{\text{пло́щадь } (S)}$$

Tire pressure **давле́ние в ши́нах** is measured in grams per square centimeter (**в гра́ммах на оди́н квадра́тный сантиме́тр**).

ATMOSPHERIC PRESSURE АТМОСФЕ́РНОЕ ДАВЛЕ́НИЕ

The illustration shows a Russian aneroid barometer, the common household kind. The words around the perimeter are also commonly found on the face of such a barometer: low pressure and storms on the left, to high pressure and dry on the right. Normal atmospheric pressure is about 760 mm. of mercury at sea level (760 *мм* **рту́тного столба́ на у́ровне мо́ря**).

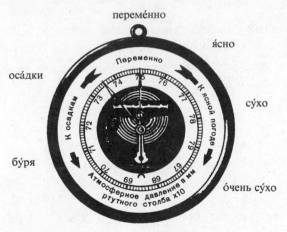

Баро́метр-анеро́ид

Speed
Ско́рость

The usual unit of speed is in kilometers per hour **в киломе́трах в час (км/час, км в час)**. In the USSR the speed limit **преде́льная ско́рость** in cities is now up to eighty kilometers per hour on major arterials unless restrictions are posted. Trucks have a speed limit of fifty kilometers per hour in cities. Outside cities no speed limit is established. (Remember, one kilometer is about five-eighths of a mile.)

The following are (1) some average speeds for various means of locomotion, from a pedestrian to a jet airplane; and (2) top speeds for various makes of cars.[11]

(1) Не́которые сре́дние ско́рости:

пешехо́д—4–5 км в час

ло́шадь ры́сью—12–13 км в час

лы́жник—18 км в час (cross-country racing speed)

по́езд—50 км в час

реакти́вный самолёт—1000 км в час

(2) Наибо́льшие ско́рости разли́чных авто-моби́лей:

грузовы́е—от 60 до 70 км в час

легковы́е

«Москви́ч»—90 км в час

«Побе́да»—110 км в час

«Во́лга»—130 км в час

«Ча́йка»—160 км в час

Ско́рость зву́ка ∼ 330 м/сек.

Не́которые реакти́вные самолёты достига́ют сверхзвуковы́х скоросте́й.

Моле́кулы га́зов дви́жутся с огро́мными ско́ростями (400–1200 м/сек), ча́сто превыша́ющими да́же ско́рость руже́йной пу́ли (865 м/сек).

Electricity
Электри́чество

Voltages **напряже́ния** in the USSR vary: the two common ones are 127 volts and 220 volts. In Moscow, 127 volts is quite common, but 220 volts is more common elsewhere. The usual voltage in the United States is 110 volts, except for major appliances, some of which operate on 220 volts. In the Soviet Union the frequency of the alternating current **частота́ переме́нного то́ка** is 50 cycles a second 50 **пери́одов в секу́нду** while in the United States the frequency is 60 cycles per second. (It can be concluded from this that all equipment run by synchronous

motors will be off by 50/60. Also, if you use electrical equipment designed for 110, especially in places wired for 220 voltage, then you will either have to replace a fuse or replace the equipment. Only a transformer can solve the problem.)

The Russian must find out what voltage his apartment house is supplied with before he moves in. The different voltages cannot be distinguished by different sized plugs. Some of the newer appliances in the USSR come supplied with a transformer switch **переключа́тель на трансформа́торе** that makes the appliance usable at either voltage.

● Электри́ческие ла́мпочки продаю́тся по свеча́м. Мо́жно купи́ть ла́мпочки в 50 свече́й, в 20 свече́й, и т. д. (Свеча́—едини́ца измере́ния си́лы све́та, излуча́емого каки́м-нибу́дь исто́чником.) Ла́мпочки то́же продаю́тся по ва́ттам.

Latitude and longitude
Широта́ и долгота́

Latitudes **широ́ты**, of course, are either northern or southern, and longitudes **долго́ты** are eastern or western.

долгота́

широта́

Гло́бус

[11] Пчёлко и Поля́к, *Арифме́тика для 4 кла́сса* (Москва́: Просвеще́ние, 1968), стр. 184. (Currently, attainable speeds are higher.)

The following text should help you read latitude and longitude indications in Russian:

● Координа́ты Москвы́—55° 45′ (пятьдеся́т пять гра́дусов со́рок пять мину́т) с. ш. (се́верной широты́) и 37° 37′ (три́дцать семь гра́дусов три́дцать семь мину́т) в. д. (восто́чной долготы́) по Гри́нвичскому меридиа́ну. О́стров Кергеле́н в Инди́йском океа́не нахо́дится на 50° ю. ш. (пятидеся́том гра́дусе ю́жной широты́), Гибралта́рский проли́в —на 5° з. д. (на пя́том гра́дусе за́падной долготы́).

And since we are involved in directions, you should know what a Russian compass looks like:

Ко́мпас

● На дне коро́бки ко́мпаса нанесены́ деле́ния, обознача́ющие гра́дусы—от 0° до 360°. Е́сли освободи́ть стре́лку ко́мпаса, то коне́ц стре́лки, пока́зывающий се́вер, бу́дет соотве́тствовать 0° − 360°, юг—180°, восто́к—90° и за́пад—270°.

Money
Де́ньги

Soviet coins **моне́ты** come in two varieties, silver coins **серебро́** and copper coins **медь**, even though the remnant of either silver or copper is relatively small.

The illustration shows various denominations of coins. One side of the coins has the state emblem, and the value of the coin is on the other. Some coins are known by alternate names. The use of the words **гри́венник** and **двугри́венный** is somewhat old fashioned but fairly common. **Полти́нник** is regularly used.

Not shown is the silver ruble (in slang, **целко́вый**). It is often minted to commemorate an event, such as the twentieth anniversary of the victory over fascism, the fiftieth anniversary of the Revolution, and so forth. But the paper ruble is more common.

The paper one-ruble bill is shown. The other denominations are: three rubles **три рубля́, тре́шница, тре́шник, трёхрублёвка**; five rubles **пять рубле́й, пятёрка, пятирублёвка**; and ten rubles **де́сять рубле́й, деся́тка, десятирублёвка**.

The size of the bill increases with the denomination, and though the markings on the bills are almost the same, the predominant color changes.

Медь

одна́ копе́йка

две копе́йки

три копе́йки

пять копе́ек, пята́к

Серебро́

10 копе́ек, гри́венник

15 копе́ек

20 копе́ек, двугри́венный

50 копе́ек, полти́нник

Оди́н рубль, ру́блик, рублёвая бума́жка, рублёвка

Old terminology for money, which you may come across in literature, includes:

алты́н 3 копе́йки
гри́венник 10 копе́ек
пятиалты́нный 15 копе́ек
двугри́венный 20 копе́ек
черво́нец 10 рубле́й

PRICES   ЦЕ́НЫ

Prices are posted in several ways depending upon the formality:

7 руб. 49 коп. *in a newspaper advertisement*
7 р. 40 к. *in a store*
7-40 *at the market*

Notice the use of a hyphen when letter abbreviations are omitted.

In 1960 there was a currency change in the USSR of ten old rubles for one new ruble. Thus, if a book cost seventy rubles before 1960, then it cost seven rubles after 1960. It was only a paper transaction, with no change in prices for goods or services, but this explains what seem to be inflated prices or wages before 1960.

12

Abbreviations and acronyms

Сокращéния

Abbreviations are presumably a convenience, but the convenience is a privilege of the native speaker. As non-Russians, we not only have the problem of expanding and deciphering the abbreviation, we often must learn how to pronounce it and whether to decline it. Unfortunately for foreigners, abbreviations abound in Russian. Many abbreviations and acronyms are products of the Revolution. New institutions, new organizations, new factories, all needed names of some sort. They got them. Professional translators, advanced students, and libraries should have at least one of several fairly large compendiums of abbreviations and acronyms. Two of the best are: *Glossary of Russian Abbreviations and Acronyms*, compiled by the Aerospace Technology Division, Reference Department (Washington, D.C.: Library of Congress, 1967); and *Russian Abbreviations*, *A Selective List*, compiled by Alexander Rosenberg, Reference Department (Washington, D.C.: Library of Congress, 1957). The former is newer, larger, and more likely to contain all conceivable scientific abbreviations. The latter is older and smaller, but it contains more acronyms in use before World War II (of use or interest to students of literature). A third excellent reference is the Soviet *Словáрь сокращéний рýсского языкá*, ред. Корѝцкий (Москвá: Гос. изд-во инострáнных и национáльных словарéй, 1963). Its major advantage is that it gives specific direction on pronouncing abbreviations. The disadvantage is, of course, that the expanded abbreviations are not translated into English.

Here the discussion must be confined to a limited description of types of abbreviations in order to elucidate some of the difficulties they present for the non-Russian. These types have been manufactured to suit this chapter's purposes so that the definitions serve this discussion alone. The types to be considered are: "literary" abbreviations (including those for measurements), "letter" abbreviations (with a section on the derivation of airplane names), and acronyms.

«Literary» abbreviations
«Усло́вные» сокраще́ния

"Literary" abbreviations are those that are encountered only when they are written: etc., Inc., Co. Therefore, the problems they present for the foreigner are relatively simple: what their expansion is and what the expansion means. Generally speaking, the problem of pronunciation does not occur. The few given here are those the reader of current prose would find it difficult to avoid. The Russian recognizes many more, and for their expansion you may refer to any dictionary of abbreviations. These abbreviations usually present fewer problems for the foreigner because generally they are not pronounced as abbreviations. When they are pronounced, such usage is very informal. The best example is и т. д., pronounced in familiar company as "итэдэ́." (However, the pronunciation of "га" for гекта́р is approaching standard colloquial usage.) There is also a large gray area in colloquial speech where common literary abbreviations, especially those indicating rank or authority, turn into words in their own right: зам, зав, пом.

Sometimes a plural is indicated by a repetition of the abbreviation; for example: в—век, вв—века́; п—пара́граф, пп—пара́графы; №—но́мер, №№—номера́.

The most common literary abbreviations are:

в.	век	century
В	восто́к	east
вкл.	включе́ние, включи́тельно	inclusion, including
вм.	вме́сто	instead of
в т. ч.	в том числе́	including
гл. обр.	гла́вным о́бразом	mostly, mainly
Ж	Же́нская (убо́рная)	women's room
ж.д.	желе́зная доро́га	railroad
З	за́пад	west
зав.	заве́дующий	manager, chief
зам.	замести́тель	substitute, deputy
и др.	и други́е	and others
им.	и́мени	named after

и пр.	и про́чее	and so on
и т. д.	и так да́лее	and so forth
и т. п.	и тому́ подо́бное	and so on, et cetera
Л.	Ленингра́д	Leningrad
М., M	метро́	subway (station)
	Москва́	Moscow
	Мужска́я (убо́рная)	men's room
м. б.	мо́жет быть	perhaps
м. г.	мину́вшего го́да	last year
напр.	наприме́р	for example
н. э.	на́шей э́ры	*Anno Domini* (до н. э. *Before Christ*)
ок.	о́коло	near, about
пом.	помо́щник	assistant
приб.	приблизи́тельно	approximately
ред.	реда́кция, реда́ктор	editorial office, editor
С	се́вер	north
с. г.	сего́ го́да	this year
сл. обр.	сле́дующим о́бразом	as follows
см.	смотри́	see, refer to
СПб	Санкт-Петербу́рг	Saint Petersburg
ср.	сравни́	compare
стр.	страни́ца	page
т. е.	то́ есть	that is
т. к.	та́к как	since
т. наз.	так называ́емый	so-called
т. обр.	таки́м о́бразом	in this way, thus
тов.	това́рищ	comrade
ул.	у́лица	street
Ю	юг	south

Abbreviations for units of measure
Сокращённые назва́ния едини́ц мер

Units of measure are often referred to by standardized abbreviations, which are most likely to appear in technical publications but are also often used in the daily press (in plan fulfillment information and the like). They almost invariably appear preceded by numbers and are not usually followed by a period. These abbreviations can have three parts: *квтч*, for example, consists of a multiple (*к—кило́*), a unit of measure (*вт*—**ватт**), and an indication of time (*ч*—**час**). The only part of the abbreviation that can appear alone is the unit of measure. Listed below are some standardized abbreviations of units of measure.

а	ар, ампе́р	*кал*	кало́рия
в	вольт	*л*	литр
вт	ватт	*лм*	лю́мен
г	грамм	*м*	метр
гн	ге́нри	*ом*	ом
гц	герц	*т*	то́нна
к	куло́н		

The following are abbreviations for multiples of the units cited above. Thus *см* for **сантиме́тр** is 1/100 meter, and *гвт* for **гектова́тт** is 100 watts. The most frequently used prefixes of this sort are:

мк	микро-	1/1 000 000
м	милли-	1/1 000
с	санти-	1/100
д	деци-	1/10
да	дека-	$10x$
г	гекто-	$100x$
к	кило-	$1\,000x$
мг	ме́га-	$1\,000\,000x$

Finally, rates and speeds are indicated by the abbreviation of a unit of time or space that follows the preceding abbreviations. Thus *гвтч* is the abbreviation for **гектова́тт-час** hundred watts per hour, and *ц/га* is **це́нтнеров с гекта́ра** centners per hectare. The use of the slash always indicates a rate, but the slash may not always appear. Thus **гектова́тт-час** can be seen as *гвтч* or *гвт/ч* or *гвт-ч*.

The commonly used time abbreviations are:

ч	час
мин	мину́та
сек	секу́нда

In some cases, the use of the slash is almost obligatory.

см/сек сантиме́тров в секу́нду centimeters per second

об/мин оборо́тов в мину́ту revolutions per minute

Combinations of these forms are numerous, and with a little practice in seeing them they are readily recognizable.

гм	гектоме́тр
дг	дециграмм
кв	килово́льт
км/час	киломе́тр в час
мм	миллиме́тр
га[1]	гекта́р

"Letter" abbreviations
Бу́квенные сокраще́ния

The other major type of abbreviation is the "letter" abbreviation—initials of institutions, projects, and even slogans. Here, the problem is not only to decipher and translate but also to pronounce; for example: **АН, ВЛКСМ, ЦУМ.**

Some abbreviations have become permanent whole words and thus are no longer necessarily in capitals: **загс, гум, вуз.** Many Russians have even forgotten what the letters **ЗАГС** stand for.

The abbreviation is pronounced as a word if there is a vowel in the middle: **ГОСТ** is pronounced **"гост"** and **ЗИЛ** is pronounced **"зил."** Otherwise, more often than not, the individual letters are pronounced as they would be in a recitation of the alphabet (see "Russians and their alphabet," Chapter 9). There are some prominent exceptions to the way letters are pronounced in abbreviations: the unaccented **"К"** is often pronounced **"кэ," "эС"** can be **"Сэ," "эФ"** can be **"Фэ,"** and **"эР"** can be **"Рэ." ВЛКСМ** is used so often that it is reduced to **вэлкесэ́м.** Sometimes the pronunciations of these letter abbreviations have become new words of their own. **СР** for **социали́ст револю́ционе́р** has become **эсэ́р:** "**Во вре́мя эсе́ровского мятежа́ он поги́б.**" Similarly, **ЧК** for **Чрезвы-**

---

[1] В разгово́рной ре́чи ча́сто произно́сится как "га" вме́сто "гекта́р."

чайная комиссия is now **чека́**: "Чеки́сты собрали́сь во Дворце́ Съе́здов."

When a new word is felt to have been formed, it is usually declined and its gender is determined by the final letter. Those ending in a consonant become masculine, those ending in an *a* become feminine, and so on. The majority, therefore, are masculine: **ЖЭК, ДОСААФ, ЗИЛ.**

In the table below only the most common letter abbreviations are given. An underscore before the abbreviation indicates that another abbreviation often precedes; for example:

__АССР—АбхАССР (Абха́зская АССР); __ССР—УССР (Украи́нская ССР); __ОНО—ОблОНО (Областно́й ОНО). An underscore following the abbreviation indicates the reverse: **ЦНИИ__—ЦНИИВТ (ЦНИИ во́дного тра́нспорта)**. Also, the abbreviations given here are for the convenience of the American reader of Russian. Some abbreviations, therefore, refer to institutions that no longer exist—**МТС, ЗИС, РАПП**. They are followed by an asterisk. Those abbreviations that have become words and are therefore declined are indicated by (d).

Abbreviation	Pronunciation	Expansion	Translation
АН	а-э́н	Акаде́мия наук	Academy of Sciences
__АССР	а-эс-эс-э́р	Автоно́мная Сове́тская Социалисти́ческая Респу́блика	Autonomous Soviet Socialist Republic
БГТО	бэ-гэ-тэ-о́	"Будь гото́в к труду́ и оборо́не"	"Be ready for labor and defense" (slogan; health and fitness standard for children)
ВВС	вэ-вэ-э́с	Вое́нно-возду́шные си́лы	Air Force
ВДНХ	вэ-дэ-эн-ха́	Вы́ставка достиже́ний наро́дного хозя́йства	Exhibition of Achievements of the National Economy of the USSR
ВКП(б)*	вэ-ка-пэ-бэ́	Всесою́зная Коммунисти́ческая па́ртия (большевико́в)	All-Union Communist Party (of Bolsheviks)
ВЛКСМ	вэ-эл-ка-эс-э́м (вэлкэсэ́м)	Всесою́зный Ле́нинский Коммунисти́ческий Сою́з Молодёжи (Комсомо́л)	All-Union Lenin Young Communist League
ВНИИ__	вний	Всесою́зный нау́чно-исследовательский институ́т	All-Union Scientific Research Institute (of ———)
ВОКС*	вокс (d)	Всесою́зное о́бщество культу́рной свя́зи с заграни́цей	All-Union Society for Cultural Relations with Foreign Countries
ВПШ*	вэ-пэ-ша́	Вое́нно-полити́ческая шко́ла Вы́сшая парти́йная шко́ла	military-political school higher party school
врио	ври́о	вре́менно исполня́ющий обя́занности	acting [official]
ВТУ	вэ-тэ-у́	Вы́сшее техни́ческое учи́лище	higher technical school
ВУЗ	вуз (d)	Вы́сшее уче́бное заведе́ние	higher educational institution
ГАЗ	газ (d)	Го́рьковский автомоби́льный заво́д	(Automobile made by) Gor'kiy Automobile Plant[1]
ГАИ	гай	Госуда́рственная автомоби́льная инспе́кция	State Automobile Inspection (State Patrol)

[1] Whence the name for the Russian jeep **га́зик.**

Abbreviation	Pronunciation	Expansion	Translation
(Continued)			
ГДР	гэдэ-э́р	Герма́нская Демократи́ческая Рес-пу́блика	German Democratic Republic
ГОСТ	гост (d)	госуда́рственный общесою́зный стан-да́рт	All-Union State Standard
ГПУ*	гэ-пэ-у́	Госуда́рственное полити́ческое управле́ние	State Political Administration
ГСО	гэ-сэ-о́	"Гото́в к санита́рной оборо́не"	"Ready for sanitary defense" (first-aid slogan and badge)
ГТО	гэ-тэ-о́	"Гото́в к труду́ и оборо́не"	"Ready for work and defense" (slogan; health and fitness standard for adults)
ГУМ	гум (d)	Госуда́рственный универса́льный магази́н	State department store
ГУ__	гу	Гла́вное управле́ние	Main Administration (of ———)
		ГУЛА́Г—Гла́вное управле́ние ис-прави́тельно-трудовы́х лагере́й	Main Administration of Labor Camps
__ГЭС	гэс (d)	Гидроэлектри́ческая ста́нция	hydroelectric power plant
ДОСААФ	доса́ф (d)	Всесою́зное доброво́льное о́бщество соде́йствия а́рмии, авиа́ции и фло́ту СССР	All-Union Voluntary Society for Assistance to the Army, Air Force, and Navy of the USSR
ДРВ	дэ-эр-в́э	Демократи́ческая респу́блика Вьет-на́м	Democratic Republic of Vietnam
ДСО	дэ-сэ-о́	Доброво́льное спорти́вное о́бщество	Voluntary Sports Society
ЖАКТ*	жакт (d)	Жили́щно-аре́ндное кооперати́вное това́рищество	housing-renting cooperative association
ЖСК	же-эс-ка́	Жили́щно-строи́тельный кооперати́в	housing construction cooperative
ЖЭК	жек (d)	Жили́щно-эксплуатацио́нная конто́ра	housing operation office
ЗАГС	загс (d)	Бюро́ за́писи а́ктов гражда́нского со-стоя́ния	civil registry office
ЗИЛ	зил (d)	Заво́д и́мени Лихачёва	(Automobile made by) Moscow Automobile Plant im. I. A. Likhachev
ЗИС*	зис (d)	Заво́д и́мени Ста́лина	(Automobile made by) Moscow Automobile Plant im. Stalin (now: ЗИЛ)
ИЛ	ил	(Изда́тельство) "Иностра́нная ли-терату́ра"	Publishing House of Foreign Literature
КВЖД*	ка-вэ-жэ-д́э	Кита́йско-Восто́чная желе́зная до-ро́га	Chinese Eastern Railroad
КГБ	ка-гэ-б́э	Комите́т госуда́рственной безопа́с-ности[2]	State Security Committee

[2] Кагебе́шник is derogatory slang for an employee of KGB.

Abbreviation	Pronunciation	Expansion	Translation
(Continued)			
КНДР	кэ-эн-дэ-э́р	Коре́йская Наро́дно-Демократи́-ческая Респу́блика	Korean People's Democratic Republic
КНР	ка-эн-э́р	Кита́йская Наро́дная Респу́блика	Chinese People's Republic
__КП	ка-пэ́	Коммунисти́ческая па́ртия	Communist party
КПК	ка-пэ-ка́	Коммуни́стическая па́ртия Кита́я	Communist Party of China
КПСС	ка-пэ-эс-э́с	Коммунисти́ческая па́ртия Сове́т-ского Сою́за	Communist Party of the Soviet Union
ЛГУ	эл-гэ-у́	Ленингра́дский госуда́рственный университе́т	Leningrad State University
МАЗ	маз (d)	Ми́нский автомоби́льный заво́д	(Automobile made by) Minsk Automobile Plant
МАИ	май	Моско́вский авиацио́нный о́рдена Ле́нина институ́т	Moscow "Order of Lenin" Aviation Institute
МВД	эм-вэ-дэ́	Министе́рство вну́тренних дел	Ministry of Internal Affairs
МВО	эм-вэ-о́	Моско́вский вое́нный о́круг	Moscow Military District
МВС*	эм-вэ-э́с	Министе́рство вооружённых сил	Ministry of the Armed Forces
МВТУ	эм-вэ-тэ-у́	Моско́вское вы́сшее техни́ческое учи́-лище (им. Н. Э. Ба́умана)	Moscow Higher Technical Institute (im. N. E. Bauman)
МГБ*	эм-гэ-бэ́	Министе́рство госуда́рственной безо-па́сности	Ministry of State Security
МГИМО (*formerly* МИМО)	мимо́	Моско́вский госуда́рственный ин-ститут междунаро́дных отноше́ний	Moscow State Institute of International Relations
МГУ	эм-гэ-у́	Моско́вский госуда́рственный уни-версите́т	Moscow State University
МИД	мид (d)	Министе́рство иностра́нных дел	Ministry of Foreign Affairs
МПВО*	эм-пэ-вэ-о́	Ме́стная противовозду́шная оборо́на	local antiaircraft defense
МТС*	эм-тэ-э́с	Маши́нно-тра́кторная ста́нция	machine and tractor station
МХАТ	мхат (d)	Моско́вский Худо́жественный акаде-ми́ческий теа́тр	Moscow Academic Art Theater
НИИ__	нии	Нау́чно-иссле́довательский институ́т	Scientific Research Institute (of ———)
НКВД*	эн-ка-вэ-дэ́	Наро́дный комиссариа́т вну́тренних дел	People's Commissariat of Internal Affairs
НКГБ*	эн-ка-гэ-бэ́	Наро́дный комиссариа́т госуда́р-ственной безопа́сности	People's Commissariat of State Security
НТС	эн-тэ-э́с	Нау́чно-техни́ческий сове́т Наро́дно-трудово́й сою́з	scientific and technical council People's Labor Union (émigré political organization)

Abbreviation	Pronunciation	Expansion	Translation
(*Continued*)			
НЭП*	нэп (d)	Но́вая экономи́ческая поли́тика	New Economic Policy
ОАГ	о-а́г	Организа́ция америка́нских госуда́рств	Organization of American States
ОБХСС	о-бэ-ха-э́с	Отде́л борьбы́ с хище́ниями социалисти́ческой со́бственности и спекуля́цией	Department for Combating Embezzlement of Socialist Property and Speculation
ОГПУ*	о-гэ-пэ-у́	Объединённое госуда́рственное полити́ческое управле́ние	Unified State Political Administration
__ОНО	оно́	Отде́л наро́дного образова́ния	department of public education
ООН	о-о́н	Организа́ция Объединённых На́ций	United Nations N Y.
ОТК	о-тэ-ка́	Отде́л техни́ческого контро́ля	department of technical control
ПВО	пэ-вэ-о́	Противовозду́шная оборо́на	antiaircraft defense
__ПКиО	пэ-кэ-о́	Парк культу́ры и о́тдыха	park of culture and rest
ПТУ	пэ-тэ-у́	Профессиона́льно-техни́ческое учи́лище	trade school
РАПП*	рап	Росси́йская ассоциа́ция пролета́рских писа́телей	Russian Association of Proletarian Writers
РККА*	рэ-ка-ка́ *or* эр-ка-ка́	Рабо́че-Крестья́нская Кра́сная А́рмия	Workers' and Peasants' Red Army
РКП(б)*	эр-ка-пэ-бэ́	Росси́йская Коммунисти́ческая па́ртия (большевико́в)	Russian Communist Party (Bolsheviks)
РСДРП(б)*	эр-эс-дэ-эр-пэ́	Росси́йская социа́л-демократи́ческая рабо́чая па́ртия (большевико́в)	Russian Social Democratic Workers' Party
РСФСР	эр-эс-эф-эс-э́р	Росси́йская Сове́тская Федерати́вная Социалисти́ческая Респу́блика	Russian Soviet Federative Socialist Republic
с.-р.*	эсэ́р (d)	Социали́ст-революционе́р	Socialist-Revolutionary
СССР	эс-эс-эс-э́р	Сою́з Сове́тских Социалисти́ческих Респу́блик	Union of Soviet Socialist Republics
__ССР	эс-эс-э́р	Сове́тская социалисти́ческая респу́блика	Soviet Socialist Republic
США SHA	ша, сэ-ша́, *or* сэ-шэ-а́	Соединённые Шта́ты Аме́рики	United States of America
ТАСС	тасс (d)	Телегра́фное аге́нтство Сове́тского Сою́за	TASS (News Agency of the Soviet Union)
ТЭС	тэс	Теплова́я электри́ческая ста́нция	thermal electric power plant
ТЭЦ	тэц	Теплоэлектроцентра́ль	heat and electric power plant
ТЮЗ	тюз (d)	Теа́тр ю́ного зри́теля	children's theater

Abbreviation	Pronunciation	Expansion	Translation
(Continued)			
УАЗ	уа́з	Улья́новский автомоби́льный заво́д	(Automobile made by) Ul′yanovsk Automobile Plant
ФБР	фэ-бэ-э́р	Федера́льное бюро́ рассле́дований (США)	Federal Bureau of Investigation (USA)
ФРГ	фэ-эр-гэ́ *or* эф-эр-гэ́	Федерати́вная Респу́блика Герма́нии·	Federal Republic of Germany
ЦИК*	цик (d)	Центра́льный Исполни́тельный Комите́т	Central Executive Committee
ЦК	цэ-ка́	Центра́льный Комите́т	Central Committee
ЦКК	цэ-ка-ка́	Центра́льная контро́льная коми́ссия	Central Control Commission
ЦНИИ_	цний	Центра́льный нау́чно-иссле́довательский институ́т	Central Scientific Research Institute (of ———)
ЦОПЭ	цо-пэ́	Центра́льное объедине́ние послевое́нных эмигра́нтов из СССР	Central Association of Postwar Emigrés from the USSR
ЦРУ	цэ-эр-у́	Центра́льное разведыва́тельное управле́ние (США)	Central Intelligence Agency (USA)
ЦСУ	цэ-сэ-у́ *or* цэ-эс-у́	Центра́льное статисти́ческое управле́ние	Central Statistical Administration
ЦУ_	цу	Центра́льное управле́ние	Central Administration (of ———)
ЦУМ	цум (d)	Центра́льный универса́льный магази́н (Москва́)	Central Department Store (in Moscow)
ЧК*	чека́[3]	Всеросси́йская чрезвыча́йная коми́ссия по борьбе́ с контрреволю́цией и сабота́жем	All-Russian Extraordinary Commission for Combating Counterrevolution and Sabotage
ЮНЕСКО	юнэ́ско	Организа́ция Объединённых На́ций по вопро́сам образова́ния, нау́ки, и культу́ры	United Nations Educational, Scientific, and Cultural Organization
ЯАЗ	яа́з	Яросла́вский автомоби́льный заво́д	(Automobile made by) Yaroslavl Automobile Plant

[3] **Чеки́ст** is an historical and respectable name for an employee of the Cheka.

Deciphering letter abbreviations
Расшифро́вка бу́квенных сокраще́ний

Since the table gives only the most common letter abbreviations, you will no doubt come across some in your reading that have not been given here. There is a method that may be useful to follow in determining what those others may stand for.

First, you should check to see if the abbreviation under consideration is a combination involving some of those listed. Thus, **ОНО́** is basic to several other forms: **РайОНО́**, **ОблОНО́**, **ГорОНО́**. Often the first part of an abbreviation will denote a geographical or organizational division. Notice, for example, **МАЗ**, **ГАЗ** (**Моско́вский**, **Го́рьковский Автомоби́льный Заво́д**); **ЛГУ**, **МГУ** (**Ленингра́дский**, **Моско́вский Госуда́рственный Университе́т**); **ГДР**, **КНДР** (**Герма́нская**, **Коре́йская Наро́дная Демократи́ческая Респу́блика**).

More likely, of course, you will find no such handy pattern; then you should look carefully at the context. Expansions of relatively unfamiliar abbreviations can often be found in an early part of the discussion in which they occur. These expansions are often not capitalized and are therefore by no means obvious.

Combining context and the abbreviations listed here is a final tactic. The **ИКП** in an article datelined "Rome" is undoubtedly **Италья́нская коммунисти́ческая па́ртия**.

Identifying airplanes
Назва́ния самолётов

Russian airplanes have rather short titles often followed by a number. In naming their planes, the Russians take this opportunity to honor the principal designer. The airplane names are the initials of the designer or designers plus a model number. Below is a listing of the most common abbreviations of this sort.

Initials	Expansion
АМ	А. А. Мику́лин
АН	О. К. Анто́нов
АШ	А. Д. Швецо́в
Г	Д. Р. Григоро́вич
ИЛ	С. Б. Илью́шин
ЛА	С. А. Ла́вочкин
МИГ	А. И. Микоя́н, М. И. Гуре́вич
ТУ	А. Н. Ту́полев
ЩЕ	С. О. Щербако́в
ЯК	А. С. Я́ковлев

Some airplanes are commonly referred to either by the abbreviation (**ТУ-104**, **ИЛ-18**) *or* the full name of the designer (**Ту́полев-104**, **Илью́шин-18**).

Acronyms
Сложносокращённые слова́

"Acronym" is being used here to mean those words that are made up of (1) initial syllables plus initial syllables (**замза́в** for **замести́тель заве́дующего**); (2) initial syllables plus whole words (**детдо́м** for **де́тский дом**); or (3) initial syllables plus "letter" abbreviations (**ГорОНО́** for **городско́й отде́л наро́дного образова́ния**).

The acronym is surely one of the flowers of the Revolution. When the old order was swept away and new institutions were set up, words, titles, and names for them were also required. These names were formed with great facility and sometimes with more enthusiasm than judgment. Even Lenin protested when **учи́тель** was to become **шкраб** (**шко́льный рабо́тник**). In the 1920's some people named children **Долка́п** for "**Доло́й капитали́зм!**"—"Down with capitalism!" One man named his daughter **Гертру́да**, thinking it an abbreviation of **Геро́й труда́** Hero of Labor. These excesses disappeared while others persist. Office, factory, and project names are almost invariably acronyms: **Азовста́ль**, **Беломо́ркана́л**, **Донба́сс**, **Шахтостро́й**, and the like. Many such names are as familiar as our "Texaco" or "Nabisco." Others belie their designation as abbreviation:

Росглавтекстильснабсбытсырьё

A list of commonly recognized acronyms would be close to endless, since the acronym identifies not only institutions but also offices, workshops, and factories. The non-Russian needs help in learning to recognize the acronym by its parts.

The following listings are meant to be read, not used as a reference. They do, however, include many of the acronyms that the Russian comes across in daily life. The first is a list of acronyms grouped according to their first element which is expanded and translated; sublists are examples. Some important or fairly frequent single acronyms are also expanded and translated here. The second list is arranged according to common acronym endings. The third lists a few factory, project, and geographical names as typical examples of the process.

Common acronyms and their prefixes
Сложносокращённые слова по пе́рвому сло́гу

а́виа- **авиацио́нный** air, airplane, aviation
авиабиле́т airplane ticket
авиамодели́ст a builder of model airplanes
авиабандеро́ль (a cover for) airmail printed matter
а́вто- **автомоби́льный** automobile, motor vehicle
автоколо́нна motor vehicle column, convoy
авточа́сть motor vehicle unit
автопокры́шка automobile tire tread
автосто́п hitchhiking (where driver is partially reimbursed with prepaid coupons **тало́ны**)
аги́т- **агитацио́нный** agitation, propaganda
агитотде́л propaganda division
агитпро́п agitation and propaganda department
бе́нзо- **бензи́новый** gasoline
бензоколо́нка gas station
бензово́з gasoline truck
бензоба́к gas tank
вое́н- **вое́нный** military, war
Военги́з Military Publishing House
военко́м military commissar
Военкома́т Military Commissariat
военру́к military instructor
военпро́м war industry
всеобу́ч **всео́бщее (нача́льное) обуче́ние** universal (primary) education
ген- **генера́льный** general
генсе́к secretary-general
геншта́б general staff
генсове́т general council
Гипро- **Госуда́рственный институ́т проекти́рования** State Institute (for ———)
Гипрогра́д State Institute for Planning and Designing Cities

Гипроазо́т State Institute for Planning and Designing Nitrogen Plants
Гипрову́з State Institute for Planning and Designing Higher Educational Institutions
Гипробу́м State Institute for Planning and Designing in the Pulp and Paper Industry
Глав- **Гла́вное управле́ние** Main Administration (of ———)
Глававтозаво́дов Main Administration of Automobile Plants
Главжелезобето́н Main Administration for the Manufacture of Reinforced Concrete Parts
Главка́бель Main Administration of the Cable Industry
Главли́т Main Administration for Literature and Publishing
глав- **гла́вный** main, chief
главвра́ч chief physician
главко́м supreme commander
главк main committee
гор- **городско́й** city
горбольни́ца city hospital
горза́гс city civil registry office
горздравотде́л city health bureau
горко́м city committee
горисполко́м city executive committee
гос- **госуда́рственный** state
Госба́нк State Bank of the USSR
Госпла́н State Planning Commission
Госстра́х Main Administration of State Insurance USSR
Госто́рг State Import-Export Trade Office
госаппара́т state apparatus
дет- **де́тский** children's
Детги́з Publishing House for Children's Literature
детдо́м children's home
детплоща́дка play yard, playground
детса́д kindergarten, nursery school
дом- **дома́шний** building, house
домко́м apartment house committee
домрабо́тница domestic servant, maid
жил- **жило́й** housing
жилпло́щадь housing space
жилотде́л housing office

зав- **заве́дующий** manager, chief

за́вуч (school) department head or vice-principal

завхо́з business manager, manager

зав- **заводско́й** factory, plant

завко́м factory committee

замза́в **замести́тель заве́дующего** deputy chief

запча́сть (заво́д) **запасны́х часте́й** spare parts (factory)

зарпла́та **за́работная пла́та** wages, pay

здрав- **здравоохране́ние** public health

здравотде́л public health department

здравпу́нкт public health station

исполко́м **исполни́тельный комите́т** executive committee

канцтова́ры **канцеля́рские това́ры** office supplies

кино- **кинематографи́ческий** motion picture

киноактёр motion picture actor

кинокарти́на motion picture

кинопередви́жка mobile motion picture theater

киносеа́нс motion picture performance

кинотеа́тр motion picture theater

ком- **команди́р, кома́ндный** commander, commanding

комбри́г brigade commander

комди́в division commander

комсоста́в command personnel

ком- **коммунисти́ческий** communist

Коминте́рн Communist International, 1919–1943

компа́ртия Communist party

комсомо́л Communist Youth League

концла́герь **концентрацио́нный ла́герь** concentration camp

край- **краево́й** "kray" (geographical and administrative area)

крайко́м "kray" committee

крайсобе́с "kray" department of social security

крайсу́д "kray" court

крайисполко́м "kray" executive committee

культ- **культу́рный** cultural

культба́за cultural activities center

Культкоми́ссия Commission on Cultural Work for the Masses

культобслу́живание cultural and educational service

культпохо́д educational field trip

легпро́м **лёгкая промы́шленность** light industry

леспро́м **лесна́я промы́шленность** lumber industry

линко́р **лине́йный кора́бль** battleship

лит- **литерату́рный** literature

литфа́к literature department (of a university)

Литфо́нд Foundation for Writers

мед- **медици́нский** medical

медосмо́тр medical examination

медпу́нкт first aid station, nurse's office

медсестра́ nurse

местко́м **ме́стный комите́т** local committee (of a trade union)

Мин- **Министе́рство** Ministry (of ———)

Минлеспро́м Ministry of the Lumber Industry

Минтяжстро́й Ministry of Heavy Construction

Минто́рг Ministry of Trade

Минсельхо́з Ministry of Agriculture

Мос- **Москва́** Moscow

Мосгорисполко́м Moscow City Executive Committee

Мосгорсове́т Moscow City Council

Мосмука́ Moscow Trust of the Flour Mill and Groats Industry

Моссове́т Moscow City Soviet of Workers' Deputies

Мосто́рг Moscow Oblast Trust for Wholesale and Retail Trade

нар- **наро́дный** people's

Нарко́м People's Commissar, 1917–46

Наркома́т People's Commissariat, 1917–46

нарсу́д people's court

нач- **нача́льник** chief

начди́в division commander

об-/обл- **областно́й** oblast (an administrative-territorial unit)

обко́м   oblast committee

облисполко́м   oblast executive committee

облОНО́   oblast public education department

орг-   **организацио́нный**   organization

оргбюро́   organization bureau

оргото́л   organization department

Осоавиахи́м   **О́бщество соде́йствия оборо́не и авиацио́ннохими́ческому строи́тельству**   Society for Assistance to the Defense, Aviation, and Chemical Construction of the USSR, 1927–48

парт-   **парти́йный**   party

партакти́в   active members of the Communist party and a meeting thereof

партбиле́т   Communist party membership card

партко́м   Communist party committee

парто́рг   Communist party organizer, secretary of CP cell

партста́ж   length of Communist party membership

пед-   **педагоги́ческий**   pedagogical, teachers'

педву́з   teachers' college

педте́хникум   "tekhnikum" for teachers (see "Vocational schools," Chapter 5)

педучи́лище   primary teachers' school

пище-   **пищево́й**   food

пището́рг   food trade office, food store

пищепро́м   the food industry

пищема́ш   food processing machinery plant

подло́дка   **подво́дная ло́дка**   submarine

полит-   **полити́ческий**   political

Политбюро́   Politburo

политгра́мота   political education

политэконо́м   political economist

политото́л   political department

политпросве́т   political education committee

политру́к   political education instructor

пом-   **помо́щник**   assistant

помза́в   assistant to the chief, assistant manager

помна́ч   assistant chief

прод-   **продово́льственный**   food

продма́г   food store

продналог   taxes in kind (for farms)

пром-   **промы́шленный**   industrial

промкомбина́т   industrial combine

промтова́ры   manufactured goods

промфинпла́н   operational and finance plan (in industry)

прора́б   **производи́тель рабо́т**   supervisor, foreman

проф-   **профсою́зный**   trade union

профакти́в   active members of trade union

профбиле́т   trade-union membership card

профбюро́   trade-union office

профдисципли́на   trade-union discipline

профо́рг   trade-union organizer

профдвиже́ние   trade-union movement

рабко́р   **рабо́чий корреспонде́нт**   workers' correspondent

рай-   **райо́нный**   "rayon" (an administrative-territorial unit)

райвоенкома́т   district military commissariat

райжилотде́л   district housing office

райздравотде́л   district health department

райисполко́м   district executive committee

райко́м   district committee

районо́   district department of public education

райсобе́с   district department of social security

райсове́т   district soviet

райфо́   district finance department

Рев-   **революцио́нный**   revolutionary

Реввоенсове́т   Revolutionary Military Council

Ревко́м   Revolutionary Committee

роддо́м   **роди́льный дом**   maternity hospital

сан-   **санита́рный**   sanitation, medical

санвра́ч   public health physician

санинспе́ктор   sanitation inspector

санобрабо́тка   medical treatment, use of sanitary measures

сану́зел   lavatory facilities in a public building

сбер-   **сберега́тельный**   savings

сберка́сса   savings bank

сберкни́жка   bankbook for a savings account

сель-   се́льский   agricultural, rural
  селько́р   agricultural correspondent
  сельма́г   rural store
  сельма́ш   agricultural machinery plant
  сельпо́   rural consumers' society
  сельсове́т   village soviet, village council

собе́с   социа́льное обеспече́ние   social security

Сов-   Сове́тский   Soviet; Сове́т   Council
  Совинформбюро́   Soviet Information Bureau
  Совнарко́м   Council of People's Commissars
  Совнархо́з   Council of the National Economy

соц-   социа́льное   social, socialist
  соцреали́зм   socialist realism
  соцсоревнова́ние   socialist competition
  Соцстра́х   Social Insurance Administration

спец-   специа́льный   special
  спецко́р   special correspondent
  спецо́бувь   work shoes
  спецоде́жда   special work clothes
  спецста́вка   increased wage rate for specialists
  спецшко́ла   special school

ссудоба́нк   ссудосберега́тельный банк   savings and loan bank

стенгазе́та   стенна́я газе́та   bulletin board newspaper

строй-   строи́тельный   building, construction
  стройматериа́л   construction material
  стройма́ш   construction machinery plant

тех-   техни́ческий   technical
  те́хникум   "tekhnikum" (see "Vocational schools," Chapter 5)
  техми́нимум   minimum level of technical knowledge
  техперсона́л   technical personnel
  техпропага́нда   technical education campaign
  техсове́т   technical council
  техсоста́в   technical staff
  техре́д   technical editor

торг-   торго́вый   trade
  торгпре́д   trade representative

торгфло́т   merchant marine fleet

трампа́рк   трамва́йный парк   streetcar depot

тяжпро́м   тяжёлая промы́шленность   heavy industry

Угро́зыск   уголо́вный ро́зыск   Office of Criminal Investigation

универма́г   универса́льный магази́н   department store

уч-   уче́бный, учи́тельский, учени́ческий   academic, teachers', student
  Учги́з   State Publishing House for Textbooks and Pedagogical Literature
  учко́м   student committee
  учколле́ктор   store (or office) for sale of teaching materials

физкульту́ра   физи́ческая культу́ра   physical culture

фин-   фина́нсовый   finance
  фининспе́ктор   tax collector, budget supervisor
  финотде́л   finance department

хим-   хими́ческий   chemistry, chemical
  химбо́мба   chemical bomb, gas bomb
  химвойска́   chemical warfare troops
  химзаво́д   chemical plant
  химфа́к   chemistry department (of a university)

хоз-   хозя́йственный   economy, household, farm, establishment
  хозрасчёт   self-supporting (enterprise) not financed by the state

центро-   центра́льный   central
  Центропеча́ть   Central Administration for Accounting, Printing, and Circulation of Printed Matter

ширпотре́б   (това́ры) широ́кого потребле́ния   consumer goods

Штаба́рм   Штаб А́рмии   Army Staff, Headquarters

штади́в   штаб диви́зии   division staff, headquarters

эсми́нец   эска́дренный миноно́сец   destroyer

юн-   ю́ный   young, youth
  юнко́р   youth correspondent
  юнна́т   young naturalist

Common acronym endings
Сложносокращённые слова́ по после́днему сло́гу

-ком   **комите́т, комисса́р**
   обко́м
   райко́м
   местко́м
   домко́м
   нарко́м

-кор   **корреспонде́нт**
   рабко́р
   селько́р
   юнко́р

-маш   **(заво́д) машинострое́ния** machine building (factory)
   углема́ш   coal machinery plant
   химма́ш
   стройма́ш

-орг   **организа́ция, организа́тор**
   профо́рг
   парто́рг

-отде́л   **отде́л** department
   женотде́л
   жилотде́л
   финотде́л

-по   **потреби́тельское о́бщество** consumers' society
   сельпо́
   райпо́

-пред   **представи́тель** representative
   торгпре́д

-пром   **промы́шленность** industry
   легпро́м
   леспро́м
   тяжпро́м

-проп   **пропага́нда**
   агитпро́п

-уч   **уче́бный** educational, academic, school
   за́вуч

-фак   **факульте́т** (university) department
   литфа́к
   медфа́к
   рабфа́к
   химфа́к

-фо   **фина́нсовый отде́л** finance department

   райфо́
   горфо́

-хоз   **хозя́йство, хозя́йственный** economy, arrangement, set-up
   леспромхо́з
   колхо́з
   совхо́з

Acronyms for practice
Упражне́ния в чте́нии акрони́мов

What follows is a small sample of some factory, project, and geographical names that are acronyms. Those with asterisks are famous.

Азовста́ль*   **Азо́вский металлурги́ческий заво́д**
   Azov Metallurgical Plant

Беломоркана́л*   **Беломо́рско-Балти́йский кана́л**
   White Sea–Baltic Canal

Внешторгба́нк   **Банк для вне́шней торго́вли**
   Foreign Trade Bank USSR

Дизельмонта́ж   **Монта́жно-ремо́нтная конто́ра Главлокомоби́льди́зеля**
   Assembly and Repair Office of the Glavlokomobil′dizel′

Днепрогэ́с*   **Днепро́вская гидроэлектри́ческая ста́нция**
   Dnepr Hydroelectric Power Plant

Донба́сс*   **Доне́цкий у́гольный бассе́йн**
   Donets Coal Basin

Жилстро́й   **Трест индустриа́льного жили́щного строи́тельства**
   Industrial Housing Construction Trust

Кузба́сс*	Кузне́цкий у́гольный бас-се́йн Kuznetsk Coal Basin		All-Union Association of the Paper and Cellulose Industry
Ленмясокомбина́т	Ленингра́дский мясно́й комбина́т Leningrad Meat Combine	Средазнефть	Объедине́ние среднеазиа́т-ской нефтяно́й промы́ш-ленности Central Asian Petroleum Association
Магнитострóй*	Госуда́рственное управле́-ние по строи́тельству металлурги́ческих заво́-дов в Магнитогóрске State Administration for the Construction of Metallurgical Plants in Magnitogorsk	Стальмóст	Заво́д стальны́х и мосто-вы́х констру́кций Fabricated Steel and Bridge Parts Plant
Метрострóй*	Госуда́рственное управ-ле́ние строи́тельства Москóвского метро-полите́на State Administration for the Construction of the Moscow Subway	Ташсельма́ш	Ташке́нтский заво́д сéль-ско-хозя́йственного машинострое́ния Tashkent Agricultural Machinery Plant
		Туркси́б*	Туркеста́но-Сиби́рская же-ле́зная доро́га Turkestan–Siberian Railroad
Росглаввинó	Гла́вное управле́ние вино-де́льческой промы́шлен-ности (РСФСР) Main Administration of the Winemaking Indus-try (RSFSR)	Урало́бувь	Ура́льский обувно́й заво́д Ural Footwear Factory
		Черноморнéфть	Объедине́ние Черномóр-ской нефтяно́й промы́ш-ленности Association of the Black Sea Region Petroleum Industry
Сибтяжма́ш	Сиби́рский заво́д тяжёлого машинострое́ния Siberian Heavy Machinery Plant		
Снабтопрóм	Контóра по снабже́нию предприя́тий тóпливной промы́шленности Office for the Supply of Fuel Industry Establish-ments	Электрострóй	Управле́ние электротех-ни́ческих сооруже́ний Administration of Electro-technical Structures
Союзбума́га	Всесою́зное объедине́ние бума́жно-целлюлóзной промы́шленности	Южуралтяжма́ш	Ю́жно-ура́льский заво́д тяжёлого машинострое́-ния South Ural Heavy Machin-ery Plant

Периоди́ческая Систе́ма Хими́ческих Элеме́нтов Д. И. Менделе́ева

Г Р У П П Ы   Э Л Е М Е Н Т О В

Пе-рио-ды	Ря-ды	1	II	III	IV	V	VI	VII	VIII			O
1	I	**1** **H** Водоро́д 1,00797										**2** **He** Ге́лий 4,0026
2	II	**3** **Li** Ли́тий 6,939	**4** **Be** Бери́ллий 9,0122	**5** **B** Бор 10,811	**6** **C** Углеро́д 12,01115	**7** **N** Азо́т 14,0067	**8** **O** Кислоро́д 15,9994	**9** **F** Фтор 18,9984				**10** **Ne** Нео́н 20,183
3	III	**11** **Na** На́трий 22,9898	**12** **Mg** Ма́гний 24,312	**13** **Al** Алюми́ний 26,9815	**14** **Si** Кре́мний 28,086	**15** **P** Фо́сфор 30,9738	**16** **S** Се́ра 32,064	**17** **Cl** Хлор 35,453				**18** **Ar** Арго́н 39,948
4	IV	**19** **K** Ка́лий 39,102	**20** **Ca** Ка́льций 40,08	**21** **Sc** Ска́ндий 44,956	**22** **Ti** Тита́н 47,90	**23** **V** Вана́дий 50,942	**24** **Cr** Хром 51,996	**25** **Mn** Ма́рганец 54,9381	**26** **Fe** Желе́зо 55,847	**27** **Co** Ко́бальт 58,9332	**28** **Ni** Ни́кель 58,71	
	V	**29** **Cu** Медь 63,54	**30** **Zn** Цинк 65,37	**31** **Ga** Га́ллий 69,72	**32** **Ge** Герма́ний 72,59	**33** **As** Мышья́к 74,9216	**34** **Se** Селе́н 78,96	**35** **Br** Бром 79,909				**36** **Kr** Крипто́н 83,80
5	VI	**37** **Rb** Руби́дий 85,47	**38** **Sr** Стро́нций 87,62	**39** **Y** Иттрий 88,905	**40** **Zr** Цирко́ний 91,22	**41** **Nb** Нио́бий 92,906	**42** **Mo** Молибде́н 95,94	**43** **Tc** Техне́ций [97]	**44** **Ru** Руте́ний 101,07	**45** **Rh** Ро́дий 102,905	**46** **Pd** Палла́дий 106,4	
	VII	**47** **Ag** Серебро́ 107,870	**48** **Cd** Ка́дмий 112,40	**49** **In** И́ндий 114,82	**50** **Sn** О́лово 118,69	**51** **Sb** Сурьма́ 121,75	**52** **Te** Теллу́р 127,60	**53** **I** Иод 126,9044				**54** **Xe** Ксено́н 131,30
6	VIII	**55** **Cs** Це́зий 132,905	**56** **Ba** Ба́рий 137,34	**57** **La*** Ланта́н 138,91	**72** **Hf** Га́фний 178,49	**73** **Ta** Танта́л 180,948	**74** **W** Вольфра́м 183,85	**75** **Re** Ре́ний 186,2	**76** **Os** О́смий 190,2	**77** **Ir** Ири́дий 192,2	**78** **Pt** Пла́тина 195,09	
	IX	**79** **Au** Зо́лото 196,967	**80** **Hg** Ртуть 200,59	**81** **Tl** Та́ллий 204,37	**82** **Pb** Свине́ц 207,19	**83** **Bi** Ви́смут 208,980	**84** **Po** Поло́ний [210]	**85** **At** Аста́т [210]				**86** **Rn** Радо́н [222]
7	X	**87** **Fr** Фра́нций [223]	**88** **Ra** Ра́дий [226]	**89** **Ac**** Акти́ний [227]	**104** **Ku** Курча́товий [264]							

* ЛАНТАНИ́ДЫ

58 **Ce** Це́рий 140,12	59 **Pr** Празео-ди́м 140,907	60 **Nd** Неоди́м 144,24	61 **Pm** Проме́тий [145]	62 **Sm** Сама́рий 150,35	63 **Eu** Евро́пий 151,96	64 **Gd** Гадоли́-ний 157,25	65 **Tb** Те́рбий 158,924	66 **Dy** Диспро́зий 162,50	67 **Ho** Го́льмий 164,930	68 **Er** Эрбий 167,26	69 **Tm** Ту́лий 168,934	70 **Yb** Итте́рбий 173,04	71 **Lu** Люте́ций 174,97

** АКТИНИ́ДЫ

90 **Th** То́рий 232,038	91 **Pa** Протак-ти́ний [231]	92 **U** Ура́н 238,03	93 **Np** Непту́ний [237]	94 **Pu** Плуто́ний [242]	95 **Am** Амери́ций [243]	96 **Cm** Кю́рий [247]	97 **Bk** Берке́лий [247]	98 **Cf** Калифо́р-ний [249]	99 **Es** Эйнштей́-ний [254]	100 **Fm** Фе́рмий [253]	101 **Md** Менделе́е-вий [256]	102 **No** Нобе́лий [255]	103 **Lw** Лауре́нсий [257]

Element 85 can be **Аста́т** or **Астати́н**. Element 97 can be **Берке́лий** or **Бе́рклий**. Element 103 can be **Лауре́нсий** or **Лоуре́нсий**.

APPENDIX A

I. On reading chemical formulas
Чтéние химúческих фóрмул

For most elements, the full name of the element is used when chemical formulas are read. The pronunciation of the chemical abbreviation is not used except in the following cases:

Element	Symbol	Pronunciation
водорóд	H	аш
кислорóд	O	о
фóсфор	P	пэ
сéра	S	эс
углерóд	C	цэ
азóт	N	эн
ванáдий	V	вэ

For some other elements, the Latin rather than the Russian name for the element is frequently used in reading.

фéррум	желéзо
плю́мбум	свинéц
кýпрум	медь
силúций	крéмний
цúнкум	цинк
арсéникум	мышья́к
аргéнтум	серебрó
стáннум	óлово
стúбиум	сурьмá
áурум	зóлото
хидрáргирум	ртуть

Examples
Примéры

$2H_2 + O_2 \rightarrow 2H_2O$ два аш два плюс о два даёт два аш два о

$H_2SO_4 + Ba(NO_3)_2 \rightarrow BaSO_4 + 2HNO_3$ аш два эс о четыре плюс барий эн о три дважды даёт барий эс о четыре плюс два аш эн о три

$2HCl + Mg \rightarrow MgCl_2 + H_2$ два аш хлор плюс мáгний даёт мáгний хлор два плюс аш два

H_2O аш два о (водá)

CO_2 цэ о два (углекúслый газ)

$2HCl$ два аш хлор (соля́ная кислотá)

$Cu(OH)_2$ кýпрум о аш двáжды (гидрáт óкиси мéди)

$Fe(OH)_3$ фéррум о аш трúжды (гидрáт óкиси желéза)

H_2SO_4 аш два эс о четы́ре (сéрная кислотá)

$Ba(NO_3)_2$ бáрий эн о три двáжды (азотно-кúслый бáрий)

II. The Morse code
Áзбука Мóрзе

Знаки Морзе	Буквы		Цифры	Знаки препинания и сигналы телеграфной службы
	Русские	Латинск.		
·—	А	Aa	·———— 1	(,) запятая ·—·—·—
—···	Б	Bb	··——— 2	(.) точка ······
·——	В	Ww	···—— 3	(;) точка с запятой —·—·—·
——·	Г	Gg	····— 4	(:) двоеточие ———···
—··	Д	Dd	····· 5	(?) вопросительный знак ··——··
·	Е	Ee	—···· 6	(№) —·———·—
···—	Ж	Vv	——··· 7	(+) он же конец депеши ·—·—·
——··	З	Zz	———·· 8	(„") кавычки ·—··—·
··	И	Ii	————· 9	( ) скобки
—·—	К	Kk	————— 0	(!) восклицательный знак ——··——
·—··	Л	Ll		(—) минус —····—
——	М	Mm		Знак подчеркивания ··——·—
—·	Н	Nn		(/) дробная черта —··—·
———	О	Oo		Знак раздела —···—
·——·	П	Pp		Перебой (исправление ошибки) ········
·—·	Р	Rr		Знак, отделяющий целое число от дроби ·—··—·
···	С	Ss		Знак предложения (начинаю передавать) —·—·—
—	Т	Tt		Знак согласия на приём ·—·
··—	У	Uu		Начало действия —·—·—
··—·	Ф	Ff		
····	Х	Hh		
—·—·	Ц	Cc		
———·	Ч	Öö		
————	Ш	Ch		
——·—	Щ	Qq		
—·——	Ы	Yy		
··——	Ю	Üü		
·—·—	Я	Ää		
·———	Й	Jj		
—··—	Ь.Ъ	Xx		
··—··	Э	Éé		

Radio amateurs (hams) are as popular in the USSR as they are here. They exchange QSL cards, have a magazine *Радио* comparable to *QST*, and must learn the Morse code, too.

III. The Braille alphabet
Áзбука Бpáйля

The following is the Braille alphabet both in Latin and Cyrillic letters:

aa	бb	цc	дd	еe	фf	гg	xh	иi	жj
кk	лl	мm	нn	oo	пp	чq	pr	cs	тt
yu	—v	щx	—y	зz	й—	ъ—	ы—	ь—	
e—		ш—	я—	ю—	э—	вw			

IV. An index of common Russian birds
Указáтель рýсских назвáний птиц

This list of common Russian birds is arranged in alphabetical order. Starred entries have been discussed in Chapter 10. Information is presented in the following order:

(1) When specified, the most common species follows the entry in parentheses: **синúца (большáя)**.

(2) When there is a commonly used word for the female, it follows without parentheses: **тéтерев, тетёрка**.

(3) The wing **крылó** length in millimeters is given merely to indicate relative size. The **синúца** (кр. 66–82 *мм*) is a tiny bird, while the golden eagle **бéркут** (кр. 595–725 *мм*) is correspondingly huge.

(4) The common name for the bird family follows if it seems necessary to the description.

(5) The scientific genus and species name is given in italics.

(6) The English translation is given if it appears in either of two books by Alexander Wetmore: *Song and Garden Birds of North America* (Washington D.C.: National Geographic Society, 1964) and *Water, Prey and Game Birds of North America* (Washington D.C.: National Geographic Society, 1965).

(7) Description or comments follow this.

(8) Finally, and in parentheses, the name for the bird is given as found in *Рýсско-англúйский словáрь*, ред. А. И. Смирнúцкий (Москвá: ОГИЗ, 1949).

The major Russian source for names and descriptions has been Б. К. Штéгман и А. И. Иванóв, *Крáткий определúтель птиц СССР* (Москвá: Наýка, 1964).

áист (**бéлый**), кр. 554–680 *мм*, *Ciconia ciconia*. Russian tradition holds that babies come from cabbage patches, but the Western notion of storks is beginning to take hold. The bird is common only in the southwest regions of the USSR. (stork)

бекáс кр. 122–36 *мм*, *Capella gallinago*, common snipe

бéркут кр. 595–725 *мм*, *Aquila chrysaetus*, golden eagle

буревéстник кр. 217–53 *мм*, *Puffinus puffinus*, Manx shearwater. Perhaps because of Gorky's "Пéсня о буревéстнике," this bird has become the herald of the Revolution. (storm petrel)

вáльдшнеп кр. 177–98 *мм*, Snipe family, *Scolopax rusticola*. This bird is commonly hunted. (snipe, woodcock)

*****воробéй** кр. 69–83 *мм*, *Passer domesticus*, house or English sparrow

вóрон кр. 385–530 *мм*, *Corvus corax*, common raven. The bird is completely black and very large.

ворóна (**чёрная**), кр. 310–75 *мм*, *Corvus corone corone*. It is more common in the south. (crow)

*****ворóна** (**сéрая**), кр. 292–340 *мм*, *Corvus corone cornix*. In color it is black with large gray patches; it is more common in central Russia. (crow)

гáга (**обыкновéнная**), кр. 258–328 *мм*, *Somateria mollissima*, common eider

гагáра (**поля́рная**), кр. 315–413 *мм*, *Gavia immer*, common loon

гáлка кр. 209–48 *мм*, Crow family, *Corvus monedula*. The bird is mixed in color, with black head, wings, and back, and the rest in various shades of gray. It flies in great flocks and is famous for making an awful noise (mainly because of its numbers): "Они орýт (úли шумя́т), как гáлки." (jackdaw, daw)

*****глухáрь** кр. 268–390 *мм*, Grouse family, *Tetrao urogallus*. It is iridescent black and very large. (capercaillie, wood grouse)

гóголь кр. 187–231 *мм*, Duck family, *Bucephala clangula*, common goldeneye: "'ходúть гóголем' —ходúть чúнно и вáжно."

гóлубь (**сúзый**), кр. 184–240 *мм*, *Columba livia*, domestic pigeon. A children's name for a pigeon is гýля. "Гоня́ть голубéй" is a game played by boys with pet pigeons. The pigeons are released and later signaled to return in the hope that other pigeons will join those originally released. The game was so popular that the expression "гоня́ть голубéй" has become synonymous with wasting time. (pigeon, dove)

*****грач** кр. 287–350 *мм*, Crow family, *Corvus frugilegus*. It is all black in color. (rook)

гусь (**сéрый**), кр. 398–495 *мм*, *Anser anser*. According to popular theory, if the goose is white, it is domesticated; if it is gray, it is wild. (goose)

дрозд (**пéвчий, пёстрый, чёрный**), Thrush family, *Turdidae*. There are three or four very common species of thrush with the same build as our robin, *Turdus migratorius*, though the Russian varieties are usually colored a speckled brown and white. (ouzel, thrush, blackbird)

дя́тел (**большóй пёстрый**), кр. 119–50 *мм*, Woodpecker family, *Dendrocopos major*. This is only one of many other woodpeckers easily recognized as such by us. (woodpecker)

*****жáворонок** (**полевóй**), кр. 99–124 *мм*, *Alauda arvensis*, skylark. (lark)

*****журáвль** (**сéрый**), кр. 520–620 *мм*, *Grus grus*. The bird is colored gray with some brown. (crane)

заря́нка or **малúновка** кр. 68–75 *мм*, *Erithacus rubecula*. This is the English robin redbreast. It is small with a brown back, red bib, and white underparts. (robin)

зя́блик кр. 85–94 *мм*, Finch family, *Fringilla coelebs*. The bird is distinctive by its coloration: gray head, orangish underparts, brown back. (finch)

úволга кр. 132–63 *мм*, Oriole family, *Oriolus oriolus*. A long bird, almost all yellow except for brown wings, it is usually found near the water and is famous for its morning song. American meadowlarks, blackbirds, and orioles are in the family Icteridae, not Oriolidae, and live only in the Western Hemisphere. (oriole) коросте́ль or дерга́ч, кр. 124–44 *мм*, Coot family, *Crex crex*. This is a wading bird with brown back, white throat, gray breast, and white side stripes. (landrail)

ко́ршун (чёрный), кр. 428–545 *мм*, Eagle and Hawk family, *Milvus korschun*. Infamous for its inroads on the chicken population, this large bird is also a symbol of fast attack: "**Что ты на меня́ налета́ешь, как ко́ршун?**" (kite, black kite)

кре́чет кр. 355–425 *мм*, Falcon family, *Falco gyrfalco*. This very large falcon has largely white underparts and brown or black top parts. (gerfalcon)

кря́ква кр. 235–95 *мм*, *Anas platyrhynchos*, mallard. The bird is so common that the phrase "**ди́кая у́тка**" probably refers to it. It is well known for its greediness: "**Она́ прожо́рлива, как у́тка.**"

*куку́шка кр. 180–246 *мм*, Cuckoo family, *Cuculus canorus*. The bird is mostly gray with some black and white stripes. (cuckoo)

кули́к This term can apply to any of a large family of small, usually long-billed and long-legged wading or shore birds (the order Charadriiformes). If it seems obvious that the use of the word indicates a specific kind of bird, then the closest equivalent is probably the sandpiper. (snipe)

куропа́тка (се́рая), кр. 139–58 *мм*, Pheasant family, *Perdix perdix*, gray partridge. It is much more common than the willow ptarmigan **бе́лая куропа́тка**. (partridge)

ла́сточка (дереве́нская), кр. 117–30 *мм*, *Hirundo rustica*, barn swallow. There are, of course, many other swallows, but this is the one people see most often. (swallow)

ле́бедь (-клику́н), кр. 560–635 *мм*, *Cygnus cygnus*. Even swans accompany spring. (swan)

Лю́ди всегда́ с волне́нием ждут лебеде́й. И когда́ они́ прилета́ют, когда́ на рассве́те поднима́ются с разли́вов со свои́м вели́ким весе́нним кли́чем "кли́нк-кланк!"—лю́ди провожа́ют их глаза́ми, кровь начина́ет звене́ть у них в се́рдце, и они́ зна́ют тогда́, что пришла́ весна́.

Юрий Казако́в, "Арктур—го́нчий пёс." (a story)

лунь (полево́й), кр. 335–98 *мм*, *Circus cyaneus*, marsh hawk. A silver gray hawk, it flies low over fields looking for its prey: "**Он как лунь седо́й.**"

овся́нка кр. 80–99 *мм*, Finch family, *Emberiza citrinella*. The bird is yellow with red brown spots. (yellow bunting)

орёл (степно́й), кр. 520–638 *мм*, *Aquila rapax*. There, as here, the eagle is a symbol of power: "**орёл—царь-пти́ца.**"

пе́репел перепёлка, кр. 97–111 *мм*, Pheasant family, *Coturnix coturnix* (quail)

ря́бчик кр. 150–64 *мм*, Grouse family, *Tetrastes bonasia*. This quail is small, mostly brown with white spots and a small black bib. It is traditionally considered to be the most elegant food. (hazel hen, hazel grouse)

Ешь анана́сы,
ря́бчиков жуй,
День твой после́дний
прихо́дит, буржу́й.

Маяко́вский

свиристе́ль кр. 107–19 *мм*, Waxwing family, *Bombycilla garrulus*, Bohemian waxwing. This very pretty bird looks like a gray cedar waxwing and is famous for eating berries, especially those of the mountain ash.

*сини́ца (больша́я), кр. 62–82 *мм*, Titmouse family, *Parus major*. The bird has a mostly green and blue back with white and yellow underparts. (tomtit, titmouse)

* скворе́ц кр. 118–35 *мм*, *Sturnus vulgaris*, starling

* снеги́рь кр. 77–97 *мм*, Finch family, *Pyrrhula pyrrhula*. This finch has orange red underparts, a mostly gray back, black head, and wing stripe. (bullfinch)

сова́ Owls are best known not for their wisdom but for their presumed (daytime) blindness and/or absent-mindedness: "**Он сиди́т, как сова́ на забо́ре**"—"He doesn't pay attention to anything." Some common Russian owls are:

уша́стая сова́ кр. 273–300 *мм*, *Asio otus*

со́вка кр. 138–60 *мм*, *Otus scops*

сыч (домо́вый), кр. 149–80 *мм*, *Athene noctua*

бе́лая сова́ кр. 395–470 *мм*, *Nyctea scandiaca*

со́кол (-сапса́н), кр. 289–390 *мм*, *Falco peregrinus*, duck hawk or peregrine falcon. The falcon is a symbol of courage, speed, and daring. Gorky's "**Пе́сня о со́коле**" is familiar to Soviet schoolchildren. (falcon)

* солове́й (восто́чный), кр. 82–92 *мм*, *Luscinia luscinia*. The bird is colored in gradations of gray. (nightingale)

* **соро́ка** кр. 175–230 *мм*, *Pica pica*, black-billed magpie.

стриж (чёрный), кр. 165–79 *мм*, Swift family, *Apus apus*. Resembling a large dark swallow, this bird is famous for its very fancy flying; its wings seem to alternate in flight. (martlet, sand martin, stone martin, swift)

* **те́терев тетёрка**, кр. 220–63 *мм*, Grouse family, *Lyrurus tetrix*. The bird is colored black with red marking on top of its eyes and some white on its wings. (heath cock, blackcock, black grouse)

трясогу́зка кр. 73–99 *мм*, Wagtail family, genus *Motacilla*. There are two common kinds of wagtail—one with yellow underparts, the other with white underparts, both of them gray on top. These rather long thin birds do wag their tails as they walk, whence their name in Russian as well as English. (wagtail)

фаза́н кр. 190–240 *мм*, *Phasianus colchicus*, ring-necked pheasant

фи́лин кр. 420–550 *мм*, *Bubo bubo*. The bird is a very large and fierce hunter. It is in the same genus as our great horned owl. (eagle owl)

ца́пля (се́рая), кр. 420–75 *мм*, *Ardea cinerea*. The common heron is smaller than the crane **жура́вль**; in flight the heron bends its neck back, while the crane will stretch out full length. The heron also has a few long feathers extending from the back of its head, while the crane has a smooth head.

ча́йка (обыкнове́нная), кр. 288–340 *мм*, *Larus ridibundus*, black-headed gull. Depending on the circumstances, the gull is either a scavenging nuisance or a rather romantic accompaniment to a sea voyage. Chekhov's *Seagull* probably had something to do with the latter. (seagull, mewgull)

чиж кр. 65–75 *мм*, Finch family, *Carduelis spinus*. Mostly yellow with brown and black accents, this small bird has been immortalized in a song known to every Russian child. There are many versions, both more and less vulgar, but the one given below seems to be standard. (siskin)

Чи́жик-пы́жик,
Где ты был?
На Фонта́нке
Во́дку пил.

Вы́пил рю́мку,
Вы́пил две.
Зашуме́ло
В голове́.

щего́л кр. 70–88 *мм*, Finch family, *Carduelis carduelis*, European goldfinch. This is a very brightly colored bird (white, black, red, yellow), often caught and kept in a cage as a pet.

я́стреб (-тетеревя́тник) кр. 299–395 *мм*, *Accipiter gentilis*, goshawk. This hawk was named after its prey, as was the smaller **перепеля́тник**. (hawk)

APPENDIX B: TRANSLATIONS OF PASSAGES NOTED BY •

p. 2   Everyone must know the structure of his body. The body consists of the head, the neck, the trunk, and two pairs of extremities: the upper extremities or arms and hands, and the lower extremities or the legs and feet.

p. 5   When a person is hot, his skin becomes covered with small drops of sweat. Sweating is very important for us. Harmful substances are eliminated in sweat. Sweat is exuded from the skin through small openings—the pores. When the weather is hot, the sweat evaporates and cools the skin.

p. 6   We breathe air. Notice what you do when you breathe. First we breathe in air (inhale), and then we breathe it out (exhale).

p. 7   We all know that the outside of our body is covered with skin. Feel your arms and legs. You will notice something soft underneath the skin. These are muscles. At the ends of muscles are tendons.

Who are they?

p. 13   They wrote in their questionnaires: year of birth—1932; family background—white-collar workers (Karpov, from a working-class family); party membership—member of the Komsomols (VLKSM) since 1947; service in wartime—none; convictions—none; do you have relatives living abroad—no; and several more no's up to the column "family status," where they all wrote—single. Their autobiographies took up half a page, and this is how they described themselves. . . .

p. 21   "Yegorovna is signaling to you," Yura whispered. . . . At the entrance [threshold] stood Agrafena Yegorovna, an old gray-haired housekeeper.

p. 26   She adored Nika. His [full] name was Innokentiy and from it she made a raft of ridiculously sweet and silly nicknames like Ínochek and Nóchenka.

p. 26   Say, [listen] mama. When I was born, how did you know that I was Yurochka?

p. 29   Day of the prophet Saint Jeremy, the martyred monk Vata, the martyred Saint Makariy, Metropolitan of Kiev (1497), the Abbot Pafnutiy of Borovsk (1477), Saint Tamara, Queen of Georgia. Day of the icon of the Mother of God of Tsarevokokshaysk or the Mironositskaya [Myrrh-bearer] Mother of God; the Byzantine and Andronikov icons.
   Reading: Acts XII, 1–11; John VIII, 31–42.
   Fourth week after Easter (Mid-Pentecost) [a church holiday midway between Easter and Pentecost].

p. 30   On the Last Syllable
   (Advice to writers of ladies' romantic novels)

I would compare the situation of the lady writer with that of mothers with many children. Before her children can begin to do something, they have to be dressed, fed, housed, and given some sort of environment. And who must do this? Why, we lady authors, of course.

Our hero has been born—we must give him a name. . . . The principles of choosing a name are not new, of course. A positive hero can be called Andrey, Aleksey, Pavel, or in an extreme case, Sergey (although in the last case our hero must die. For some reason Sergeys always die.) To call a positive hero Ivan, Pyotr, or even worse, Kuz′má or Prókhor, is not recommended—the reader might stop reading. These names are used for lesser types: Andrey (or Aleksey or Pavel) can have a friend, a nice guy from the working class (railroad worker, poet, farmer, graduate student at an agricultural college—cross out those not applicable). His job is to hear out the scientific views, technical ideas, and the cherished hopes of the positive hero. Usually our lady readers skip these pages.

Semipositive heroes, humanized by a shortcoming or two, can have names like Igor, Leonid, or Anatoliy. The nicknames derived from these names depend on which element in the hero is greater—the positive or the negative. In the first case Leonid can be called Lyónka or Lyókha by his friends and family. But if he has more bad traits, then he is given a strange-sounding nickname like Leonídik or Lyúsik. If there is a negative mother-in-law in the novel, she will call her son-in-law Leó, with the stress on the last syllable, the way the French do.

The names of negative heroes have been well worked over; they are Edvard (Edik), Arnol′d, or even perhaps Vadim. Such names are given to profligates, cowards, and Ph.D. recipients, who, as everybody knows, can't possibly be positive heroes. Debauchees and abstractionists must have elaborate last names, like Kedro-Livanovich [Cedar of Lebanon] or Vénezuelskiy. Suppressors of criticism and building managers can be given last names like Glyga and Shchup [feel out].

Women's names also have their subtleties and nuances. Do you think your work is done once you have named your heroine Elizaveta? If she is a positive character, then Elizaveta will be called Liza; if she has a restless, proud spirit, then she can be Lika; but if she is outright negative, then she must be Lil′ka or, Heaven forgive us, Lizzi. A femme fatale whose passport name is Elizaveta can also be called Veta.

I am simply amazed at some beginning authoresses who do not understand the abyss that separates Anastasiya, who at home is called Nastya (large gray eyes, reinforced concrete chastity, irreconcilable to this and that), from her other namesake Anastasiya, who at home is called Asta (green, almond-shaped eyes, a tight black turtleneck sweater, conversations about Kafka and uncommunicability).

p. 53 The person entering an apartment wipes his feet on the entrance rug, takes off his galoshes and his coat, and only then enters the room. If he is not wearing galoshes, then he wipes his shoes on the doormat on the stairway.

p. 56 It is best to wash dishes and silverware with soap and a brush under a stream of hot running water. But, unfortunately, not all houses yet have plumbing with hot water or a water heater. Therefore dishes are sometimes washed in dishpans. In any case the children should learn the right methods: they will simplify and speed up the entire washing process. The dirty dishes should be on the right, a dishpan of warm water (with a solution of mustard or soda) should be in front of the dishwasher, and next to it should be another dishpan with hot water for rinsing. The dishes that have been done should be placed on the left.

p. 63 The gingerbread man got tired of lying there, so he rolled from the window to the bench, from the bench to the floor, along the floor to the door. He jumped over the threshold to the entrance room, from the entrance room to the porch, from the porch to the yard, from the yard through the gate—farther and farther.

p. 64 The gingerbread man got tired of lying there. He rolled from the window to the "zavalinka," from the "zavalinka" to the grass, from the grass to the road, and on down the road.

p. 67 Kerosene is used [burned] in just a few houses. The others are lit by burning sticks or [the people] go to bed early [before dark].

p. 67 Special bathrooms have begun to appear only very recently in the newest buildings. For this purpose they wall off one of the ends of the walkway in the "barn" [dvor]. Old houses had no special lavatories; the entire "barn" [dvor] was used for this purpose.

p. 68 Of interest to us is the invitation issued to the yard spirit and the house spirit when the peasants move to a new place. The owner stands in front of the courtyard gates, bows three times in different directions, turns his head over his left shoulder and calls: "Father house spirit, mother house spirit, father yard spirit and mother yard spirit, with the whole family, come with us to our new house, to live with us."

The concept of the house spirit and yard spirit is still quite alive among the peasants. They are often pictured as doubles of their masters. They appear every once in a while but for no good purpose, and their faces resemble that of their owner. And their character and tendencies are also like their owner's. If he is careless about the livestock, then the yard spirit will play pranks; but one must, in any case, treat these spirits with respect or they might go away.

p. 71   According to the census of 1897, 29.3 percent of the men were literate and 13.1 percent of the women were literate in Russia; at the same time 59.9 percent of the men workers [as opposed to peasants] were literate, and 34.9 percent of women workers were literate.

p. 72   According to the census of 1897, even in the European part of the country, for every 1000 people, 227 men were literate and 117 women were literate.

p. 72   A special place in the general education of adults was occupied by "workers' schools." They were organized for the first time in 1919 at several colleges. The decree of the Council of People's Commissars, "On Workers' Schools," which was passed in September, 1920, secured their formation throughout the country. The workers' schools were assigned the task of preparing workers and peasants for study at the university level, of huge significance in the creation of a new Soviet intelligentsia.

Until the middle of the 1920's the secondary education of adults grew rather slowly and was mostly due to the workers' schools. . . . In the 1928–29 school year there were 107 workers' schools in the RSFSR with 39,900 pupils, while in 1932–33 there were 609 schools with 204,900 pupils.

p. 73   A decree of the Central Committee of the Communist party of July 25, 1930, established universal primary education beginning with the 1930–31 school year; a seven-year universal education was established in cities and towns. (Obligatory universal seven-year education was established in the Russian Federation in 1949.)

p. 77   TRADE SCHOOL NO. 70
        IS ACCEPTING YOUNG PEOPLE

The school prepares highly qualified specialists:

PLUMBERS
SHEET METAL WORKERS [fitters of industrial ventilating equipment]
PIPE-LAYERS
BOOKKEEPERS (10th-grade [complete] education)
DRAFTSMEN-DESIGNERS (10th-grade education)

Young men and women with an 8th- or 10th-grade education are accepted.

Length of study: 1, 1½, or 2 years.

Classes begin in September.

Students accepted by the school receive state support [uniforms and meals]; and students studying drafting and bookkeeping receive a stipend. Study time is included in work seniority [computations]. People from areas outside of Moscow who study pipe-laying will be given a dormitory space and permission to live in the environs of Moscow when they have finished their course.

Applications are accepted daily from 9 to 5.

Telephone inquiries: 154–75–31.

Public transportation: subway station "Vodnyy stadion"; bus No. 123 to the stop "Avtomotornaya ul."

p. 78   The Moscow Institute of Electronic
        Machine Building Announces that
        It Is Selecting First Year Students
      Day Students in the Following Specialties:
"SEMICONDUCTOR AND ELECTRIC VACUUM MACHINE BUILDING,"
"PRECISION MECHANICAL EQUIPMENT,"
"AUTOMATION AND REMOTE CONTROL,"
"CALCULATING DEVICES AND INSTALLATIONS,"
"THE DESIGN AND PRODUCTION TECHNOLOGY OF RADIO EQUIPMENT,"
"ELECTRONIC EQUIPMENT,"
"AUTOMATED CONTROL SYSTEMS,"
"APPLIED MATHEMATICS."

Evening students [will be accepted] in all the above specialties except "Automated Control Systems." For the specialty "Applied Mathematics" evening students are accepted if they have a higher technical education.

The Institute does not have a dormitory.

Applications are accepted:

For day study—until July 31.

For evening study—until August 31.

The applicant must present: a high-school diploma (original, not a copy), a character reference, a medical clearance (form #286), 5 photographs (3 centimeters by 4 centimeters), work record, passport, draft card or military status card.

Entrance exams are on mathematics (written and oral), physics (oral), Russian and literature (written).

WILL BE HELD:

For day students—from August 1 to 20,

For evening students—from August 11 to September 10.

Address of the Institute: B. Vuzovskiy pereulok 3/12.

Public transportation: subway stations "Kirovskaya" or "Novokuznetskaya"; streetcar "A,", 3, 39 to the stop Kazarmennyy pereulok; trackless trolley 25, 41, 45; bus 3 to the stop "Pokrovskiye vorota."

p. 83   Question Set No. 5

(1) Gorky's early revolutionary-romantic works, their ideological direction and artistic originality.
(2) Turgenev's *Fathers and Sons*: the idea behind the title and the distinctive features of the composition. The depiction in the novel of the sociopolitical struggle of the 1860's.

p. 83   Question Set No. 13

(1) A. A. Blok's poem "The Twelve." The idea. The structure, vocabulary, and rhythm of the poem.
(2) Chernyshevsky's civic heroism.

p. 83   Question Set No. 24

(1) Sholokhov's portrayal of the beauty of spirit and strength of character of Soviet man as warrior and worker in *The Fate of a Man*.
(2) The ideological aim and artistic originality in Saltykov-Shchedrin's satire. Saltykov-Shchedrin's characterizations in Lenin's works.

p. 83   III.

(1) Solve the inequality:
(2) Find all the real solutions for each real number a in the equation:
(3) A man bought several identical notebooks and identical books. He bought 4 more books than he did notebooks. He paid 72 kopecks for all the notebooks and he paid 6 rubles 60 kopecks for all the books. If each notebook had cost as much as each book cost, and if each book had cost as much as each notebook cost, then the man would have spent 4 rubles 44 kopecks less than he did. How many notebooks did he buy?
(4) In a right-angle trapezoid $ABCD$, angles A and D are right angles, side AB is parallel to side CD, and the length of the sides are as follows: $AB = 1$, $CD = 4$, $AD = 5$. On side AD the point M is taken so that the angle CMD is twice the angle BMA. In what ratio does point M divide side AD?
(5) A sphere is inscribed in a right-circular cone. The ratio of the volumes of the cone and the

sphere is two. Find the ratio of the total surface of the cone to the surface of the sphere.

p. 99   Cherkutino used to be a large trading center; the peasants from the surrounding villages would come to attend the fairs on St. Peter's Day or during carnival week [Shrovetide].

p. 99   They used to work hard gathering hay between St. Peter's Day and St. Elia's Day.

p. 100

Kolyadá, kolyadá
Open the gates,
Snow[s] have fallen on the ground
From time to time.
Christmas has come
To the master's window.
Get up, master,
Wake up the mistress.
Be hospitable to us,
[Feed us with bread and salt],
Show us the road.
What sleek calves our mother has!
They jump over the garden beds,
Clicking their hoofs,
Not touching the ground.
Our mistress has
Thick cream,
Rich sour cream,
[And] yellow butter . . .
We will take not a ruble, nor fifty kopecks,
One twenty-five piece,
A pie and a tart,
A gold piece.

p. 101   The household servants were dressed up as bears, Turks, innkeepers, and lords, both frightful and funny. They brought the cold and their gaiety in with them, at first huddling timidly in the entrance hall, then, hiding behind one another, they moved to the ballroom. Bashfully at first, and then more gaily and friendlier, they began to sing, dance, and play Christmas games. The countess recognized the faces, laughed at costumes, and went off to the drawing room. Count Ilya Andreyich sat in the ballroom with a radiant smile, approving the players. The young people vanished somewhere.

In half an hour another old lady in a hoop skirt appeared among the other mummers in the ballroom —this was Nikolai. Petya was a Turkish woman. Dimmler was a clown, Natasha was a hussar, and Sonya was a Circassian, with a mustache and eyebrows drawn with burnt cork.

p. 101   At Christmas and Shrovetide the mummers go from house to house and then have a party with the food and money they have collected. Thus, during the Christmas holidays in 1960 in Klimovo, women went around the village dressed up as fighters or a bear and his trainer, and the children dressed up as gypsies.

. . . It was about five o'clock. Suddenly there was a knock at the door, laughter, and footsteps pounding on the porch. Gypsy children burst into the room. There were three of them: a girl with soot on her face about ten to twelve years old and dressed up in a fancy "sarafan," shawl, and a bundle in her hands; another girl, a little bit smaller, and a boy, both of them with soot on their faces and dressed up in rags. They giggled, became embarrassed, and pushed one another.

"Well, go ahead, ask!" the hostess urged them.

"Give us, please give us, a wee bit of meat."

We gave the children some candies.

"They used to get dressed up more," Anna Ivanovna said, "as beggars, gypsies, Death."

p. 101   "Fortune-telling in the bathhouse, that was frightening!" said an old maid at the supper table who lived with the Melyukóvs.

". . . Once a young lady took a rooster and two place settings and sat down, just as she was supposed to. She sat for a while just listening. Suddenly, something is coming . . . with bells ringing. A sleigh arrives. She hears someone coming. Something in human form enters, very much like an officer. He sits down at one of the place settings."

"Oh!" screamed Natasha, her eyes staring in horror.

"What is he like? Does he talk?"

"Yes, he's like a man; everything is just the way it's supposed to be; he begins to persuade her. She should have tried to get him to talk until early morning, but she got scared and put her hands over her face. So he grabbed her. It's a good thing the girls came running in. . . ."

"Well, what do you want to frighten them for!" said Pelageya Danilovna.

"Mother, you told fortunes, too," said the daughter.

"How do they tell fortunes in the barn?" asked Sonya.

"Well, even nowadays they go to the barn and listen. It depends on what you hear: if you hear hammering or banging, that's bad; if you hear grain fall, that's good; but sometimes . . ."

p. 102   Once on Epiphany Eve
The girls were telling fortunes;

They took off a shoe and
Threw it over the gate;
Drew designs in the snow;
Listened at the window;
Fed counted grains to a chicken;
Melted unbleached wax;
Into a cup of pure water
They put a gold ring
[or] emerald earrings;
They spread out a white kerchief,
And over a cup
Sang fortunetelling songs.

p. 102   The Christmas holidays ended with Epiphany. On that day a "procession of the cross" would go "to Jordan," that is, a hole broken in the river ice. After the water had been blessed, some of the people swam the river.

p. 104   On Easter they would go out walking in the streets, swing on the swings and roll painted eggs; the young men played "gorodkí," "laptá," "bábki," and other games. . . . One of the basic parts of these spring holidays was the group dances, indulged in by the young. The dances ["khorovody"] usually took place outside the village proper. The dance would begin with songs that invited people to come and have a good time. Then there were various dancing and game songs, mostly the same ones they had at Christmastime. They ended with songs that said it was time to go home.

p. 109   The rural public is carrying on an active fight with this harmful remnant of the past. The introduction of new customs helps the population reject the "altar holidays."

p. 112   Those who say that the city is nothing but shoving and long lines are just not humanitarians. I, for instance, love crowds. . . . I won't get on an empty trolley. Why ride in an empty trolley? Might as well take a taxi. There you can at least talk to the chauffeur for your money. I love to ride public transportation in the mornings. . . . There you can get squashed, squeezed, crushed. . . . "It's all over, that's the end," you think. But no! They throw you out at your stop, you straighten up, and you feel . . . you're still alive! Such a joy comes over you, such enthusiasm. . . . You feel you can move mountains! . . . You get on the trolley and go in the opposite direction.

p. 116   The following are some of the administrative penalties; they depend on the kind of infraction of the law and the consequences thereof:
(1) oral warning;
(2) fine;

(3) the driver's traffic violation card will be punched;
(4) temporary suspension of the right to drive;
(5) in cases where noncompliance with the law has resulted in an accident with damage to people or state or personal property, then those guilty are subject to criminal prosecution.

p. 116   Foreigners arriving in the USSR with their own automobiles or motorcycles must have:
(1) documents for the automobile (motorcycle);
(2) an international driver's license or an insert to a national driver's permit;
(3) a national registration license number and a country-of-origin plate as specified in the International Convention.

p. 118   (I) Caution signs
 (1)   Railroad crossing without barrier
 (2)   Railroad crossing with barrier
 (3)   Intersection
 (4)   Intersection with secondary road
 (5)   Arterial road ahead
 (6)   Traffic signals ahead
 (7a) Road turns to the right
 (7b) Road turns to the left
 (8)   Winding road
 (9)   Steep hill
 (10) Bumpy road
 (11) Slippery road
 (12) Road narrows
 (13) Drawbridge
 (14) Two-way traffic
 (15) Pedestrians
 (16) Children playing
 (17) Men working
 (18) Animal crossing
 (19) Warning of other danger

p. 118   (II) Prohibitory signs
 (1)   Do not enter
 (2)   No thru traffic
 (3)   Automobile traffic is prohibited
 (4)   Truck traffic is prohibited
 (5)   Motorcycle traffic is prohibited
 (6)   Horse-drawn traffic is prohibited
 (7)   Tractor traffic is prohibited
 (8)   Bicycle traffic is prohibited
 (9)   Load limit
 (10) Axle load limit
 (11) Clearance height limit
 (12) Clearance width limit
 (13) Stop (before continuing)
 (14a) No left turn
 (14b) No right turn
 (15) No U-turn

(16) No passing
(17) Trucks may not pass
(18) Speed limit
(19) Do not sound horn
(20) No stopping
(21) No parking
(22) End to limitations

p. 119   (III) Limiting signs
 (1)   Permissible direction of traffic
 (2)   Detour
 (3)   Traffic circle
 (4)   Automobile traffic only
 (5)   Truck traffic only
 (6)   Motorcycle traffic only
 (7)   Bicycle traffic only

p. 119   (IV) Informational signs
 (1)   Parking
 (2)   U-turn
 (3)   (Automobile) camping site
 (4)   Food
 (5)   First aid
 (6)   Repair station
 (7)   Telephone
 (8)   Gas station
 (9)   Arterial
 (10) End of arterial

p. 119   (V) Signs used with other signs
 (1)   Distance sign is in effect
 (2)   Distance to object
 (3)   Time that the sign is in effect
 (4)   Direction of detour
 (5)   Type of conveyance
 (6)   Dangerous railroad crossing
 (7)   Danger, train

p. 119   (VI) Route indicators
 (1)   Name of place
 (2)   Direction
 (3)   Distance
 (4)   Highway route indicator
 (5)   Route number
 (6)   Distance along route

p. 121   In connecting five seas, the White Sea–Baltic Canal, the Lenin Volga–Baltic Waterway, the Moscow Canal, and the Don Navigation Canal, named after Lenin, formed a unified deep-water system for the European USSR.

p. 121   Many tourist itineraries begin at Moscow—from the Khimki River Terminal. There are new river terminals in Gorkiy, Kazan, Ulyanovsk, and Osetrov. The three-decker, diesel electric ship *Lenin* sails between Moscow and Astrakhan. It is the flagship of the river fleet and is designed for 439 passengers.

p. 121 The *Ivan Franko* is one in a series of passenger liners in the USSR commercial fleet. It has more than 300 cabins for 750 passengers. The speed of the liner is 20 knots.

p. 126
The moon breaks
Through the billowing fog,
Pouring [its] sad light
On the sad fields.

Along the tedious winter road
A swift troika runs,
Its monotonous sleighbell
Rings on [wearisomely].

Something sounds of home
In the driver's long songs,
Now [songs of] abandon,
And revelry . . .

Then heartfelt melancholy.
Neither a light nor dark hut,
Silence and snow in front of me [facing me] . . .
Only striped roadmarkers
Appear one after another.

p. 127   Yo, heave ho! Yo, heave ho!
Once again, once again!
We will uncurl the birch tree,
We will uncurl the curly one . . .

p. 131 "I told my husband that I would immediately come home from the resort if I didn't get a letter from him every day."
"What did he do?"
"He writes twice a day!"

p. 136 On Sunday, Zelenin took Inna to the club.
"What's going on there today?"
"First there's a lecture on how to be well dressed. The lecture is interesting, we're going to show slides of Czechoslovakian fashions. . . . We decided to wage a war for good taste."
"Who's 'we'?"
"The directors of the club."

.   .   .

A concert began after the lecture. Zelenin appeared on the stage from time to time. Sometimes he did some announcing; with a glued-on beard he played, in a skit, the role of a professor who was the father of a dissolute son; he also gave a poetry reading. . . ,

Zelenin recited verses, Timofey played slow waltzes on the accordion, Dasha sang "chastushki" [sung doggerel, competitively composed], and Boris did an acrobatic étude with a thin little girl whom others described later as a cement layer. Then all of a sudden, Zelenin stepped to the edge of the stage and said loudly, "The next number will be a Chopin nocturne played by Inna Zelenin."

p. 142   (1) [We] only show the square that the piece is moved to.
(2) If a pawn makes a capture, [we] note the vertical on which it stood and then the vertical that it went to as a result of the capture.

p. 143 *Master of Sport:* Use no more than 156 sticks on 90 "gorodki" figures and accomplish this twice in one year—once at contests not lower than the municipal level that are participated in by no less than three sports organizations of various departments and the Voluntary Sports Society; and the second time at USSR championship games, championships and regional competitions of the republics, Moscow and Leningrad, all-union championships of departments, and championships of the central and republic councils of the Voluntary Sports Society.

OR

Set a new USSR record in the number of sticks used on 15, 30, 45, 60, or 90 "gorodki" figures in single or team competitions.

First Class: Use no more than 165 sticks on 90 figures.
Second Class: Use no more than 140 sticks on 60 figures or 216 sticks on 90 figures.
Third Class: Use no more than 165 sticks on 60 figures or 90 sticks on 30 figures.
First Youth Class (16–18 years): Use no more than 175 sticks on 60 figures or 85 sticks on 30 figures from a distance of 13 meters.
Second Youth Class (up to 16 years): Use no more than 105 sticks on 30 figures or 50 sticks on 15 figures from a distance of 10 meters.

p. 146   Burn, burn brightly,
So that it won't go out.
Look at the sky.
The birds are flying,
The bells are ringing!
One, two—don't gape [dawdle],
Run like fire!

p. 148   On a golden porch there sat:
A tsar, his son; a king, his son;
A shoemaker; a dressmaker.
Answer, which are you?

p. 148   This little basket
Has cosmetics and perfume,
Ribbons, lace, and shoes—
Everything your heart desires
  [your soul requires].

p. 149   "Posidelki" occur mostly in places where there are still too few cultural establishments or where [these establishments] are not working well enough.

p. 152   A stranger need only come into the room and in the first ten minutes I can tell his cultural biography; I can tell whether he is well read and whether he moves in cultivated society or whether he is a drunk who keeps company with numbskulls.

p. 168   Matryona had another big chore when her turn came to feed the goatherds: one of them was a solidly built deaf-mute and the other was a kid with a wet, homemade cigarette eternally on his lip. Her turn came once every month and a half, but Matryona had to pay dearly for it. She went to the country store, bought canned fish, and paid out money for sugar and butter, which she herself was not used to eating. It turned out that the women would try to outdo each other in feeding the herders.

p. 171   In the USSR medicinal leeches are caught mostly in Krasnodarskiy Kray, in the Moldavian, Ukrainian, Georgian, and Azerbaijan republics. They are also raised in laboratories.

p. 171   Butterfly, moth
Many people collect butterflies.
There are four stages in the life of the butterfly: (1) egg, (2) caterpillar, (3) chrysalis, (4) butterfly.

    Ladybug
"Ladybug, fly away to the sky.
There your children are eating cutlets." [!]
[*Earlier version:* Fly away . . . bring us some bread.]

    Beetle
The beetle is any insect with hard wings.

    Moth
Same as the butterfly, but it appears outside at night.

    Gnat
Gnats appear mostly in the evening, at sundown.

Ant
The ant works day and night; it is a symbol of industriousness. Ants live in anthills.
    Spider
Spiders spin webs.
    Wasp
Don't touch a wasp nest or there'll be disaster.
    Bee
Bees live in hives. The queen is the largest bee; she lays eggs. The worker bee collects honey, and the drone doesn't do any work. The swarm follows the queen bee.
    Cricket
Crickets often live in houses near the stove; earlier, it was thought that crickets talk to the house spirit. Sometimes they are identified as the house spirit himself.
    Firefly
Fireflies come out at night.
    Dragonfly
Read "The Dragonfly and the Ant" by Krylov.
    Bumblebee
Bumblebees are like bees, only bigger.

p. 172   Cabbage moth
Cabbage moths lay eggs in cabbage stems, and then their grubs eat the stems.
    Tick
The forest tick transmits encephalitis.
    Mosquito
"I itch. A mosquito bit [me]."
    Grasshopper
[A ditty] Little green grasshopper, with his knees [bent] back;
He's excited, chirring, for some reason very happy.
    May beetle
The May beetle eats birch trees. The May beetle is destructive to agriculture.
    Sow bug
Sow bugs are very repulsive; they are thought to be dirty.
    Moth
Naphthalene may be used against moths.
    Fly
Be sure to read "Mukha tsokotukha" by Chukovskiy.
In order to get rid of flies, they use fly swatters and [fly] paper.
    Locust
They attacked the table like locusts. (They ate up everything very quickly.)

Cockroach
Cockroaches are very unpleasant and are hard to get rid of.

Aphid
(The word for aphid is used mostly in the singular.) Aphids have come out. Aphids are crawling there.

Earwig
According to superstition, the earwig will burrow into [one's] ear and even into the brain.

p. 172   Flea
"Why are you jumping like a flea?"

Louse
Lice live off the blood of man and mammals. Three kinds of lice are parasitic on man: head lice, clothes lice, and pubic lice.

Nit
Nits are louse eggs. They are small, white, and they don't move.

Bedbug
Bedbugs are feared less than lice, since they usually live in [furniture] rather than on the body.

By the way, DDT powder is the most common weapon [means] in the battle with household parasites.

p. 173   When in danger, lizards save themselves by "losing" their tails.
He crawls like a turtle. (He is going very slowly.)

p. 173   According to superstition, people get warts from toads.

p. 173   "What kind of fish are there here?"
"Fish? All kinds of fish. . . . There are crucian carp in the deeper pools, pike, and, well then, those perch, roach, bream, and then tench. Do you know tench? It's fat as a little pig. First time I caught one myself, my mouth fell open."

p. 177   Among the larger game birds are the gray partridge, the hazel grouse, the black grouse, the wood grouse, the pheasant, the wild goose, and the duck; among the smaller game birds are the quail, snipe, great snipe, and the woodcock.

p. 179   "There are the cranes! [Look] how near they are! What marvelous birds they are! And their legs—like long sticks!"
. . . One crane took off.

p. 180   The next day Nikífor went to hunt with his dog. The dog began to bark. This was a special bark,
the one by which a commercial hunter immediately recognizes that the dog has treed a squirrel. The squirrel jumps from tree to tree. The dog runs around below and barks plaintively and impatiently, and the hunter only has to follow the bark.

Soon a gray squirrel appeared in a tree. Almost immediately the dog jumped out of the bushes, continuing to bark incessantly. The squirrel was not afraid of the dog; an enemy on the ground is not fearsome to a squirrel sitting in a tree. It descended to a lower branch and began to snort at its persecutor. The dog jumped up and down and trampled the snow, and the squirrel angrily growled and hissed.

Then Nikífor appeared from behind the bushes. He unhurriedly rested his rifle against a notch in a tree trunk and took aim at the squirrel. The squirrel didn't notice the hunter; its attention was riveted on the dog.

Nikífor shot. The dead squirrel hung from a branch by its claws. The hunter hit the squirrel down and immediately began to remove its hide. He cut the hide with a sharp knife and then began to peel off the fur, turning it back just the way one takes off stockings.

After skinning the animal, he threw the naked carcass to the dog. The dog ate it hungrily.

The hunters stayed four months in the taiga. They killed many squirrels.

In the middle of March Nikífor and all his group returned home.

p. 205   Celsius—A thermometer with a scale [showing] 100° from the melting point of ice to the boiling point of water. Water freezes at 0°. Water boils at 100° Celsius.

p. 207   Electric light bulbs are sold by candle power. One can buy light bulbs at 50 candle power, 20 candle power, and so forth. (A candle is a unit of measure of light emitted by a source.) Bulbs are also sold according to their wattage.

p. 208   The coordinates of Moscow are 55° 45′ latitude north, and 37° 37′ longitude east of Greenwich. Kerguelen Island in the Indian Ocean is located at 50° latitude south, and the Strait of Gibraltar is located at 5° longitude west.

p. 208   The face [on the bottom] of the compass has divisions that indicate degrees—from 0° to 360°. If the compass needle is freed, then the end of the needle that points to the north will correspond to 0°–360°, the south to 180°, the east to 90°, and west will be 270°.

List of Illustration Sources

p. 29 *Отрывной календарь на 1960 годъ* (Париж: Изданые Зарубежнаго Союза Русскихъ Военныхъ Инвалидовъ, без даты).

p. 35 Феликс Лев, *У самого Белого моря* (Москва: Малыш, 1970).

p. 44 *Домоводство,* 4ое изд. (Москва: Колос, 1965), стр. 438.

p. 45, p. 47 left, p. 48 top (художник) Н. Виноградова, «Мужской костюм Архангельской губернии», «Костюм девушки Архангельской губернии», «Женский костюм Тульской губернии», (Москва: «Изобразительное искусство», 1969).

p. 46 Токарев, *Этнография народов СССР,* стр. 79.

p. 47 С. А. Токарев, *Этнография народов СССР* (Москва: Изд. Московского университета, 1958), стр. 74.

p. 47 *Народы европейской части СССР* том I, ред. В. А. Александров и др., в серии Народы мира (Москва: Наука, 1964), стр. 375.

p. 48 Александров, *Народы европейской части СССР,* стр. 372.

p. 52 Игорь И. Середюк, *Культура вашей квартиры* (Киев: Будивельник, 1967), стр. 17.

p. 53 Е. и М. Никольские, *Книга о культуре быта,* 2ое изд. (Москва: Профиздат, 1967), стр. 27.

p. 53 Там же, стр. 96.

p. 54 Федорова и др., *Домоводство: Пособие для учителей* (Москва: Просвещение, 1967), стр. 34.

p. 56 Е. В. Белова и Л. Р. Тодд, *English, 7th Form,* 11ое изд. (Москва: Просвещение, 1967), стр. 127.

p. 60 *Русские народные сказки,* ред. А. Нечаев и Н. Рыбакова, 3ое изд. (Москва: Детская литература, 1967), стр. 17.

p. 60 А. С. Пушкин, *Сказки* (Москва: Детская Литература, 1953), стр. 61.

p. 61 Александров, *Народы европейской части СССР,* стр. 299.

p. 61 Там же, стр. 302.

p. 62 Е. Э. Бломквист, «Крестьянские постройки русских, украинцев и белорусов», *Восточнославянский этнографический сборник,* ред. С. А. Токарев, Труды института этнографии им. Н. Н. Миклухо-Маклая, новая серия, том XXXI (Москва: Академия Наук, СССР, 1956), стр. 215.

p. 62 Там же, стр. 139.

p. 63 Т. В. Станюкович, «Внутренняя планировка, отделка и меблировка русского крестьянского жилища», *Русские,* ред. Александров и др. (Москва: Наука, 1970), стр. 69.

p. 64 Токарев, *Этнография народов СССР,* стр. 64.

p. 64 *Русские народные сказки,* стр. 367.

p. 65 Александров, *Народы европейской части СССР,* стр. 397. Г. С. Маслова, «Пища и хозяйственная утварь», *Материалы и исследования по этнографии русского населения европейской части СССР,* Труды института этнографии им. Н. Н. Миклухо-Маклая, новая серия, том LVII (Москва: Академия Наук, СССР, 1960), стр. 167.

pp. 66 Е. Э. Бломквист, *Восточнославянский этнографический сборник,* стр. 273.

p. 67 Н. Яснецкий, «Деревенское строительство в Печерском крае», *Материалы и исследования по этнографии русского населения европейской части СССР,* стр. 311.

p. 68 Л. А. Анохина и М. Н. Шмелева, *Культура и быт колхозников Калининской области* (Москва: Наука, 1964), стр. 125.

p. 76 *Вечерняя Москва,* 9 июня 1969, 8 августа 1969.

p. 77 Там же, 12 августа 1969.

p. 78 Там же, 4 июля 1969.

p. 79, 80 Там же, 9 июня 1969.

p. 92 М. В. Антропова, *Школьная гигиена* (Москва: Медицина, 1970), стр. 271.

pp. 106, 108, 110 Tass from Sovfoto.

p. 115 А. И. Манзон и Г. Е. Нагула, *Пособие по правилам движения,* 4ое изд. (Киев: Техника, 1967), стр. 52.

pp. 118, 119 Там же, вкладка.

p. 122 Перышкин и др., *Физика: Учебник для 6го класса,* 9ое изд. (Москва: Просвещение, 1967), стр. 80.

p. 123 Tass from Sovfoto.

p. 125 Соловьева, Карпинская и Щепетова, *Родная Речь I,* 24ое изд. (Москва: Просвещение, 1967), стр. 79.

p. 125 *Товарный словарь,* ред. И. А. Пугачев, том 7 (Москва: Гос. изд. торговой литературы, 1956–1961), стр. 998.

p. 125 Там же, стр. 999.

p. 125 *Товарный словарь,* том 8, стр. 717.

p. 125 *Товарный словарь,* том 2, стр. 710.

p. 126 Александров, *Народы европейской части СССР,* стр. 361.

p. 127 *Soviet Life,* from Sovfoto.

p. 139 *Вечерняя Москва,* 26 июня 1969.

p. 140 *Спортивные игры,* том I, ред. М. С. Козлов, 2ое изд. (Москва: Физкультура и спорт, 1955), стр. 60.

p. 140 *Вечерняя Москва,* 26 июля 1969.

p. 142 *Спортивные игры,* том II, ред. М. С. Козлов, 2ое изд. (Москва: Физкультура и спорт, 1955), стр. 336.

p. 143 Там же, стр. 333, 334.

p. 155 А. М. Финкель и Н. М. Баженов, *Курс современного русского языка,* 2ое изд. (Киев: Радянска школа, 1965).

p. 156 А. Е. Супрун, *Русский язык советской эпохи* (Ленинград: Просвещение, 1969), стр. 49.

p. 174 Fotokhronika Tass, Sovfoto—M. Redkin.

p. 178 Е. И. Никитина, *Родное слово: Книга для чтения в 1 классе,* 2ое изд. (Москва: Просвещение, 1969), стр. 72–73.

p. 190 Harbrace.

p. 200 Перышкин и др., *Физика: Учебник для 6го класса,* стр. 44.

p. 202 *Расписание движения поездов и вагонов международного сообщения* (Москва, 1967), стр. 19 и 46.

p. 203 *1968, Календарь школьника,* ред. Р. Петрова и Г. Алимова (Москва: Политиздат, 1967).

p. 204 U. S., War Department, *Dictionary of Spoken Russian,* TM30–944 (Washington, D. C.: Government Printing Office, 1945), p. 563.

p. 205 Перышкин и др., *Физика: Учебник для 6го класса,* стр. 133.

p. 206 Н. А. Максимов, *Физическая география: Учебник для 5го класса* (Москва: Просвещение, 1967), стр. 96.

p. 207 Там же, стр. 21.

p. 208 USSR Magazine from Sovfoto.

p. 209 Sovfoto—Harbrace.

When more than one illustration appears on a page, the order of the listing is left to right, top to bottom.

INDEX

Page numbers in italics refer to illustrations.

E 9
F 0
G 1
H 2
I
J 3